THE PARADOXES OF PLANNING

New Directions in Planning Theory

Series Editors
Gert de Roo, University of Groningen, The Netherlands
Jean Hillier, RMIT University, Australia
Joris Van Wezemael, University of Fribourg, Switzerland

Ashgate's series, New Directions in Planning Theory, develops and disseminates theories and conceptual understandings of spatial and physical planning which address such challenges as uncertainty, diversity and incommensurability.

Planning theories range across a wide spectrum, from questions of explanation and understanding, to normative or predictive questions of how planners should act and what future places should look like.

These theories include procedural theories of planning. While these have traditionally been dominated by ideas about rationality, in addition to this, the series opens up to other perspectives and also welcomes theoretical contributions on substantive aspects of planning.

Other theories to be included in the series may be concerned with questions of epistemology or ontology; with issues of knowledge, power, politics, subjectivation; with social and/or environmental justice; with issues of morals and ethics.

Planning theories have been, and continue to be, influenced by other intellectual fields, which often imbue planning theories with awareness of and sensitivity to the multiple dimensions of planning practices. The series editors particularly encourage inter- and trans-disciplinary ideas and conceptualisations.

The Paradoxes of Planning
A Psycho-Analytical Perspective

SARA WESTIN
Uppsala University, Sweden

Routledge
Taylor & Francis Group
LONDON AND NEW YORK

First published 2014 by Ashgate Publishing

Published 2016 by Routledge
2 Park Square, Milton Park, Abingdon, Oxfordshire OX14 4RN
711 Third Avenue, New York, NY 10017, USA

First issued in paperback 2016

Routledge is an imprint of the Taylor & Francis Group, an informa business

British Library Cataloguing in Publication Data
A catalogue record for this book is available from the British Library

The Library of Congress has cataloged the printed edition as follows:
Westin, Sara, 1979-
    The paradoxes of planning : a psycho-analytical perspective / by Sara Westin.
     pages cm. – (New directions in planning theory)
    Includes bibliographical references and index.
    ISBN 978-1-4094-4803-7 (hardback)
1. City planning–Social aspects. 2. Cities and towns–Psychological aspects.
3. Architecture–Human factors. 4. Architecture–Psychological aspects. I. Title.
    HT166.W4825 2014
    307.1'216–dc23

                        2013045810

ISBN 13: 978-1-138-27183-8 (pbk)
ISBN 13: 978-1-4094-4803-7 (hbk)

Contents

List of Figures

Preface

> In language, in religion, in art, in science, man can do no more than to build up his own universe – a symbolic universe that enables him to understand and interpret, to articulate and organize, to synthesize and universalize his human experience.
>
> Ernst Cassirer

When I contemplated how to start this preface, for a while I considered beginning with the words 'I love cities'. But then I realised that the statement is too vague – cities can be so different. I love cities, but not all cities. Nor do I love all parts of the cities I love; on the contrary, some stir up an almost inexplicable feeling of anxiety. Then one day I was reading a story about a woman who papered her walls with pictures from New York. She, too, loved cities, but that was not what caught my attention – it was the words she used to describe herself: *pulse addict*. This book is written by that kind of person, a pulse addict. The meaning of this term cannot be explored in a few sentences, maybe not even in a book. But to the reader of this book, a meaning will hopefully emerge. However, at this point, I can say that what the pulse addict desires is not so much cities in general but *urbanity*.

Urbanity. What, then, is this multi-faceted phenomenon? This question permeates the book. But early on, my quest to capture and understand the phenomenon was accompanied by another quest, the quest to understand how we – people in general and scientists in particular – understand. How we describe something depends on who we are and what we want to do with our description, and since I am not only a *flâneur* (to use a word more well-known than *pulse addict*) but also a scientist, my exploration has required both breadth and depth. And since it is not only human geographers that find an interest in urbanity but also architectural theorists, sociologists, economists, historians, anthropologists and psychologists, the broad approach has been even more necessary. All this has led me out into an ocean of literature – to which the long list of references testifies. If I were to categorise this book in only a couple of words, I would probably call it an *intellectual excavation*. Since the landscape is so vast and the material to dig up, virtually endless, I – like any other researcher taking on an interdisciplinary research subject – have had to choose areas of specialisation and limit the depth of the pits I dig. It is a well-worn insight that the more you learn, the more you realise there is to learn – something that makes it possible to regard the reference list not as too long but as too short.

As the reader may have already noticed by leafing through the first pages of this book, the table of contents provides no guidance on which parts of the book are empirical and which are theoretical, nor is there any information about when I am being descriptive and when I am being analytical. Classifications of this kind may be prohibitive rather than facilitative if you – as I have done in this study – have chosen to follow a problem wherever it leads. Many of the book's points are born from the cross-fertilisation that took place in the meeting between seemingly disparate thought traditions. If I allow myself a stretch, I would describe the ideas as a meeting between the Enlightenment and Romanticism, between science and art, between positivism's quest for exactness and poetry's need to transcend boundaries.

Architectural researcher Lars Marcus (2000b: 7) presents his book *Architectural Knowledge and Urban Form* with the following words: 'At the heart of this thesis is the relation between the architect and the city'. To a certain extent, this statement functions as a description of the book in hand as well. How do architects and planners – these so-called 'experts' – relate to the city and to the challenge of building attractive and lively cities? Answering this question has not been an end in itself; rather, it has been a means to explore another, more fundamental problem: the gap between vision and reality in urban planning. The background is today's attempts in Sweden to build 'city-like' areas (*stadsmässiga områden*); the point of departure is my personal experience of them. Of the examples discussed in the book, Hammarby Sjöstad in Stockholm appears most often. Here, I want to emphasise that this is not a book about Hammarby Sjöstad; its role in the work is precisely to serve as an example: it is through Hammarby Sjöstad I attempt to understand *something else*, something broader.

The book can be read on two levels: first, it is a study of the city and urban planning, and second, it is an analysis of how we understand these phenomena. Ultimately, it embodies a planning critique, a relatively thorough one, as it puts under the microscope – or, rather, lays on the couch – the very rules of reason that planners as well as the majority of planning critics conform to. The inquiry into what counts as knowledge has also made the book into a critique of scientific reasoning. Last but not least, the book can be seen as part of a wider critique of contemporary society because it is grappling with the problem of alienation in modern society. Why is it that this phenomenon – or neurosis, to use Sigmund Freud's terminology – is so prevalent in Western cities? The book is an attempt to answer this question.

Author's Note

This book was originally published in Swedish in 2010 with the title *Planerat, alltför planerat. En perspektivistisk studie i stadsplaneringens paradoxer*. Since I have translated it myself, with the valuable help of line editor Rebecca Ahlfeldt, I have had the opportunity to revise it slightly. All translations of quoted material from Swedish and Norwegian are also my own unless noted.

Acknowledgements

I would like to thank the Institute for Housing and Urban Research (IBF), Uppsala University, for helping me to fund parts of the translation work. I am also grateful to the anonymous referee for valuable comments on the manuscript, and to my commissioning editor, Valerie Rose, for turning the manuscript into a book.

It is true that the truth lies. It is also true that this is a paradox, since the claim denies its own starting point. If the claim is true, then it is false, and if it is false, it is true. Mixed messages! Confusion! In the paradox something happens on the road from the argument's premise to its conclusion. This is a common situation in urban planning and architecture because here, too, we see 'peculiar changes on the way from good intention to mechanised realisation' (Olsson 1980b). The contradiction chafes: How can something come out of its opposite?

Introduction
The Gap

Whenever I step foot in Mourenx I am filled with dread. Yet the new town has a lot going for it. The overall plan (the master blueprint) has a certain attractiveness: the lines of the tower blocks alternate horizontals and verticals. ... The blocks of flats look well planned and properly built; we know that they ... offer their residents bathrooms or showers, drying rooms, well-lit accommodation ... Our technicists and technocrats have their hearts in the right place, even if it is what they have in their minds which is given priority. ... Yet every time I see these 'machines for living in' I feel terrified.

Henri Lefebvre

In the same way the two strivings – for individual happiness and for human fellowship – have to contend with each other in every individual; so too the processes of individual and cultural development are bound to come into conflict and dispute each other's territory.

Sigmund Freud

Wrestling with paradoxes is ... the only way to learn, for genuine paradoxes can be neither solved nor ignored.

Gunnar Olsson

The origin of this book is fairly trivial; it began with a feeling. It all started with a visit to Hammarby Sjöstad – a newly built area in Stockholm – one day in May, 2002. I arrived as a student in urban studies. I had read the planning documents describing Hammarby Sjöstad as an extension of the inner city and, specifically, of the district of Södermalm, located across the Hammarby waterway. I had previously lived on Södermalm and had enjoyed it immensely, and this made me all together sympathetic to the new project, at the time about halfway completed. 'Finally!' my reaction had been when reading the plans; finally the planners and politicians had decided to 'build a city' and not another 'residential area'. However, when I arrived on the ferry, I was confused. Where was the city life that the planners had talked about? Where was the urban atmosphere that characterises the inner city? Why did I get the feeling of being in a ghost town, or in the middle of some sort of theatrical propped-up scenery? But, most of all, my question was this: How did what was described as an attractive, urban neighbourhood appear, in its reality, as a ghost town, an area without life?

Figure I.1   Hammarby Sjöstad
Source: Author's photograph from 2009.

The gap between vision and reality in planning – the problem's name – has been noted before, specifically in reference to attempts in Sweden to create 'city-like' areas.[1] Since the 1980s the planning discourse has been characterised by political enthusiasm for a radically new planning ideal: to break with the paradigm of modernist city planning, which has spawned residential suburbs with no street life, and instead build 'city-like' areas with the inner city as a model ('Det nya Stockholm' 2006, *Stockholm* Översiktsplan 2000, Kallstenius and Pemer 2005: 21). But as the critique puts forth, there has been no 'urban renaissance'; what is being built is the *image* of a city. And the question remains: How can this be?

How Can We Study the Gap?

> Just as one does not judge an individual by what he thinks about himself, so one cannot judge … a period of transformation by its consciousness. (Marx 1977: Preface)

---

1   See, e.g., Franzén (2004), Hellström and Gullbring (2001), Klarqvist (1995), Marcus (1992; 1998; 2000a; 2000b), Nyström (1999), Rådberg (1997), Söderlind (1998) and Westin (2005a; 2005b; 2010). Journalistic examples are Andersson (2010a; 2010b), Hadley-Kamptz (2002), Johansson (1989), Rabe (2004) and Svensson (2004).

Figure I.2   Hammarby Sjöstad
Source: Author's photograph from 2009.

Urban environments where silence reigns abound in today's Western cities. Sociologist Lyn Lofland (1998: 97) has explored why this is so. According to her, it is partly because areas like these are relatively simple to create and partly because their creators – architects and planners – simply have wanted them this way: '[I]t is quite likely that they fully intended to create empty spaces', and for this, she says, there is 'evidence' (ibid.: 205). Le Corbusier, for example – one of the biggest sources of inspiration in post-war urban planning – was explicit with his craze for the totally intersection-free – and thus conflict-free – city. In sum, Lofland (1998: 208, my emphasis) concludes that 'the post-war agents of transformation *knew exactly* what they were doing'.

Lofland is talking about urban environments in post-war America, but the idea that explicit anti-urban tendencies lie behind the Swedish suburbs' general lack of city life is not hard to accept. These were designed as alternatives to the traditional city and as a solution to what was considered cities' problems (Lilja 2006: 113). Thus, to disperse people's movements and, thereby, reduce conflicts was a conscious and explicit goal. However, we do not need to think very hard to realise how badly this explanation fits when it comes to the kind of urban development project that is our focus. 'City-like' planning projects claim to be 'for' and not 'against' urbanity, which means that we cannot rely on either Lofland's or Jane Jacobs's (1992) reference to anti-urban 'attacks' on public space – attacks that openly categorise the street as a bad place. The problem has changed. We can no longer interpret what we see as an outcome of clear intentions; what we are dealing with is something more subtle and elusive. What we are facing is nothing less than a paradox. The planners say one thing and do another.

'To understand how buildings are formed, we must look at the knowledge behind them', writes architectural theorist Björn Linn (1992: 55). So far, I have no objections. But what is this knowledge and how do we study it? One option would be simply to interview architects and planners and ask them questions such as, 'What do you and your colleagues mean by urbanity and how do you implement the goal of creating it?' Such an approach assumes that the planners are capable of answering such questions fully and accurately. In other words, it requires an Enlightenment-infused image of man as rational and transparent to himself. It also assumes that knowledge is something we can talk about and transfer. It presupposes a view of knowledge as something a person *has*. It equates knowledge with information, thinking with the knowledge of facts.

In my book I have chosen not to follow this route. The reason is the same as Sigmund Freud's, when he chose not to ask his patients: Why do you make yourself ill?

A Psycho-Analytical Perspective

> [I]n western culture ... [k]nowledge of the material world has become detached from knowledge about ourselves. ... We know the cosmos, but we do not know ourselves. (Hulme 2013: 306)

The book is a psycho-analytically inspired ideology critique of contemporary urban planning, which means that I am less interested in what planners think and more interested in how they think. The empirical material consists of texts and published interviews with individuals – well known and less well known, Swedish and international, historical and contemporary – who in one way or another contribute to the shaping of the physical environment.

In short, a psycho-analytic understanding helps to illuminate the conflicted nature of man and of the world. It points to a lengthy but usually well controlled conflict between the individual and her social environment as well as between different parts within the individual. Other ways to describe this form of understanding are dynamic, dialectical or Dionysian. Herbert Marcuse characterised the dynamic as two-dimensional, as one of 'a world antagonistic in itself ... a world afflicted with want and negativity constantly threatened with destruction' (cited in DeKoven 2003: 266).

As it becomes evident in the opening quotation, when philosopher and sociologist Henri Lefebvre describes his dread during a visit in the well planned French working-class area of Mourenx in the 1960s, the problem of the gap is neither isolated nor new. Urban planning is steeped with good intentions – and yet, Lefebvre was terrified. '[S]o much of urban planning and design in the twentieth century has failed to deliver on its claims', to borrow a formulation from Marcus (2008: 135). It is an old sociological insight that bureaucratic organisations – of which urban planning is an example – can develop a way of working that is contrary to their foundational objectives (Israel 1971: 324, Weber 1994: 362). In fact, the problem is a version of a more general philosophical problem, namely, the question of how something can emerge from its opposite.

Human geographer Gunnar Olsson (2007: x) has highlighted this problem by likening planning to the classic tragedy – 'everything beautifully right at the beginning; everything horribly wrong at the end; no one to blame in between'. If we are to believe Friedrich Nietzsche (1986a: §1), 'almost all the problems of philosophy once again pose the same kind of question as they did two thousand years ago: how can something originate in its opposite, for example rationality in irrationality, the sentient in the dead, logic in unlogic, disinterested contemplation in covetous desire, living for others in egoism, truth in error?'

So far I have put forth my experience of the vision-reality gap. But experiencing is not the same as understanding. Therefore, it is my aim to explore ways to make the gap intelligible. Put another way, the study represents an attempt to gain greater clarity about the problem of contra-finality in urban planning. If the goal is to create an urban atmosphere, how is it that the result resembles a ghost town characterised by boredom? In the preface, I emphasised the similarities between my book and Marcus's (2000b) *Architectural Knowledge and Urban Form*. Both have emerged against the backdrop of 'city-like' building (see ibid.: 35ff). Both are captivated by the vision-reality gap (see ibid.: 37f). Both aspire to study architectural knowledge – that is, architects' attitudes, preferences, and dispositions. But while Marcus's (ibid.: 43) method can be described as archaeological (he studies the artefacts of architecture), I look at the architects' words.[2] And it is because the architects' knowledge is largely tacit, unspoken – even unconscious – that I have made my critique psycho-analytical.

> Architecture is a product of an accumulation of knowledge that has been going on for thousands of years. Experience has been stored in memory, transmitted to new generations, processed and built. Through the transfer of knowledge between generations we have worked our way up to levels that were impossible to reach within the framework of one generation. (Linn 1992: 20)[3]

The book rests on two assumptions. The first is that man has a tendency to make himself unhappy. The second is that the relationship between society and the individual is conflicted. In Freud's words, 'Just as the planet still circles round its sun, yet at the same time rotates on its own axis, so the individual partakes

---

2   Actually, this is also a type of archaeology, since the study of words is the study of characters, not meanings. However, my reason for distinguishing between an analysis of artefacts and an analysis of words is pedagogical.

3   See also Cuff 1992, Hillier et al. 1972, Lundequist 1991, Sternudd 2007.

in the development of humanity while making his own way through life'
(Freud 2002: 100).

The study begins with a contradiction, and the focus is on the boundary
between society and the individual, a boundary that in Chapter 2 is expressed by
the dualism in The Eye of the Architect – The Body of the *Flâneur*. I agree with
Olsson (1980a: 8b) when he says that 'the subject matter of the social sciences is
neither man nor society but man and society conceived relationally'. The boundary
is embodied in every individual, but it chafes in different ways. However, it turns
out that the feeling has a name: alienation. Therefore, in Chapters 3 and 7 and in
the Conclusion, I will discuss this phenomenon.

To say that we are facing a complicated problem is to state the obvious, but I do
want to emphasise its complexity. Like most problems, the vision-reality gap can
be confronted in different ways, and it is not my aim to provide a comprehensive
or definitive answer. What I will do is to invite the reader on my epistemological
journey towards a better understanding. When I use the term 'we', it is not to say
that you are me and I am you but to invite the reader to be a critical partner in my
own thinking.[4] It is my hope that this study is relevant even for those who have
other interests besides cities and urban planning. My scope is broader than that
of producing knowledge about the city and urban planning; I want to understand
how we understand. A tool in this work is the continual changing of perspectives
– perspectivism – a mode of analysis described in Chapter 1.

In this book I direct attention to the planner's knowledge. When I write
'planners' or 'architects', I am referring to the practical perspective, professionals
working in the field of urban planning, and this perspective is the main focus of
Chapters 2 and 3. But I am also interested in how researchers of urban planning
look at urbanity. The practical perspective is therefore complemented by what I
call a scientific perspective, here represented by the architectural theory of space
syntax.[5] This perspective is discussed rather late in the book, in Chapter 6 – not
because it is less interesting but because this order makes sense chronologically.
Space syntax is fundamentally a critique of the practical perspective in architecture,
and, as Stuart Hughes (1958: 37) wrote, 'in order to understand a new tendency in
thought, we must first look at what the revolt is directed against'.

My reason for examining space syntax is two-fold. Firstly, as we will see in
Chapter 4, the starting point of space syntax is similar to the starting point of this
book: a feeling of confusion and frustration over the gap between vision and reality
in urban planning. Secondly, the theory is very much preoccupied with a question
that sits at the heart of human geography: the relation between form and process.

---

4   This formulation owes much to Richard Sennett (2009).
5   Space syntax is both a theory and a method, with contributions from a number
of researchers; sometimes it denotes a research tradition, sometimes a concrete urban
design practice. In this book I focus on its theoretical underpinnings. Well aware that it is a
generalisation, I use the expression *proponents of space syntax* or *space syntax researchers/
theorists* mostly when referring to the works of two people: Bill Hillier and Lars Marcus.

Geographer Jacqueline Beaujeu-Garnier (1976: 9) writes, 'From the outset, the founders of modern geography sought to understand the interrelationships between human activity and the physical environment'. It is therefore in light of insights acquired in human geography (and related social sciences) that I will examine space syntax. The results will hopefully be cross-fertilising.

Although my aim is to show how the perspective of the space syntax theorist differs from the practitioner's perspective, I will also highlight similarities between them. For example, both are based on an implicit belief that the world is an arena of more or less calculable forces, where if you do *this*, you can achieve *that* (Gullberg 1986: 4, Olsson 1990: 84). In addition, they both express the idea that urban planning is a means to achieve stated ends. Here the gap between vision and reality is implicitly formulated as a technological problem, and the task becomes to refine technology. Overall, this is an example of the reasoning we call logic – a thinking that characterises the majority of scientific research (social and natural), as well as our everyday understanding.

Since I am interested in the taken-for-granted – in society and in the individual – I (metaphorically) put the space syntax theorist on the couch, too: or, rather, her reasoning rules. And to illuminate what I find, I view the result in the light of dialectics, a way of reasoning that many urban geographers and urban sociologists share. Basically, space syntax researchers and dialectical urban theorists are interested in the same thing: the relationship between the built environment, on the one hand, and social processes, on the other. But the way they handle this relation differs – something we will see in Chapters 5, 6 and 7. For now, let me just note that this book not only deals with the problem of contra-finality but with the general philosophical-geographical problem of form and process as well.

The book finds inspiration in a range of disciplines: human geography, architecture, psychology, philosophy, critical theory, sociology, anthropology and literature. The approach is broad because at the forefront I have placed my research problem – not my discipline. The problem of the vision–reality gap – as well as the relation between form and process – is so multi-faceted that it cannot be exhausted by a single discipline, let alone by one individual.

The main sources of inspiration have been Friedrich Nietzsche, Sigmund Freud, Henri Lefebvre and Gunnar Olsson but also Martin Heidegger and Norman O. Brown. Three things unite these thinkers: First, they are critics of power and of Enlightenment thinking; their focus is on the shadow side of human life, to borrow William Barrett's (1962: 22) expression. Second, but related to the first, they emphasise the importance of the body for power and knowledge. Third, they all deal with paradoxes. In turn, this means that they – to a varying degree of voluntariness[6] – make room for the contradictory and dialectical in our

---

6 This reservation is written with regard to Freud, who said, 'I always envy the physicists and mathematicians who can stand on firm ground' (in Flyvbjerg 2001: 26f). While science generally sees contradictions as a weakness, psycho-analysis builds on them, which is one explanation to why Freud, who was inspired by both Enlightenment and Romanticism

understanding of the world. This necessarily involves a challenging of conventional science,[7] whose ultimate aim is to eliminate the ambivalence of human existence (see, e.g., Østerberg 1966: 15). Like good skaters they take advantage of the slipperiness of the ice instead of trying to defeat it. As Nietzsche (2010: 173) writes: 'Smooth ice/A paradise/For those who dance well'.[8]

As the reader has probably already understood, it was not without irony that I used the word trivial when I described the book's origin. Without regard to emotions and moods – phenomena that have to do with the body – it is hard to understand the problems that face social scientists. But as Western philosophy since the seventeenth century has been characterised by the Cartesian split between mind and body, emotions have been regarded as the enemy of reason (Marcuse 1955: 144, 1968b: 161). This attitude is traditionally found in geography as well: '[O]n the surface the discipline of geography often presents us with an emotionally barren terrain, a world devoid of passion ... [G]eography, like many of its disciplinary siblings, has often had trouble expressing feelings' (Bondi et al. 2005: 1, see also Ley 1977: 8).

Outside the personal sphere, emotions are generally considered irrelevant. Perhaps they are a matter for the arts (Coolidge 1941: 449). In addition, emotions are awkward to study because they lack physical extension (Svendsen 2005: 108). But as Olsson (1980a: 45b) states, '[T]o deny being to concepts like hope and fear, joy and sadness, is to extract from life precisely that element of autonomy which makes it worthwhile' (see also Lowenthal 1967: 1). An overall aim of the book is to deal with issues that conventional science cannot handle and thus represses:[9]

(Ricoeur 1970: 262), had a difficult time finding acceptance for his ideas within the scientific community of clinical psychology (Schorske 1981: 184). 'By the end of his life he had become at least as much a philosophical and literary figure as a man of science and of medicine. The positivist vocabulary remained – but the positivist mentality had been largely sloughed off' (Hughes 1958: 135). Although Freud strived to find the 'ultimate foundations that can be said to determine psychological progress', he often experienced logical reasoning as a straitjacket (Sjögren 2001: 34; 38, see also Greenberg 1994: 232 and Johansson 2011).

7 By 'conventional science', sometimes just 'science', I mean modern (natural) science that emerged during the seventeenth and eighteenth centuries; a thought tradition on which the social sciences were built (MacMurray 1957: 36). Georg Henrik von Wright (1986: 45ff) identifies its three basic features: 1) a dualistic view of the relationship between man and nature, objects, human subjects, which means that humans are partly observers, partly manipulators, 2) a clear distinction between facts and values, and 3) a view that nature has regularities that the scientist can discover by formulating laws, according to causes and effects. Furthermore, science is associated with a quest for truth, that is, a correspondence between claim and reality (Liliequist 1997: 9). Once generated, truth is believed to guide the prediction of future outcomes (Johnston 1989: 61).

8 This is more elegant in the German original: 'Glattes Eis / Ein Paradeis / Für den, der gut zu tanzen weiß' (Nietzsche 2007: 8).

9 *Repression* is a psycho-analytic term that denotes an unconscious defence mechanism to prevent memories, feelings or desires from becoming conscious (Brenner 1970: 80).

subjective and bodily experiences, immaterial phenomena, contradictions and that which is considered out of bounds. In this way I hope to highlight some of the negative consequences that may result from repression.

Some decades ago geographer Torsten Hägerstrand (1986: 42) called for an expansion of geography's focus from 'the merely visible' to 'the human actors, their knowledge and intentions, which not even natural geographers can ignore anymore'. Today, the growing field of emotional geography indicates that we should not only take into account man's intentions but also his emotions[10] (see Anderson and Smith 2001, Bondi et al. 2005, Davidson and Milligan 2004, Pain and Smith 2010). However, I want to emphasise that I do not consider emotions and knowledge as different but, rather, as highly interwoven phenomena.

It is hardly surprising that calls to disregard personal experience often come from individuals in a higher position (social or professional), from individuals in positions of power (politicians, teachers, parents and so on). From these positions, such talk might appear threatening, since it can uncover power relations (Anderson and Smith 2001: 7, Listerborn 2002: 74). However, personal experience is especially important in studies of urban planning. For what is urban planning if not an 'extraordinary example of human action' (Olsson 1985)? And, as we learn from anti-psychiatrist R.D. Laing (1967: 21), human experience and human action 'occur in a social field of reciprocal influence and interaction'.

By now, the absurdity of the labelling of urban planners as 'neutral experts' should be clear. Nevertheless, this is the way that many urban planners regard themselves (Johansson and Khakee 2008: 205).[11] In its most basic form, this book is a challenge to this view, a questioning of both the words 'neutral' and 'expert'. But to see that the emperor is naked, we must first discover his disguise; we must reveal his perspective, his vantage point. And since perspectivism plays a central role in my book, I will discuss it in the first chapter.

As mentioned in the preface, the question 'what is urbanity?' permeates the book. It also became clear in the preface that this question is personally motivated. But this is not the whole story. On an academic level, the question has grown out of a frustration with how the social sciences in general and human geography in particular tend to overlook the physical dimension in the discussions of the urban. Briefly put, the urban is either depicted as a mental state, as a kind of floating

---

10   Related to the concept of emotion is that of feeling. In the science community – including fields such as psychology, sociology, history, medicine and neuroscience – there is no consensus as to whether there is a difference between these concepts and what their respective meanings are. In the book I will use them interchangeably and not go into their respective ontology (that is, whether they refer to something biological or cultural). In relation to these concepts, there is the concept of affect. On the topic of emotions and affect in recent human geography, see Pile (2010).

11   In a study of different ethical aspects within the urban planning profession, Johansson and Khakee (2008) sent out a survey to 150 planners in 20 Swedish cities. 94 of them responded.

spirit independent of the morphology of physical reality, or the term is used as a synonym for 'the city' in general. A consequence of the latter is that the urban is equated with the rather bland term 'urban area'. In both cases, the definition covers almost anything and, hence, means nothing. How can we capture the urban as a socio-material phenomenon in a way that takes into account both its tangible and intangible dimensions? This is where the theory of space syntax is helpful, and the book can be seen as an introduction of this theory into urban geography research.[12]

In this introduction I have built a platform for what is to come. However, this platform is still somewhat unstable, which is why some further clarifications are needed.

Some Clarifications of Concepts and Perspectives

Planning/Architecture

> There exists a coherent action called town planning which, although it is
> sometimes empirical and often uses the concepts and methods of other disciplines
> (demography, political economy, geography, etc. …), approximates a scientific
> and technical approach in the same manner as an established discipline such as
> economics. (Lefebvre 1977: 339)

Planning and architecture. And the slash / in the title above; the symbol that signifies both identity and difference. In this book I lean towards and draw on the identity aspect of the symbol. In other words, I do not separate 'planners' and 'architects' but use the terms interchangeably to denote individuals that on scientific or artistic grounds are considered to have the know-how in assessing how the city, or parts of the city, are to be formed (see Strömgren 2007: 37f). They are considered *experts*.

Although in some contexts it might be appropriate to highlight the differences between planning and architecture (for example, scales and working procedures),[13] it would not only be irrelevant but also counterproductive to do so here. This would distract from the fundamental similarities between these two activities (Grant 2000: 171). '[T]he design professions of architecture, urban planning, and urban design have at their base a visionary charge and a utopian agenda' (Cuff 2000: 31). We are dealing with a specific 'planning mindset', regardless of whether one is designing a house, an office interior design or an entire city. This broad definition of planning or architecture is also used by Marcus (2000b: 7), who

---

12   Earlier introductions include Soja (2001) and Seamon (1994; 2004; 2007).

13   The answer to the question of whether architects are planners and vice versa generally varies between different countries. For studies on the architect's and/or planner's role and responsibilities, see Cuff (1992), Grange (2013), Imrie and Street (2008) and Knox and Ozolins (2000).

argues that architectural knowledge is not necessarily restricted to individuals with a degree in architecture. Rather, it is a matter of 'a certain disposition in individuals to look at things, or design things, or even formulate questions on things, in a way that differs from other individuals' (ibid.). The architect/planner is a part of a thought collective; she is a bearer of a particular thought style (Fleck 1979). A thought collective can be defined as 'a community of persons mutually exchanging ideas or maintaining intellectual interaction' (Fleck 1979: 39). A thought style is something that develops over time, consisting of different layers, developed by several generations, and influencing how the individuals in the thought collective think and act.

Lastly and most importantly, both architecture and planning are political and, thus, power-ridden activities. As Max Weber (1994: 311) underscores, politics – in its broadest sense – is a will to power or a desire to influence the distribution of power. Exercises in power make up an essential aspect of all politics; the quest for power is one of its main driving forces. Putting these ideas together, 'No planning can exist if there is no instrument of power to force the individual into obedience and submission' (Améen and Lewan 1970: 41) – be this instrument of power tangible or intangible.

The Planner's/Architect's Acting Space and Responsibility

> Stockholm lacks the tools necessary to meet the new building boom. The distribution of responsibility is uncertain. When not even the City Hall politicians can answer who has authority over planning, you realise that no one knows who is responsible. Perhaps no one wants to shoulder the responsibility today. (Larsson 2010: 60)

At this point, perhaps the reader of this book is wondering what the planner's/ architect's role in today's urban planning process is exactly. This 'expert' attempts to facilitate a process in which a range of concerns must be met, including building codes, referral agencies, citizens, interest groups, environmental goals, developers' demands and, last but not least, economic conditions. Is the gap between vision and reality really a function of the planner's doings and not-doings? The question is not unwarranted, especially since the sheer number of considerations that the planner must deal with has dramatically increased during the twentieth century to include safety, environment, accessibility, health and so on (Imrie and Street 2008). As planning theorist Anders Gullberg (1986: 5) points out, the view of planning as an activity in which the subject's will and determination reigns is unreasonable. The opposite view that the structures of society dictate the course of events is also unreasonable. The only reasonable thing to do would be to combine these perspectives – the rationalist and the structural – and then assess how big the planner's acting space really is.

However, this is not the question I have set out to answer. Moreover, the question of the planner's 'real' acting space is deeply problematic. How do you investigate this? And how would you handle the conflicting answers you would most certainly get? In Sweden alone there are architects that describe their situation from diametrically different perspectives. One says, 'The project I am working on … is an example that shows that many factors apart from the architect's intentions have influenced the results' (in Sörenson 2005: 93). Another says, 'We have gone from a time when no one listened to the architects to a period when the architects are running the development' (in ibid.: 87).

Two of the architects I quote in the book, Jan Inghe-Hagström and Aleksander Wolodarski, have both been powerful actors in urban planning in Stockholm during the past 40 years. Wolodarski has worked as a planning architect at the Stockholm City Planning Office since 1968 (Andersson 2009b, Gullbring 2002: 19) and Inghe-Hagström has been responsible for, among other things, Minneberg, Södra stationsområdet and Hammarby Sjöstad. Erland Ullstad (2008: 70; 59), representative of the Swedish Architects, emphasises that urban development is a complex game with many actors but also says that the city architect and her team are the ones that should enable the making of good architecture and good environments. Herein lays the mission of the expert, a mission that entails both freedom and responsibility.

Closely linked to power is responsibility. I regard responsibility as something that, at the end of the day, only can be held by the individual. In the words of A.C. Armstrong (1907: 120): 'In fine, is not each man responsible for his own deeds, whether he acts by himself or along with others … ?' Planners are partly cogs in the wheel of a bureaucratic organisation whose rules they are obliged to follow. At the same time, we should not forget the fact that they also – regardless of what they believe – are 'arbiters of other people's patterns of life' (Evans 2003: 29). Being a 'neutral' city planner is thus impossible.

To act, as defined by von Wright (1968: 38), 'is intentionally ("at will") to *bring about* or to *prevent* a *change* in the world (in nature)'. Hence, '[T]o forbear (omit) action is either to *leave* something *unchanged* or to *let* something happen' (ibid.). To execute a command (from someone higher up in the bureaucratic and/ or political hierarchy) is also a choice. The refusal or failure to act is also an act. Planners are members of a social system, which means that they can influence it (Israel 1971: 20, see also Taleb 2007: 163). To assert one's neutrality as a planner is the same as claiming that you are a passive object, whose role has been imposed on you. Human beings are sometimes subjects, sometimes objects but never just one or the other (Israel 1980: 203, Arendt 1998). In the words of Cassirer (1972: 11): 'Contradiction is the very element of human existence. Man has no "nature" – no simple or homogeneous being. He is a strange mixture of being and nonbeing. His place is between these two opposite poles'.

Therefore, we can now say this: asserting our neutrality is the same as depriving ourselves of what makes us human. Naturally, there is a price for refusing to do what is asked: expulsion from the system, resignation or the like. But the fact that a price exists shows that planning is a game that the players – that is, the planners – have agreed to play. Being a planner is to play a role, a role that the individual chooses. There are, of course, limitations to this game, but 'those limitations must be chosen by the player since no one is under any necessity to play' (Carse 1986: §12). The role as a planner is simply not imposed on the individual; it is freely taken on. And with freedom comes responsibility.

As we leave this section, it should be noted that the issue of the planner's responsibility has not been exhausted; on the contrary, the problem permeates the book. The planner here plays the role of the tragic hero: although other forces seem to determine her fate, she remains the author of her actions.

Continuity – Not Change

> In Swedish planning politics there are no tendencies of post-modern planning reasoning. (Strömgren 2007: 248)

Modern Swedish urban planning is commonly thought to have oscillated between two different types or ideals: first, a modernist ideal, dominant between the 1930s and the 1980s, and second, a more traditional type, prevailing before the 1930s, and then after the 1980s and onwards (see Kallstenius 1986). In the 1980s, with the critique of modernism in general and The Million Programme[14] in particular, construction of a more traditional urban environment was resumed (ibid.). The type of neo-traditional building that has prevailed since then is called 'city-like' building or planning; early examples of planning projects include Skarpnäck, Södra stationsområdet and Hammarby Sjöstad.

As argued elsewhere, today's 'city-like' building is, in fact, modernism in disguise[15] (Marcus 2000, Westin 2004; 2005a; 2005b). The planners may claim that they have left the central ideas of modernism behind, but a closer look at their reasoning reveals references to modernist solutions such as to open up, to loosen up, to tear down the old and to separate different functions. Thus, the contention that 'city-like' planning represents a complete paradigm shift in the history of urban planning is misleading.

Marcus (2000b: 36f) gives a more reasonable picture. If you look at how these neo-traditionally built environments *function*, he argues, they are no different from modernist-built environments. In fact, the neo-traditional and the modernist planning traditions belong to one and the same category. The period between approximately 1900 and the 1930s also belong to this category. Hence, no break has occurred – neither in the 1930s, nor in the 1980s – if you take into account how the urban environment *functions*. However, there is a clear difference between

---

14   The Million Programme refers to the large housing programme implemented in Sweden between 1965 and 1974 by the Social Democratic Party. The aim was to build a million affordable dwellings in ten years in order to solve the massive housing shortage. At the same time, a large proportion of the older housing stock was demolished.

15   Or functionalism, which is the name modernism got in Sweden. I will use them interchangeably.

environments built before 1900, and environments built after 1900. After 1900, urban development has given rise to relatively similar environments in terms of function, although the goal in recent years has been to build traditional, urban environments of the type found in the older, inner parts of the cities.

What happened around 1900 that changed urban planning so much? It was at this point that architects started to gain increased influence. In 1901 the first modern urban planning competition was organised in Sweden (ibid.: 32), and this served as a starting point not only for the meeting of architectural knowledge and urban form but also of architectural knowledge and everyday life (Östnäs and Werne 1987: 28). The change of the architectural profession's traditional tasks during this time was considerable. From having created unique solitary monuments for centuries, the responsibility was suddenly extended to homes, workplaces and entire neighbourhoods (Eriksson 2001: 88; 172, Habraken 2005: 31). '[U]rban planning and design in the twentieth century differs substantially from urban planning and design in previous centuries, in that, to a degree never encountered before, it is the result of architectural knowledge' (Marcus 2000b: 193).

In sum, twentieth-century urban planning can be seen more in terms of continuity than change. The problem of modern urban planning – that is, the activity that was born in late nineteenth century and culminated after World War II – is of such a general nature that it never really disappears. Support for the continuity thesis is not only found in works by architectural theorists Marcus (2000b: 32), Sternudd (2007: 149) and Habraken (2005: 10, 31) but also in a paper by human geographer Ola Söderström (1996), which shows that urban-planning instruments have remained relatively unchanged since the 1940s and that some of their roots go back to the nineteenth century. In addition, political scientist Andreaz Strömgren (2007) has examined Swedish planning politics between 1945 and 2005 and has found that the Planning and Building Act, the comprehensive plan and zoning legislation, continue to exert influence on planning regardless of any paradigm shifts taking place on a discursive level.

A Pessimistic Planning Critique

> Urban-renewal administrators frequently speak of 'citizen participation' and 'planning with people'. Yet, the final decisions after the public hearings are made by those in power. (Goodman 1972: 54)

The book is a critique of planning. But in what way is the book a critique? It is to this question we now turn. To begin to answer this question, I will clarify what I am *not* trying to do.

All planning critique is more or less normative. Planning critics – in the most basic sense, and regardless of whether they do it explicitly or not – call for a different, better kind of planning. And they usually do so in one of the following two ways (though one does not exclude the other). Either they criticise planning with regard to its objectives, what planners are trying to achieve (garden city, dense urban neighbourhood and so on), whereby they propose a new, 'better' goal (garden city, dense urban neighbourhood and so on),[16] or they criticise – in a broad sense – the planning process in itself, whereby they propose another, 'better' type of planning. This latter form of criticism can in turn be divided into two subtypes, one that succinctly calls for a more just and democratic planning process in which marginalised groups are given voice,[17] and one that suggests other measures – preferably evidence based – that will ensure the realisation of goals regardless of what objective is being pursued.[18]

Although this schematic summary does not do the individual studies justice, there are problems with all mentioned forms of planning critiques. The problem with the first type – the one that proposes a new and 'better' goal of planning, and thus offers a new version of what counts as a 'good city' – is that it rarely acknowledges that 'good' is a value judgment and that there are a variety of definitions of what a 'good' living environment is. The second form of critique – the one that criticises the planning process in itself and proposes another, 'better' type of planning – has embraced this insight on subjectivity (and often goes on to criticise the former on exactly this point), but it is problematic in a different way. The assumption behind a critique of the planning process is that *it is possible* to conduct planning that is democratic and just. One could say that what this kind of critique calls for is non-authoritarian planning, planning conducted by 'humble experts'. This call is exemplified in the following excerpt by Bradley et al. (2004):

> As we reject dogmatic modernist planning, let us not make the same mistake and put our faith in a universal grammar that dictates how we build. We must maintain an ongoing discussion where we look at both the global and local conditions to understand how we can develop better communication and an urban planning that meet people's needs and desires. We put our hope in a new generation of planners and architects; an ethnically, socially and sexually mixed corps that is not marked by the settlement with modernism and the Million Programme, and that is able to think multi-dimensionally, beyond simple formulas.

---

16   See, e.g., Arnstberg and Bergström (2001), Gehl (1991), Jacobs (1992), Katz (1994), Nyström (1999), Rådberg (1997) and Söderlind (1998). Rådberg (1997: 114) writes: 'What we need is a theory of urban planning that tells how we build good suburbs'. Nyström (1999: 42) calls for an urban politics that can change the urban landscape around the Swedish cities into 'good and worthy living, working and cultural environments for the future'. Gehl (1991: 32) too pleads for a city that is 'good in all possible ways' and he has compiled a check list for 'the good city'. For a challenge of the normative prescriptive role of planning practice, see Gunder and Hillier (2009: 39–56).

17   See, for example, Bradley (2009), Bradley et al. (2004), Davidoff (1996), Fainstein (2010), Forester and Krumholtz (1990), Healey (1992; 1996), Sandercock and Forsyth (1992), Steffner (2009) Thomas (1996), Tunström (2009; 2010) and Wilson (1992a).

18   This type of critique is best exemplified by space syntax.

The condensed message is this: if only a new generation of planners would gain influence, urban planning would be just. That is to say, if only the 'right' planners get power – those who are able to 'think multi-dimensionally' and justly – planning will meet human needs (and desires!). This idea of non-authoritarian planning is widespread, but, in fact, it is a contradiction in terms.

Generally, we can say that most planning critique adopts a critical perspective based on the content of planning, while its basic form is more or less left unquestioned. By basic form I mean the perception of planning both as something essentially positive and as an activity that can lead to something good for the individual and for society in general. If only the 'right' planners are mobilised, or if only the 'right' measures are taken, we can prevent any shortcomings in planning. As Oren Yiftachel (1998: 396) has noted, planners are generally regarded – both by practitioners and theorists – as 'do-gooders'.

It should now be clear that my interest is in the 'the dark side of planning' (Flyvbjerg 1996, Yiftachel 1998). But in what way, more precisely, do I understand planning as 'dark'? This is a restatement of another question: In what respect is the criticism formulated in this book new? The book differs from other planning critiques in emphasising that it is not necessarily so that a given group (male, heterosexual, white and so on) through urban planning measures oppress other groups (women, ethnic minorities, homosexuals and so on).[19] Rather, there is a guerrilla war being waged between those who we will meet in Chapter 2 as Homo Faber and Homo Ludens, ocnophils and philobats, Sunday lovers and Sunday haters. But the problem is even more complex than that. What psycho-analysis, the individual perspective and the Chiasm (introduced in Chapter 7) helps us to discover are man's tendencies towards neurotic suffering, which are a consequence of him oppressing not so much other people but himself.[20]

A pessimistic picture of planning, indeed. The purpose of painting this picture has not been to argue against state planning or to reject the critique mentioned. Society is a collective, and planning is needed to promote the collective good.[21] What would the alternative be? At the same time it should be remembered that the statement 'planning promotes the collective good' points to the plural (collective), not the singular (individual). If we apply the singular form, the picture is different – and much more complex. Planning cannot escape the predicament of contra-finality; this is how one could summarise the points made in this section but also the message of the book as a whole. In short, 'We are damned if we do

---

19   This form of critique is widespread and draws mainly on Michel Foucault's philosophy. See Yiftachel (1998: 397–9) for an overview.

20   Planning critics that have expressed similar ideas in other ways are Olsson (1980a; 1990), Nordström (2008), Ramirez (1995), Lefebvre (1995) and Sennett (2008). For an explicit Lacanian analysis of spatial planning, see Gunder and Hillier (2009).

21   See Klosterman (1985) for an exposé of common arguments for and against planning.

and damned if we don't' (Olsson 1980a: 11e). A slightly longer answer to what the human predicament means is given by Sören Kierkegaard (1987: 38f):

> Marry, and you will regret it. Do not marry, and you will also regret it. Marry or do not marry, you will regret it either way. Whether you marry or you do not marry, you will regret it either way. Laugh at the stupidities of the world, and you will regret it; weep over them, and you will also regret it. Laugh at the stupidities of the world or weep over them, you will regret it either way. Whether you laugh at the stupidities of the world or you weep over them, you will regret it either way. Trust a girl and you will regret it. Do not trust her, and you will also regret it. Trust a girl or do not trust her, you will regret it either way. Whether you trust a girl or do not trust her, you will regret it either way. Hang yourself and you will regret it. Do not hang yourself and you will also regret it. Hang yourself or do not hang yourself, you will regret it either way. Whether you hang yourself or do not hang yourself, you will regret it either way. This, gentlemen, is the quintessence of all the wisdom of life.

With these clarifications made, it is time to move on. Since the book embodies an attempt to understand, we begin with a closer look at Friedrich Nietzsche's perspectivism, a philosophy that is intimately intertwined with understanding.

Chapter 1
Perspectivism

In so far as the word 'knowledge' has any meaning, the world is knowable; but it is *interpretable* otherwise, it has no meaning behind it, but countless meanings. – 'Perspectivism'.

Friedrich Nietzsche

Turn your eyes inward, look into your own depths, learn first to know yourself! Then you will understand why you were bound to fall ill; and perhaps you will avoid falling ill in the future.

Sigmund Freud

Perspectivism is a metabelief that ... characterizes the discipline of geography.

Gunnar Olsson

What you see depends on where you stand and how your mind is moulded; if you and I do not understand each other, we most likely experience the world from different vantage points. This is the essence of Nietzsche's philosophy of perspectivism,[1] and the message is that we should look first and foremost into our rules behind our reasoning if we want to understand why we become surprised, amazed, puzzled. Or as Olsson (1991: 6) puts it: 'To understand is to condense a thought position into a point and place it in relation to other points'.

When I reflect upon my expectations before my first visit to Hammarby Sjöstad, I realise they rested on the assumption that the concept of urbanity has the same meaning for the planners as it has for me. But how can we be sure that we are all thinking about the same thing when we are dealing with a kind of nebulous phenomenon like urbanity? Considering perspectivism, I have come to see the vision-reality gap as a gap between, on the one hand, my understanding of the urban and my way of relating to the built environment and, on the other, the planners' understanding. Therefore, I have established two fixed points: the eye of the architect and the body of the *flâneur*, and these are the focus of Chapter 2. There, I ask what characterises these forms of understanding.

One of the basic assumptions in my book is the deceivingly simple thesis that the city – well, actually everything – appears differently depending on whether

---

1 Nietzsche explicitly discusses perspectivism in *The Will to Power* and *Beyond Good and Evil*. For an introduction, see Megill (1985: 84ff). The concept of perspectivism was founded by Gustav Teichmüller in 1882 but was later elaborated on by Nietzsche (Jay 1994: 188).

you relate to it primarily with your eyes or with our body (see e.g. Heil 1983: 5). Another assumption is that the planner and the *flâneur* want different things from the city; behind every interpretation lies a set of preferences. Chapter 2 also illustrates how the city – to the planner – first and foremost is a conceived space, shaped by different visualisation tools, while for the *flâneur*, it is a multi-sensory lived space. In light of Henri Lefebvre's (1991) philosophy of space, I then relate these spatial dimensions to each other.[2] In practice, this means analysing statements of planners and *flâneur*s, and determining what characterises the different perspectives.

Since conceived space is materialised in buildings that, in turn, 'enter into and help shape and direct life' (Dewey 2005: 241), the conceived space of the planner is here seen as a power tool that subordinates the user's lived space as well as human experience. Or, as Robin Evans (2003: 29) puts it, '[I]t is in the present nature of things that planners or architects have thrust on them the onerous task of being arbiters of other people's patterns of life, whether they find this right and proper, or peculiarly unenviable'.

To better understand the lived space of the *flâneur*, on the other hand, I turn to fiction writers, with Virginia Woolf and August Strindberg in the foreground. Inspired by Nietzsche's idea that each utterance is a hiding place, that every word is a mask (Berg Eriksen 2005: 154), it follows that everything explicitly formulated can be studied in order to access a feeling, a desire, an attitude. Although I sometimes speak of unconscious beliefs or unconscious ideas, it should be emphasised that I do not mean ideas in a Platonic sense. As Freud says (in Brown 1959: 7), 'We remain on the surface as long as we treat only of memories and ideas. The only valuable things in psychic life are, rather, the emotions'.

Philosopher Lars Svendsen (2005: 111f) stresses that there is a link between cognition in general and our interests and that cognition must be interpreted in light of moods. This means a challenging of the distinction between objective descriptions and subjective values, exemplified by the following thought-provoking question: 'Can we ... clearly distinguish between whether something *is* boring or if it only *feels* boring?' (Svendsen 2005: 108). This leads us to the next section, in which I discuss the epistemological basis of my book.

A Solipsistic Starting Point

> Essential: to start from the body and employ it as a guide. It is the much richer
> phenomenon, which allows of clearer observation. (Nietzsche 1968: §532)

---

2   Besides lived space (spaces of representation) and conceived space (representations of space), Lefebvre's (1991) trialectical theory of space includes the dimension of perceived space (spatial practices). How these are related is a study in its own right. As Merrifield (1995: 110f) has said, Lefebvre himself is 'vague about how spatial practices *mediate* between the conceived and the lived, about how spatial practices keep representations of space and spaces of representation together, yet apart'.

Can there be a world that is not characterized by any sort of attunement, any mood? In this case, I will argue that the answer is a categorical no. (Svendsen 2005: 107f)[3]

Each attempt at understanding necessarily starts from subjective experience. The Greeks seemed to understand this, considering the word *empeiria* originally meant human experience (Nordström 2008: 91, Ramirez 2003: 62). I chose Woolf and Strindberg as principal guides in the lived space of the *flâneur* because their depictions of the city fascinate me; like an ally I walk in their footsteps. By making the *flâneur*'s perspective my own – my own the *flâneur*'s – I appropriate, as Elizabeth Wilson (1992a) before me, what is usually described as a classic masculine approach to the city (Prendergast 1992, Tester 1994, Wolff 1985). The choice to anchor my writing in my own experience is ultimately the result of a desire to take seriously the fundamentally solipsist philosophers who have inspired this book. For Nietzsche (1968: 301), the metaphysical question 'What is it?' was reformulated into 'What is it *for me*?' (see also Deleuze 2006: 77).

To use personal experiences instead of collecting data about other people's experiences is an appropriate method when the aim is to reach a deeper understanding of how we perceive our physical and social environment (see Frers 2007, Schroeder 2008). Furthermore, the method I have chosen represents a way around the problem summarised by Laing (1967: 16): '[T]he experience *of the other* is not evident to me, as it is not and never can be an experience of mine' (see also Cioran 2012: 18, Østerberg 1966: 69f).

In science, there is an implicit but widespread perception that for descriptions to be accurate, the personal and subjective should intervene as little as possible. It is assumed that the subjective distorts the perception of what something 'really' is (Brenner 1988: 9, Molander 1995: 123). This assumption, however, is seldom explicitly discussed. This is natural since ideas that are taken for granted are rarely or never discussed, and things we rarely or never discuss tend to remain unchanged. But since Immanuel Kant, we have had almost three-hundred years to incorporate the following insight: Subjectivity is not a threat to knowledge and, therefore, something that ought to be corrected and controlled; subjectivity is the prerequisite for knowledge (Daston and Galison 2007: 374, Barrett 1962: 181). And it is the body that is 'the very "stuff" of subjectivity' (Grosz 1994: ix, see also Eagleton 1990: 235). Since perspectivism means that what you see depends on where you stand, and since no one can stand in exactly the same place as another, it follows that no one can really speak for anyone else. Perspectivism and solipsism are therefore two sides of the same coin.

Overall, my method is chosen in light of the phenomenological notion that '[a]ll my knowledge of the world, even my scientific knowledge, is gained from my own

---

3   This question is a reformulation of Wittgenstein's statement that 'the world of the happy is a different world from the world of the unhappy' (in Svendsen 2005: 107).

particular point of view' (Merleau-Ponty 2002: ix).[4] And the focus of Nietzsche's philosophy was not ideas or concepts, but 'the unique experience of the single one, the individual' (Barrett 1962: 13). In pinning down the urban, I have not only used texts by writers but also my own experiences of living and being in urban environments. A part of this endeavour has been to mesmerise myself; that is, to listen to my body and to temporarily set aside (too much) logical thinking. This is difficult, since I am a scientist trained in a Cartesian scientific tradition that teaches that knowledge is 'in the head rather than in the body' (Merrifield 2006: 109). But I am left to try. The results of these experiments appear most in the three intermezzos in Chapter 2.

The search for the urban-according-to-me or urban-according-to-the-body thus requires a return to a more primitive way of thinking that has not yet been subject to the laws of logic – a way of thinking that is characteristic of children: 'The child's best-loved and most intense occupation is with his play' (Freud 1953: 25, see also Winnicott 1989). 'The child sees everything in a state of newness, he is always *drunk*', writes Baudelaire (1995: 8), and continues: '[S]ensibility is almost the whole being'. In a state of play, thoughts take their own paths, and they are immediately and strongly influenced by all kinds of emotions. The 'adult' thinking that develops later in life is subject to reason; it keeps emotions in check (Laing 1967: 22f). Furthermore, adults, in general, rely mostly on the visual: 'When we talk of the world ... we usually mean the world that we see when we use our eyes' (MacMurray 1957: 105).

But even if the child's primitive way of thinking fades as she grows up, it does not disappear completely (Palmgren 1997: 54). In typical adults primitive thinking usually emerges in dreams but also in play and in ecstasy (ibid.: 55).[5] One strategy that I have used in the investigation of lived space is to record sounds from walks in different parts of Stockholm. By listening to the tape afterwards, I have been able to ignore the visual and reinforce the auditory impressions instead.[6]

The use of fiction as research material is normally associated with humanistic geography. As Marc Brosseau (1994: 346) points out, this is usually motivated by a striving for realism. That is, novels, poems and short stories are used as instruments for accessing a supposed reality outside the text, such as the nature of different historical places. When I turn to Strindberg's and Woolf's texts, however, it is not for their depictions of, for example, turn-of-the-century Stockholm or

---

4   As Merleau-Ponty (2002: viii) himself argues, phenomenology existed as a thought tradition 'before arriving at complete awareness of itself as a philosophy', and the tradition can be traced in Hegel, Kierkegaard, Marx, Nietzsche and Freud.

5   At least this pertains to the more Dionysian art forms; such as music and poetry. Architecture and sculpture, however, are Apollonian art forms (Vattimo 1997: 24).

6   In the past decades, research on the acoustic and auditory dimensions of man's environment has become increasingly common, especially in the wake of Raymond Murray Schafer's (1993) concept of *soundscape* from 1977, not least in geography (see Butler 2006).

inter-war London but because they formulate an approach to the city that contrasts to the planner's. My reading of these authors is thus selective.

The roots of perspectivism can be traced to Kant and his subject-centred epistemology, which calls into question the concept of man and knowledge that has dominated from Plato to Descartes: 'Kant's Copernican revolution in thought centres the world upon the human subject ... making that whole register of experience less marginal, gratuitous or supplementary than it might otherwise appear' (Eagleton 1990: 102, see also Crary 1992: 69f). Before Kant, human capability for knowledge was considered through the lens of idealism, as potentially all-encompassing and primed to uncover the world's essence (Berg Eriksen 2005: 152). But Kant, inspired by David Hume, knew that the human capability for knowledge has limits, which contributed to a shift in focus from *what* we know (the object) to *how* we know (the subject). Kant's revolution was partly influenced by Romantic philosophy that acknowledged humans' creative and spontaneous imaginations as the root of knowledge (MacMurray 1957: 44f). This represented a move away from a Cartesian understanding of knowledge as a purely factual, reason-based discovery of what already exists in the world to a view of knowledge as a more or less fictitious synthesis made by a human's 'productive imagination' (ibid., see also Arendt 1998: 286ff, Entrikin 1977: 215): 'The resulting viewpoint is not a perspectiva naturalis but a perspectiva artificialis, a case of nature mirroring thought rather than thought mirroring nature' (Olsson 2007: 221). Thus, it was within a Kantian tradition that Nietzsche argued that we can never understand the world on its own terms; that there is a difference between reality and our knowledge of reality (Megill 1985: 25; 69).[7]

Perspectivism is a tradition with a visual origin that can be traced to the Renaissance. Latin *perspectiva* derives from *perspicere*, which means to see clearly, to investigate, to see through (Jay 1994: 53). Nietzsche was fully aware of this origin, but his use of the concept was meant to emphasise the problematic and subjective nature of interpretation in general (Guillén 1971: 367). Perspectivism was born as a criticism of what has been called the Cartesian *perspectivalism*, the belief in a transcendental, reason-based and non-physical way of seeing, which dominated from the Renaissance to the end of the nineteenth century (Jay 1994: 150). So, although there is a potentially confusing connection between perspectivism and perspectivalism, the former – as it hopefully has become clear – means something more than *seeing* in a literal sense; it refers to a way of experiencing and interpreting the world in which the body plays a crucial role.

Nietzsche is the forerunner of the thought tradition often referred to as post-modernism (Livingstone 1992: 344, Wood 2005: 67), and post-modernism

---

7 Even though Kant was important to Nietzsche, Nietzsche rejected his philosophy: '[I]t is high time to replace the Kantian question, "How are synthetic judgments *a priori* possible?" with another question, "Why is belief in such judgments *necessary*?" – in effect, it is high time that we should understand that such judgment must be *believed* to be true' (Nietzsche 1997: 8, see also Megill 1985: 53).

is built on some of the same fundamental assumptions as perspectivism: 'In the Nietzschean universe, men are irremediably shut out from "reality"' (Megill 1985: 49f). Genuine knowledge – that is, knowledge of how things really are – is hence unattainable; truth, or, rather, 'truth', is something achieved through language (Olsson 2007: 93; 225, Nietzsche 1997: 8).

I use perspectivism in my analysis of planning because it may have a therapeutic effect in helping us to 'break out from a deadening routine' (Megill 1985: 345); Nietzsche's philosophy acts as a distorting mirror, which may say something about our world and the possibilities to change it (or rather: change ourselves).

There are many reasons why a human geographical study of urban planning ought to ask philosophy for help. Philosophical thinking can be said to have 'effective mastery over science, since science depends on philosophy as much in its purpose as in its methods' (Kremer-Marietti 1999: 91, see also Marcuse 1964: 91, Olsson 1991: 30, Russell 1946: 11). Philosophical thinking centres on itself, its object of study is ultimately the knowledge-seeking subject (Cassirer 1972: 1).

Thus, instead of collecting seemingly objective facts about the world, I turn my attention to the net with which we seek to capture this world. Since perspectivism teaches us that what we see depends on where we stand, it is utterly central to the discipline of geography (Olsson 2002: 247).[8] What you call east is west for me and the kind of place you think is heaven on earth may well be my hell. Or, as Henri Bergson (2004: 43) puts it: 'As my body moves in space, all the other images vary, while that image, my body, remains invariable. I must therefore make it a centre, to which I refer all the other images'. In sum, perspectivism holds that any mapping of reality is our own interpretation, not an objective set of facts about how reality is. But does this render reality descriptions obsolete? Let me explain why this is not so.

Perspectivism and Reality

> [A]bsolute objectivity is a chimera, and ... absolute relativity is self-defeating.
> But why do we have to choose either? (Brown 1992: 140)

Nietzsche is sometimes seen as a proponent of the irrational, as an enemy of reason – even as an enemy of humanity in general, since his philosophy has inspired many of the lines of thought during the twentieth century that question objectivity and absolute values (Lukács 1980: chap. 3, Bloom 1987). This picture, however, is one-dimensional. Perspectivism does not imply that the one who claims a multitude of perspectives cannot or should not choose among them (Vattimo 1997: 115). As Edgar Sleinis (1999: 67) writes, '[T]here is no doubt whatever that Nietzsche

---

8   As shown by, most prominently, Olsson (2007: 274), Farinelli (1992) and Abrahamsson (2008), geography is central to philosophy too. On the map as a metaphor for knowledge, see Nordström (2008: 77ff), Pickles (2004).

frequently sees himself as revealing and rejecting the irrationalities and absurdities in belief and in human affairs that he takes others to have either missed or ignored'. The fact that Nietzsche is sceptical of rational thinking and reason does not mean that he represents a kind of 'emotional philosophy' or that he fundamentally rejects reason (Berg Eriksen 2005: 26). On the contrary, one could say that he shares the following insight – here expressed by philosopher Kojin Karatani (1995: 9): '[I]t is only reason itself that can deconstruct reason'.

Nietzsche thus believed in reason. But he knew that if we are not careful, it can lead us astray. Therefore, he wanted to limit its impact (Sleinis 1999: 69). So, perspectivism does not imply that all interpretations are equally just – a criticism often levelled against (the in itself diverse and often undefined idea of) relativism (Holmqvist 2009). To formulate a critique based on perspectivism means that you take yourself as a starting point. And from there you see the world through that lens. In this book, my starting point is the *flâneur*, and it is from this particular perspective I formulate my critique. In general, this critique is directed against what I – like many others but far from everybody – regard as a problem in cities in the Western world: the lack of urbanity.

In light of the above discussion, I can now say this: Although the philosophy of perspectivism allows me to, in this book, say that the definition of urbanity is different depending on where you stand, it is not my intention to reject attempts to formulate a precise and universal definition of the urban; on the contrary, in Chapter 5 this is precisely what I will try to do. For this book is partly motivated by a dissatisfaction with how planners talk about the phenomenon of urbanity, and one of my aims is to articulate what I – as a researcher in urban studies *and* as a pulse addict – perceive as urbanity's 'essence', if you will.

Before we continue, I should specify what I mean by 'reality'. It refers to *both* something that is common to all, *and* something that differs from person to person. Different people perceive reality differently – this truism is indisputable. Nevertheless, it is meaningful to speak of a reality. To say that there is a reality is to make an ontological stand. The idea that there – despite different views on what reality is like – is a common reality, whose characteristics and aspects we can have collective knowledge about, is based on the very existence of language. Because if reality were not congruent, we would not be able to use language at all (Israel 1980: 41). At the same time there are various descriptions of reality, both at the group level and at the individual level. Our descriptions of reality, which are specific to each and every one of us, are more often than not universal enough to allow us to convey them to and discuss them with others.

Take, for example, the psycho-analytic conversation between analyst and analysand. It is the job of the former to listen and to express understanding of the latter's reality descriptions. But the reverse is also true. That is, the psycho-analytic conversation is very much a matter of analyst and analysand together discussing their way towards deciding what is 'real' and what is not – that is to say, what can be considered realistic reactions, on one hand, and what in the context of the external reality seems to be greatly exaggerated delusions made up of past experiences, on the other. In essence, analysis is a continuous counselling or oscillation process that takes place between 'outer' and 'inner' reality – a sphere Donald Winnicott (1989: 134ff) has called the sphere of play. The analyst's challenge is – succinctly put – to teach the patient to play (not *how to* play, but *to* play). We ought not forget that a common reason behind the analysand's seeking of the analyst's help is that she experiences difficulties in managing the external reality (i.e. social relations and/or other aspects of everyday life). Overall, it should now be clear that in psycho-analysis, as well as in this book, 'reality' by no means plays an insignificant role.[9]

Any system of knowledge – including the one that this book embodies – consists of both 'active' and 'passive' connections. These are Ludwik Fleck's (1979: 10) concepts, and by active connections he means those that can be explained psychologically, historically, culturally and socially, while passive are the ones that seem 'real', 'objective' and 'true'. The passive connections, however, cannot exist isolated from the active. Against this backdrop, we can now ask this: When I, in the beginning, described Hammarby Sjöstad as a ghost town or a staged set impregnated with boredom, is this an active or passive connection? Put another way, is boredom a property of the space itself or is it just something I attribute to the space in light of my own state of mind? This question is – not surprisingly – difficult to answer. Svendsen (2005: 44) says,

> It is impossible to say if something is boring because one happens to be in a state of boredom or whether one begins to feel bored because the world is [boring[10]]. It is impossible to make any clear distinction between the respective contributions made by the subject and object to boredom, because the emptiness of the subject and object is so interwoven.

Hilary Putnam (1987: 26ff) is another philosopher who has argued for why we can sometimes gain from giving up the distinction between what 'really' exists in the world and what we 'only' project onto it. We find the ultimate support for this idea in the work of Heidegger, whose phenomenology allows no distinction between the experiencing subject and the perceived object. This relaxation of boundaries is important, especially in a book like this, where we are dealing with emotions and (other) immaterial phenomena. If we were to place these immaterial phenomena exclusively in the internal, mental sphere, and not in the world 'out there' (too),

---

9   Here it is interesting to note Paul Kingsbury's (2004: 119) explanation of why geographers turn to psycho-analysis: 'Geographers choose psycho-analytic approaches because they show how the restrictive binaries (self versus other, material versus ideal, and subjective versus objective) that are operationalized in culture are always out of sync'.

10   The word 'boring' is mine; in the English text – which is quoted above and which is a translation from Norwegian – it says 'bored'. In the original, however, it says 'kjedelig' (boring) (Svendsen 1999: 45) and in the Swedish translation it says 'tråkig' (boring) (Svendsen 2003: 52).

the city – my other object of study – would fall out of sight. As summarised by Svendsen (2005: 110), Heidegger argues that:

> precisely the fact that we are subject to moods indicates that they are *not* mere inner states that are projected onto a meaningless world. We cannot determine if a mood is something 'interior' or 'exterior' to the subject, as moods go beyond such a distinction and must be taken as a basic characteristic of our being-in-the-world.

That within social scientific urban research there is not one clear definition of urbanity but several ambiguous definitions (Andersson 1987) suggests that urbanity is not a thing that you and I can see and talk about in a unequivocal way, like a table or a chair (see Olsson 1980a: 44b). It is easier to agree that a figure on a piece of paper is a rectangle than to say what love is. To ask what urbanity is basically means grasping for a qualitative and critical meaning – a meaning that is sensed rather than thought, that resides in the body rather than in the head and that tends to slip through our fingers as soon as we try to capture it with a logical explanation or link it to concrete things (see Merrifield 2006: 110). But although urbanity is an intangible quality conditioned by historical, cultural and psychological factors, it isn't just *anything*. As Gottlob Frege says, 'It cannot well be denied that humanity has a common treasure of thoughts, which is passed from one generation to another' (in Olsson 1980a: 49b). Realism and perspectivism is not necessarily mutually exclusive. Realism, to some degree, means to rank different perspectives by their ability to deal with the reality in which we live (C. Taylor 2003: 174).

A text that combines relativism with realism is Jane Jacobs's classic book *The Death and Life of Great American Cities* from 1961. Jacobs was a journalist, but her aim is formulated in the spirit of scientific empiricism; the purpose is to describe 'how cities work in real life' (Jacobs 1992: 4) and she continues: 'Which avenues of thinking are apt to be useful and to help yield the truth depend not on how we might prefer to think about a subject but, rather, on the inherent nature of the subject itself' (ibid.: 428). This suggests a conventional-essentialist view of knowledge and truth as a correspondence between statement and reality. However, she then declares, 'Also, to be frank, I like dense cities best and care about them most', and, 'systems of thought, no matter how objective they may purport to be, have underlying emotional bases and values' (ibid.: 16: 221). As these quotes demonstrate, Jacobs is epistemologically inconsistent. But is this a problem? My answer is no.

In science, consistency is generally highly valued because it is a means to avoid confusion and mixed messages. 'Be consistent!' is something that most students writing their first scientific essay are told. Consistency is good. But it is also possible to see consistency as an expression of an anxiety that prevents us from actively reconsidering yesterday's insights. Ralph Waldo Emerson (1841) has challenged the commonsensical notion that consistency is always good; consistency, he claims, is '[a] terror that scares us from self-trust'. And he continues: 'Suppose you should contradict yourself; what then?'

'I hope any reader of this book will constantly and sceptically test what I say against his own knowledge of cities and their behaviour', writes Jacobs (1992: 16) as a humble contrast to her otherwise sharp attacks on the planning profession. What else can she do but say that what she is experiencing is reality? I am inclined to agree with Olsson (2007: 406) when he says, 'To any mapper of ... knowledge solipsism remains the only honest philosophy'.

However, Jacobs's book is problematic in that she rejects planners' statements as 'folly' (Jacobs 1993: xii). For a criticism to be constructive, it must take a detour through understanding, not condemnation (Olsson 1991: 20). As Sleinis (1999: 69f) writes, 'In general, interpretations which can explain how other interpretations have naturally arisen are better than those that are entirely silent on the matter, or worse than those that force one to condemn other interpretations as simply mad, bad, or stupid'.

Let me stress that I do not understand feelings as something we should 'also' focus on – 'in addition to' knowledge. This would mean reproducing the conventional view of feelings as something apart from science and planning. As Nietzsche (2003: 86) says, '[T]he switching off of the emotions all and sundry, granted that we could do so, what! [*sic!*] would not that be called intellectual *castration*?' Inspired by Nietzsche, but also Freud, I understand knowledge – in a wide sense – as a way to appropriate the world.

Perspectivism does not rule out criticism – it presupposes it. To not take a stand, as Carl Becker emphasised following Nietzsche, is to be dead before one's object of study (Holmqvist 2009: 265). Knowledge is a matter of appropriating the world – an effect of a human's will to power – and it is our emotions and attitudes that influence our interpretations (Berg Eriksen 2005: 153). Hence, when analysing the planners' perspective, one task is to examine what kind of drive or attitude a certain statement manifests (ibid.: 156).

In this chapter, I present my book's main epistemological assumption: the notion that the need for more facts is lesser than the need to evaluate what we think we already know (Olsson 1980a: 4, see also Asplund 1979, Bonnier 1997: 223, Cassirer 1972: 22, Ramirez 1995). Overall, it is in the nature of the book's subject that I will not come to a precise answer to my research problem, the gap between vision and reality, nor will I deliver solutions for how this gap can be bridged. My overall aim is to understand the problem. That is why I say that my goal is to make an analysis, not to stage a therapy session.

What, then, is the purpose of psycho-analysis? 'The purpose of analysis', Janet Malcolm (1981: 76) writes, 'isn't to instruct the patient on the nature of reality but to acquaint him with himself'. Hence; anyone who expects formulations of 'best practice' or 'good examples' in urban planning will be disappointed. This is not to say that good examples do not exist. But to point to good examples is not the critical social scientist's job. It is a common belief that whoever criticises something is also required to formulate an alternative. Here I would like to borrow

Magnus Eriksson's (2010: 8) words and say that, for this, there is 'no reasonable intellectual basis'. In fact, the question of 'what do you want instead?' is an effective way to put an end to intellectual work. And even though it is not enough to recognise and analyse problems of urban planning – planning needs solutions as well – the same person does not have to do everything. This is probably an idea that Kierkegaard (1987: 36) would subscribe to. He compares himself to the Lüneburger swine and says: 'My thinking is a passion. I am expert at rooting up truffles for others; I find no pleasure in them myself. I take the problems on my nose, but I can do no more with them than to throw them back over my head'.

What we are concerned with here, as I see it, is the difference between thinking and technology – or for that matter: between analysis and therapy.[11] As argued by Heidegger, the modern age is 'devoid of thought', Megill (1984: 178) sums up, and continues:

> We are dominated, [Heidegger] maintains, by a 'calculative[12] thinking', a thinking that is entirely technological, that concerns itself solely with the imposition of man's will upon the world. In calculative thinking, in the hustle and bustle of the present day, we never really think. Calculative thinking, Heidegger concedes, is indispensable; but instead of stopping and collecting itself, it 'races from one prospect to the next'.

This kind of thinking is in fact a *flight* from thinking – from 'recollective, meditative thinking' (ibid.), from reflection – by Heidegger (1977: 180) defined as 'calm, self-possessed surrender to that which is worthy of questioning'. Against this backdrop, I hold that the requirement that criticism must be followed by constructive solutions reveals a confusion of these two forms of thinking. Critical social theory makes no promises and shows no success; 'it remains negative' (Marcuse 1964: 167). Here, I also think of Foucault (1984: 343), who says: 'I am not looking for an alternative ... What I want to do is not the history of solutions, and that's the reason why I don't accept the word *alternative*. I would like to do

---

11   The concepts of analysis and therapy are often used synonymously. It might, however, be useful to distinguish between them. I do it in order to highlight the fundamental differences between the psychodynamic and the psychotherapeutic thought tradition. Although not necessarily mutually exclusive, but sometimes rather complementary, they demonstrate important epistemological, ontological and ethical differences. In short, these differences stem from the fact that the psychotherapeutic worldview is purely scientific (e.g. Cognitive Behavioural Therapy), while psycho-analysis is more dynamic-dialectical. It is debated which one of these schools offers the most effective treatment of mental illness. In Sweden, there has in recent years been a change in attitude among politicians and institutions towards a favouring of psychotherapy (Reeder 2010a).

12   To calculate means to 'to compute, to estimate by mathematical means', from Latin *calculus* 'reckoning, account' originally 'pebble used as a reckoning counter', diminutive of *calx* (genitive *calcis*) 'limestone' (*Online Etymology Dictionary* 2013-04-22).

the genealogy of problems, of *problématiques*. My point is not that everything is bad, but that everything is dangerous'.

Foucault's claim that 'everything is dangerous' is ultimately justified by the intimate connection between knowledge and power, between epistemology and ethics, between society as a fact- and truth-producing institution, on the one hand, and the individual, on the other.

Psycho-Analytical Scepticism as a Guiding Principle

> In the course of time we have come to realize that we are not so reasonable after all as the Eighteenth Century, with its worship of reason and its naive optimism, thought us. (Huizinga 2003: Preface)

It is time to say something more about the way in which Freud's psycho-analytical ideas have inspired me in writing this book.[13] Like Nietzsche, he developed his philosophy during the late nineteenth century – a time when an increasing number of intellectuals began to question positivism's emphasis on materialism, mechanism, rationality, the visual and free will (Hughes 1958: 37f).[14] 'The happy consciousness' – which in Marcuse's (1964: 54; 61) words 'facilitates acceptance of the misdeeds of this society' and believes that 'the real is rational and that the system delivers the goods' – was now met with scepticism. Against the mechanistic world view, upheld by the natural sciences, an alternative movement was born, a movement that reduced the role of the rational and that called for new insight into regions of man's soul that until now had been denied or controlled by an oversized reason (Sjögren 2001: 40). The movement is exemplified by Strindberg's (2000) play *A Dream Play* from 1901 – presented a year after the publication of Freud's *Interpretation of Dreams* – in which man's entire existence is put to trial. As literary theorist Gunnar Ollén (1949: 406) says, Strindberg's dream is steeped in pessimism, but most of all in life's contradictory 'both/and': '[I]t turns out that there is nothing that does not have its sad downside ... All opinions are refuted, all faith followed by doubt, all the fun by remorse'. Although Strindberg is not officially regarded as a part of the intellectual tradition known as 'the school of

---

13   What I will present here is the academic answer to this question. A more personal answer is given in an interview in the journal *Arche* (Caldenby et al. 2012). In reality, these stories are intervowen.

14   Freud, who had an ambivalent relationship to philosophy, did not engage in any thorough studies of Nietzsche. This, however, was not due to differences in thinking but rather because of the many similarities. Nietzsche, Freud explains (in Lehrer 1995: 174f), 'was for a long time avoided by me on that very account; I was less concerned with the question of priority than with keeping my mind unembarrassed'.

suspicion' (Ricoeur 1970: 32, see also Nietzsche 1986a: 13), Freud – along with Nietzsche and Marx – definitely are.[15]

But what is the nature of these suspicions or doubts? How do they differ from the doubt that is normally associated with Descartes? Ricoeur (1970: 33) gives an answer to this question:

> The philosopher trained in the school of Descartes knows that things are doubtful, that they are not such as they appear; but he does not doubt that consciousness is such as it appears to itself; in consciousness, meaning and consciousness of meaning coincide. Since Marx, Nietzsche and Freud, this too has become doubtful. After the doubt of things, we have started to doubt consciousness.

Thus, there should be no doubt as to why the present study, which is a criticism of power and an examination of how we understand the city and the urban, can find inspiration in Freud's work. The similarities between psycho-analysis and ideology critique are striking: both seek to abolish a false objectivity. Both psycho-analysis and ideology[16] analysis have as their general aims 'to bring about awareness that things are not what we believe them to be' (Krogh 1992: 95).[17]

When the ambition is to get behind what the planners explicitly express, to explore their statements as the hiding places they are and to understand the phenomenon of contra-finality in urban planning, there simply is no way around Freud since he was the first to formulate an ambitious and comprehensive theory of the unconscious.[18] While there are many geographers who have been inspired by Marxism – whose parallels with psycho-analysis has been highlighted not least by the Frankfurt school (see Krogh 1992: 96) – relatively few geographers have made psycho-analytically inspired analyses.[19] '[P]sychoanalysis remains a marginal resource for geographers – it seems to be an unnecessary, unpleasant

---

15 There is no evidence that Strindberg was ever familiar with Freud and psychoanalysis, but it is documented that Freud knew about Strindberg. In a footnote, added in 1917 to *Psychopathology of Everyday Life*, he pointed out that Strindberg possessed a faculty for understanding the secret nature of parapraxes (Johansson 2003).

16 In the book, inspired by Olsson (1990: 62), I adopt a broad definition of ideology as a way to understand and interpret the world. For without ideology, we would not know how to categorise.

17 Hence, psycho-analysis as a thought tradition can be seen not only as an anti-Enlightenment project, as I indicated earlier, but also as a product of the Enlightenment. Freud criticises religion, but more importantly, his 'aim of making the unconscious conscious relates to the Enlightenment idea of change as a result of knowledge. Through gaining knowledge of something that I previously did not know about, something can change' (Johansson, forthcoming).

18 As Freud (2008: 274) acknowledges, psycho-analysis was not first to recognise unconscious mental processes; an important forerunner was Arthur Schopenhauer, whose unconscious 'Will' can be likened to the mental instincts of psycho-analysis.

19 For an exposé of exceptions, see Kingsbury (2004) and Rose (2000).

experience, just like measles' says Steve Pile (1996: 81). Nevertheless, 'Psycho-analysis enables powerful *critical explanations* at various geographic scales' (Kingsbury 2004: 119).

In order to access the analysand's unconscious, Freud listened to her story. And he listened carefully. As Jacques Lacan (2001) points out, the linguistic analysis in Freud's writings is given more and more room the more the unconscious is directly affected. 'The costume of language is by no means only an exterior' – it involves a way of thinking and understanding (Asplund 2002: 9). It is a psycho-analytic view that humans always *mean* something by what they do or say; their words and actions are intentional (Malcolm 1981: 19, Sandell 1993: 1). But this cannot be understood without taking into account one of psycho-analysis's basic ideas: that there are mental phenomena – beliefs, desires – that we are normally unaware of, but which nonetheless affect the way we act. What once was intentional tends, over time, to end up in the background. For the analyst – and for the scientist – language becomes a tool, a compass. In the words of Olsson (2007: x): '[S]how me your map and compass and I shall show you who and where you are, when you came and where you are heading'.

With Freud's idea that listening is a more important tool than observing, psycho-analysis represents a step away from the visual. In particular, this is manifested in Freud's insistence that the couch should be facing away from the analyst in order to avoid eye contact. The analyst, he realised, is a visual distraction, a hindrance to inward listening (Jay 1994: 334).

After years of listening, Freud began to discern an underlying complaint that united all analysands; a complaint that can be summarised as this: 'In my own attempt to figure out how to live, something is going wrong' (Lear 2005: 10). What came to interest him was something that could be called man's aptitude for irrational behaviour. Freud's insight, Lear (ibid.: 4) tells us, is that 'humans tend toward certain forms of *motivated irrationality* of which they have little or no awareness'; in other words, people are not satisfied just because their conscious wishes are fulfilled (Brown 1959: 18). Fundamental to Freud's philosophy is that humans, in all their restless strivings, have no idea what they really want (Brown 1959: x). Many of our wishes are unconscious. And even if they would become conscious, and they would be fulfilled, there is no guarantee we would be satisfied, for the situation or the problem might have changed. First, we must be aware that a problem even exists. Put another way, we have to acknowledge the chafing feeling that we have – or, mental 'itch' – as a problem. Second, we need to identify what the problem is; this is easier said than done. It typically requires introspection, something that is generally not encouraged in Western culture. So, if we take into account the fact that planning is 'a reflection and interpretation that corresponds to strongly perceived problems' (Gullberg 1986: 53), it would seem not only reasonable but very much necessary to apply a psycho-analytical perspective on planning.

To hear what Freud has to say is undeniably – in the words of Brown (1959: xi) 'a shattering experience for anyone seriously committed to the Western traditions of morality and rationality'. And what is contemporary Swedish urban planning, if not an example of an Enlightenment-imbued tradition made up of thoughts about rationality and social ethics (see Nordström 2008, Strömgren 2007)?

Overall, these roads lead us to the following question: How can a person be defeated by her own means? It is this question that psycho-analysis seeks – if not to exhaust – then at least to understand better. This difference between to exhaust and to understand is more important than we might first think. Freud expressed the hope to find the ultimate basics that determined spiritual progress. He spoke, for example, about 'fully explaining' a dream, and that a person can be 'completely analysed' (Sjögren 2001: 34). But, as psycho-analyst Lars Sjögren (ibid.) points out, this is a misleading illusion: anyone who expects a full explanation, a fixed and finished analytical statement, is going to be disappointed. Psycho-analysis, whether directed at an individual or, as in this book, at planners as a thought collective, is likely to experience a disillusionment process. The choice is then to either abandon the illusion or to abandon the analysis. A positivist-inspired researcher would probably hold onto the illusion and abandon a deeper analysis. However, if we choose to go on with the analysis, it is necessary to throw the illusion out. It was in this latter way I handled my own disillusionment process in connection to my visit to Hammarby Sjöstad. It was only when I abandoned the illusion of a complete and simple explanation of the relationship between urban form and urban life as well as between intentions and outcomes that my epistemological journey towards understanding began.

It was not only in the individual that Freud (2002) noted self-destructive acts but also in society at large. And indeed this is an interesting observation. How will people know what is best for others when they do not even know what is best for themselves? Thus, Freud's ideas are highly relevant not only for psychology but also for philosophy and the social sciences. In fact, as Martin G. Kalin (1974: 117, 120) writes, 'Freud's depth psychology includes a sophisticated social theory' and that 'psycho-analysis not only permits but also encourages interpretation as speculative social theory'. But philosophers have been slow to recognise this. 'The problem is not with unconscious motivation per se', Lear (2005: 10f) explains, and adds: 'Philosophers from Socrates and Plato to Kant, Kierkegaard and Nietzsche believed that humans are not transparent to themselves; that much goes on in us unconsciously. The difficulty is in seeing how this affects our most fundamental concerns ... our freedom, our happiness'.

The analyst's job is to listen to the analysand's statements in order to reach behind what is immediately said into the analysand's unconscious: 'The division of the psychical into what is conscious and what is unconscious is the fundamental premise of psycho-analysis; and it alone makes it possible for psycho-analysis to understand the pathological processes in mental life, which are as common as they are important' (Freud 1995: 630).

There are not only similarities between Freud and Nietzsche but also between these philosophers and Lefebvre, another central figure in this book (see Merrifield 1993, Pile 1996: 211ff). As Philip Wander (2007: ix) points out,

Lefebvre makes us aware of the cracks in modern, pale, everyday life – cracks caused by that which cannot be completely repressed: '[t]he awakening of sexual desire and love, the undeniable delights of play, and the allure of the festival'. In the process, I will metaphorically lay urban planners as a thought collective on the couch when trying to reach their taken-for-granted. This applies to both practitioners and researchers. As Louis Wirth (in Ley 1977: 8) has pointed out, the most important thing we can know about a person is in his or her taken-for-granted. The same goes for insights about society because 'the history of civilization reflects the formation of the human personality' (Kalin 1974: 118f). What for Freud began as a quest for the unconscious discourse of the individual later came to include the search for a collective unconscious narrative (Sjögren 2008: 12, see also Brown 1959: xi). 'The analogy between the development of civilization and that of the individual can be significantly extended', Freud (2002: 100) said, raising the following question:

> If the development of civilization so much resembles that of the individual and operates with the same means, is one not entitled to proffer the diagnosis that some civilizations or culture epochs – possibly the whole of humanity – have become 'neurotic' under the influence of cultural strivings? (Ibid.: 104)

The parallel between the repealing of neurosis and the dismantling of ideology is clear: In both cases, we are faced with the task of becoming aware of the unconscious (Krogh 1992: 95, Lear 2005: 5). Psycho-analysis is a way out of 'the nightmare of endless "progress"', a way out of the neurosis that the Faustian ideal of progress has led humanity into (Brown in Berman 1983: 79). Since a whole collective and its history cannot be placed on the couch, the way into the unconscious must be taken through individual statements. A collective, however, is more than the sum of its individuals (Sjögren 2008: 32), which means that any conclusions inevitably take the form of speculation.

Psycho-analysis has been criticised for representing what is usually called psychologism, that is, the tendency to trace all human social activity to man's psychological mechanisms (Israel 1971: 333). It has also been criticised for its biologism, which refers to the tendency to explain behaviour through innate biological processes (Israel 1967: 117f). Still, its sociological relevance is obvious, partly due to its claim that society requires that individuals repress their biological instincts (for example, marriage requires monogamy). Furthermore, psycho-analysis *does* take into account society and the impact that social norms have on individual motivation and thoughts through the idea of the superego. For the ego is nothing more than an incorporation of social values (communicated via parental figures). In short, while psychologism overemphasises individual motivation and takes it as an explanation of all social activity, its antithesis, sociologism, portrays social phenomena as something situated outside the individual and the individual's control. Aware of these pitfalls, in the book I have sought to find a middle way: a both/and rather than an either-or, but with a bias towards psychological explanations. This is because I want to avoid reification, which sociologism often leads to and which makes individuals into objects, thereby principally depriving them of their responsibilities (ibid.: 400).

As I stated in the introduction, the book is a study of the reoccurring problem of something arising from its opposite (Nietzsche 1986a: §1), how reason can become unreason, how 'better knowledge' can turn into stupidity (Adorno and Horkheimer 1981: 242), how a rational society can become neurotic and how we can be defeated by our own means (Brown 1959, Freud 2002, Olsson 1980c: 20).[20] It is important to remember that psycho-analytic theory is not just about psychopathology, that is, of morbid mental function. Rather, its insights concern the psychic functioning and development of man and society in general (Brenner 1970: 9).

While Enlightenment thinkers help us see how planning *should* work, anti-Enlightenment thinkers help us see how planning *really* works (Flyvbjerg 1998: 3; 2001: 97, Strömgren 2007: 251). This approach implies a problematisation of the taken-for-granted idea that a better and more just society can be constructed with the help of precise knowledge of human behaviour and needs (Hall 1988, Dear 1986) – an idea that is essential, especially for Swedish urban planning. In Strömgren's words (2007: 248; 246), '[It] is still assumed to be central, that universal values are governing society's physical design ... [T]he Swedish planning system has continuously been ... motivated by the idea that it promotes the collective good'. But, as Barrett (1962: 26) writes, '[E]nlightened and progressive thinkers are equally blind when they fail to recognize that every major step forward by mankind entails some loss, the sacrifice of an older security and the creation and heightening of new tensions'.

An anti-Enlightenment perspective, then, helps us look closely at the supposedly sensible activity of planning. 'Sapere aude! Have courage to use your own reason!' Kant (1992: 27) exclaims when he summarises the motto of Enlightenment. In other words, we must become aware of our shadow so it does not overtake us, says psycho-analyst Carl Gustav Jung (in Palmgren 1997: 62). In order to illustrate the many contradictions that this book struggles with – in the city, in space, in planning and in the individual – I have looked to Greek mythology and the ancient symbols of Apollo and Dionysus appropriated by Nietzsche (1999) in *The Birth of Tragedy*. As Megill (1985: 38f) emphasises, the dichotomy is slippery and difficult to pin down, but the hallmark is that the Apollo-Dionysus duality itself contains three different pairs of opposites. The first is form versus formlessness, the second, the visible versus the invisible and the third, illusion versus reality. In the book, the Dionysian does not only represent the urban, the body, desire and the

---

20 Given its general nature, it is not surprising that the problem of contra-finality has been noted in a number of different contexts, not least within organisation philosophy (see e.g. Fogh Kirkeby 2000: 221f). See also Jean Paul Sartre's (2004; 2006) use of 'counter-finality' (*contre-finalité*).

dialectic, but also life itself in all its contradictions. It symbolises everything that cannot be captured in the net of logic.

Dionysus is the god of wine but also of darkness, and his 'barbaric' nature is best approached by the analogy of intoxication (Nietzsche 1992: 84; 1999: §4, §1). Apollo is a god who requires moderation from his followers (Nietzsche 1999: §4). The dichotomy has also inspired Lefebvre, who – like Nietzsche – indulged in Dionysus while acknowledging how fundamental both forces were to man: 'The Nietzschean distinction between Apollonian and Dionysian echoes the dual aspect of the living being and its relationship to space' (Lefebvre 1991: 178). Megill (1985: 47) describes Apollo and Dionysus as 'opposed yet allied symbols' and says that they can be seen as two different sides of life, of man and society – that is, as metaphors for both our civilization and our personalities (Merrifield 2006: 116). A basic assumption of this book is that both of these forces are needed; with only one of them, we would be crazy or unhappy.[21]

Exaggeration also plays a role in this book. Why are humans defeated by their own means? How is it that we have a talent for making ourselves unhappy? Why is urban planning neurotic? All of these questions are reformulations – as well as exaggerations – of the original problem of the vision-reality gap in urban planning; all draw the problem to its head. The same state of exaggeration applies to the question of the conventional scientist's goal and the question of what urbanity is. For example, to even ask – as I do in Chapter 5 – such a question as whether the urban is a *thing* or a *not-thing* is a rather black-and-white formulation; a forced binary conceptualisation. However, exaggeration has a thought-provoking function; it can make us see what we otherwise take for granted: '[O]nly the exaggerations can shatter the normal complacency of common sense and scientific sense and their comforting limitations and illusions' (Marcuse 1968b: 227, see also Brown 1991: 179). Inspired by Nietzsche, I have tried to follow my insights in a certain direction to make a point (see Megill 1985: 91). Exaggeration plays a central role not only in the works of Nietzsche but also of Freud, Olsson and Lefebvre. As Adorno (in Brown 1991: 179) writes, 'In psycho-analysis the only true thing is the exaggerations'. Freud's theory of the superego, the ego and the id is a mythology – a mythology with a great poetic force because it has changed the

---

21   The dichotomy has been used in an architectural context before. In Swedish discourse in the 1940s, it was used as a symbol of the contradiction in attitude towards architecture in the architectural profession: 'Apollo represented the logical analyst, while Dionysus was the sensual and spontaneous' (Rudberg 1992: 71f). Some claimed that Apollo controlled too much, while others – especially those who wanted more room for personal, artistic attitudes – argued that Dionysus was not sufficiently expressed in architecture. Everyone, however, agreed that Apollo and Dionysus ought to exist in a happy symbiosis in the architectural work (ibid.). While I also emphasise a balance between them, my use of the dichotomy differs from the aforementioned, as I interpret *all* architecture as Apollonian (see Vattimo 1997: 24). The Dionysian, on the other hand, I view as something that very much stands in opposition to architecture and planning.

way we interpret our experiences: 'It was not Freud's theory of the unconscious that led him to Oedipus, but the myth of Oedipus that shaped the way he listened to his patients' (Carse 1986: §95). Freud (in Ricoeur 1970: 281) himself wrote that '[w]hat follows is speculation, often far-fetched speculation, which the reader will consider or dismiss according to his individual predilection. It is further an attempt to follow out an idea consistently, out of curiosity to see where it will lead'.

My book has taken its form through a process of borrowing; I have borrowed voices from scientists, novelists and poets and mixed them with my own. The way I use other people's texts is instrumental rather than declarative; I use them mainly to weave my own fabric, in order to – in return – provide a deeper understanding of the gap. When the aim is to deepen our knowledge of human experience and man's relations to society and his environment, the sphere of poetry cannot be ignored. Poetry – as Anna-Lena Renqvist (2013) writes in an essay on philosopher Friedrich W.J. Schelling – 'is not only a source of knowledge among others; it is the true document of philosophy and man's first and major teacher'.

The form of the book goes hand in hand with my view on science and truth: What is said cannot be separated from how it is said. In this respect the study falls into the category of the essay which – inspired by Robert Musil – can be defined as the strictest that you can achieve in an area where you just cannot be strict (Isenberg 2006: 97). The essay is a form of science that crops slices of reality and seeks common features in order to 'show, not to prove, and to be valid, but not definitive' (ibid.). The argument is driven by means of examples rather than through a systematic and detailed review of the study material. Some examples may seem insignificant, but as Nietzsche says, it is the 'little things' that are important if we want to understand problems associated with politics and social organisation. Why? Because the little things are 'the basic concerns of life itself' (Nietzsche in Flyvbjerg 2001: 133, see also Freud 1989: 40, Geertz 1995: 40).

The essay as a form means repetition, anticipation, cross references and – of course – contradictions. Thus, the essay is a perfect form for the discussion of paradoxes. What is so fascinating with the paradox is that it requires a constant change in perspective; what is true is also false, what is logical is also illogical, what is my ceiling is another person's floor.[22] Even the reverse is true, for one of the things that makes perspectivism so interesting is that it is 'incapable of expressing itself without contradiction' (Ricoeur 1970: 33). If we are to believe Gary Shapiro (1993: 141) in his interpretation of Nietzsche, it is precisely in the dialogue, in the alternating between (apparent) opposites, that thinking takes place: '[T]hought occurs neither in the glaring Platonic sunlight, nor in its all too facile negation, but in the flickering, twilight play of light and shadow'. We are now ready to move on.

---

22 I owe this last formulation to Nils Ferlin (1933) and his poem 'Infall'.

Chapter 2

The Eye of the Architect – The Body of the *Flâneur*

Architecture – to me – means comfort and harmony … Sometimes you need very strong forms to turn chaos into order.

Aleksander Wolodarski

Today order is primarily where nothing is – an absence revealed.[1]

Berthold Brecht

Between the buildings here / there was this silence / that I could never really endure[2]

Tomas Andersson Wij

In the preface to the 1993 edition of *The Death and Life of Great American Cities* Jacobs makes a distinction between two kinds of people: 'foot people' and 'car people'. The former describes people who prefer to do their daily errands on foot or would like to do that if they lived in a place where it was possible. The latter is a name for those who prefer to get in the car when they run errands (or else they would like to do it if they had a car). What Jacobs does here is to indirectly refer to perspectivism, the idea that what you see – in both the literal and the non-literal sense of the word – depends on where you stand. As a *flâneur*, you are *in* the street. When driving a car, on the other hand, you are protected, or cut off; from sounds, smells and sensations of touch; from the friction of asphalt under your feet (Appleyard et al. 1967: 77, N. Taylor 2003: 1616f).

Our experience of the world is not only dependent on the point where our body is located or on the senses with which we perceive the world; most importantly, our experience is linked to what we as individuals – for the moment and/or in general – prefer. Worldview and attitude are inseparable phenomena; subjectivity is not something that exists outside or beyond knowledge – it is the prerequisite of knowledge. This Nietzschean idea is evident in Jacobs's discussion of foot people and car people.

In the previous chapter, we learned that every uttering is a hiding place; every word is a mask (Berg Eriksen 2005: 154). The words and statements that we use

---

1 'Ordnung ist heutzutage meistens dort, wo nichts ist. Es ist eine Mangelerscheinung' (Brecht in Feyerabend 2000: 25). Translated from German by Gunnar Olsson.

2 'Det fanns en tystnad mellan husen här / som jag aldrig riktigt kunde leva med'

explicitly and implicitly reflect our perspective on the world. And by perspective I do not only mean its literal meaning – that is, how we see – but also how we understand. Understanding, in turn, is an activity connected to our emotions, our attitudes; it is our will to power. In this chapter, I begin from two fixed points and continuously alternate between them. I have chosen to call them the eye of the architect and the body of the *flâneur*. By analysing these – or rather, how the city appears from these perspectives respectively – I hope to gain a better understanding of the problem studied in this book: the gap between vision and reality in planning.

Intermezzo

I walk into the display area, I study the plans, I look at the detailed blueprints, I hear the planners talk. Something does not feel right; I do not want to live in the world they are creating. But I myself have no plan, no model, no powerful rhetorical tool that makes it possible to enter into the discussion. I do not have anything concrete and material, anything present to point to; I just have a feeling. This feeling is not allowed in a model because it cannot be represented by a thing. How do we talk of that we cannot see? Given the limits of a scientific inquiry, I have no choice but to turn to writers, poets and musicians and reproduce their stories.

This chapter is based on a variety of sources. Although I frequently use statements about the Hammarby Sjöstad project to access the planner's perspective, the empirical material is not limited to this project. The statements referring to Hammarby Sjöstad are mixed with statements from planners from other geographical and temporal contexts. As I stated earlier, I use examples to drive the argument forward, which is why the review of the material is not systematic.

Since I regard words as clues, etymological investigations are regular features. What does it mean, for example, that planners often talk about people's *needs*? What is up for discussion, and what is left out? Since my study is both psycho-analytical and perspectivistic, I try to relate words and statements to ways of seeing, to different preferences, dispositions, or to more or less primitive attitudes. And this is for a good reason: 'Primitive attitudes towards the world surrounding us have always been one of the main topics for psycho-analytic research' (M. Balint 1959: 11). Primitive attitudes are, as a rule, associated with children, but they continue to live on in the human unconscious and are also observable in 'ordinary everyday adults' (ibid.: 13). What, for example, seems to lie behind modernist architects' fondness for open space? And why does the *flâneur* seek the crowd? It should be said that I do not pretend to exhaust what the individuals in question 'really' want or desire. As Brown (1959: x) writes, '[M]ankind, in all its restless striving and progress, has no idea of what it really wants. Freud was right: our real desires are unconscious'. The obscurity of our strivings is clearly conveyed by Virginia Woolf (in Gordon 2006: 5), when she writes, 'I have some restless searcher in me'.

As a way into the *flâneur*'s perspective, I use my own and others' experiences of walking in the city. Texts by Virginia Woolf and August Strindberg emerge most strongly, but I also go to more famous *flâneurs* such as Charles Baudelaire, the nineteenth-century Parisian poet, and his main interpreter Walter Benjamin. The choices of Woolf and Strindberg as representatives for the *flâneur* are justified: in them I find the passionate attitude towards the urban that I am looking for. This attitude is evident in Lefebvre's writings, too. In Woolf's texts we can see traces of 'a struggle against boredom' – a struggle that Lefebvre engaged in from the day he first visited Mourenx (Merrifield 2009: 941). But what was this struggle directed against? According to my interpretation, the answer is a specific type of urban environment, usually referred to as 'the suburbs'.[3] Mourenx filled Lefebvre (1995: 118) with dread; Putney[4] depressed Woolf: 'The streets of villas make me more dismal than slums', she wrote (Woolf in Moorcroft Wilson 1987: 157). To clarify what kind of boredom I mean, we can look at an excerpt from Richard Sennett's (2008) book *The Uses of Disorder*. The passage is long but worth quoting in its entirety, not least because it contains references to psycho-analytical thinking:

> This boredom is … rather strange. Most animals live by instinctual routines quite well; few men in agricultural, pre-industrial walks of life suffered from boredom, although their lives were hard and the rhythms of life fixed. The peculiar character of a secure, affluent routine is that it does not arise from the needs of adaptive survival with the environment or with other members of the race. It arises instead out of the fact that affluence permits men, through coherent routines, to hide from dealing with each other. Rather than face the full range of social experience possible to men, the communities of safe coherence cut off the amount of human material permitted into a man's life, in order that no questions of discord, no issues of survival be raised at all. It is this 'escape from freedom', in Erich Fromm's words, that ultimately makes a man quite consciously bored, aware that he is suffocating, although he may refuse to face the reasons for his suffocation. The boredom that rises out of this is quite natural, for it is, as Nietzsche said, the voice of the creature in each man trying to make itself heard. (Sennett 2008: 186)

Here we see how Sennett – by referring to Nietzsche – points to boredom's, or alienation's critical potential: it renders a particular situation or a particular state of mind deeply unsatisfactory (see also Svendsen 2005: 22).

Woolf was by all accounts someone who responded intensely to the physical as well as the social environment. As biographer Jean Moorcroft Wilson (1987: 17) has noted, Woolf exhibits 'a pronounced sense of place, which emerges most clearly in

---

3   If I were to anticipate the discussion in Chapter 6, where I discuss space syntax and parts of its terminology, I would use the concept of *disurban environments* here.

4   Putney is a suburb in London where Woolf's parents-in-law lived.

her writing'. In her texts[5] we witness how inner space is intertwined with external space – something that gives birth to what Anthony Vidler (2001) would call 'a warped sense of psychological space'. In this intertwining process, urban space becomes a projection of the psychological, inner space (Westerståhl-Stenport 2004: 25). 'London', Moorcroft Wilson writes (1987: 125), 'is very rarely used as a convenient setting. … [T]he outer world serves in almost every case as a reflection of the inner world which so fascinated Virginia'. In Strindberg's writing too, the outside world is given resonance in the inner world and vice versa, notably in the short novel *Alone:*[6]

> Though I burn with the desire to get down to work, I must first go out for my walk. When I reach the street door, I know immediately which way I'll take. Not only do the sun, the clouds, and the temperature tell me, but some inner sense acts as a barometer and thermometer to inform me how I stand with the world. … I soon sense which way I am to go. If I feel at peace with myself, the air caresses me and I look for company. (Strindberg 1998: 171)

The choice of Strindberg and Woolf as representatives for the *flâneur*, is not self-evident; there is debate as to *who* the *flâneur* is. The concept is characterised by an ontological ambivalence; sometimes it refers to a literary figure, a kind of mythological ideal type who is not easily tied to a sociological reality (Shields 1994: 62). Other times it represents actual people (e.g. Baudelaire, or, in the Swedish literary canon, Hjalmar Söderberg).

Since this is neither a historical nor literary study, it is not my intention to exhaust the who-where-how of the *flâneur*. Nevertheless, my choice of Strindberg and Woolf as windows into the *flâneur*'s point of view challenges three more or less accepted beliefs that I will now briefly present. The first is the one that portrays the *flâneur* as an indifferent and dispassionate being (Kjellén 1985: 178, Parkhurst Ferguson 1994: 26, Westin 1999: 171). Presumably, this idea is coloured by urban sociologist Georg Simmel's (1995) image of modern man as a creature who is fighting the amount of sensory input in the city through psychological withdrawal. But we only have to go to Baudelaire's writings to see that the *flâneur* is the opposite

---

5   In the survey, I have used both diary material and fiction as windows into Woolf's approach to the city. This choice is supported by the fact that Woolf herself did not seem to draw a sharp line between these two writing forms. 'I wonder', she asked, 'whether I … deal … in autobiography and call it fiction?' (in Gordon 2006: 7).

6   As argued by Boel Westin (1999: 169), *Alone* has an 'autobiographical aura'. Nevertheless, she continues, its narrative ego is not a 'real' *flâneur*, which is why she uses the word 'walker' (*vandrare*) instead. This is motivated by his 'empathetic and passionate attitude', she says, and since he has a way of 'opening up his senses to fantasy and fiction', he has little in common with the 'cool indifference' of the literary *flâneur* (ibid.: 171). Kjellén (1985: 178) has also emphasised Strindberg's 'active nature' as a sign of him being different from the *flâneur* – 'the observing and often dreamy drifter'. For a literary-scientific study of the relation between Strindberg's texts and representations of urban space, see Westerståhl-Stenport (2004).

of blasé; rather, she is '[a] passionate lover of crowds' (Baudelaire 1995: 5, see also Shields 1994: 73). Words and phrases such as 'passion', 'immense joy', 'flesh', 'pleasures', 'passionate', 'lover' and 'energy' (Baudelaire 1995: 9f) suggest that the *flâneur* is a highly passionate and desiring being. The *flâneur consumes* – in all dimensions of the word – the city (Buck-Morss 1986, Smart 1994).[7]

When Karin Johannisson (2009: 139–145), historian of ideas, portrays the *flâneur*, it is as a distant, dispassionate figure. '[H]e is a consumer without desire', she writes (ibid.: 139). However, between the lines in the following excerpt we can see an opening to the interpretation that the *flâneur* may not at all be a dispassionate being – on the contrary: 'There seems to be a way of life dominated by comfortable distance. But there is an underlying hunger' (ibid.: 140). This interpretation is further strengthened when Johannisson (ibid.: 138) describes the *flâneur*'s boredom as a 'wild' feeling. The writer Fyodor Dostoyevsky used similar language; he described boredom as a 'bestial and indefinable affliction' (in Svendsen 2005: 45). The aloof attitude often attributed to the *flâneur* is rather misleading and seems to hide a starvation, a deep hunger of some kind. This hunger can best be described as idleness, loneliness, emptiness, restlessness or boredom – feelings or moods for which the act of *flânerie* is an act of compensation or an escape. Although it is possible – as Johannisson and several others do – to interpret *flânerie* as an expression of indifference, it is also possible to draw the opposite conclusion; namely, that the restlessness and boredom is an expression of a hunger, a craving. In the next section, I will address the question of *what* the *flâneur* desires, but for now it suffices to say that the *what* question is secondary to the *that* statement: the fact *that* the *flâneur* desires.

The second idea that my book challenges is that the *flâneur* disappeared with Baron Haussmann's rebuilding of Paris during the latter part of the nineteenth century (see Parkhurst Ferguson 1994: 32, Prendergast 1992: 9). The disappearance of the *flâneur* was also a theme in the Swedish public discourse, although not until the 1930s (Kjellén 1985: 7). As I interpret *flânerie*, it is not a historical or nationally distinct activity but something essentially universal and timeless[8] – it is an expression of an attitude, a passion towards urban life.

---

7   Speaking of consumption, shopping is probably the activity mostly associated with urbanity. However, it is debated whether shopping is an activity for a 'real' *flâneur* (see Parkhurst Ferguson 1994: 27). It is doubtless, though, that Baudelaire loved window-shopping. To him, it was as a 'supreme Parisian pleasure' (Prendergast 1992: 36). And Wilson (1992b: 101) says that 'shopping and/or window-shopping was a key element in the identity of the *flâneur* as far back as 1806'. Rem Koolhaas et al. (2001) take it one step further when they say that shopping has infiltrated, colonised and replaced all other forms of urban life. Shopping, they claim, is the very essence of the modern city. Nevertheless, the fact that we today are able to shop from home and in shopping malls outside of cities makes it clear that shopping does not alone capture the urban (see Hall 1998: 17f). On the relation between retail and urban space in contemporary Western society, see Kärrholm (2012).

8   Kjellén (1985: 14), for example, claims that there were *flâneurs* in the cities of antiquity.

As already attested by my use of personal pronouns, the third and final idea I dispute is that *flânerie* is a gendered activity; that the *flâneur* can only be a man (Buck-Morss 1986, McDowell 1999: 154, Parkhurst Ferguson 1994: 27, Wolff 1985). My challenge has to do with my interpretation of the *flâneur* as a timeless and passionate creature who embodies an attitude. Here I choose to quote Wilson (1992a: 10) – one of those who have argued against the idea of 'the invisible *flâneuse*':[9]

> For a woman to make an argument in favour of urban life may come as a surprise. Many women and much feminist writing have been hostile to the city, and ... tended to restrict themselves narrowly to issues of safety, welfare and protection. ... This is a mistake, since it re-creates the traditional paternalism of most town planning. ... safety is a crucial issue. Yet it is necessary also to emphasise the other side of city life and to insist on women's right to the carnival, intensity and even the risk of the city.

Flânerie is partly an escape from the private sphere of the home (Tester 1994: 5). The idea of *flânerie* as a masculine activity is linked to the idea of public space as masculine and private space as feminine (Wolff 1985).[10] Paradoxically, it is precisely for this reason that I not only regard women as possible *flâneurs* but as very apt ones, too. For if anyone has a need to escape the home, is it not the one who, according to society's conventions, should stay there?[11] This especially applies to Woolf, who grew up as part of the privileged middle class in Britain during the early twentieth century. During this time, the male ruling class did everything it could to impose restrictions on the presence of women in the public sphere (Wilson 1992b: 93). This proved to be impossible when it came to prostitutes and women from the working class, but, as Wilson (ibid.) points out, '[t]he movements of middle-class women were more successfully restricted'.

Maybe it is precisely this idea and/or fact – that the home is women's sphere and the public men's sphere – that made Woolf into a *flâneur*? Woolf, who referred to herself as 'shabby, city haunting Virginia' (Moorcroft Wilson 1987: 149), wrote: '[T]o escape is the greatest of pleasures; street haunting in winter the greatest of

---

9   The expression comes from an article title by Janet Wolff (1985). The message in this article was criticised by Wilson (1992b). Others who have challenged the idea of *flânerie* as a male activity are Epstein Nord (1995), Gleber (1999), Heron (1993), Parsons (2000) and Selboe (2003).

10   For a problematisation of the idea of separate spheres, see Wilson (1992b), Marcus (1999), McDowell (1999: 71–95; 148–69) and Parsons (2000: 40f).

11   Here we can remind ourselves of one of the most important arguments of feminism: that the private sphere, which is traditionally associated with recreation and rest, is primarily constructed for the convenience of men. For women, the home is not only a workplace but also an instrument of patriarchal oppression (Wilson 1977:8; 1992b: 98). The latter argument has been criticised by hooks (1990). See also McDowell (1999: 88f).

adventures' (Woolf 2005a: 15). *Flânerie* was a part of her rebellion, her attempt to escape the social conventions that characterised her childhood in Kensington: 'Of all the places Virginia inhabited, she least liked Kensington. Associating it as she did with the special respectability of her youth, she found it, in retrospect at least, suffocating' (Moorcroft Wilson 1987: 150).

Support for the idea of *flânerie* as a revolt is found in Woolf's novel *Night and Day*, in which the physical world is interwoven with the social; different parts of the city represent not only different social strata but also different ways of living. In the centre of the story is Katharine, a woman from an intellectual, middle-class home in affluent Chelsea. Katharine is a woman who 'has it all' – beauty, intelligence and money – but she is bored in her role as hostess in her father's house. As a counterweight and possible refuge is her lover, Ralph. Ralph is working class and also younger than Katharine, thus outwardly inappropriate. The antithesis to Katharine's safe but convention-ridden life in Chelsea is embodied not only by Ralph but also by the street life in Central London. It is here, more specifically, at Lincoln's Inn Fields in Holborn, near Bloomsbury, that Woolf lets her main character unite with her lover:

> Here was the fit place for their meeting, she thought; here was the fit place for her to walk thinking of him. She could not help comparing it with the domestic streets of Chelsea. With this comparison in mind, she ... turned into the main road. The great torrent of vans and carts was sweeping down Kingsway; pedestrians were streaming in two currents along the pavements. She stood fascinated at the corner. ... the great flow, the deep stream, the unquenchable tide. (Woolf 1992: 374)

Woolf's choice to let the buzzing street life embody Katharine's desire for Ralph is nowhere more apparent than when she weaves Katharine's longing together with the stream of traffic and people at Kingsway: 'Her wants were so vast, now that she was in communication with Ralph, that the pencil was utterly inadequate to conduct them on to the paper; it seemed as if the whole torrent of Kingsway had to run down her pencil' (Woolf 1992: 375).

In recent decades it has become increasingly common to incorporate feminist considerations into issues of women's safety in cities. 'Women's fear' is an established interdisciplinary field of research, particularly in cultural geography (see Davidson 2003, Listerborn 2002, Valentine 1989). The issues that this field focuses on are certainly valid, but there is a risk that this discourse, which is larger and more diverse than what I express here, reproduces the idea that public space is masculine and private space is feminine and that a woman is expected to be scared of urban life or at least not enjoy it. This line of thought has historical roots, and as an illustration we can remember that Woolf's husband and doctor urged her to settle in the country since they interpreted her depressive condition as caused by 'the "excitement" of the city' (Bender 1999).

The problems embedded in the discourse on women's fear have been recognised by Liz Heron (1993), Linda McDowell (1999) and Hille Koskela (1997), among others. Koskela (1997) notes that in the current discourse, a scared woman is a normal woman. The opposite – to be bold – is regarded as deviant and risky. Not only are women lumped together in one single category; the discussion obscures a recognition of another 'right', namely the right to avoid 'the malaise of suburban family life', to borrow Sennett's formulation (2008: 72). Much of today's urban planning, in Sweden as well as internationally, is influenced by Oscar Newman's idea of 'defensible space' presented in the 1970s: the idea that some form of enclosure is the solution to the problem of fear in the city, as it is believed to provide transparency and control of strangers (Listerborn 2002: 104ff). This has had paradoxical results. As Sennett argues (2008: xxi): '[T]he fear of cities ... leads itself to a terrible limit on human freedom'.

Not only the city but also passion, in general, has been characterised as oppressive to women. Feminism has since the nineteenth century 'sported an anti-romantic bias' (Nehring 2009: 5f) – a bias that accelerated in the 1970s. Passion was described as a pathological condition, 'which compels women to submit to a diminishing life in chains' (Dworkin in ibid.). Overall, it is this that lies behind cultural critic Cristina Nehring's observation that '[w]e live in an age of emotional correctness' (ibid.: 15). Passion is very much regarded as a threat to feminist demands for symmetry and equality because it involves danger, darkness, fear and struggle for power in relationships that most often are asymmetrical (Wigorts Yngvesson 2009). 'If [a woman] felt deeply, she cannot, we seem to assume, have *thought* deeply', Nehring writes (2009: 3). The same applies to the notion that women in public space find men's gaze unpleasant and undesirable – as something that 'we' women at all costs want to protect ourselves from. '[I]n many contemporary Western societies ... women are frequently more likely than men to be subjected to an intrusive and objectifying stare' (Davidson 2010: 382). Again, a normal woman is a troubled woman. A troubled woman is a normal woman.

Woolf's escape from the home into the role of the *flâneur* can be seen as a quest for the right to passion and the act of desiring – a quest that finds its counterpart in Lefebvre's idea of the right to the city. This effort can also be seen in the song lyrics of Frida Hyvönen (2008) – especially in the song 'London!' from the album *Silence is Wild*. On 'the new British dandy' – a figure akin to the *flâneur* – she sings: 'I wanna be like them, I don't care if they are men'. A longing to appropriate typically masculine attributes, activities or properties is also expressed when she sings 'I wear my clothes like Sherlock Holmes'. And it is to the city of London that she addresses the following words: 'Do you think you don't care about me? / You're wrong! / If I disturb you what about it? / You keep me hanging on / to life' (ibid.).

Woolf and Hyvönen – as well as Strindberg quoted earlier – express a right to the city. But what does this mean? What is it that the *flâneur* desires? Again, although the *what* question is subordinate to the *that* statement, we can no longer avoid this question.

The Right to the City

> The *right to the city* cannot be conceived of as a simple visiting right or as a return to traditional cities. It can only be formulated as a transformed and renewed *right to urban life*. (Lefebvre 1996: 158)

> The labour of the *flâneur* is pleasurable, but it is not easy. And it cannot be performed just anywhere. ... Not all streets are ... the proper grazing ground for the *flâneur*'s imagination. (Bauman 1994: 147)

The right to the city is about the right to urbanity, to urban life. But how do we define these ideas? The question arises again and again. Indeed, this shows that Lefebvre was right when he said that '[t]he concept of the urban itself is unclear' (Lefebvre 1996: 207). But at this point in the book we know that ambiguity does not equal insignificance. As with all phenomena that 'cannot be derived either from ontological or scientific-rational conditions', the phenomenon of urbanity cannot 'logically claim universal validity and realization', to borrow a formulation from Marcuse (1964: 99). Implied here is the risk that urban life continues to be an ideal, while its concrete, critical content is lost. Even worse, the ideal – if we are not cautious when seeking its realisation – results in its opposite. Since the question of what the urban is permeates the book, I will not give an exact answer here and then move on. Nevertheless, I hope to make some clarifying points.

'What scope has an "industrial society" if it fails to produce a fruitful urban life?' Lefebvre asks (in Wander 2007: ix). The answer he gives is 'None'. Why? Intuitively, I understand his response, but how do I capture the idea in a way that submits to a scientific form? '[P]oetically dwells man upon this earth', as Johann Wolfgang von Goethe said (in Heidegger 1977: 34). The urban – as well as the lack of it – is a phenomenon that cannot be captured under a clear label or number. But ignoring the human desire for the urban, as Merrifield (2009: 942) writes, is nothing else than a devaluing of humanity's great artwork. And 'artwork' in this context does not mean something that hangs in a museum but rather 'a canvas smack in front of our noses' (ibid. 2006: 69). The urban is an essential part of what it means to be alive, to be human. My words and formulations are deliberately dramatic; they aim to underscore the idea that urbanity is not a need like other needs – for example, the need to have a house and a job – but something else. As Lefebvre writes, the right to the urban is the right to 'qualified places, places of simultaneity and encounters' (Lefebvre 1996: 148, see also Merifield 2006: 71).

Inspired by Heidegger, Lefebvre speaks of urban life as *becoming*, as something dynamic and progressive (Merrifield 2006: 68; 2009). Being in a city is more than just physically being there – it is to take part in life, to be included in processes of becoming (ibid.). Once again, what I am looking for is something that cannot be pinned down; however, to try to put it simply urbanity primarily refers to something emotional, rather than material. Thus, the struggle for the right to the city springs from an emotional rather than a material poverty (Sennett 2008: 107). It is a poverty that coincides with what Marcuse (1964) once described as one-dimensionality. And the one-dimensional man is 'the perfectly alienated man' (Israel 1971: 172). We will return to the concept of alienation in Chapters 3 and 7.

In his interpretation of Jacobs (1992), social psychologist Johan Asplund (1991: 59) says that urban planning must create a city that is a 'viable alternative' to Ferdinand Tönnies' (1957) Gemeinschaft – roughly defined as rural, private life. 'He who chooses the city rejects Gemeinschaft. It is not a choice like any other' (Asplund 1991: 58). Under what circumstances, then, is the city not a viable alternative to Gemeinschaft? When it is sprawling and impoverished. When it is emptied of life, of urbanity (ibid.: 59). This is what Jacobs (1992) warns us of when she argues why twentieth-century orthodox urban-planning ideology destroyed the city by destroying its life. The backdrop for her criticism was the dissatisfaction with 1950s' major planning projects, influenced by Le Corbusier's ideas of the conflict-free city and consisting of high-rise buildings and large green areas, aimed to improve and to modernise the city. 'These projects will not revitalize the downtown; they will deaden it', Jacobs wrote, continuing, 'They will be spacious, park-like, and uncrowded. They will feature long, green vistas. They will be stable and symmetrical and orderly. They will be clean, impressive, and monumental. They will have all the attributes of a well-kept, dignified cemetery' (Jacobs 1958).

The consequences of benevolent urban planning projects were, as we have seen, also noted by Lefebvre when he visited Mourenx. There, he asked himself, 'Here, in Mourenx, what are we on the threshold of? … Are we entering the city of joy or the world of unredeemable boredom?' (Lefebvre 1995: 119).

The right to the urban is the right to difference, to desire, to a life beyond basic needs, to anonymity and freedom from social conventions and private bonds. It is a right not to hear your own footsteps when you walk along a lonely path, to escape the boredom that can appear in the sphere of the home or in an environment where everything is put right, to avoid being protected from the noise of the traffic and from the 'chaos' that often occurs when pedestrians, cyclists and cars share the same space. Woolf's (2005) short story *Street Haunting: A London Adventure* can be interpreted as a criticism of the Apollonian dimensions of life. The street belongs to Dionysus, the private house to Apollo. It is in the home – and by extension in the suburbs – that Apollo seals himself around our personality. In the crowded street the opportunities to be someone else, to meet someone or something else, are endless. In the twentieth century, with the construction of neat residential areas like Mourenx, more and more people are denied urban life. The environments that are being built offer a life based on security, but also on isolation and monotony (Merrifield 2009: 941).

The right to the city – or more correctly: the right to the urban – is about 'the will … to party and to encounter others in public' (ibid.). It is not the kind of legal right that is enshrined in the United Nations Declaration on Human Rights. A look at the latter quickly reveals how different rights conflict each other.[12] In fact, after studying this document, one could conclude that the term 'entitlement' has no universal meaning. Rather, its meaning is a question of power – about who wins. Lefebvre's message, Merrifield writes, is that 'one must struggle for one's right to the city' (ibid.: 944). This struggle can be fought with words, and Jacobs (1993: xii), for example, knew this well; she describes her critique against orthodox urban planning as 'helpful ammunition' against so-called experts, who have power when it comes to shaping the city's physical environment. And if words can be likened to ammunition, it follows that language not only says something about our perspective on the world but also influences and, thus, helps to shape it. Herein lies one of the reasons I choose to put the language of the *flâneur* – that is, poetry – in contrast to that of the planner.

> Plato knew all about the dangers of dreamy poets in our midst, inciting and transmitting powerful feelings and latent desires, destabilizing accepted notions of order and restraint, of cool rationality. Poetry … is like politics: it expresses something *hot*; it voices hotness from the margins. (Merrifield 2009: 946)

Poets, Plato stressed, are from the state's point of view dangerous because they challenge the intellect's ability to say what is real and not, and they show that 'what seems necessary is only possible' (Carse 1986: §49).[13] One could say that in an ideology critique such as this, I use poetry – in the words of Merrifield (2009: 946) – to express something *hot*. That is, poetry is used as a contrast to or challenge of the planner's supposed objectivity. And the difference is important: 'True poets lead no one unawares. It is nothing other than awareness that poets – that is, creators of all sorts – seek' (Carse 1986: §49). Here we find, as I see it, one of the most significant differences between poets, on the one hand, and planners, on the other.

The Conceived – The Lived

> [It] is … clear that Lefebvre means something completely different by the 'urban' than what authorised urban planners do. (Bergman 1974: 322)

---

12   For example, §17 and §25 are both relevant for the city. The former speaks of the right to own property, the latter of the right to a healthy life with sufficient food, clothes, housing and medical care. Merrifield (2009: 943) points to the dilemma that occurs when these rights are combined: '[E]verybody has a right to adequate housing and well-being, but property owners have the private right to deny such a universal right, because no one can deprive them of their property'.

13   But as Carse (1986: §49) points out, Plato himself was an artist; a poet. We cannot deny, Carse writes, that 'behind the rational metaphysician, philosophy's great Master Player, stood Plato the poet, fully aware that the entire opus was an act of play, an invitation to readers not to reproduce the truth but to take his interventions into their own play, establishing the continuity of his art by changing it'.

Many have noted the central role that vision has played in the history of Western thought (Crary 1992, Crosby 1999, de Certeau 1984, Haraway 1991, Heidegger 1977, Jay 1994, Jonas 1954, Levin 1993, MacMurray 1957). The eye is the sensory organ that most resembles the intellect; it requires distance and order (Berg Eriksen 2005: 255). '[Practices of seeing] not only dictate how the world looks but also what it is' (Daston and Galison 2007: 368). Thinking is often understood as a kind of inner vision (MacMurray 1957: 105), and '(t)he fusion of vision with knowledge in general ... persists until the present day' (Guillén 1971: 287, see also Nordström 2008: 73). Martin Jay (1994: 1) strikingly illustrates how vision as a metaphor for knowledge is deeply embedded in language:

> Even a rapid glance at the language we commonly use will demonstrate the ubiquity of visual metaphors. If we actively focus our attention on them, vigilantly keeping an eye out for those deeply embedded as well as those on the surface, we can gain an illuminating insight into the complex mirroring of perception and language. Depending, of course on one's outlook or point of view, the prevalence of such metaphors will be accounted an obstacle or an aid to our knowledge of reality. ... I hope by now that you, *optique lecteur*, can see what I mean.

This quote contains no less than twelve visual metaphors, many of which are embedded in words that no longer seem to denote the visual. For example, the word *vigilant* is derived from the Latin *vigilare*, which means 'to watch' and is akin to the French *veiller*, which, in turn, is the basis for the word *surveillance* (Jay 1994: 1). Parallel with Western philosophy and the history of science's rewarding of sight as the noblest of all senses, the body has been neglected and reduced to something untrustworthy or irrelevant (Sigurdsson 2006: 294f).[14] With Bergson and Nietzsche as forerunners, many thinkers – most often French – have questioned the noble position of sight and emphasised the importance of the body (Jay 1994). Lefebvre (1991: 75f), for example, points to the following risk when favouring the visual: 'People *look*, and take sight, take seeing, for life itself'.[15]

Just as vision traditionally has been ranked higher than the other senses and that perception equals vision, the conceived dimension of space, to use Lefebvre's terminology, has been equated with space in general. We can find an example of how such confusion occurs today in the following lines by architect Erland Ullstad (2008: 69):

---

14   For an interesting reflection on why the body is relatively absent in the history of Western philosophy, see Leder (1990: 125) and Sigurdsson (2006: 305).

15   In recent times, there have been a number of approaches that problematise the link between geography, the pictorial and vision (Cosgrove 2008: 4). See Crang (2003), Driver (2003), Gregory (1994), MacPherson (2005), Matless (2003), Rogoff (2000), Rose (2003), Ryan (2003) and Smith (1997S).

With a simple sketch, many characteristics of the whole are instantly captured. A picture communicates more than a thousand words. With today's technologies, three-dimensional architectural drawings can be made as lifelike as photographs. The discussion deepens. An idea can be presented to a larger audience.

As several scholars before me have stated, architecture and planning are visual activities (de Certeau 1984, Goodman 1972, Lefebvre 1991, Pallasmaa 2005, Rasmussen 1964, Söderström 1996). The ideal city, Aristotle claimed, was one that 'can be taken in with a single view' (in Prendergast 1992: 48). Kant (2005: §51) argued that architecture, which is a kind of beautiful formative art, is about an aesthetic idea – and archetype – given physical extension. And that the beautiful arrangements of this art form are 'only apparent to the eye, like painting; the sense of touch cannot supply any intuitive presentation of such a form' (ibid.). In this chapter, I will discuss the consequences this may have for the urban as well as illustrate the ways in which the architect's perspective differs from that of the *flâneur*.

As already noted, my critique of urban planning coincides with the critique of the visual, more generally. Talking about the eye and the body when it comes to urban planning is a way to talk about conceived space and lived space, about the authority that planning exercises on the body of the user. Lefebvre (1991), who coined the terms conceived space and lived space, is deliberately vague in his definitions. This is because he – with dialectics as his guide – lets the epistemology of space follow the rhythm of what he perceives as the ontology of space. The reason why I avoid a systematic review of Lefebvre's concepts is because this would alter the essence of the philosophy in which they are embedded (see Merrifield 2009: 947 and Brown 1968: 246). Instead, I put them in direct contact with my material, my *empeiria*, and hope that something will grow from it (see Nietzsche 1992: 40). The expression 'to take something seriously' here gets a new, non-literal meaning; it denotes more than anything else a matter of 'letting be' (see Hollier 1989: 26; 177).

The power dimension of the planner-*flâneur* relationship is clear. We can summarise the reasons in three points. Firstly, planning is politics and '[a]nyone engaged in politics is striving for power' (Weber 1994: 311). Secondly, planners belong to a kind of techno-bureaucratic social stratum, whose power rests on professional skill – which is considered essential in today's 'developed' society. In addition, this group controls its own recruitment. Planning professionals also largely determine the meaning of political and technically heavy concepts of rationality and efficiency, which means they can easily reject criticism. As sociologist Joachim Israel (1971: 311) writes, 'By referring to their own expertise and to the lack of technical knowledge among their critics, the tautological circle of defending actions – by using exactly the same criteria upon which they are based – is fulfilled'.

This more or less closed circle of self-referential activity is illustrated by the reward system in architecture. As Robert Goodman (1972: 156), self-critical architect, emphasises, the closeness of the reward system contributes to the profession's increasing intolerance for 'non-expert opinions'. The indoctrination begins in school: which is evident in the following quote, where Mark Howland (in Cuff 1992: 118) describes how architectural training affected him and his fellow students:

> The long hours of work in a common studio space forged us into a close knit group of men and women who were marked by our dedication, endurance and talent. We shared the excitement of learning to see the world in a new way, of learning to distinguish between well and poorly designed glasses while our friends were drinking coffee unaware from styrofoam cups.

At long last, we come to the third and final reason why the power dimension of the planner-*flâneur* relationship is clear. It is because the conceived dimension of space is the one that has the greatest practical consequences; it contributes to the shaping of the physical environment (Lefebvre 1991: 42). Lived space, however, 'merely' produces symbolic works: art, poetry and fiction (ibid.). The conceived space of the architect gets transformed into stone, which in turn creates boundaries to what the *flâneur* can and cannot do. Its abstractions 'rides roughshod over everyday life', as Lefebvre (1995: 120) puts it. The *flâneur* needs to submit to the authority of those in power. As Lefebvre (1995: 118) writes, 'Our technicists and technocrats have their hearts in the right place, even if it is what they have in their minds which is given priority'.

Besides Lefebvre, Lofland (1998), Wilson (1992a), Franzén (1982; 1987) and not least Sennett (1990; 1992; 1996; 2008), have pointed to the gap between architects and laymen when it comes to interpreting and evaluating the built environment. They have also demonstrated how destructive conceived space can be. And this gap seems to be born – and grow – during training (see Cuff 1992, Goodman 1972, Groat 2000, Nasar 1989, Nyman 1989, Steffner 2009, Sternudd 2007). Architects are there taught to flout the opinions of laymen, for they lack education and thus knowledge on the subject matter (Norberg-Schulz 1963: 14; 24, Östnäs and Werne 1987: 23).

One of the first to call attention to the gap was, however, Jacobs (see Goldberger 2006). But instead of talking about car people and foot people, I choose to talk about the eye of the architect and the body of the *flâneur*, and – as we will eventually see – of philobats and ocnophils. But the point is essentially the same; the experience of a contradiction between what the 'expert' thinks, on the one hand, and what I – as an individual, a layman in the midst of life's poetic mess – feel, on the other.

To illustrate what I mean by saying that our statements reflect our perspective, I want to give an example from the Hammarby Sjöstad project. On one occasion the director of the planning project talked about 'axes ... made of grass', when he described that which I perceived as a quiet and boring path way (in Hultin and Waern 2002: 37). His choice of words awoke the idea that what he has in front of his inner eye must be *a line on a blueprint* – a line that leads from point *A* to point *B*. And indeed; on a drawing you notice little difference between a

Figure 2.1   **'Man walks in a straight line because he has a goal and knows where he is going' (Le Corbusier in Carter 2002: 28). Hammarby Sjöstad**
Source: Author's photograph from 2009.

line representing a path way (made of grass) and a line representing a street. But in reality, the 'axes' that the planner was talking about are very real pathways, with edges – not only a beginning and an end (see Figure 2.1). Unlike a street that weaves together dwelling and movement (Franzén 1982: 15), that makes it possible to also move sideways, in the pathways in Hammarby Sjöstad my body moves either forwards or backwards in one given direction. That the planner does not seem to pay attention to this distinction between drawing and reality becomes clear in the following quote:

> Many claim that the classic grid structure generates safety. But the argument that a tree structure like this one would prevent safety – I do not believe. The grid is here, it is just that one axis is made of grass instead of asphalt. I do not believe that safety would decrease just because there are no cars there. (Inghe-Hagström in Hultin and Waern 2002: 37)

Looking at Figure 2.1, which illustrates one of these 'axes', we can recall Le Corbusier's (1986: 187) statement that architecture is based on axes, and an axis is defined as 'a line of direction leading to an end'. This view of architecture rhymes with his vision of modern man as a rational creature, in stark contrast with the pack-donkey, the animal who 'meanders along, meditates a little in his scatter-brained and distracted fashion, … zigzags in order to avoid the larger stones, or to ease the climb, or to gain a little shade' (ibid.).

Both Hammarby Sjöstad and Södra stationsområdet were planned with urbanity as an ideal. We get clues as to how the planning director (the same for both projects) interprets this ideal from an article in the journal *Arkitektur*, where he speaks of 'the spatial qualities of the dense city' (Inghe-Hagström 1987: 32). These seem to be about 'the formation and design of urban space, the material of the external environment, the architecture of the buildings and the layout of the apartments'. The blocks are made of 'traditionally city-like constructions that walk the line between flat and house' and the houses 'should be designed with architectural details that have affinity with the architecture of the inner city'. These details are 'base sections, window, balcony fronts and cornices but also roofing materials and colours' (ibid.: 32f). The reference to forms and details in contemporary discussions on urbanity is not unusual; on the contrary, at one point 'city-like lanterns' are discussed (see Gestaltningsprogram för Kvarnbergsplan 2005). According to architect Aleksander Wolodarski, urbanity is ultimately about forms. He writes, 'I think that urbanity is mainly created from the integrity of the architectural form. It is therefore first of all the form that determines whether an environment is urban or not' (Wolodarski 2003: 150). And when interviewed, he says (in Andersson 2009a),

> Many believe that urbanity is created by a mixture of content. But this is damn wrong; this is not how it is. First, there is urban form, and that includes many levels, from the urban structure down to the smallest detail.

As Inghe-Hagström, Wolodarski uses the word 'axes': 'In order to restore the city, certain specified conditions must be met: City blocks, clear place formations and street axes are main elements' (in Gullbring 2002: 21).

To create urbanity, to seek the diversity of the inner city appears to be a challenge that the planners do not really know how to handle. The Hammarby Sjöstad project was initially criticised by politicians for not being sufficiently urban, or 'city-like'. According to the director of the project, this criticism was partly based on the belief that 'it is city-like with streets on four sides and closed blocks' (in Hultin and Waern 2002: 34). But he did not want to build this way. The planners' response to the criticism was instead to try to pursue a mixture of functions to a greater extent than before (ibid.). 'To integrate new businesses in order to succeed in building a city' is highlighted as a major challenge (Inghe-Hagström 1997: 34). In addition to investing in a diversity of uses, narrow openings along Hammarby Allé were replaced with closed glass and balcony sections, and – interestingly – names were revised; 'alleys' (*gränder*) became 'streets' (*gator*) and (*BoStad02* 2002: 31).

Intermezzo

Götgatan on Södermalm, one of Stockholm's busiest streets. I used to lived there, between Högbergsgatan and Medborgarplatsen on Götgatan's north part where car traffic is still allowed, and where pedestrians, cyclists and motorists share the same space. With windows facing the street, I learned to recognise how the different days of the week sound. As expected, Sundays were the quietest of them all – especially in the mornings, when you could hear the ticking of the traffic lights at the pedestrian crossing just down the street. It was a sound that came to signal silence since it otherwise was lost in the general noise. Friday and Saturday nights were – of course – the busiest. Then you had to keep the windows closed if you wanted to hear the TV or the radio. Saturday mornings were a mixture of, on the one hand, the kind of calm that can only come after an outburst of energy (Friday night before), and, on the other hand, a slowly rising, almost playful expectation. All this brought a feeling of being connected to something else, beyond myself, with other people, contemporary as well as historical. Sometimes I found it relaxing to work when the festive atmosphere in the street was at its highest, and I could hear the buzz and the music from the bar below. But mostly I followed its rhythm – it was as if I did not wake up alone; it was me and the whole city that awoke to meet the day. This brought about a tremendous sense of well-being.

Planners act by virtue of legality, that is, by virtue of belief in appropriate competence founded on rationally established rules (Weber 1994: 312). The fact that people have become accustomed to this, does – as Kaj Nyman (1989: 5) writes – not make the problem less severe. The discomfort and the suffering are still there – 'although it is denied' (ibid.). The spaces of the users are lived, not primarily conceived, not just represented through maps and drawings. Plato, one of Western philosophy's most influential thinkers, took sides with thinking against the body, against passion. Since Plato, bodily passion has been regarded as a force that both gods and men have sought to control, especially in relation to rational thinking and the activities that form the basis of social order and security, family, tradition, and so on (Sigurdsson 2006: 291). As Lefebvre (1991: 363) has noted, lived space is marginalised in Western thinking, and therefore he wants to restore the body, to recover the non-visual and the sexual – in the sense of sexual energy.[16]

As an aid to understanding the urban from the perspective of the *flâneur*, we can look at Lefebvre's idea of the moment. The moment relates to what is left over after 'all the sums have been totalled, after everything has seemingly been accounted for: the moment is a philosophical anti-concept, an affirmation of *residue*, of remainders, of marginal leftovers, of the power and radicality of the ragged and the *irreducible*'

---

16   Sexuality is a multi-faceted word. It can be seen both as a drive, an act and as a matter of identity (Grosz 1994: viii). Psycho-analysis is undisputedly the most developed theory in understanding sexuality as a drive. It is also in this way I use the term. Characteristic of this approach is that sexuality is interpreted broadly, which means that it is closely associated with desire (ibid., see also Roazen 1979: 119ff).

(Merrifield 2009: 939). The moment is irreducible; it escapes categorisation and reification and is always excluded from totalising systems. The moment is a potentiality, an opportunity waiting to be taken, something geographical and temporal, intense and absolute while at the same time fluid and relative. In fact, the moment – and, thus, the urban – resembles nothing less than sex, 'the delirious climax of pure feeling, of pure immediacy, of being there and only there, like the moment of festival, or of revolution' (ibid.). Sarah Jessica Parker, actress and co-producer of the TV series *Sex and the City*, has said: 'In New York City, you walk out the door and you do not know what is going to happen. There's such potential for poetry' (in Sanders 1996: 266, see also White 1999: 29).

Both urbanity and the sexual act involve a crossing, a collapsing of boundaries, a definition that renders the urban not only as a sexual but also as a poetic phenomenon.[17] Poetry has a disruptive and destabilising potential, of which Plato, so long ago, was aware. Poets have always possessed the ability to challenge the accepted order and cool rationality (Merrifield 2009: 946). The moment represents presence, and thus it is an opposite to alienation, to which we will return, but for the moment we can define alienation as absence. Lefebvre's moment expresses a sense of freedom and passion – a moment that only has a certain amount of time. The instantaneous and the formless, the trans-boundary and the dissolvable – all of these features of the urban can be met in Woolf's novel *Mrs Dalloway*. There we see how Clarissa Dalloway, one of the main characters, virtually blends with the surroundings when she is walking through London. The fusion is made to the point that she confuses external events with internal: '[S]he cannot distinguish the pause between heartbeats from the silence before the Big Ben strikes, the heart beating from the bell ringing' (Squier 1985: 95f). Clarissa feels a kinship with all the residents of the city when she walks along the streets, for with them she shares not only London but also life, and the moment: 'Life; London; this moment of June' (Woolf 1996: 6). At this moment she transcends class boundaries, 'affirming a community including even the "veriest frumps" and drunks "sitting on doorsteps"' (Squier 1985: 96). This boundary-dissolving that Woolf depicts between Clarissa and the environment, and between her person and other people (see e.g. Woolf 1996: 10f), shows Woolf's attitude that the urban environment 'by its disparate, varied nature, nurtures egalitarian social relations' (ibid.). To Woolf, the urban was an opportunity to break away from her own personality. To her, this meant freedom.

> [W]hat greater delight and wonder can there be than to leave the straight lines of personality and deviate into those footpaths that lead beneath brambles and thick tress trunks into the heart of the forest where live those wild beasts, our fellow men? (Woolf 2005: 15)

---

17   Related to the issue of sexuality is flirting – defined by Simmel (in Carter 2002: 58) as 'the act of taking hold of something only in order to let it fall again, of letting it fall only to take hold of it again'. According to Simmel, flirting – as well as the adventure and the meeting – is a kind of social commodity that the city offers (ibid.: 57).

The urban has a fluid character. This is emphasised in Jacobs' (1992: 376) choice of metaphor for the city: a large field in the dark, where

> many fires are burning. They are of many sizes, some great, others small; some far apart, others dotted close together; some are brightening, some are slowly going out. Each fire, large or small, extends its radiance into the surrounding murk, and thus it carves out a space. But the space and the shape of that space exist only to the extent that the light from the fire creates it.

The fires, as I understand it, symbolise the crowd; people in motion, activities in the spaces of the city that obtain their public character as a result of human presence (see Altay 2007). Jacobs is not the first to use the metaphor of fire to describe the urban. To the writer Honoré de Balzac, Paris was a world 'in perpetual motion', a field of fire (Prendergast 1992: 55; 57).

Let us now consider the fixed points on which the chapter is based: the eye of the architect and the body of the *flâneur*. The names suggest that the architect is the one who sees, while the *flâneur* is the one who feels. This is based on an artificial separation of the senses and it is a simplification. It is only in theory that sensory inputs can be isolated (Dewey 2005: 130, Gibson 1969: 60). What, then, motivates this division?

The Eye of the Architect – The Eyes of the Flâneur

Both the architect and the *flâneur* have eyes to see. And not only the *flâneur* has a body. Nevertheless, I speak of the architect as if she had no body and of the *flâneur* as if she had no eyes. In this section, I will explain why this distinction is justified. To begin with, this is a scientific analysis, and the very meaning of the word analysis is decomposition. But the reason for this dichotomy is not just abstract. The most important thing is that the planner's and the *flâneur*'s way of seeing is different, and this difference can be understood through psychologist James J. Gibson's (1950) concept of *visual field* and *visual world*.[18] The *visual field*, which in this case refers to what the planner sees, is demarcated; it includes the picture or the drawing she has in front of her. The *visual world*, on the other hand, is the world of the *flâneur,* and that is not limited – it is also behind her and above her. This is illustrated in the following quote by Priscilla Parkhurst Ferguson (1994: 27): '*Flânerie* urbanizes observation by making the observer part of the urban scene ... [T]he *flâneur* is observed while observing. He is himself an integral part of the urban spectacle. He looks up and around, pokes his head about, and walks endlessly'.

---

18   The difference between the planner's and the *flâneur*'s way of seeing can also be highlighted by David Levin's (1988: 68) idea of *assertoric* and *alethic* gaze (see also Jay 1994: 275).

As the *flâneur* is in the city, her way of seeing differs from the planner's, who sees the city from a distance, through her visualising instruments (Certeau 1984: 92f). The visual world is crowded with sensory impressions other than the visual. That is why Gibson (1950: 42) notes that 'although the visual field is *seen,* the visual world is only *known*'.[19]

In essence, the two forms of visualisation that we are dealing with are differently power-ridden (Bauman 1994: 141, Berg Eriksen 2005: 256, de Certeau 1984: 93, Jacobs 1992: 379, Pinder 1996, see also Foucault 2004). When referring to the eye of the architect, I have chosen to use 'the eye' in singular and not the architect's eyes in the plural because the architect seems to operate with a Cartesian or transcendental eye, a kind of internal, disembodied eye synonymous with the intellect (Berg Eriksen 2005: 255, Harries 1973: 37, Jay 1994: 81, Merleau-Ponty 2002: 230). I interpret the planner as an unembodied self – 'an onlooker', an observer of what the body does, without being in direct contact with anything (Laing 1965: 69, see also Imrie 2003) – while the *flâneur* is an embodied self, 'implicated in bodily desire and the gratifications and frustrations of the body' (Laing 1965: 67).

Planner's visualisation tools are an important element in the decision of what counts as knowledge, and their use of them is one contributing factor to the gap between planners and users.[20] General plans, detailed plans and models are powerful rhetorical tools or instruments of persuasion; they demonstrate '*savoir faire* and seriousness' (Söderström 1996: 252). Or, as it was expressed at a meeting of an urban renewal project in Boston in the 1970s, when the city planners had finished their introduction and were on their way to presenting the details, one of the residents in the audience said: 'Uh, oh, here comes the maps' (Goodman 1972: 57).

One thing visualisation tools do is that they create distance (Ley 1977: 10). As many before me have stated, vision means distance; our eyes must be at a distance from the object in question for us to see it (Jay 1994: 378f, MacMurray 1957: 107, Pallasmaa 2005: 25). It is through our eyes that we determine what is far away and are warned about what will come. Although the ears, too, can help in this general spatial orientation process, they work differently. Sounds – like light – do come from outside, but sound itself is close and intimate; it literally makes our body shake (Dewey 2005: 246). Here we can remember that it is not the visual impression of her lover, but her voice, that makes poet Karin Boye (1994) 'tremble like a leaf'. The voice of her beloved 'pierces' her, tears her 'into rags and pieces'. Visual stimuli evoke emotion indirectly, while sound 'agitates directly, as

---

19   That the *flâneur*'s way of observing by no means is limited to seeing in a literal sense, but that she is also immersed with – or distracted by – sounds, smells and the tactile contact with objects, was something that Benjamin insisted on (Frisby 1994: 93).

20   On drawing as a fundamental activity in the building of the architect's knowledge, see Robbins (1997). On the panorama as a form of representation and its effects on our understanding of the city, see Prendergast (1992: chapter 3).

a commotion of the organism itself' (Dewey 2005: 247). When Malte, the central figure of Rainer Maria Rilke's novel *The Notebooks of Malte Laurids Brigge* (2009: §2), lies in his bed in Paris with the window open, he comments on the noise from the street: 'The trams rattle jangling through my room. Automobiles drive over me'.

It is not only in the physical sense that vision means distance. In psycho-analysis, it is well known that visual impressions between the analyst and analysand can prevent the attachment process that is so crucial for analysis. I have already noted that Freud placed the analyst behind the part of the couch where the analysand rests her head in order to avoid eye contact. This is because the more the analyst is shrouded in shadow and mystery, the greater the intensity of the analysand's experiences of mental and emotional closeness (see e.g. Malcolm 1981: 38). Vision, metaphorically speaking, can make us blind; we learn this not only from Freud but from André Breton too, the surrealist writer who comments, 'I have discarded clarity as worthless. Working in darkness I have discovered lightning' (in Jay 1994: 211). In this context, we understand that it is hardly a coincidence that Lefebvre chose to describe the technocrats' office with the adjective 'silent'. In the introduction to *The Production of Space*, he writes, 'I shall return later to the peculiar kinship between ... mental space and the one inhabited by the technocrats in their silent offices' (Lefebvre 1991: 6). While architecture, Peter Zumthor (2005: 7) posits, is 'a way of looking at things', Lefebvre (ibid.: 313) knew that '[s]omeone who knows only how to see ends up ... seeing badly'.

When architects through the design of facades are trying to create urbanity, it is the eye and not the body they are addressing. They are creating '[s]igns and images of the urban, of "urbanness"', as Lefebvre puts it (ibid.: 389). But the result is a deceptive world; 'indeed the most deceptive of all worlds – the world-as-fraud' (ibid.). An example that shows both how planners emphasise the visual and how the visual implies a distance comes from one of the architects of the Minneberg area in Stockholm: 'Most people will experience Minneberg from the outside, far away from bridges and other parts of the city and from the water. The structure of the silhouette then, of course, becomes important' (Brunnberg 1987: 4) (see Figure 2.2 below).

It seems that planners still see themselves as 'vigilant guardians', borrowing the words Le Corbusier (1948: 132) used when describing his profession.

Despite the dominance of the visual, there are of course other factors that architects take into account when creating or evaluating a building (Rasmussen 1964: 9, see also Dyrssen 1995). The tactile experience of different materials, the sound of footsteps on the floor, the smell of wood in a summer house – all this plays a role in the design process, too (see Hellström 2003; 2010, Hedfors 2003). Nevertheless, as philosopher John Dewey (2005: 53) has argued, architects are handicapped relative to other artists (see also Evans 2003: 7; 156, Lawson 1997: 25, Rasmussen 1964: 14). The handicap is due to the gap between drawing and building – a problem we will now turn to.

Figure 2.2   If we are to believe the planners, this is how 'most people' will experience Minneberg, Stockholm
Source: Photograph by Leif Strååth, by courtesy of Stockholm City Planning Office.

Drawing/Building

> A spider conducts operations which resemble those of the weaver, and a bee would put many a human architect to shame by the construction of its honeycomb cells. But what distinguishes the worst architect from the best of bees is that the architect builds the cell in his mind before he constructs it in wax. (Marx in Merrifield 2006: 66)

As hinted above, the architect is handicapped relative to other artists. This is because she – unlike the painter, writer and composer – is unable 'to build up simultaneously the idea and its objective embodiment' (Dewey 2005: 53). It is only when the building is finished that she can experience it with all her senses. The same applies if we meet a person about whom we previously have had only a vague idea. We may have seen a photo or heard the person's voice, but when we experience the person in physical space, our senses work together in a way that makes us really *take her in*. In this fundamentally emotional process, we are often caught off guard by character traits we never imagined: 'We realize that we never knew the person before; we had not seen him in any pregnant sense' (Dewey 2005: 54).

Behind every architect-designed building or neighbourhood is imagination. The word itself – *imagination* – indicates the process by which the architect makes the absent present in the form of an inner *image*. 'When I think about architecture, images come into my mind', says Zumthor (2005: 7). This image is available only to the (inner) eye, while it – by definition – is unavailable to our sense of touch, smell, hearing and taste (Levin 1988: 116, Merleau-Ponty 2002: 235).

In sum, we can say that the pictures that the architect have in her head are transformed into drawings and models, which in turn get projected on real projects – such as Hammarby Sjöstad. It is not until then that they can be experienced, lived. This means that the architect does not work directly with her object of thought like the painter or the writer. She lacks the ability to simultaneously build both the idea and its embodiment.

This handicap, caused by the gap between drawing and building, can be highlighted by the following excerpt from the architect Ragnar Uppman's autobiography, *Arkitektens* öga (translates into *The Eye of the Architect*):

> In the eye of the architect there are two images. The original version, influenced by dreams and intentions, and the final version, which harshly demonstrates the result. The two images chafe against each other, like a double exposure. You really only see that which is deviant, that which did not turn out as intended. (Uppman 2006: 110)

The gap, Uppman says, can only be experienced by the architect herself. But, as Eiler Rasmussen (1964: 40) notes, 'Anyone who has first seen a place in a picture and then visited it knows how different reality is'. It is because of this that Rasmussen (ibid.: 33) posits that it is not enough to *see* architecture; you have to experience it as well. What he does not note, however, is that this is only possible with existing architecture, that is, realised drawings. Nor does he acknowledge the fact that the consequences of this gap can be severe – especially when the scales of the projects are large.

The drawing-building gap is rarely problematised in urban-planning discussions today. There are two plausible explanations for this. As mentioned in the section 'The Conceived – The Lived', planners rely on new, advanced technology and software to present 'lifelike' pictures. Another explanation is that this gap is an essential and thus taken-for-granted aspect of planning itself. What is most obvious is often the least noticeable. When discussing the planning of Norra Stationsområdet in Stockholm, Wolodarski says, '[T]he yards in Norra Stationsområdet *will be perceived as* intimate rather than cramped' (in Andersson 2009b, my emphasis). Similarly, architect George Lundquist writes that Hammarby Sjöstad '*will not be confused with* suburbia or the independent satellite' (in *BoStad02* 2002: 76, my emphasis). Naturally, it is the experts' job to be persuasive, to give citizens the illusion that they have something that mere mortals do not have: the ability to see into the future. But what is ignored here is not only the gap between the drawing and the finished building, between the visual field and the visual world, but also the gap between the architect and the user, between society and individual, between your perspective and mine. In this conflict, planning is never neutral; the Swedish word for planning, *samhällsplanering* (literally 'society planning'), already underscores a bias (Olsson 1985). In light of this understanding, it is hard not to see the manipulative aspect in the slogan, which the city of Solna is trying to market the newly planned Järvastaden: 'Järvastaden – this is where I want to live!' ('Solna – the City of the Future' 2010: 41).

Homo Faber/Homo Ludens

> It seems to me that next to *Homo Faber*, and perhaps on the same level as *Homo Sapiens*, Homo Ludens, Man the Player, deserves a place in our nomenclature.
> (Huizinga 2003: Preface)

I have already argued why architecture and planning can be seen as power-ridden activities. In practice this can be seen in city architect Per Kallstenius's (1998: 244) comment: 'The feeling for nature and the need to live in its proximity was manifest among those who moved into the outer city suburbs. This deep sense of the green city that the citizens of Stockholm share must be one of the most important issues for the future'.

By way of using language, Kallstenius produces his perspective not as a perspective but as the given truth. 'Only those occupying the positions of the dominators are self-identical, unmarked, disembodied, unmediated, transcendent, born again', writes Donna Haraway (1991: 193). For the city architect quoted above, we learn, for example, that 'a reasonable scale, light and transparency' count as 'qualities' (Kallstenius 2006: 127), and that the green structure is 'an essential part' of the city, that 'nature-proximity building' and 'separated pedestrian and bicycle paths' are 'unique qualities' (Kallstenius 1998: 244; 246). Finally, we learn that 'the suburbs of Stockholm as a whole [are] attractive'. Why? Because unlike the 'chaotic jumble' of many European cities, Stockholm has a 'systematically developed suburban area' (ibid.). He continues, claiming that it is important to maintain Stockholm's soul and character: 'If one can wish for anything in the future architecture of Stockholm, it will be the bright, light, maybe colourful, with nature on our doorstep and an affirmation of the Nordic light' (ibid.: 247). Between the lines we can hear the echoing of the words of functionalist architect Uno Åhrén (1928: 174): 'The cities are too cramped. The traffic squeaks, people's nerves are tried hard, the houses have inadequate air and light'.

Another example of power's freedom to define reality – a reality that the planning documents project onto the future – is the following statement by the planning director behind Hammarby Sjöstad: 'We want to avoid the classic cons of the inner city; the goal is to reduce the amount of asphalt and provide more greenery' (in Hultin et al. 1992: 22). This not only classifies asphalt as something negative, but the adjective 'classic' implies that this view is a given. As pointed out elsewhere (Westin 2005a: 25, Mattson and Wallenstein 2009), planners often present their ideas as objective truths, as logic, as rationality-based conclusions of logic. Perhaps it is against this type of debaters that Nietzsche (2001: §57) directs his words:

You sober people, who feel armed against passion and phantastical conceptions ...
[you] insinuate that the world really is the way it appears to you: before you alone
reality stands unveiled, and you yourself are perhaps the best part of it ... But
aren't you too in your unveiled condition still most passionate and dark creatures,
compared to fish, and still all too similar to an artist in love?

Inspired by the idea that words are hiding places, I will now try on a perspectivistic
rewriting of the director's statement. In this way I hope to underscore how
something that is presented as taken for granted is but one opinion among others,
that it is an expression of an individual's attitude and desires. Perhaps he is saying:
'I want to avoid making the area too much like the inner city, because I think that
it has so many disadvantages; among other things I think it has too much asphalt,
and I like it best with more greenery around me'.

If we deepen the analysis further and stop at the word asphalt, it evokes
associations with the *flâneur* – a figure who, using Benjamin's words, 'goes
botanizing on the asphalt' (in Prendergast 1992: 134). *Flânerie*, he continues,
is not an activity like any other but one that very much expresses an *attitude*
(ibid.). Given the planning director's negative attitude towards 'asphalt', it is not
unreasonable to assume that he is of a different attitude; that he simply values
other things – in his surroundings and in his life – than the *flâneur*.

The concept of attitude derives from the Latin *aptitudinem* – a variation of
the word *aptus*, which translates as 'adapted' or 'inclined to'. Originally, *attitude*
was a technical term in art to describe a particular body posture, which implied
a certain mental state. Later, the more general meaning of the word was noted:
'a behaviour, reflecting a feeling or an opinion' (*Online Etymology Dictionary*
2009-09-18). '[T]he prime requisite of an expert *flâneur*', states writer Henry James,
is 'the simple, sensuous, confident relish of pleasure' (in Prendergast 1992: 4).
Another writer and renowned *flâneur*, Balzac, described his food orgies in the
Paris restaurants as a feast for the gastronome, for the body (ibid.: 19). Pleasure
and enjoyment, in general, is something that is far from suppressed in nineteenth-
century literary and poetic depictions of the city.

Where has this line of reasoning taken us? When the planning director behind
Hammarby Sjöstad speaks negatively about 'the asphalt' in the inner city, we can
interpret this as a sign of him having a different attitude or feeling towards the
urban than the *flâneur* has. That is to say, his attitude is different from someone
who has a passionate relationship to the urban and its pleasures and is more than
happy to botanise 'the asphalt'. The point of departure for my reasoning is the
planner's wish to 'reduce the amount of asphalt', and my train of thought runs
like this: asphalt–*flânerie*–attitude.[21] As writer Aldous Huxley (1963: 14) states,

---

21 It should be noted that this does not say anything about what the planner
'really' prefers, for that would assume a clear and transparent subject. But it does say
something about what the planner in question values in terms of professional aspirations to
political fulfilment.

'Human life is lived simultaneously on many levels and has many meanings'. In the planner's professional world, it is likely that the goal is to create an environment in which good citizens may engage in predictable and decent behaviour (get to and from work, do grocery shopping, exercise in parkland, drop off and pick up the kids at school), rather than creating an unpredictable and chaotic 'city of pleasure' that can satisfy the daydreaming *flâneur*. Here we are again confronted with the conflict between the individual and society. In Marcuse's (1968b: 178) words,

> If left to itself, pleasure as the immediate gratification of the merely particular interest must come into conflict with the interest of the hypostatized social community. In contrast to the isolated individual, society represents what is historically right. It demands the repression of all pleasure that violate the decisive social taboo. It forbids the satisfaction of those wants which would shatter the foundations of the established order.

Furthermore, it is likely that control over her task is central for the planner – as for virtually all professionals – so that she can get a clear picture of what will happen where in the new area that she is planning; that all functions are in place and that every need of the citizens is satisfied. The planner must be factual and sober because she serves a cause: society's best interest. Soberness, or, as Weber (1994: 353) writes, '[p]assion in the sense of *concern for the thing itself (Sachlichkeit)*', is one of the pre-eminently decisive qualities for a politician. Being sober or objective is the same as having and keeping a distance – to things, to other people, but also to oneself. Therefore, Weber (ibid.) concludes, 'Politics is an activity conducted with the head, not with other parts of the body or soul'.

'The risk for chaos is greater than for monotony', says the director of Södra stationsområdet (Inghe-Hagström 1987: 33). Probably it was this fear that lay behind the decision to separate the traffic in the area: 'One side of the blocks face a park area. Parks, gardens and walkways form a large contiguous green space that is separated from car traffic' (ibid.: 32). The director also says that Richard Bofill, the Italian architect who had been invited to participate in the drawing of Södra stationsområdet, was 'obviously attracted to execute a project in a planned urban environment, not just a stand-alone monument in an otherwise chaotic urban area' (ibid.: 33). One does not have to read many planning documents today to understand why Sennett (2008: 98) characterises urban planning as a kind of purification mechanism that seeks control: 'Real disorder is a problem, planners think ... Planners' sights are on that urban "whole" instead; they are dreaming of a beautiful city that exists somewhere other than in the present, a beautiful city where people fit together in peace and harmony' (see also Boyer 1997, Hall 1988: 11).

For example, Kallstenius (1998: 245) advocates for emphasising the following advantages when planning Stockholm: 'beauty, the moderate scale, the green city and the clean environment'. Purity, sobriety and greenery are thus assumed to displace or replace... well, what? Ugliness, overindulgence, asphalt and dirt? Can we take for granted the hierarchy in city values that Kallstenius posits?

The urban walker or *flâneur* belongs to the asphalt and is aesthetically stimulated by the very confusion and clash of the different elements of urban life. Displaced to the park-like garden city, the *flâneur* loses his dynamic relationship with specifically urban streets. In fact, the ultimate result of Le Corbusier's city is to prevent human movement ... and human contact with the street surface; thus threatening human autonomy. (Parsons 2000: 13)

Here it may be interesting to recall that order (*Ordnung*) was one of the most frequently used words in the literature on German architecture during the National Socialist era (Taylor 1974: 182). The architects' stated task was to create order, as this was seen as a desirable quality in German society. And as argued by human geographer Irene Molina (1997: 67), the Swedish idea of Folkhemmet (literally *The People's Home*) was a social normalisation project characterised by a way of speaking and thinking in a series of dichotomies like order-disorder, purity-filth and so on. *Folkhemmet*, it was said, would be everyone's home – security, solidarity and community would be accessible to all. In reality, this project has led to stigmatisation and discrimination (ibid.).

In light of these ideas, it is motivated to ask what it means that architects of today, who are ostensibly committed to promoting urbanity and diversity, speak so warmly about *order*? Should we take this as cause for concern for the citizens? 'With compassion and a sense of beauty, such is our motto. ... Making diversity thrilling and rich, not cluttered and chaotic', says the architect Jacob Cederström (1985: 16). Here we can recall the quote at the beginning of the chapter, in which Berthold Brecht likened order to an absence revealed (*Mangelerscheinung*). And as Sennett (2008) has argued, a planning that puts primary emphasis on creating ordered cities runs the risk of suffocating people.

To plan and to *flânerie* – are these two different activities performed by two different types of people? To plan is to engage in rational consideration; to take steps that will benefit the society of tomorrow. This makes the planner a true Homo Faber – that is, a working, producing human who judges everything 'in terms of suitability and usefulness for the desired end, and for nothing else', and whose highest goal is 'to make the world more useful and more beautiful' (Arendt 1998: 153; 208). The bureaucratic structure exerts a constant pressure on the employee to be 'methodical, prudent, disciplined', and to have an attitude appropriate for the system (Merton 1968: 252). Homo Faber – 'the fabricator of the world' (Arendt 1998: 126), 'the technological animal' (Barrett 1962: 20) – is trying to live up to her ideals of stability and endurance.[22] In her world, everything must prove its utility and be used as a means to something else (Arendt 1998: 153). To *flânerie*, on the other hand, is to play, to act according to personal whims and fancies; 'The joy of strolling in the city', Bauman (1993: 169) writes, 'is the joy of playing'.

---

22 When and where the expression Homo Faber first was used is unclear, but according to Jean Leclercq (in Arendt 1998: 136), Henri Bergson popularised it.

Therefore, the *flâneur*'s alternate name is Homo Ludens – the playing man – a *lekman* in the literal sense (*lekman* is Swedish for 'layman'; *lek* means *play*). Man does not play 'in order to ... '; his play is not a means; it has no goal beyond itself. Its opposite is not seriousness but utility (Asplund 1987: 55). Planning, however, is fundamentally a means to achieve a pre-formulated end. The end of planning, in its most basic form, is to bring order, to build a predictable society. Modernity, to quote Bauman (1993: 8), 'is about conflict-*resolution*, and about admitting of no contradictions except conflicts amenable to and awaiting resolution'. The result is therefore not uncommonly what may be called '[a] product of tidy minds' (Ley 1977: 11).

As Laing (1965: 66) sees the embodied and the unembodied self as 'two different ways of being human', I interpret the *flâneur* and the planner as two different ways of being human. We are all Homo Fabers, and we are all Homo Ludens; we normally have both of these attitudes within us. The question is to which of these we allow most influence. However, the authors behind the functionalist manifesto *acceptera* from 1931 claim that 'the normal person'[23] feels comfort 'when faced with the well-arranged, the well-organized' (Asplund et al. 2008: 237f). Looking at planning documents today, one can see that this longing for order is still very much manifest.

The question of attitudes takes us to Walter Gropius, founder of the influential Bauhaus school in Germany (1919–1933). Gropius, who later, in 1937, became professor at Harvard, said in his opening lecture: 'It is not so much a ready-made dogma that I want to teach, but an attitude toward the problems of our generation which is unbiased, original and elastic' (Gropius in Gelernter 1995: 251). This statement reveals that the philosophy of the Bauhaus school – here represented by Gropius's statement – is based on a paradox: First you teach the students an attitude; then you learn them not to acknowledge this attitude as an attitude but as an 'unbiased' approach worthy of an expert. And as Mark Gelernter (1995: 254) has shown, this philosophy dominates many architectural schools today.

The strategy can be illustrated by another example: Lúcio Costa – one of the architects of Brasilia – deliberately hid his political and social intentions in his city plan; they were not published until years later. As Holston (1989: 74) explains, the reasons were rhetorical: '[W]ithin the context of the state-sponsored design competition, it was impolitic to make explicit his (and Niemeyer's) political and social presuppositions about Brasilia'. The subjective is made objective – Platonism in a nutshell. As I highlighted in the introduction to this book, urban planners of today consider themselves to be 'neutral experts' (Johansson and Khakee 2008: 205). The power of persuasion and the potential exercise of power in Platonism – as well as in modernism – is hitherto unmatched (Czarniawska 2009).

---

23   This is my translation from the Swedish 'varje normal människa' (Asplund et al. 1980: 97). The translator of the 2008 English edition – David Jones – uses the expression 'the average person' (Asplund et al. 2008: 237), but I think 'the normal person' is closer to the original and more suitable here.

In the discussion above I have illustrated how supposedly objective statements can hide an attitude, a disposition. Most importantly, I have shown how the attitude that the planner often espouses is different from that of the *flâneur*. Now, it is time to introduce two new concepts, philobatism and ocnophilia, to better understand the vision-reality gap. It is these concepts that I will use to deepen the analysis of both the planner's and the *flâneur*'s approach to the city. But in order to facilitate an understanding of these concepts, I will start by saying a few words about the more familiar concept of agoraphobia. The reason I have chosen to address this (as well as the related concept of claustrophobia) is that it can contribute to a deeper understanding of how we – as psychological beings – relate to the city. Since these phobias are related to our relationship with the external as well as to the internal environment, they are indeed relevant for geographical studies. Despite this relevance, the area has been relatively unexplored.[24]

Agoraphobia/Claustrophobia

Most people are familiar with the meaning of the word agoraphobia (*agorafobi* in Swedish, or the more common expression *torgskräck*, where *torg* translates as 'town square' and *skräck* as 'fear'). When I at one point asked people around me what they associated with the word *torgskräck*, the answers were roughly the same: a fear of places. When I asked them to clarify what types of places they had in mind, the answers varied between 'big', 'open' and 'empty' spaces. Then I asked them what exactly it is about these places that you are afraid of if you

---

24 One of the exceptions is Davidson (2003). However, I see two problems with her book. The first is that she refers to the idea of agoraphobia as a fear of open, empty places as a 'misunderstanding' (ibid.: 9). Agoraphobia is a fundamentally *social* anxiety, she affirms: 'Contrary to popular opinion, the condition of agoraphobia actually relates to public and social, as opposed to 'open' spaces' (ibid.). As I see it, to reject this second meaning of the term is a drastic and misleading 'solution' to the problem of the ambiguity inherent in the very word *agora*. The ambiguous nature is not something that Davidson discusses. The rejection appears as even more problematic if one takes into account that a fear of emptiness is the original meaning of agoraphobia: '[N]o fear without the void', as Henri Legrand du Saulle stated in 1878 (in Vidler 2001: 30). According to Davidson (2010: 376), Sitte, who also emphasised this meaning of agoraphobia, was 'simply mistaken'. The other problem is that she reproduces the stereotypical idea that women are afraid of the city – specifically crowded public places. Drawing on Wilson (1992a), I would like to emphasise the desire for the urban as a human, not necessarily gendered, desire. Davidson's largely sociological interpretation of agoraphobia bears a resemblance to feminist psychologists, who see agoraphobia as 'a symptomatic reaction to the social, economic and political construction of women in patriarchy' (Carter 2002: 209). Davidson (2003; 2010) thus relates to agoraphobia as a female phenomenon, but as shown by Callard (2006: 885), the link between agoraphobia and 'models of femininity' is a later invention (after the nineteenth century).

suffer from *torgskräck*, whereby they responded 'you are afraid to walk cross the square', and 'you are afraid of being alone in the square'.

Agoraphobia is a clinical term coined in 1871 by German psychiatrist Carl Otto Westphal as a way to describe a fear arising out of 'the sight of a large room, a long street or a wide square' (Carter 2002: 16). However, definitions vary somewhat – its meaning is not as simple as one might think. The *Swedish National Encyclopaedia* defines *torgskräck* as an 'intense fear of leaving a safe place, usually the home, and of staying in public places or in places where many people gather, e.g. on bridges and in shops'. The word *or* is interesting here because it indicates ambiguity; either the word means a fear of places in themselves, or it indicates a fear of the crowd that is often associated with these places. Hence, there is confusion regarding the exact meaning of agoraphobia. The ambiguity is found in the Greek word *agora*, which can mean both/either a crowd of people, and/or the places in which people gather (*phobos* means fear – an irrational and disproportionate fear). Like Lefebvre's concept of *space*, Marx's *value* or Freud's dream symbols, *agora* carries opposite meanings. The ambiguity is particularly evident in Freud's description of agoraphobia, where he simply translates the word to 'fear of space':

> Those patients who suffer from agoraphobia (topophobia, fear of space), no longer reckoned as an obsessional neurosis but now classified as anxiety-hysteria, … fear enclosed spaces, wide, open squares, long stretches of road, and avenues; they feel protected if accompanied, or if a vehicle drives behind them, and so on. Nevertheless, on this groundwork of similarity the various patients construct individual conditions of their own … One fears narrow streets only, another wide streets only, one can walk only when few people are about, others only when surrounded with people. (Freud 1970: 281)

As Paul Carter (2002: 16) underscores, the meaning(s) of agoraphobia can be sorted into two main categories. In the first, it is said to denote a fear of the crowd, and here agoraphobia is ultimately a fear of getting lost, to 'drown' in the crowd. In the second meaning, agoraphobia is simply a fear of open spaces; that is, it is primarily the street or the square that invokes fear. The latter meaning is the original and that which I take note of, but rather quickly after the coining of the concept, it came to include the former meaning as well (Vidler 2001: 31). Whether it is a question of a fear of crossing large, empty places, or if it is a fear of losing oneself in the crowd, the universal symptom of agoraphobia is, as Carter (2002: 16) says, a *movement inhibition*. It is probably easier to see how a crowd, rather than an empty square, can prevent movement, but Carter (ibid.: 17) explains how the latter might be possible: 'Immobility is produced not by a lack of directions, but by an excess of them'. Westphal (in Carter 2002: 17) draws on stories from his patients when describing the feeling:

> They all felt a peculiar uneasiness or anguish in crossing over wide squares or free, unenclosed spaces. One of the patients compared it to the feeling of a

swimmer crossing a lake, uncertain whether he will be able to reach the other side ... The feeling of distress was sometimes overpowering, and prevented them crossing many of the wide streets and squares.

When agoraphobia is said to mean a fear of getting stuck in the crowd, its kinship with another word becomes obvious: claustrophobia (*claustrum* is Latin for a locked room). This may seem strange because, when coined in 1879 by Benjamin Ball, claustrophobia was described as agoraphobia's 'apparent opposite' (Carter 2002: 32). The ambiguity becomes clear if we look at the German word for agoraphobia: *Platzangst* (*Platz* translates as 'town square' and *angst* as 'fear'). In everyday language, this word is used to describe claustrophobia, but it can also mean agoraphobia, depending on which dictionary you use. Not infrequently both meanings are stated.

Psychiatrist Emanuel Miller (1930) took note of this entanglement after having observed his patients, noting that agoraphobia and claustrophobia are two sides of the same kind of anxiety. Therefore, he coined the term *agora-claustrophobia*. Because if agoraphobia means a fear of the crowd, we recognise its kinship with claustrophobia, which means a fear of being trapped in an enclosed space, a feeling of being unable to move. As philosopher and sociologist Dag Østerberg (2000: 68) writes, 'The bodies of others deprive me of the most important thing of all: being a functional being'. Østerberg (2000: 68; 70) again:

> [T]here are those who feel the *phobia* of congestion, that they are surrounded by human bodies that impede their ability to move ... The feeling of hopelessness can reach climax if the driver – besides himself with impatience – is trying to get out of the traffic jam and realises that it is impossible.[25]

To the architect Camillo Sitte, who is said to have suffered from agoraphobia (Carter 2002: 46), agoraphobia meant a fear of large, empty spaces. He called it *Platzscheu*. Sitte was critical of the emerging modernist urban planning, which he believed was the cause of the disease (ibid.: 31). And he was not alone: 'In traditional cities, with their small, intimate and human-scaled spaces, the illness was unknown' (Vidler 2001: 28). According to Sitte, Ringstrasse in Vienna – one of the first examples of modernist city planning (Schorske 1981: 64) – embodied 'the worst features of a heartless utilitarian rationalism' (Vidler 2001: 28). The broad street not only isolated buildings but people as well. The open urban space ought to be replaced by the intimate, enclosed and human space, he said; '[t]he essential thing of both room and square is the quality of enclosed space' (Sitte 2005: 421).

Both agoraphobia and claustrophobia are 'distressing disorders of mental function' (Miller 1930: 253) – far from static and far from concerning only the

---

25   Perhaps there is no better example of a claustrophobic fit than that which strikes the character William Foster in Joel Schumacher's (1993) movie *Falling Down*. Another example is *Noise* by Henry Bean (2007). In the latter case, claustrophobia is triggered by sound.

mentally ill. In principle, anyone can suffer from it – including those who are considered 'normal'. These disorders do not take on any dramatic expression, nor are they always noticed (see Trotter 2004). Depending on who we are, where we are in life, our mood and what our goal is, we tend to prefer either open places where we can move freely in all directions or more enclosed places where we are accompanied by things and other people. Severe forms of agoraphobia and claustrophobia are, of course, obsessive compulsive disorders, pathological obsessions, or kinds of idée fixe. As Marina van Zuylen (2005) has shown in her book *Monomania. The Flight from Everyday Life in Literature and Art*, the obsession fills a function for those who suffer from an anxiety-filled relationship with both the internal and the external world; the idée fixe transforms the chaotic reality into a meaningful whole. Although agoraphobia and claustrophobia are undesirable syndromes, they can – paradoxically – be comforting: 'The idée fixe is an infinite source of comfort; not only does it provide unshakable boundaries, but it lures the subject into a sense of agency. In contrast, in the confusion of everyday life, with its chance encounters and unanticipated challenges, formlessness prevails, rupturing our hold over things' (van Zuylen 2005: 6).

If we choose to see agoraphobia as an idée fixe, we find that it is not so much an external emptiness that one fears, but an inner *horror vacui* (Latin for 'fear of empty space') (ibid.: 22). The pulse and movement of the street can be a welcome distraction from one's own thoughts; it can even alleviate existential loneliness. The agoraphobics' comfort in the crowd can be understood as an escape from the confrontation with 'their brittle selves' (ibid.). Johannisson (2009: 142) has noted how the *flâneur* (who in many respects resembles an agoraphobic) often carries a '[l]oneliness, an indefinite melancholy and a restless anxiety that must be kept at bay. … *Flânerie* becomes compulsive, one aimlessly floating around'.

The agoraphobic can also be said to have a temporal sibling: the Sunday hater. 'The universe transformed into a Sunday afternoon', philosopher E.M. Cioran writes, 'is the very definition of ennui, and the end of universe' (Cioran 2012: 22, emphasis removed). Sundays are occasions for rest and tranquillity, and just like an empty square, Sundays can bring a sense of restlessness, a sense of boredom.

> Time and space are interrelated, and in boredom the temporal *horror vacui* also becomes a spatial *horror loci*, where the emptiness of this particular *place* torments me. In the same way as one wants the time to pass in a state of situative boredom,[26] one also wants to escape the place where one is located. (Svendsen 2005: 112)

---

26 'Situative boredom' is a form of boredom that is caused by something specific (Svendsen 2005: 111), like Sundays or empty streets (see Johannisson 2009: 138 on what she calls 'Sunday neurosis'). In contrast, 'existential boredom' has a more unclear cause (Svendsen 2005: 111). As Svendsen (ibid.) writes, while the former is an emotion, the latter is a mood. This latter form of boredom is said to be characteristic of the *flâneur* and is often referred to as *spleen* (Johannisson 2009: 139–45). For further analyses on the subject of boredom and melancholy, see Goodstein (2004), Hammer (2006) and Spacks (1995).

But, is it really the agoraphobic who is the Sunday hater's sibling? Both suffer from a sense of emptiness – yes. But when we read the following lines by Svendsen (2005: 40), we see that the Sunday hater is akin to the claustrophobic, too: 'Time in boredom is not something that has been conquered: time is imprisoning'.

As Sennett (2008: 64f) has pointed out, happiness and well-being are usually associated with serenity. Social compositions that are characterised by conflict are often considered problematic. However, we ought to challenge this view, Sennett (ibid.) holds, and we only have to read Plato to understand that the assumed link between tranquillity and happiness is debatable. Historian Richard Seaford (2006: 106) writes:

> Plato knew that mothers calm their babies not by stillness but by rocking and a kind of singing, and compares this, as a cure, to the effect of dance and song on those who are 'out of their mind' in a Dionysiac frenzy. In both cases, the state to be remedied is a kind of fear, which is by external motion transformed into peace (*galênê*) and calm (*hêsuchia*) in the soul ...

The word agoraphobia is related to *ago* – Greek for 'I act' (Carter 2002: 72f). The crowd makes it possible to be someone else. As we saw when discussing Woolf's writings, this was one aspect of urban life that she appreciated: 'to leave the straight lines of personality' (Woolf 2005a: 15) and (pretend to) walk in someone else's shoes. She continues, 'Into each of these lives one could penetrate a little way, far enough to give oneself the illusion that one is not tethered to a single mind, but can put on briefly for a few minutes the bodies and minds of others' (ibid.: 14).

Intermezzo

In the small community in the north of Sweden where I grew up, the opportunity to be someone else was limited. It was partly for this reason my enthusiasm for an upcoming visit to Östersund – the largest city in the region – was so great. 'Mom, can I wear my high heeled shoes then?' I asked, every time. Why I did not wear high heeled shoes in the community where we lived was not something I reflected upon; it was just unthinkable. Partly because everyone knew everyone else there, which ruled out the ago project entirely, partly because there hardly was any well-used *agora* in which one could *ago*. In a city you dress up (in whatever way you may; you can dress down too) because there are people to dress up (or down) for. In the city you react to the motion of the crowd, accompanied by the sound of shoes that meet the pavement: click-clack, click-clack, click-clack. This was part of my early, unspoken understanding of the urban.

To the agoraphobic – here in the sense of someone who fears open, empty spaces – the crowd is not a threat but a possibility for a sense of community, for freedom. Matter does not only weigh us down – it can also set free, Østerberg (2000: 97) writes, continuing, 'many are reluctant to go into an empty restaurant because they want the other guests to strengthen their own presence' (ibid.: 118). Other people in the same public place can offer a certain sense of anonymous, shared joy. In contrast, stillness – which characterises both the empty restaurant and Sundays – becomes oppressive; we feel alone and loneliness is nothing less than the 'facticity of our sociality' (ibid.: 80).

As previously mentioned, a discussion of agoraphobia and claustrophobia helps us to learn more about how humans, as psychological beings, relate to the city. In the following I will extend this analysis using two related – and in my opinion even more interesting – concepts developed within the psycho-analytic tradition.

Philobats and Ocnophils

From Emanuel Miller's connection of agoraphobia and claustrophobia, the conceptual distance is not far to the psycho-analyst Michael Balint's (1955; 1959M) study of people's primitive attitudes towards the world. After studying his patients he drew the following conclusion: People can, in general, depending on how they relate to the world, be divided into two different categories: philobats and ocnophils. Before I explain what these terms mean, it should be emphasised that these are theoretically pure cases derived from extreme empirical cases. In most people, we find a mixture of these two attitudes in different proportions, and often one attitude is used to alleviate the other (Balint 1955: 228; 236).

In short, we can say that the ocnophil needs objects – both physical and human. She simply cannot live without them: 'Like a drowning man clutching at a straw, [the ocnophil] clings to whatever will give him immediate emotional and physical support' (Carter 2002: 32). Empty spaces and places are therefore experienced as frightening – something that emphasises the ocnophil's kinship with the agoraphobic (M. Balint 1959: 136). 'There constantly [has] to be someone, not necessarily the same person, to whom she [can] turn for sympathy, understanding, and help, if she [comes] up against a difficulty' (Balint 1955: 225). For the ocnophil the world consists primarily of objects and the gap in between them are perceived as intimidating.[27]

The philobat, however, usually sees objects – physical and human – as a disturbance (Balint 1955: 226). And as Balint (M. 1959: 136) points out, there is a risk that philobatism can lead to claustrophobia. Objects are fundamentally dangerous and unpredictable, which is why the philobat takes her refuge in the 'friendly expanses'. The philobat's world can therefore be described as a space populated by scattered objects. To the philobat, it is empty space that provides a sense of security. Both cases refer to an emotional attitude – not only towards the outer, physical world but also towards alleged dangers in the inner, mental world (Balint 1955: 226f).

---

27   Suddenly, the following statement by space syntax theorist Lars Marcus (2008: 136) gets a deeper, psychological meaning: '[W]e live in cities so that we can get close to many different things' (see also Niedomysl 2006: 13; 18).

A look at the etymology of these words can shed additional light on their meaning. Philobat comes from the Greek word *akrobat*, which literally means 'one who walks on his toes', away from the safe earth (ibid.: 227). Ocnophil comes from *okno*, which means to shrink, to hesitate, to stand back (ibid.). 'Whereas the ocnophilic world is structured by physical proximity and touch, the philobatic world is structured by safe distance and sight' (ibid.: 228). The ocnophil would consequently touch/feel; the philobat, see/look. Enid Balint[28] discusses the two types' respective relation to proximity and distance:

> The ocnophil avoids the distances between objects and satisfactions and tries to deny their existence; the philobat transfers parts of his libido from direct satisfaction to a skilful overcoming of the unsatisfactory spaces and times between satisfactions. (E. Balint 1959: 131, emphasis removed)

Now that we have a rough picture of these two world views, it is natural to ask this: Where do they come from? Since Balint is a psycho-analyst, he gives a psycho-analytically inspired answer. He also gives an answer to his own question, which of these worldviews that comes chronologically first; that is, which one developed out of which. Before we go into that, let us briefly recall one of the fundamental ideas of psycho-analysis, namely that a person's life – her thoughts, feelings and actions – are largely formed in early childhood. Memories (which in no way are static phenomena) from this period reside in our unconscious and continue to affect our lives in ways we are not consciously aware of. Characteristic of childhood is a person's first and largest trauma: the separation from the parent – or, as Balint (1955: 235) writes – 'the painful discovery of the independent existence of important objects'. In other words, trauma results from the realisation that the objects around me – including my mother's breast and/or the hand that gives me a baby bottle – exists independently of me (ibid.: 233).

At a superficial glance, it is easy to categorise the ocnophilic world as the most primitive. It is easy to understand the ocnophil's attachment to objects that represent the parent. Similarly, it is easy to understand that the ocnophil is afraid of voids and finds them frightening because in the void there is no mother/father; '[c]linging is therefore both an expression of an anxiety and an attempt to prevent its outbreak' (ibid.: 232).

As easy as it is to judge the ocnophilic world as primitive, it is also easy to see the philobatic world as highly developed. Superficially, this is correct, for the philobat has accepted reality, the inevitable separation from her parents (ibid.: 233). She sees the world 'in true perspective' and has come to terms with the realisation that the world consists of separate objects (ibid.). The philobat seems mature and sophisticated. But she has merely found other strategies to satisfy her needs. One of these is sublimation, a phenomenon I will discuss in more detail in Chapter 3.

---

28 Michael Balint's wife, also psycho-analysis. When I write Balint, it is Michael Balint that I am referring to because I only refer to Enid Balint this one time.

'[Sublimation] means the creation, in place of our faithless original objects, of new ones, or the acceptance as objects for our love and hate of things that have but little in common with our original ones' (ibid.). Sublimation demands of the individual – in this case the philobat – a certain degree of skill. She has to construct a world that she knows, that turns reality into a sort of fairyland in which things are arranged according to her own wishes. '[In philobatism] the individual must develop some personal skills ... in order to retain, or regain, the freedom of movement in, and harmony with, the objectless expanses, such as mountains, deserts, sea, air, etc.'. (Balint 1979: 70). Balint exemplifies with the worlds created by dancers, actors, skaters and musicians, but he also stresses that a philobat may also take refuge in more mundane objectives such as learning how to drive: 'The philobat apparently firmly believes that his skill will be sufficient to cope with all the hazards and dangers, and that everything will turn out all right in the end. It is up to him to conquer the world' (Balint 1955: 234).

Philobatism thus requires skill. In order to maintain a fantasy of the friendly expanses, she must make an effort. The primary skill is acquired when the child learns how to walk. This is no easy task, and it often occurs in stages – initially the child throws herself across the floor between secure items, the father's arms, the mother's legs, and so on, 'cutting their sojourn in the unsafe empty spaces as short as possible, that is to say, behaving in a truly ocnophilic way' (ibid.). Learning to appreciate the void between objects instead of seeing it as frightening is thus a process of maturation. Note that this does not make philobatism a non-neurotic orientation.

The ocnophil generally finds it more difficult to accept her independence. She continues to deny the existence of separate objects and handles her trauma auto-plastically; to compensate for not being held she clings firmly to the objects. Ocnophilia is a fixation caused by a trauma, and by the act of clinging, the ocnophil can create the illusion that she and her objects are still one and the same. The philobat's feelings and actions are also reactions to this trauma, but she – as we have just seen – handles it differently. She re-establishes the harmony between herself and the world – paradoxically enough through a constant repetition of the original trauma, – by surrounding herself with empty space that separates her from the environment.

Ocnophilia and philobatism both contain the word *philo*, which means 'love' in Greek. Balint (1955: 235) explains why this is so: 'By this I wanted to stress that they are not true opposites, although in some respects they may appear so. In my mind they are both secondary stages, developing out of the archaic phase of primary love as reactions to the traumatic discovery of the separate existence of objects'.

Both types have an ambivalent relationship to objects. The ocnophil is always suspicious, distrusting and critical. The philobat is always superior, condescending (ibid.). Both run the risk of constantly destroying their relationship with their beloved objects 'by exactly the same method by which they gained their favour; the ocnophil by the use of too much dependent clinging, the philobat by the use of too much superior skill' (ibid.: 236). What Balint here points to, as I interpret it, is an overarching risk of contra-finality in both the ocnophil's and the philobat's way to go about.

Before we continue to the next section – in which I connect Balint's concepts to the fixed points of the present chapter – I want to address the issue of sound and silence. For the ocnophil's and the philobat's problematic relationships are not only with visible objects. Auditory impressions – or lack thereof – can bring (dis)comfort as well. Balint (1955: 239) speaks of two different kinds of silences. Silence can be harmonious, confident and serene, but it can also be perceived as a rejection, as pervaded by suspicion and aggression: 'In everyday life we meet people who adore silence, seek for solitude, and need it; on the other hand people who hate silence are only happy in noisy places' (Balint 1955: 239).

An explanation of why silence can be perceived as daunting is given by ethnologist Karin Eriksson (2007: 30): 'In silence there is a sense of fear, a feeling of being outside, of not being heard or not understanding what you hear. People who have ever been accustomed to feel safe when hearing certain sounds can experience deep loss when these are taken away'.

The parallels between Balint's two kinds of silences, on the one hand, and 'the horrid empty spaces' and 'the friendly expanses', on the other, are striking. The ocnophil's longing to be held needs not only be directed towards objects in the traditional sense (house, other people's bodies and so on), but also towards various forms of sound. Eriksson, the ethnologist quoted above, expresses a form of sonic ocnophilia as she explains how she feels 'enveloped' by the sounds of Istanbul's streets (K. Eriksson 2007: 27–29): 'I was protected by the sounds, I found myself inside the sound bubble ... Even if you do not join the commerce of the bazaars, you feel quite involved in its atmosphere. The sounds of Istanbul have evolved into a romance'.

Balint's idea of philobatism and ocnophilia is interesting because it offers a way to understand and talk about people's primitive attitudes towards the world, which, in turn, can deepen our understanding of a range of common human experiences (M. Balint 1959: 136; 12). Next, I will use this knowledge to deepen our understanding of the gap between vision and reality in urban planning – the chief problem of this book, which I in this chapter have chosen to view as a gap between the perspective of the planner and the perspective of the *flâneur*.

The Philobatic Architect – The Ocnophilic *Flâneur*

> Life is so hideous ... that the only way to endure it is to turn it into art. (Flaubert in van Zuylen 2005: 16)

> The role of architecture is therapeutic: Forms of envelopment (room and roof) and forms of exposure (façade) minister to our incipient agora-claustro-phobic panic. (Carter 2002: 181)

According to Sitte (2005: 414), Aristotle said, 'A city should be built to give its inhabitants security and happiness' (see also Bartetsky and Schalenberg 2009: 7). Aristotle may have been right, but as the perspectivistic geographers we are in this investigation, we know that what you regard as happiness may not necessarily be happiness for me. Moreover, it is a dubious manoeuvre to even clump these feelings or (mental) conditions – security and happiness – together into one positive value. In what follows I will formulate a thought experiment. Admittedly a simplification, it can be summarised as follows: The planner is first and foremost a philobat and the *flâneur* is primarily an ocnophil.

The first quote at the beginning of this section is from a letter by the writer Gustave Flaubert. To his friend he wrote about his approach as a writer and likened it to that of the architect. Flaubert could not stand lived experiences – they were too chaotic and changeable. Therefore, he fled into the sphere of art and writing and made his creative endeavour a corrective – a sense-making activity – that compensated for the many inadequacies of life. For it is true that it is easier to handle a monologue than a dialogue. In his writing, Flaubert searched – like an architect – for 'a divine form, something as timeless as a principle' (in van Zuylen 2005: 16). Flaubert personifies the monomaniac – an individual who, for one reason or another, cannot stand life as it is and who takes refuge into the world of art, where life can be arranged according to self-designed principles and harmonies. Van Zuylen (2005: 205) explains: 'All these attempts to simplify and to unify protect the self from the intolerable pressure of being cast out in a realm where division reigns. Retreating into one's solipsistic world provides a simultaneous sense of autonomy and subordination'. However, monomania is an ambiguous phenomenon; while the artist assumes control over her world (that is, her art work), she remains a slave to her own principles.

Flaubert's identification with the architect's modus operandi is interesting for our study. A possible motivation is found in the following quote by architect Åhren (1928: 173): 'It is really a sad state of lack of clear principles we live in'. The motto of modernist urban development reads, 'Organise!' (Råberg 1970: 106). After World War I, Le Corbusier observed the traffic on Champs-Elysées and noted that it was 'as though the world had suddenly gone mad' (in Carter 2002: 26). It is no wonder, then, that one of modernism's fundamental ideas is that the city 'must be re-organised' (Johansson 1930) and that the remedy for the impending madness is spelled architecture.

The idea that architecture is a kind of cure for feelings of insecurity and anxiety is supported by Wolodarski, quoted in the beginning of this chapter: 'Architecture – to me – means comfort and harmony ... Sometimes you need very strong forms to turn chaos into order' (in Andersson 2009a). When asked what makes good architecture, he replied that architecture should 'bring harmony to places. In the chaotic times in which we live, architecture must provide a peaceful and harmonious setting' (in Kazmierska 2010).

It is interesting to contemplate Wolodarski's depiction of the city and the times we live in as 'chaotic'. As we have seen, he is not the only planner who shares this view. Where does the idea come from? Here we can recall what Freud (1989: 13) said about the neurotic. A neurotic is an individual who in one way or another is fixated to a previous trauma. She is, as Freud says, unable to 'get free of the past and for its sake [she] neglect[s] what is real and immediate' (ibid.). When applying this perspective, we can say that urban planning as an activity largely arose as a reaction to a kind of trauma: namely, the rapidly growing industrialised city with its crowds and traffic problems (see Eriksson 2001, Hall 1988). Today, in the wake of modernism, cities are rather facing the opposite problem: crowd congestion on the street pavement has been replaced by empty pathways and squares. Urban planning is still, however, fixated with yesterday's trauma: the city is all the same perceived as 'chaotic'.

Architecture can be seen as an obsession or an idée fixe that the individual in question uses as a powerful weapon against life's tyranny, the threat of chaotic disintegration, and 'the dictatorial nature of materiality' (van Zuylen 2005: 6). In this sense, we can understand the ideas that '[c]onstruction is the art of making a meaningful whole out of many parts' (Zumthor 2005: 11). Hereby, the architect – the philobat she is – creates a kind of fairyland in which things are arranged according to her wishes. Zumthor (2005: 24) again: 'I carefully observe the concrete appearance of the world, and in my buildings I try to enhance what seems to be valuable, to correct what is disturbing, and to create anew what we feel is missing'.[29]

The fact that architecture and planning basically involves a kind of primitive desire for comfort, peace and balance to the creator in question is also attested by Sennett (2008: 96) who writes, 'Buried in this hunger for preplanning along machine-like lines is the desire to avoid pain'. For it is not without a sense of relief that one of the architects behind Hammarby Sjöstad says that the area is located 'at a safe distance from Södermalm', which is a part of the inner city (*BoStad02* 2002: 76). This is interesting, because just before he stated this, he expressed a desire to 'link the area with the inner city'. And if we continue our close reading of the architect's statement, we realise that it is through their eyes that people will experience Hammarby Sjöstad's connection with the inner city: Södermalm can be reached 'at a glance', he writes (ibid.). When reading this, I cannot help thinking that it is the distance – the empty space (in practice, water) between Hammarby Sjöstad and the inner city – which bestows for the architect a sense of security. Philobatic tendencies indeed. These tendencies are also present in the functionalists' planning philosophy, where the detached house in the city's outer, greener area is held as the ideal form of living since '[t]he demand for light, fresh air, and peace and quiet can be satisfied there more easily' (Asplund et al. 2008: 217). These are described as 'priceless assets' and it is our longing for these assets that 'compels us to seek the outskirts of our cities' (ibid.). To ensure greenery adjacent to residential houses, the houses would thus ideally be detached

---

29   It is interesting also to note how Zumthor in this quote, almost in passing, reasons from 'I' to 'we' – *the* rhetorical device of power (see e.g. Cioran 2012: 5).

and the blocks would be opened up. This desire is prominent in the plans for Hammarby Sjöstad as well: '[Y]ards, parks and shorelines are connected into a coherent system which loosens up and structures the city' (*BoStad02* 2002: 23) and in the sub-area Sickla Udde the open block model is further developed into 'detached town houses' along the shoreline (ibid.: 28). The director of Hammarby Sjöstad has planned Minneberg, too – a residential suburb I mentioned earlier (Figure 2.2). As he says in an interview about the latter, the place where he was living at the time, the advantage of the area is that it is 'green and quiet, peaceful and beautiful' (Inghe-Hagström in Hultin et al 1992: 26).

To Strindberg – but also to Woolf – urbanity is in many respects a reservoir of energy that makes it possible to connect with humanity. This same idea comes through when Judith Walkowitz (1992: 16) quotes Henry James: '[O]ne may live in one "quarter" or "plot" but in imagination and by a constant mental act of reference … [inhabit] the whole'. The *flâneur* – like the ocnophil she is – seeks refuge in the crowd; the crowd is 'the veil through which the familiar city is transformed for the *flâneur* into phantasmagoria' (Benjamin 1999: 10). And it is '[t]o the arcades [in Paris] people came to linger and mill around' (Bauman 1993: 175). The crowd is sometimes landscape, sometimes living room; it is for the *flâneur* 'as the air is that of birds and water of fish' (Baudelaire 1995: 9):

> His passion and his profession are to become one flesh with the crowd. For the perfect *flâneur* … it is an immense joy to set up house in the heart of the multitude, amid the ebb and flow of movement, in the midst of the fugitive and the infinite. To be away from home and yet to feel oneself everywhere at home; to see the world, to be at the centre of the world, and yet to remain hidden from the world – such are a few of the slightest pleasures of those independent, passionate, impartial natures which the tongue can but clumsily define. … Thus the lover of universal life enters into the crowd as though it were an immense reservoir of electrical energy. (Ibid.: 9f)

One of Woolf's characters, Jinny in *The Waves*, thrives at the Piccadilly tube station, for it is a point 'where everything that is desirable meets … The great avenues of civilization meet here and strike this way and that. I am in the heart of life' (Woolf 2004: 128). The sense of excitement for meeting with the unexpected is described in the following lines:

> The train slows and lengthens, as we approach London, the centre, and my heart draws out too, in fear, in exultation. I am about to meet – what? What extraordinary adventure waits me, among these … swarms of people … I feel insignificant, lost but exultant. (Ibid.: 129)

To Woolf, the centre of London was 'a symbol of life' (Moorcroft Wilson 1987: 13). It is frequently the sounds that Woolf portrays when she talks about her desire for London – because sound means life:

Figure 2.3   **'I walked along Oxford Street. ... To walk alone in London is the greatest rest', Woolf (2008: 279) writes in one of her diaries. Oxford Street, London**
Source: Author's photograph from 2008.

I decided to go to London, for the sake of hearing the Strand roar, which I think one does want, after a day or two of Richmond. Somehow, one can't take Richmond seriously. One had always come here for an outing, I suppose; and that is part of its charm, but one wants serious life sometimes. (Woolf 2008: 11)

In *Night and Day* she writes: 'The great torrent of vans and carts was sweeping down Kingsway; pedestrians were streaming in two currents along the pavements. She stood fascinated at the corner. The deep roar filled her ears' (Woolf 1992: 374).

With the rise of modernism, architects, inspired by abstract artists such as Pablo Picasso, began to strive for immateriality and weightlessness (Lefebvre 1991: 303). Maybe, I ask, it was his philobatic tendencies that motivated Le Corbusier to do away with walls? Le Corbusier claimed to be concerned with 'freedom' – the freedom of the facade in relation to the inner and the outer room; the dissolution of boundaries; the creation of open, unbounded space (ibid.). Modernist architects and urban planners, Lefebvre states (ibid.: 308), offered 'an empty space ... ready to receive fragmentary contents'. The impression of weightlessness and immateriality is connected to the dominance of the visual. For the visual is not felt; it is observed. Perhaps it was also for this reason that Wolodarski used the word 'delicate' (*gracilt*) to describe the impression of the two skyscrapers he had drawn for Norra Stationsområdet in Stockholm. The project was cancelled, but the plan was to make them 145 meters high. This height is necessary, said Wolodarski (in Andersson 2009c), in order to create a 'delicate silhouette'. The choice of words places the discussion in the category of aesthetics, for no one in their right mind would call two towers of 145 meters 'delicate' if it were not for something other than the concrete materiality of these objects. When placing the issue in the realm of aesthetics, the planning of the towers seems fairly innocent because the only question that is discussed is whether they are delicate to the eye or not.[30] And architects are experts on aesthetics. And aesthetics – however innocent and irrelevant the topic may seem to the general public and the users of the city – is a currency of power. As long as the powerful players in the urban debate – architects, architectural critics, politicians, journalists and others – continue to talk about architecture in aesthetical rather than political-ideological terms, architecture can be used as an effective means to achieve political-ideological goals (Goodman 1972: 153). The reason is simple: This discussion creates the illusion that architects do not mess around with people's lives; they merely provide them with a beautiful living environment by emphasising the qualities of order, security and harmony.

Modernism, which still characterises Swedish town planning (Westin 2005a, Andersson 2010b), has open space as one of its most central principles (Råberg 1970: 103). Le Corbusier (in Carter 2002: 28) defended this principle against its critics, including Sitte, with the following words: 'Man walks in a straight line because he has a goal and knows where he is going; he has made up his mind to reach some particular place and he goes straight to it'. Thus, again, it is not farfetched to say that Le Corbusier and his successors are philobats. The plan for Hammarby Sjöstad states that the area should be characterised by 'openness, views, brightness, water and greenery' and that these properties take their expression in the 'semi-open neighbourhood, where some links in the street structure are green' (*BoStad02* 2002: 23; 25). The yards are broken up 'because there are great qualities in both directions; water on one side and trees on the other' (Hultin and Waern 2002: 37). In Hammarby Sjöstad, the blocks were designed with 'generous openings to the outside world' (*BoStad02* 2002: 23; 76). The director of the project says in an interview that at one stage in the planning

---

30   This makes me think of Goodman's (1972: 134) story of Marcel Breuer' skyscraper Grand Central Tower, near Grand Central Station in New York. According to Breuer, the tower would make 'a calm background' for the façade of the terminal. As Goodman says, architectural considerations were here reduced to the question of 'how a tower will relate visually to the terminal building below it' (ibid.). This happened in the 1960s, but as the Wolodarski example demonstrates, history repeats itself.

process, they received a lot of criticism from the Social Services for the large yards. 'Social Services said it was far too large in scale, too large yards', he says and continues: 'I do not think that reflects reality. I think the yards are pretty nice' (in Hultin and Waern 2002: 37).

The modernists found it necessary to abandon the closed block system of the inner city when building new housing (Asplund et al. 2008). They presented their plans as necessary adaptations to the new demands of the future – a rhetoric that motivated almost all measures:

> Modern people appreciate open-air life more than their parents did. This finds expression mainly in sports but also in the requirement for a more open design in housing. Today's ideal is no longer a form of fortified enclosure. We have no fear of the outside world and do not withdraw into our shells. … We allow the room to interact with the landscape outside to create a feeling of space and freedom, and we open our homes to the fresh air, sun, and the city's greenery. (Ibid.: 204)

It seems that what the modernists recognised as 'the demands of the new era' were in fact their own philobatic/claustrophobic predilections. 'The cities are too crowded', Åhrén writes (1928: 174). And streets – which the modernists wanted to eliminate – are always defined by a certain degree of spatial confinement (Holston 1989: 109). Is it not, then, plausible to say that Hammarby Sjöstad is an environment primarily tailored to meet the philobat's need for the friendly expanses?

Earlier, I pointed to *flânerie* and planning as activities related to a certain attitude. This association is in line with the view of knowledge I developed in Chapter 1; that knowledge is a will to power and a way to appropriate the world. When I analyse the planners' perspective, I apply the Nietzschean-inspired 'tragic method' (Deleuze 2006: 78), which is about relating a concept to the will to power, or to a drive, thus making it a symptom of a will, without which the concept could not even be imagined. It is our emotions that largely determine our perspective (Berg Eriksen 2005: 153). The task is therefore to examine what emotional attitude a certain thought might manifest. When we look at Miller's (1930: 253) definition of agoraphobia and claustrophobia, we clearly see that these are attitudes:

> [T]he state of anguish which supervenes upon the discovery of being in an enclosed space or in the wide open world arises on the perceptional level dominantly, and it is the use that a certain emotional attitude makes of these precepts that constitutes the manifest side of the phobia.

Let us now return to the planning director's statement that Hammarby Sjöstad's 'axes' are 'made of grass' (in Hultin and Waern 2002: 37) and its parallels to Le Corbusier's idea of architecture as based on axes. The connection to modernism can be illustrated with another example too: In Costa's pilot plan of the city of Brasilia in 1957, the word 'axis' (*eje* in Portuguese) is used repeatedly, while the word 'street' (*rua*) is not used at all. When the director of Hammarby Sjöstad uses the word 'axes', consciously or unconsciously he expresses something that can be called 'the ideology of the straight line' (Carter 2002: 39).

> To walk in a straight line, Le Corbusier assumed, is to think ahead. It is to have a goal. In the straight line, reason and the will fuse perfectly. Their fusion is powerful: instead of responding to the lay of the land, taking the line of least resistance, the intellectually upright and forward-looking logical walker can push aside all resistances. (Ibid.)

The ideology finds its origin in Descartes (1988: 32), who argued that if you find yourself lost in the woods, you should walk in a straight line in a certain direction (*any* direction), whereby you eventually will end up in a place that is at least better than where you started. Benjamin has criticised this ideology for what it has given rise to: a void (Carter 2002: 40). The modern architect, whom Benjamin exemplifies with Adolf Loos, is a later version of Descartes' rational creature. Modern architects embody the ideology of the straight line; they do not encounter obstacles as ordinary mortals do but see a way everywhere: 'Because he sees a way everywhere, he has to clear things from it everywhere' (Benjamin in ibid.). One explanation for this difference between the architect and ordinary mortals is found partly in the fact that the architect has transcended her own physicality and has become a thinking, creative eye ('he *sees* a way').

As Benjamin argued, the ideology of the straight line results in a void. And for the architect – at least for the modernist-trained architect – space seems to be a void; nothing more and nothing less. A void is universal and endless. In it objects are placed here and there. Zumthor (2005: 22) uses the expression '[a] mysterious void' when he describes space. He continues:

> I do not claim to know what space really is. … About one thing, however, I am sure: when we, as architects, are concerned with space, we are concerned with but a tiny part of the infinity that surrounds the earth, and yet each and every building marks a unique place in that infinity. (Ibid.)

Another influential architect who carries obvious philobatic traits and for whom architecture has a therapeutic effect is John Lautner. In the video documentary *Infinite Space* (Grigor 2008), we learn about the creation of his villa, the Arango Residence, in Acapulco, Mexico in 1971: 'I felt that the best thing that could be done there was to keep the beauty of the Acapulco bay and the sky with no interference', he says. And when Frank Escher, architect and Lautner-connoisseur, describes Lautner's approach to his buildings, he says, 'He never thought about his buildings as objects in the landscape – it's always about the space, how the architectural space connects with the landscape' (ibid.). Hence, it is space, infinite space, or rather the void, that Lautner pursued. The objects themselves are thus of secondary importance; they are, rather, perceived as obstacles. 'One of the main ideas is to improve human life by creating truth and beauty and infinite space',

Lautner explains when he sums up his views on architecture. And he continues: 'I have designed from within all my life' (ibid.). As historian Nicholas Olsberg says in the same documentary, Lautner's design has been criticised for being arbitrary. But Olsberg defends Lautner by saying, 'It took him 35 years to develop this level of precision; to frame the view and direct your eye to the far horizon'. So, it is the eye that should reach the horizon, without barriers.

Ultimately, the modernist-trained architect wants the facade to be a kind of membrane that erases the boundary between the private and the public (Lefebvre 1991: 147). The principle of transparency – one of the guiding principles of modernism – makes all buildings 'penetrated from all sides by light and air' (Vidler 2001: 61). The private is opened up for public view – as in Hammarby Sjöstad, with its large windows. What happens, then, to public space, one might ask? Since public space can only exist as a contrast to private space, the transparency principle weakens the public status of public space, as it has been described by Jacobs (1992), Holston (1989) and Sennett (1992).

The terrace surrounding Lautner's Arango Residence has no railings. Instead, it is bordered by a basin of water. If children fall, Lautner says (in Grigor 2008), the only thing that happens is that they get wet. Even the stairs and the little bridge over the basin leading to the terrace lack railings. All of these examples support the idea that the modernist architect – here represented by Lautner – is a philobat. Objects are obstacles; they have to give way to infinite space, to the friendly expanses.

I can only think of how horrified Strindberg would have been had he visited Lautner's villa. In his essay *Deranged Sensations* – which could have been called 'Confessions of an Ocnophil' – he writes,

> Now I have to cross the Place d'Armes. This vast semicircle gives one the impression of a sea, and when I have embarked upon it, I feel myself a prey to an indefinable fear. The great building draws me to it as large bodies attract small ones; but the open area terrifies me like empty space. I search in vain for a focal point. A cab comes towards me; I follow it a short distance but it passes me almost in the same moment as I hasten my steps. A policeman gets slowly nearer; I catch him up and attach myself to him; I feel protected by his presence, in so far as I experience a feeling of well-being under the influence of the animal warmth that emanates from him, invisibly and, moreover, indiscernibly. ... Instinctively I turn about, brought to life again by the fear of being suspected of God knows what, and find refuge in an enormous lamp post which rises up there like a lighthouse on its rocky cob out at sea. I cling tightly to this iron post; the sun's rays have warmed it, and I fancy I can feel how this rise in temperature has softened it ... (Strindberg 2008: 124f)

Another place where Strindberg probably would have experienced discomfort is Brasilia – the city that most clearly embodies modernist urban planning and the ideology of the straight line. Some of the social consequences of this ideology have been documented by anthropologist James Holston (1989), who, after years of ethnographic research, tells of the shock that people experience when they move to this city from other cities in Brazil: the absence of crowds. The social life they expected to find in the city's public spaces simply was not there:

> Brazilians expect to experience the daily life of crowds in cities not only because they anticipate a larger population in cities than in the country, but even more because they expect to find streets in a city and because the street is the customary arena of *movimento* – of the public display and transactions of crowds. (Holston 1989: 107)

A city and its streets are inseparable phenomena. In Brazil, 'streets' (*ruas*) exist only in the city; rural places have 'roads' (*estradas*) and 'paths' (*caminhos*). Therefore, 'going downtown' in Portuguese is *vou à rua* – literally 'going to the street'. Street corners are called *pontos de convivência social*, which translates as 'points of sociality'. As Brasilia lacks streets and street corners, the city has gotten a reputation for lacking human warmth (Holston 1989: 105, see also Lefebvre 1991: 312). The lack of street corners caused people to develop an 'allergy to Brasilia', and many expressed a sense of isolation.

Berlin is another city marked by a modernistic quest for open space. To an ocnophil, this is terrifying. When I visited the city in 2008, it was precisely the open spaces and lack of crowds that made the strongest impression on me, and it made me think of the writer Vilhelm Ekelund, who wrote, '[Berlin] is no city where you *flânerie*; a concept that here seems completely unfamiliar, as long as one does not – to the parodic users of this noble art – include the poor children, who are chasing each other back and forth on [Unter den] Linden' (in Kjellén 1985: 13f).

Where in the modernist city, then, can the *flâneur* find her place – the creature whose home is the crowd? As Carter (2002: 46) interestingly notes, agoraphobia – whose ultimate expression is a movement inhibition – can be seen as a resistance to the ideology of the straight line. By refusing to think and act in a straight line, through a void, and instead stroll in the midst of other human beings and things, the agoraphobic embodies a protest against modernist urban planning visions. 'A modern city lives by the straight line', wrote Le Corbusier (1971: 16), who found walking a daunting task because of the ever-increasing traffic. The modernisation of the city has made the walker 'a hunted animal', to quote Carter (2002: 46).

As we remember from the previous section, the ocnophil fears the void not only in a physical but also in a sonic sense. This was very much true for Woolf and Strindberg but also for the singer and songwriter Tomas Andersson Wij, who seems to prefer the sounds of the city to the stillness of the suburbs. This is how he depicts his childhood in Aspudden, a suburb in Stockholm, in the song 'Tommy och hans Mamma' (Andersson Wij 2004):

> this smell of chestnut and grass / the pizza house and the gravel dust / These cold modernist houses / and all the benches where no sober man ever sits / I'm

Figure 2.4   Berlin, Karl Marx Allée
Source: Author's photograph from 2008.

Figure 2.5   The open, empty space – the ocnophil's nightmare.
**   Berlin, Hauptbahnhof**
Source: Author's photograph from 2008.

back where it all started / It was a different life, it seems / the same sound when the subway stops / I'm the same man, yet completely changed ... It was an Aspudden summer / childhood's last summer / Watch out for the doors, doors are closing / We rushed forward through the tunnels / Forward ... their refrigerator was humming / the evening paper crossword and football at three / Between the houses here / there was this silence / that I could never really endure / I remember an Aspudden summer / I remember the bright light against yellow facades / And I was already on the way to something else / I remember the rain on an empty street[31]

Here we can recall Malte, the character in Rilke's (2009: §2) novel, in Paris, and his difficulty sleeping: 'That I cannot give up sleeping with the window open!' he thinks to himself, and then describes all the sounds that keep him awake. It is only when the rooster crows in the morning that he suddenly falls asleep. 'Those are the sounds I hear', he says, '[b]ut there is something more fearful still: the silence' (ibid.: §3). The *flâneur*, whose home is the crowd, is afraid of silence because '[n]oise [is] the corollary of crowds' (Corfield 1990: 144). Strindberg too speaks negatively about silence. In *Alone*, where sight and hearing are the two dominant senses (Westin 1999: 177), he writes:

My neighbors in the apartment house have moved to the country, and the building seems cold and empty. I feel as if all the tension and all the life had gone from it. These vectors of force that exist in every family in the shapes of man, wife, children, and servants, these components of energy have gone and left only an empty diagram behind them. And the house, which always seemed to me an electric generator that I could plug into, has had a power failure. I stop dead. My contact with people is broken off. I miss all the little sounds from the different apartments that used to stimulate me. Even the dog who woke me up for my nocturnal meditations or aroused my wrath, got me good and mad, healthy mad, has gone and left me desolate. The singer is silent, and I can no longer hear Beethoven. Nor do the telephone wires in the wall sing to me, and when I climb up and down the stairway I hear my steps echoing through the empty rooms. Every day is as quiet as a Sunday, and in the place of the sounds I used to hear I hear a ringing in my ears. (Strindberg 1998: 198f)

---

31   'Den här doften av kastanj och gräs / Pizzerian och grusvägsdammet / Dom här svala 50-talshusen / Och alla bänkar där ingen nykter människa sitter / Jag är tillbaka där det började en gång / Det var i ett annat liv, känns det som / Samma ljud när tunnelbanan stannar / Samma människa, ändå en helt annan ... Det var en Aspudden-sommar / Barndomens allra sista sommar / Se upp för dörrarna, dörrarna stängs / Vi rusade framåt genom tunnlarna / Framåt ... Deras kylskåp som brummade / Expressens korsord och fotboll vid tre / Det fanns en tystnad mellan husen här / Som jag aldrig riktigt kunde leva med / Jag minns en Aspudden-sommar / Jag minns skarpt ljus mot gula fasader / Och att jag redan var på väg mot något annat / Jag minns ett regn över tomma gator'.

As I will elaborate in Chapters 5 and 6, there is a point in distinguishing between different types of urban environments and ascribing them with 'essences' that can be said to represent their least common denominator. In discussions about Stockholm a distinction is often made between the inner city (*innerstaden*) and the suburban parts of the city (*förorten*).[32] It is interesting to note that Woolf did the same with London: 'It is quite clear that Virginia ... divided London mentally into three – the centre, the suburbs and the slums', Moorcroft Wilson (1987: 146) writes, and continues: 'Of these she certainly preferred central London ... Just as she adored central London for its vitality so she preferred the slums to the suburbs, theoretically at least, because they seemed to her more alive'.

Life in the suburbs Woolf described as 'a life spent, mute and mitigated' (ibid.: 104). Central London seems to have given her a sense of freedom and a variety of impressions, which served as fuel for her writing. 'It is clearly the lack of vitality which irritated Virginia in Putney' (Moorcroft Wilson 1987: 158). Woolf and Andersson Wij are different people: Woolf was a woman who lived in London during the early twentieth century, and Andersson Wij is a man who grew up in Stockholm at the end of the twentieth century. Despite these differences, we can discern a common denominator in what they seem to prefer as their habitat; judging by the above-quoted excerpts, they apparently prefer an urban environment with sound, life and movement instead of a built environment where this is lacking or at least hidden from the senses. Here, we ought to recall Svendsen's observation (2005: 12; 153), that 'boredom is a very serious phenomenon that affects many people'; it is 'a major problem in modernity'.

The architect is a philobat – this we have already established. The *flâneur*, on the other hand, can be primarily understood as an ocnophil. Previously we saw how Le Corbusier described modern man as the opposite to the pack-donkey, with its scatter-brained and distracted way of moving around. Or is it the *flâneur* that he attacks? Modern man walks with firm steps from *A* to *B* and does not want to be held up. Therefore, intersections must be avoided if possible. But is this a universal preference? Woolf, for example, treasured the traffic[33] of London, as shown by the following two quotes:

---

32   Although there are more precise terms (as we will see in Chapter 6), this division is not irrelevant. It speaks of a difference in how these respective urban environments work, how they function. In Stockholm, the division between the inner city and the suburbs coincides with the old system of city tolls, which lasted until the beginning of the nineteenth century. Thus, the inhabitants of Stockholm still refer to the inner city as 'innanför tullarna' (*inside the tolls*). Most suburbs were built during the twentieth century, and the largest portion is from the 1960s and onwards.

33   According to Nigel Taylor (2003: 1623), 'most people's aesthetic experience as they move about the city is *dominated* by their experience of road traffic'. Therefore, he concludes that 'our aesthetic experience of the modern city is synonymous with our aesthetic experience of motor traffic'. What was earlier said about shopping thus seems to pertain to traffic as well; it is an essential part of the urban, although it cannot exhaust the meaning of the phenomenon.

it is life that matters. London is enchanting. I step out upon a tawny coloured magic carpet, it seems, and get carried into beauty without raising a finger. And people pop in and out, lightly, divertingly, like rabbits; and I look down Southampton Row, wet as a seal's back or red and yellow with sunshine, and watch the omnibuses going and coming, and hear the old crazy organ. One of these days I will write about London. (Woolf 2008: 181)

A fine spring day. I walked along Oxford Street. The buses are strung on a chain. People fight and struggle. Knocking each other off the pavement. Old bareheaded men; a motor car accident ... To walk alone in London is the greatest rest. (Ibid.: 279)

The *flâneur* does not act according to the ideology of the straight line. She seeks the anonymous company of the crowd and has a different purpose for moving around in public space than taking the most efficient path between two points; the street – to her – is a space for dwelling, not primarily for transportation. A *flâneur* wants to see and be seen; *flânerie* is 'a *crowd practice*' (Shields 1994: 65).

That the *flâneur* wants to become one with the crowd becomes evident in Woolf's writings; she loved '[the] stir and colour [of the Soho markets] ... The noise and crowds helped rouse in her the visions needed for her books' (Moorcroft Wilson 1987: 153f). When she (in ibid.: 127) describes how she misses central London, where 'pedestrians [are] streaming in ... currents along the pavements', she expresses a sense of paralysis, a movement inhibition:

Oh to be able to slip in and out of things easily, to be in them, not on the verge of them – I resent this effort and waste ... oh to dwindle out [our short years of life] here, with all these gaps and abbreviations! Always to catch trains, always to waste time ... when alternatively, I might go and hear a tune, or have a look at a picture, or find out something in the British Museum, or go adventuring among human beings. Sometimes I should merely walk down Cheapside. But now I'm tied, imprisoned, inhibited ... For ever to be suburban. (Woolf in Moorcroft Wilson 1987: 104)

To the *flâneur*, the crowd is thus a prerequisite for movement – not an obstacle. This seems reasonable when one considers that the crowd, by definition, is 'on the move' (Carter 2002: 73). As we see in Woolf's writings, she expresses a feeling of confinement when she is unable to walk in the city. This feeling can be described in Johannisson's (2009: 128) words as a 'claustrophobic discomfort of being imprisoned in a world defined by bourgeois narrow-mindedness'. The boredom that the *flâneur* experiences and against which the act of *flânerie* stands as a remedy is a feeling of being paralysed and pacified, shut out from one's own opportunities (ibid.: 134). Furthermore, here we get yet another insight into the dialectical relationship between agoraphobia and claustrophobia. What I have concluded here also sheds light on the fact that a city with narrow streets and many people may – and indeed does – encourage movement.[34]

Woolf has told how she associated her childhood in Kensington with feelings of claustrophobia and that the move to Bloomsbury in central London provided her with 'a sense of enormous liberation' (Moorcroft Wilson 1987: 11). The sense of confinement in Kensington made her frequently depressed (ibid.: 157). Here I come to think of Marcuse's (1968b: 165f) somewhat simplified but, nevertheless, interesting comment on what happens in the human psyche when we in some way are prevented (or have prevented ourselves) from living out our passions: 'In an order of unfreedom … passion is deeply disorderly and hence immoral. When not diverted toward generally desired goals, it leads to unhappiness'.

In the previous chapter I underscored that language is not an external 'suit'; it is a way of thinking and understanding. And architecture is a visual language (Nyman 1989: 6). The planner's 'adult' thinking submits itself to reason, relies on visual input and can be described as disembodied. As Merrifield (2009: 939) writes, '[R]eason and rationality expulses irrationality and spontaneity'. The main objective of the Hammarby Sjöstad project was to stop 'the ongoing spontaneous transformation' of the area (*BoStad02* 2002: 18f). 'The street is no longer a living room' (Asplund et al. 2008: 328), the functionalists assertively exclaimed – as if they were speaking to a group of children. The paternalistic feature of functionalism is well documented (see Mattsson and Wallenstein 2009, Miller Lane et al. 2008, Wilson 1992a). That was then, someone might say, but in 1999, the planners behind Hammarby Sjöstad stated that their aim is to meet the requirements for 'a good living environment with light and greenery, modernity and rationality' (Detaljplan för Sickla Kaj 1999: 27).

The *flâneur*'s way of thinking, in contrast, can be described as evocative, primitive and bodily: 'The *flâneur* is intoxicated with life in the street – life eternally dissolving the patterns which it is about to form' (Kracauer in Vidler 2001: 111). To illustrate the *flâneur*'s language and thinking, we can call to mind Woolf's novel character Katharine, who was hoping to run into her lover Ralph after he had finished work at Lincoln's Inn Fields (Woolf 1992: 373ff). She waits and waits, but he does not turn up. When Woolf weaves together Katharine's longing and growing impatience with depictions of life in the streets of London, it is interesting to notice her choice of words. The experience is framed in terms that make it difficult to mistake the fact that the one who is pronouncing them is a bodily I; a desiring I, 'who is never for a moment without the genius of childhood' to borrow Baudelaire's (1995: 9) words. It is as if Dionysus himself speaks. Whether consciously or not, at one point in *Night and Day*, Woolf (1992: 374–7) uses the word 'child' in various forms no less than four times in four pages.[35] The following

---

34 Just think of how extremely popular the medieval Old Town in Stockholm, for example, or Visby, are to tourists.

35 Page 374: *children*, page 375: *child*, page 376: *children*, page 377: *childhood*.

words and expressions – selected and put together by me – from one and the same page (page 376) can be highlighted as an illustration of this thinking:

> Child / dream / desire / imagination / strangeness / darkness / London / back street / children / roused herself impatiently / rapidly / rapidly / desires / powerful / unreasonable force / muscles / crushing her gloves / anxiously / faces / curiosity / forgot / desperate desire

Being among strangers is one of the fundamental traits of urbanity (Asplund 1991: 53). When the narrator in Strindberg's *Alone* (1998: 168) had not spoken to a soul for three weeks straight, he began feeling restless: '[M]y solitude seemed like an exile'. Therefore, he sat down on a streetcar 'just to get the feeling of being in the same room with other people'. He continues: 'I listened to their talk as if I were at a party and had a right to participate in the conversation, at least as a listener. When the car became crowded, it was a pleasant sensation to feel my elbow making contact with a human being' (ibid.). The same search for impersonal interaction we find in Hjalmar Söderberg's novel *Doctor Glas* (2002: 54): 'This is why I mostly stay in town, summer and winter. I do this the more willingly, having the solitary person's constant desire to see people around me – *nota bene*, people I do not know and so do not have to speak to'.

So far we can conclude that one of the joys of urbanity, from the *flâneur*'s perspective, seems to be '[p]eople-watching – seeing and being seen' and to be 'surrounded by the hum of conversation' (Lofland 1998: 92; 89). To endure their self-chosen solitude, the narrators in Strindberg's and Söderberg's novels need urban life. As I stated earlier, fundamentally, *flânerie* is something not time nor gender specific. A century after Strindberg and Söderberg, the French writer Anna Gavalda (2007: 151) describes how the main character in her novel *Hunting and Gathering* is drawn to the crowds in Paris:

> She decided to walk back, but took a wrong turn without realizing it. Instead of heading left down the boulevard Montparnasse as far as the Ecolé Militaire, she went straight and ended up on the rue de Rennes. It was because of the boutiques, the Christmas garlands, the atmosphere. She was like an insect, drawn to the light and the warm blood of the crowds.

Gavalda's main character does not behave like Le Corbusier's rational man, who knows where he is going and goes 'straight to it' (in Carter 2002: 28). Having a goal for your walks is essential according to the ideology of the straight line (Carter 2002: 39), which means that if you do not have a goal, you at some level protest against it. But this need not necessarily be the case, for the *flâneur* can have an excuse, a cover. Let us look at an example. In *Street Haunting: A London Adventure* Woolf (2005a: 1) tells how she constructs a goal as an excuse for her walks: to buy a pencil:

No one perhaps has ever felt passionately towards a lead pencil. But there are circumstances in which it can become supremely desirable to possess one; moments when we are set upon having an object, an excuse for walking half across London between tea and dinner. As the foxhunter hunts in order to preserve the breed of foxes ... so when the desire comes upon us to go street rambling the pencil does for a pretext, and getting up we say: 'Really I must buy a pencil', as if under cover of this excuse we could indulge safely in the greatest pleasure of town life in winter – rambling the streets of London.

By referring to the need for a concrete object, Woolf distracts attention from the real – but less comprehensible and not as socially acceptable – goal for her walk: the desire for ... well, what? '[R]ambling the streets of London' (ibid.)? But what kind of goal is this? And what is it *good for*? These are questions I imagine that Le Corbusier and other straight-line ideologists would ask. At the end of the novel, when Woolf (2005a: 15) has reported on her adventures and is home again, she contemplates on the concrete – and undeniably trivial – quarry that her walk brought forth: a pencil.

What we can remember from this last argument is that when Woolf wants to go out 'street-rambling', she refers to the need for an object; most likely because people in her environment, but perhaps also herself, would have difficulties accepting as well as understanding her desire for the urban.[36] This can be understood as an attempt at Apollonian restraining a Dionysian force. The result is moderation and understandability. I will return to the need-desire question further on; the time has come to round off this chapter.

Conclusion

In Hammarby Sjöstad and in Södra stationsområdet, the planners speak of facades that have an 'urban character', and in the St Erik area, Wolodarski has aimed at enhancing the 'public character' of the space between the residential buildings by the placement of an old chapel (Wolodarski 1997: 40). In conclusion, it is thought that these *things* will symbolise urbanity and a public atmosphere. A symbol is something that only the eye can perceive. If we look at what the *flâneur*,

---

36   More than once, Woolf shows how the construction of a goal can make the act of *flânerie* more acceptable. In *Night and Day*, for example, Katharine decides to find out Ralph's address, and this becomes a goal: 'The decision was a relief, not only in giving her a goal, but in providing her with a rational excuse for her own actions' (Woolf 1992: 377). As literary theorist Tone Selboe (2003: 185) has pointed out, this is likely due to the fact that Woolf is a woman, and thus does not 'belong' in public space: 'As a strolling woman in the twentieth century, she must fabricate an excuse; invent a necessary errand'. Interestingly, Strindberg too, or at least his narrative ego in *Alone*, finds it important to have a goal for his walks (see Westin 1999: 189).

in contrast, associates with the urban, it seems to be primarily the crowd, the sounds of the traffic, the bodily sensation of the animal warmth of other people, or: life itself. Of these things there are not many that are possible to literally see, nor is it correct to refer to them as 'things'. Hereby, the urban is not something you can easily delineate on a piece of paper, an observation that reinforces its Dionysian character. 'Dionysus reveals himself by concealing himself, makes himself manifest by hiding himself from the eyes of all those who believe only in what they can see, in what is "evident before their eyes"' (Vernant and Vidal-Naquet 1990: 391).

We have also seen how the planner's and the *flâneur*'s perspectives differ when it comes to their relationships to objects in general. Like the philobat, the modernist architect exhibits a tendency towards claustrophobia and therefore seeks open spaces. '[O]ur hearts are always oppressed by the constriction of its enclosing walls' (Le Corbusier in Vidler 2001: 61). Objects – which can act as barriers both for the eye and for the rationally minded human on her way to her destination – must be eliminated from the philobat's horizon. The philobat's goal is to create a fairyland without any disturbances, where she can feel at home. The *flâneur* too wants to feel safe, at home. But because she has a different approach to the city, the architect's expanses, to her, are not friendly but daunting. Rather, it is the crowd – in constant motion – that gives the *flâneur* enjoyment. Since she is not afraid of objects but needs them for her well-being, she finds pleasure in a more or less chaotic street scene with cars, pedestrians and buses moving back and forth.

It is also because of the visual dominance of urban planning as an activity that planners often associate the urban with chaos. The problem was acknowledged already by Jacobs (1992: 372ff), who argued that the bustling streets seem chaotic from the planner's point of view, while foot people see a 'natural' order. This diametric difference in perception is explained by the difference in perspective. An architect, who looks at the world artistically, does not see as a lay person; she is concerned with a perceptual whole (Dewey 2005: 141). The architect certainly distinguishes between individual objects and buildings but only to relate them to other parts of the visual field. Hence, it is not difficult to understand that a busy street with people and traffic moving around can cause perceptual confusion. Nor is it difficult to understand that the visual perspective is related to a desire for order. 'When masses are balanced, colours harmonized, and lines and planes meet and intersect fittingly … Even at a first glance there is the sense of qualitative unity. There is form' (Dewey 2005: 141).

The eye of the architect organises, classifies and systematises (Pallasmaa 2005: 25) – it seeks form. Chaos – visual chaos – is a threat to form. I have already noted the dominance of the visual in Western thought. Related to the visual dominance is the idea of form as primary. Forms and contours are generally regarded as stable and intelligible, while processes and atmospheres are seen as fluid and illogical (Dewey 2005: 120f). To see, to observe, means 'an exploration of the form-seeking and form-imposing mind, which needs to understand but cannot unless it casts what it sees into manageable models'

(Arnheim in Söderström 1996: 249). And from Kant (2005: §14) we learn that true beauty is only found in the beauty of form; it is only through the form that an object is beautiful. In architecture, as in all formative arts, 'the *delineation* is the essential thing', Kant writes, and continues: '[H]ere it is not what gratifies in sensation but what pleases by means of its form that is fundamental for taste'. Nature, says Carse (1986: §82), is neither chaotic nor orderly; chaos and order describe the cultural perception of nature.

The architect's desire for form, order and visual beauty makes it possible to liken her with Apollo, the formative power that values balance and moderation. The urban, however, as it has appeared in this chapter, is a Dionysian phenomenon, where the Dionysian means a force that 'cannot be pinned down in any form ... the epiphany of Dionysus elude[s] the limitations of visible forms and shapes' (Vernant and Vidal-Naquet 1990: 397f). The fact that the planner looks for order (see Boyer 1997, Choay 1997, Rådberg 1991) is interesting from a psycho-analytical perspective because – as Marcuse (1955: 149) points out – the word *order* has a 'repressive connotation'. Given that the planner speaks and acts as if she knows the needs of all citizens – what activities that are appropriate and where they should be carried out – she is acting as a kind of 'moral guardian' (Sjögren 2008: 32), a superego of society. The function of the superego in humans' psychic life is to say how we should think and behave. For this reason, there are clear parallels between the superego, on the one hand, and architecture and planning, on the other. In the next chapter I elaborate on this analogy.

Chapter 3
Planning as a Neurosis

Architecture is the expression of every society's very being. ... [But] only the ideal being of society, the one that issues orders and interdictions in the strict sense of the word.

Georges Bataille

[T]he essence of society is repression of the individual, and the essence of the individual is repression of himself.

Norman O. Brown

Neuroses ... depend only upon an alteration in the balance of the forces at work in mental life.

Sigmund Freud

Jane Jacobs (1992: 9f) tells in *The Death and Life of Great American Cities* a fascinating story about a city planner she knows in Boston. Jacobs calls him up from a restaurant during a visit to Boston's North End to ask some questions about the neighbourhood, which she found 'the healthiest place in the city' with its crowded streets, many small businesses and excellent food stores. 'Why in the world are you down in the North End?' he wondered and informed her that the district was the worst slum in the city. But despite calling the North End 'terrible slum', he also affirmed Jacobs's positive impression of the area; 'I often go down there myself', he said, 'just to walk around the streets and feel that wonderful, cheerful street life'. And then he said, 'But of course we have to rebuild it eventually. We've got to get those people off the streets' (ibid.). This is how Jacobs (1992: 10f) comments on this anecdote: 'My friend's instinct told him that North End was a good place ... But everything he had learned as a physical planner about what is good for people and good for the city neighborhoods, everything that made him an expert, told him the North End had to be a bad place'.

Jacobs calls this story 'curios' (ibid.: 10). But is the story really that curious? Are we humans not always – consciously or unconsciously – experiencing a conflict between what we want and desire, on the one hand, and what we must and ought to, on the other? If we are to believe Freud, this ceaseless struggle is characteristic of human existence – an idea that breaks with Descartes' view of the subject as a stable and irrefutable fact (Berg Eriksen 2005: 169). Freud's view rejects the Enlightenment view of the self as free individuality and instead depicts it as a provisional arrangement constantly mediating between conflicting entities; he shares this view with Nietzsche. The self is thus a 'secondary product of the conflicts between what one is and what one ought to be' (ibid.: 167). On one side of the conflict is a kind of drive, a primitive desire or a feeling; on the other side is our conscience, the adult concerns, one's self-image (Sandell 1993: 2). Man has reason, but at best it plays a peripheral or superficial role – this is the general understanding in psycho-analysis. Brown (1968: 147) captures this idea when he writes, 'Every person … is many persons; a multitude made into one person; a corporate body; incorporated, a corporation'. The idea is also expressed by poet Gunnar Ekelöf (1949): 'Each person is a world, populated by blind creatures in shadowy rebellion'.[1] Consciousness is a field where different parts of the self confront each other; the self is the scene in which the moral drama of life unfolds, where different and conflicting impulses are struggling against each other (Vattimo 1997: 70f, Cassirer 1972: 11). Or, as Woolf said, 'How queer to have so many selves' (in Gordon 2006: 6).

These ideas stretch as far back as Plato, who argued that in the soul of man, there are two[2] principles,[3] although Plato – unlike both Nietzsche and Freud – saw reason, not sexual desire, the body or the will to power, as the only directive agency (Berg Eriksen 2005: 168). From the dialogue between Socrates and Adeimantus:

> 'Now, would we assert that sometimes there are some men who are thirsty but not willing to drink?' 'Surely', he said, 'many and often'. 'What should one say about them?' I said. 'Isn't there something in their soul bidding them to drink and something forbidding them to do so, something different that masters that which bids?' 'In my opinion, there is', he said. 'Doesn't that which forbids such things come into being – when it comes into being – from calculation, while what leads and draws is present due to affections and diseases?' 'It looks like it'.
> (Plato 1991: §439)

That this complexity in man is often neglected in science is a result of the strict Cartesian division between spiritual and non-spiritual, between body and mind. Descartes and French rationalism equated the psyche with conscious, rational thinking, which has contributed to the shaping of the idea that a (normal) human being is altogether sane: 'The unconscious with its devils, demons and desires did

---

1   'En värld är varje människa, befolkad av blinda varelser i dunkelt uppror'.

2   Here it may be noted that Freud later in his career saw the human psyche as divided into three – not two – parts: the ego, the id and the superego. The fundamental conflict, however, is still between the pleasure principle and the reality principle. It is the ego that ends up under fire from both directions, and neurosis is a result of too strong of a contrast between the two forces.

3   Freud took his concept of Eros (which represents love, sexuality and the life instinct – also known as libido) from Plato and in many ways he shared Plato's view. For a comparison between Plato's and Freud's views on love and rationality, see Gould (1963: 15f; 173–6).

not belong in this picture of the soul of man' (Sjögren 2001: 118). Freud's thinking, which can be described as a powerful reaction against the body-mind dualism, calls into question the view of man as entirely rational, consistent and fully aware of his thoughts, desires and actions. The only constant is a person's sex drive, Freud asserted; Nietzsche said it was the will to power (Berg Eriksen 2005: 167).

Reducing man's conflicting parts neglects the conflict between individual and society that is embodied in each individual, as well as the chafing feeling that this conflict has the propensity to generate. The whole of a person will not fit into the sphere of reason: 'The gratification of his wants and capacities, his happiness, appears as an arbitrary and subjective element that cannot be brought into consonance with the universal validity of the highest principle of human action', Marcuse (1968b: 159f) writes.

The contradiction between reason and happiness (in the most general sense of the term), between society and the individual, is clearly reflected in the example of Jacobs's planner friend. 'My friend's instincts told him the North End was a good place', she writes. But *everything that made him an expert* told him that it had to be a bad place.

'There is no such thing as a single human being, pure and simple, unmixed with other human beings. Each personality is a world in himself, a company of many', writes psycho-analyst Joan Riviere (in Brown 1968: 147). When the architect stands on her own feet after finishing school, she can be likened to a child who has grown up; and growing up means incorporating the requirements of parental figures, their values and attitudes, and making them one's own. The role models in architectural school are the architect's parents; they form her professional self, far from easily demarcated from her personal self. Freud (1995: 655) posited that 'The super-ego arises ... from an identification with the father taken as a model'. The superego has a general character 'of harshness and cruelty exhibited by the ideal – its dictatorial "Thou shalt"' (ibid.). We have already noted that the city planner embodies 'adult' thinking and that there, in the functionalists' manifesto, *acceptera* projects a strong paternalistic attitude. For this reason the architects' professional attitude, which is largely unconscious, is a superego that puts demands on the individual and convinces her to (again, unconsciously) make decisions that may be contrary to her wishes. The superego's task is to establish and maintain norms (Sjögren 2008: 28). Functionalism can be seen as the superego of contemporary urban planning; functionalists saw as their duty to 'transform the chaos of the big city into a neat and transparent order' (Rådberg 1998: 96). Therefore, Rådberg notes that 'modern urban planning is ... *anti-urban* – its edge is directed towards the city and city life' (ibid., see also Bergman 1980: 160).

Often and decidedly, Freud (2002) pointed out that nothing in the individual disappears; perceptions and beliefs are moved to the background and become more or less invisible as they – metaphorically speaking – merge into the air a person breathes. 'The unconscious', Sjögren (2008: 32) notes, 'takes a long time to change'. And since the development of society can be likened to the psychological development of the individual, this is also true for the collective. There are also signs that the architect's learned ideology is like an iceberg; it is larger below than above the surface. This is because architects largely think in pictures. 'When I think about architecture, images come into my mind' Zumthor (2005: 7) writes, and Apollo – to whom we have likened the planner – is 'the god of all image-making energies' (Nietzsche 1999: §1). According to Kant (2005: §51), an aesthetic idea is an archetype – in Swedish *urbild* (Kant 2003: §51), which literally means 'original picture' – in the artist's head. These images are linked to a learned repertoire of solutions that the architect more or less unconsciously chooses from when she designs (see Cuff 1992, Hillier et al. 1972, Lundequist 1991: 67, Sternudd 2007: 153). According to Freud (1995: 633), thinking in images is closer to the unconscious than thinking in words: 'Thinking in pictures is ... a very incomplete form of becoming conscious. In some way, it stands nearer to unconscious processes than does thinking in words'.

Regarding, Fleck (1979) explains the tendency of thought styles towards inertia, using the example of how the modern concept of syphilis originated. At first, syphilis was seen as a 'carnal scourge' (*Lustseuche*), and this idea from the fifteenth century lingered for 400 years until it finally was revised and clarified (ibid.: 2). There were no empirical observations underlying this idea; instead, 'special factors of deep psychological and traditional significance greatly contributed to it' (ibid.: 3). Here we can refer to Olsson's (1990: 23) observation: '[T]hat which lets itself be said often enough eventually becomes credible. And that which enough people believe is enough credible, gradually becomes a truth. This is nothing new, just a reminder of how people and ideologies mutually mold and are mutually molded'.

From journalist David Brooks (2010) comes another example of the inertia of ideas; in New York City in the 1960s and 1970s, crime increased dramatically. 'Things are different now', he writes, 'but some of the certain psychological effects remain'. He continues: 'The people who grew up afraid to go in parks at night now supervise their own children with fanatical attention, even though crime rates have plummeted. It's as if they're responding to the sense of menace they felt while young, not the actual conditions of today' (ibid.). Gradually taken for granted, these previously formed thoughts run the risk of exerting an even greater influence on the individual's mind and actions than if they had been made explicit. Therefore, Marcuse (1964: 162) writes: 'We are possessed by our images, suffer our own images. Psycho-analysis knew it well, and knew the consequences'.

Let us return to the example of Jacobs's planner friend. Assume for a moment that he had an executive position and implemented the plans to sanitise North End. Then he would no longer be able to enjoy its atmosphere (that he claimed to appreciate), because few – if any – of those people and businesses that were on the streets would remain. What should be said about such a decision? Was it wise? Was it for the good of society? Did he act professionally when he – consciously or unconsciously – ignored his own experience? In an enlightening interpretation of Freud's message in *Civilization and its Discontent*, Michael Smith (1980: 68) writes:

Freud makes clear that modern civilization, rather than inducing joy in conformity, instead relies on a continuous sense of guilt to maintain the social bond. Herein lies the double bind. People experience unhappiness of guilt both when they conform and when they deviate from social controls.

Jacobs's friend chose duty first. Or can we say 'chose'?

> Morality is preceded by *compulsion*, indeed it is for a time itself still compulsion, to which one accommodates oneself for the avoidance of what one regards as unpleasurable. Later it becomes custom, later still voluntary obedience, finally almost instinct: then, like all that has for a long time been habitual and natural, it is associated with pleasure – and is now called *virtue*. (Nietzsche 1986a: §99)

To continue this problematisation of the 'right thing to do', I would like to quote Laing's (1967: 99) pointed formulation: '[S]ocial adaptation to a dysfunctional society may be very dangerous. The perfectly adjusted bomber pilot may be a greater threat to species survival than the hospitalized schizophrenic deluded that the Bomb is inside him'.

In psycho-analytic theory, the superego is the individual's (or society's) moral function; the agency that pushes the ego to think and act modestly (Israel 1967: 116). That which challenges the superego's standards of how things should be is repressed. Furthermore, this process of assessing acceptable actions is often done unconsciously; the superego is an incorporation of external standards (parents', society's, teachers'), which over time has been taken for granted. If, or when, these standards are allowed to control too much – paradoxically because they have been repressed – the mind's balance is disturbed and the risk of neurotic suffering increases.

> The idea that morality promotes human happiness or fulfilment is, Freud thinks, exposed as a wishful fantasy. For the psychic structure that morality fosters is a structure of individual human suffering: a punishing superego is set over against an inhibited ego. Outwardly and consciously, the person may be an upstanding member of society. Inwardly, and perhaps unconsciously, he is inhibited from pursuing his desires; and thus lives in frustration. Virtue is decidedly not its own reward. (Lear 2005: 196)

Perhaps we today are paying the price for the domination of the superego in urban planning during the twentieth century? Just ponder Lefebvre's story (1995: 117ff) about the dread he felt when visiting Mourenx. Everything was set up for the needs of the citizens, yet he experienced not only discomfort but dread. Herein lies the great paradox of 'good' urban planning, a paradox that can also go by the name of alienation. What we can say about Jacobs's story is that it is a striking illustration of modern man's alienation from his own experience. This phenomenon is relevant to the present study because it highlights the damaged relationship between experience and actions (Laing 1967: 65). We act according to *what we believe* is the best way to act, but since we do not tune into our own bodies nor our own experience, we run the risk of making ourselves unhappy. 'Rationality' works *against* instinct. '"Rationality" at any price as dangerous, as a force undermining life!' Nietzsche cried (1992: 49), well aware that it is the body that is 'the mind's corrective' (Olsson 2007: 102).

As we saw in the previous chapter, the planner and the *flâneur* interpret the city in different ways – they want different things. At least, the planner's professional aspirations differ from the *flâneur*'s. Reason, which is what the planner relies on, seeks immutability[4] (Berg Eriksen 2005: 160) – the *flâneur*'s body desires becoming. Where the planner by all accounts is looking to control the environment, to reduce complexity and to avoid conflicts in order to create a safe and secure environment for the residents and establish truths about the present and the future, the *flâneur* longs for and welcomes movement, unpredictability, bodily pleasures and a myriad of impressions. This longing is manifest in Woolf's writings. '[T]he fiercer the London scene, the more refreshing Virginia finds it', Moorcroft Wilson (1987: 14) writes. The contrast is clear if we look at the following statement by the director of the Hammarby Sjöstad project: 'If you are to do a project out of this, you have to control the chaos here' (in Hultin et al. 1992: 22). We can bring these opposing attitudes together in the following dichotomy: Where planner *x* is seeking to control the environment, reduce complexity, avoid conflicts and develop facts and predictions about the present and the future, private person *x* longs for movement and unpredictability, for '[the] sudden capricious friendships with the unknown' – yes, perhaps even to 'rub against some complete stranger' (Woolf 2005a: 10; 9). Professionally, planner *x* perhaps speaks of the importance of sunlight and open spaces, privately, she longs – again with the words of Woolf – for 'the irresponsibility which darkness and lamplight bestow' (ibid.: 1).

It is not my intention to portray this duality as a defect or as a character trait that only applies to planners. Rather, I want to shed light on a paradox: As a private individual the planner inhabits the multi-faceted world that all other people also inhabit (see Huxley 1963: 11, Taleb 2007: 54). The planner's instrument is the map/plan/drawing, which creates a distance – but 'it is in the ground-level haze that we live, and move, and have our being' (Ley 1977: 11). Since knowledge is power, the planner – through knowledge of what happens in the imaginary world of building codes, visualisation tools, statistical calculations, transport logistics and particle values – has the power to control and modify the world in which she lives as a private person. This is where she runs the risk of making herself unhappy.

---

4   The reasoning rules of logic are based on and require stability since they are ill-adapted for handling qualitative change. The conventional approach to studying change is to compare what one regards as one and the same phenomenon at two different points in time, whereby one calls the difference between them change. As Ollman (2003: 64) emphasises, this is not change as it takes place, but a comparison between two static conditions.

Passion, as Susanne Wigorts Yngvesson (2009) writes, drawing on Cristina Nehring's *A Vindication of Love. Reclaiming Romance for the Twenty-First Century* (2009), 'is an outdated phenomenon, a trace of the wild'. Passion poses a threat to the safe, orderly People's Home (Folkhemmet), against institutions that want to control and systematise. Modern society is characterised by instrumentality, which means that everything should have a purpose, a goal; otherwise, it is meaningless. Passion – and *flânerie*, I would like to add – is without goal, without purpose. They exist and are performed for their own sake, for the sake of pleasure. This purposelessness is something that the planning, producing human being does not appear to understand. Moreover, passion and pleasure is closely associated with pain and conflict, with loss of control. Passion, in essence, lays bare our inability to avoid pain. So no wonder that modern society, when seeking to create a safe environment for its citizens, is trying to avoid and control passion. But this is not just a loss, Wigorts Yngvesson (2009) concludes; it is a tragedy.

The parallel I draw between modern urban planning and the superego is explored in Lefebvre's work. The abstractions of modernity and the conceived space of the planner have

> lost all ability to … produce or reproduce anything living, but [are] still capable of suppressing it – the father figures who feel they have to be cruel to be kind: the state, the police, the Church, God (and the absence of God), the gendarmerie, the caretakers, offices and bureaucracy, organization (and lack of organization), politics (and all its shortcomings). (Lefebvre 1995: 120)

Here it may be worthwhile to recall that the classic concepts of psycho-analysis – the unconscious, the ego, the id and the superego – are abstractions with a dynamic place and task within a given theory. This means that none of the concepts denote essences that can be understood by themselves (Sjögren 2008: 36). Therefore, I let the concepts define themselves as I use them. However, some clarifications can be made. The superego can best be understood in relation to the ego. The German word for superego is Überich, literally 'above ego', and it shows that we are dealing with an instance that is superior to the ego (ibid.: 25f). This is to be understood metaphorically, as a power relation. Although the superego has as its utmost goal to protect the ego, to avoid suffering by controlling its behaviour within socially acceptable limits, it contains more or less cruel features, which can be harmful to the ego as a whole. The term ego does not denote a readily delineated essence but a process; an ongoing quest to understand and balance our inner and outer realities into a functioning whole (ibid.). From the beginning of life, it is a centre of conflict, and it desires peace. The ego is usually that which we identify as ourselves: we are familiar with it, and in our lives the ego is what we rely on.

Simply put, when the balance is good, we feel at ease. When it is not good, we feel anxious. The ego must take into account and mediate between different demands. From the inside – from the instance that is called the id – come primitive desires for immediate gratification. These demands can be said to originate in the body, and they often clash with the demands of external reality for deference, fidelity and other societal expectations – requirements which originally come from both the parents and the wider community and that have been internalised in the individual in the form of the superego. The superego can be defined as 'an inner force of the commandments, prohibitions, encouragement and punishment, a force with its roots in the perception of the external world but also the product of a highly personal interpretation of this world' (ibid.). As the ego is exposed to events beyond its control, the balance of the ego is not always easily maintained – often because of the adherence of the unconscious to old ways. The superego, as we touched on earlier, is understood as a kind parent to the ego, which implies we all have a parent and a child within us. But a curious thing with this inner parent is that it was born chronologically after the ego.

The same applies to cities. Cities existed long before the birth of modern urban planning. In the same manner that Freud argued that the ego – despite its indispensable social function – interferes with the ego's inner work towards balance, we can, inspired by Jacobs (1992), Sennett (2008) and Lefebvre (1995), say that the meticulous urban planning of the twentieth century tends to disrupt the city's 'natural' or inherent order.

The conscious ego, which is governed by what Freud called the reality principle, adapts to the environment and displaces the id's desires and wishes that are in conflict with society. And repression is a defence mechanism, designed to keep memories, thoughts and feelings at a distance but which nonetheless remain a part of the individual (Brenner 1970: 78, Brown 1959: 4). The superego, the part of us that is subject to the reality principle, is associated with what the Greeks called *Ananke*: necessity (Sjögren 2008: 28). The superego thus stands for what is believed to be necessary, and it interferes with the ego, which must take into account the primitive desires of the id. When primitive desires are repressed, they will instead present themselves in the form of fantasies, dreams and neurotic symptoms, which act as substitutes for the pleasures that the ego has denied herself. Hereby, the yearning for pleasure turns into pain; it is relegated to a symptom. Society encourages repression – it is a necessity. This poses problems because if repression is the cause of humankind's universal neurosis, it follows that there is an intrinsic link between social organisation and neurosis (Brown 1959: 9) – and, thus, between planning and neurosis.

Let us review what is meant by planning and neurosis, respectively. Broadly defined, planning is an activity – fundamentally human – whose purpose is to improve life and increase prosperity for society and/or the individual (Strömgren 2007: 28). Since I do not distinguish between planning and architecture in this book, it may be interesting to look at what Joseph Esherick (1984: 26) writes when he interprets Vitruvius – the architectural theorist of the first century: '[A]rchitecture and the work of architects is for the welfare of society in general and for the health, security and enjoyment of individuals in particular'.

A neurotic person is someone whose ego 'has become weakened by the conflict with its internal enemies as well as by its responsibilities as the mind's emissary to external reality' (Malcolm 1981: 32). A sign of neurotic behaviour is when an individual's or a society's compensation acts, which are meant to avoid suffering, causes a greater suffering than the suffering the compensation act was originally intended to protect from. Since all human beings are characterised by mental conflicts, Freud saw only a difference in degree, not in type, between neurotic and so-called normal people (Brown 1959: 6, Freud 1989: 56, Malcolm 1981: 21). In the words of Laing (1967: 23f), 'What we call "normal" is a product of repression, denial, splitting, projection, introjection and other forms of destructive action on experience ... The condition of alienation, of being asleep, of being unconscious, of being out of one's mind, is the condition of the normal man'.

As Olsson (1980a) points out, human life is characterised by an oscillation between certainty and ambivalence, a perpetual pendulum movement that Freud expresses as the pulls between the forces of the pleasure principle and the reality principle, the id and the superego, desire and conscience, the individual and society (Malcolm 1981: 32). Freud was convinced that 'the mind worked according to fundamental principles. He saw his neurotic patients as essentially conflicted and hypothesized that the conflicts arose from conflicting principles at work in the mind' (Lear 2005: 162, emphasis removed). In this book, I use psycho-analytic theory to understand the contra-finality tendencies of urban planning, because – as mentioned earlier – psycho-analysis highlights the conflict between individuals and their social environments (Kalin 1974: 121). 'Psycho-analysis has a debunking effect on any ideology that sides unconditionally with society against the individual' (ibid.: 184).

Freud diagnosed many of his patients with the same diagnosis I tentatively give contemporary urban planning: a strict superego, which, in its pursuit of certainty, order, cleanliness and beauty, seeks to defeat what is perceived as chaos. The goal of psycho-analysis as a form of therapy is often this: '[T]o oppose the superego and attempt to lower its demands' (Freud 2002: 103, see also Smith 1980: 72). And in this context, to oppose means to make visible, to make conscious. We find an example of the stern and restrictive thinking of the superego in the planning documents behind Södra stationsområdet. Here it is stated that deviations from the structure of the inner city were necessary, since 'the requirements on the urban environment design have ... changed since the nineteenth century – for example when it comes to traffic safety, accessibility, accessibility, open spaces, lighting conditions and hygiene' (*Södra stationsområdet* 1984: 4). Whose claims are the planners taking into account when they refer to 'changing requirements'? The functionalists'? The public's? Decision makers'? When contemplating where the watchful eye of the superego comes from, Laing's words can be illuminating. For this reason, I let them begin the next section.

Whose Requirements?

[We have alienated ourselves] from our experience, our experiences from our deeds, our deeds from human authorship. Everyone will be carrying out orders.

Where do they come from? *Always from elsewhere.* ... Within this most vicious circle, we obey and defend beings that exist only in so far as we continue to invent and to perpetuate them. What ontological status have these group beings? This human scene is a scene of mirages, demonic pseudo-realities, *because everyone believes everyone else believes them.* How can we find our way back to ourselves again? Let us begin by trying to think about it. (Laing 1967: 66, my emphasis)

As sociologist Robert Merton (1968) points out, all bureaucratic systems bear within themselves the seed of a *circulus vitiosus*. The individual in a bureaucratic organisation runs the risk of displaying a 'ritualistic behaviour'; eager to do the right thing, she follows the rules literally. Hereby, submission to the rules becomes a goal in itself, which may prove to complicate the implementation of the original task. In the case of planning, this task would be the creation of a human environment: 'Behavior becomes rigid, and the individual has difficulties in adapting himself and his behavior to the demands of the job, at which point there occurs what Merton calls 'trained incompetence''[5] (Israel 1971: 324).

It is noteworthy that among today's planners, there is an idea that submission to rules is the same as having an ethical approach. 'Some planners' view of ethics revolves mainly around the strict adherence to rules and regulations', Johansson and Khakee (2008: 31) witness in their study on Swedish urban planners' views on ethics. It seems that Nietzsche (1986b: §40) has a point when he highlights the important role that *forgetting* plays for the moral sensation:

The same actions as within primitive society appear to have been performed first with a view to common *utility* have been performed by later generations for other motives: out of fear of or reverence for those who demanded and recommended them, or out of habit because one had seen them done all around one from childhood on, or from benevolence because their performance everywhere produced joy and concurring faces, or from vanity because they were commended. Such actions, whose basic motive, that of utility, has been *forgotten*, are then called *moral* actions: not because, for instance, they are performed out of those *other* motives, but because they are *not* performed from any conscious reason of utility.

In this context it might be interesting to look at a report from 1965 called *Increased requirements for space in the urban environment,*[6] published by the Royal Building Society in conjunction with a conference in Örebro, Sweden, the same year. It provides an example of the problem of the ambiguous nature of the requirements or needs planners are trying to satisfy. The main argument of the

---

5   'Trained incompetence' is Thorstein Veblen's expression and is developed by Merton (1968).

6   The report is in Swedish and the original title is Ökade *ytbehov i stadsbygden.*

report can be summarised as follows: In the Nordic countries, economic prosperity and the standard of living increased in the period between 1929 and 1965. People have more leisure time and there is an increased demand for 'comfort'. As leisure time 'has become more active and as more and more time is dedicated for outdoor activities', greater land area is required for these activities; that is, specific areas must be reserved for outdoor activities (p. 53). It is argued that 'society must be seen as having a great responsibility to promote outdoor recreation' and that this will be implemented through finding appropriate areas of land and water (p. 55). Based on the fact that leisure time and land area has increased, it is concluded that even in the future there will be an increased demand for more land area where the usual (or preferred?) type of recreation – hiking – can be exercised. It is not only the recreational function that requires a greater area of land; this function also creates a need for business and traffic space. And more space for traffic means more space for noise protection walls and for parking (p. 49).

The experts behind the report not only reify when translating (leisure) time into land area, but they also – like the economist and sociologist Vilfredo Pareto (see Olsson 1980a: 9b) – make the jump from *is* to *ought*. *Increased requirements for space in the urban environment* (1965) – a text that is meant to be used as a basis for future planning – is based on how things are right now; that is, on the 'existing development and current trends in the Nordic countries' (p. 65). Based on current conditions, people are looking to 'roughly calculate future urban land needs' (p. 6) and thus 'obtain a better basis for physical community planning' (ibid.). In brief, the argument is as follows: since the land area for parks, recreation areas and sports facilities, has increased significantly – significantly more than the size of the population – this means that people have called for/needed/required this. This, in turn, is interpreted as a sign that people in the future will call for/need/require more land area.

The upward curve seems to be interpreted as a law of nature that humans face passively. Therefore, the experts conclude by saying that the '[t]endency will probably ... be a continued increase in urban green space through sprawling within neighbourhoods and through urban residents' increased demands on nearby recreation areas for their increased leisure time' (p. 58). Note that the sprawling of the city is identified as a consequence of the urban residents' demands. But is it not rather so, I wonder, that the sprawling is due to urban planners' demands? That is, demands that were formulated in for example *acceptera* from 1931? The functionalists clearly expressed that it is their – the experts' – requirements, and no others', that should guide urban development. Any resistance from the citizens was rejected on the grounds that they did not understand what was in their own good and that they would get used to the new conditions. *acceptera* has a special section where they respond – or more correctly put down – common criticism of the new ideals. For example, the following 'standing objection' – '[L]et us go on living in slightly cramped and inconvenient conditions – all that about hygiene is not that dangerous after all – but do not deny us comfort. Leave us the beautiful – that suits our own tastes!' – is met with these words: 'Yes, this is the standing objection. ...

To this we could respond brutally, "It is very unfortunate, but necessary, alas"' (Asplund et al. 2008: 233). Subsequently, the authors of *acceptera* state that 'comfort' is first and foremost dependent on 'adequate space' (ibid.: 237).

But the increased demand for space – whose demands are these again? What the experts behind *Increased requirements for space in the urban environment* from 1965 refer to as the city residents' demands seem to be the functionalists' demands as they were formulated three decades earlier instead (although no explicit references to, for example, *acceptera* are made).

Today we can conclude that these requirements have, since then, been realised in urban development projects – the amount of space between the buildings increased significantly after 1965 – which the experts, in turn, would interpret as a sign that future city residents will continue to require even more space. And as we saw earlier, this idea persists; in 1984 the planners behind Södra stationsområdet referred to the increased demands for 'open space, lighting conditions and hygiene'. The source of this requirement is unclear. Maybe they have forgotten? That we humans forget why we do the things we do, or say the things we say, does not mean that we stop doing or saying it. It is a psycho-analytical insight that '[w]e live our lives according to the repetition compulsion, and analysis can go only so far in freeing us from it' (Malcolm 1981: 108). Here we can refer back to Fleck's idea (1979: 10) of passive and active connections. The example above shows how easily an active connection (a human-made idea) gradually turns into a connection that is considered passive (a natural-given fact).[7]

Sometimes it is easy to identify where the requirements come from. This does not mean that they are justified. When The Swedish National Board of Housing, Building and Planning (Boverket) in a document provides recommendations for what they call 'safety distance' in detailed planning, they refer neither to empirical investigations nor previous research (Bergdahl and Rowan 2001: 16). As an expert institution on issues related to living environment and cities, the Board's need to argue for and support their statements is almost non-existent; it suffices that they are experts. Here we can say that the Board utilises its position as 'parent' in the urban planning family. Parents have power over their children simply due to their position. And those who find themselves in such a position – that is, in one that is higher up in the hierarchy than the rest – are more often than others believed – or at least obeyed: 'The titled are *powerful*. Those around them are expected to yield, to withdraw their opposition, and to conform to their will – in the arena in which the title was won' (Carse 1986: §27).

The more power an actor or a thought collective has, the lesser is its need to justify its statements and actions. If we are to believe Olsson (2007: 178), we find the ultimate example of this in the Bible story of Abr(ah)am – the foundation of all Western monolithic religions. Here we are told how God rules over the people;

---

7   This confusion is evident in the very meaning of the word fact; the Latin word *factum* literally means 'thing done', i.e. something humans have made, but it in the modern world it has gradually come to mean its opposite.

it is by being unpredictable, by not giving any reasons, that God is so effective in exerting his power.

From what we have so far learned about the superego – that it is a control instance that tells us what is right and wrong – we can conclude that its motives are moralistic. Another name for moralism is Apollonian ethics (Coolidge 1941). Let us explore what this means.

Apollonian Ethics

> The architects are experts not only on how buildings will look but also on how to live in them. (Nyman 1989: 5)

> Since the Apollonian artist is characteristically optimistic, he seldom lacks confidence in his own powers of persuasion. 'This is the world of my dreams. Can anyone fail to find it beautiful?' He waits for no negative reply. If he heard one he could do nothing about it. He has not presented an argument but has attempted to move mankind by the portrayal of what is pleasant to himself. (Coolidge 1941: 457)

When I pointed out above that Apollonian ethics is another name for moralism, I wrote *moralism* and not *ethics*. There is an important difference. But let us start by looking at the concepts of *morality* and *ethics*. Linguistically, these have same meaning. Morality is derived from the Latin *mos*, closely related to the Greek éthos, meaning custom or behaviour (Andersen 1997: 21, Hermerén and Lynöe 2008: 9). In every day speech they are often used interchangeably – but this is also true among some researchers (e.g. Andersen 1997, Rockcastle 2000). Others point to a difference between them and believe that morality concerns man's practical and actual behaviour, while ethics is the reflection of more general human values and actions (Hermerén and Lynöe 2008: 9, Johansson and Khakee 2008: 27). Thus, according to some, we are dealing with moral acts and/ or ethical theories. In our study, this difference is not relevant, partly because I am reluctant to make a clear distinction between thoughts and actions (see Chapter 7), and partly because I want to draw attention to another distinction: the difference between ethics, on the one hand, and moralism, on the other. It is not, of course, my ambition to exhaust the meaning of ethics; my exploration of this concept is basic. However, it is important for our study to highlight ethics's degenerated sub-species: moralism.

When philosopher Svend Andersen (1997: 10) summarises Aristotle's considerations in ethics, he writes: 'Ethics is a critical reflection on our beliefs about what is the right or good human action and way of life'. Or as social theorist Nikolas Rose (1999: 178f) describes it, ethics is about 'the active and practical shaping by individuals of the daily practices of their own lives in the name of their own pleasures, contentments and fulfilments'. Ethical thinking represents an antithesis to attempts at translating ethical judgments to supposedly objective, scientific and rational terms. Ethics is not a question of learning the rules of what is right and wrong and then subordinating to these rules. Rather, to act and live ethically is something else, something more than 'knowing the rules'. It is only natural that ethical challenges – the process of arriving at what is most ethical to do in a given situation – are elusive and difficult.

Moralism, however, can be described as the malady of ethics; its 'misfunction' (Katz 1955). Moralism means obeying externally established rules about thinking and behaviour with the collective's best interests in mind. Or, to put this another way, it is about ensuring that others (often the public) behave morally (Osborne and Rose 2004: 220). For this reason, moralism lies closer to politics than ethics. Politics is originally 'statecraft', that is, 'the art of taking responsibility for, managing and defending a society, giving it stability through statutes and laws' (Hermerén and Lynöe 2008: 11). Moralism can be described as 'micro-management', that is, the kind of policies that seek to control citizens' behaviour in detail (Rose 1999: 193). While ethics is about every individual finding her place and the best ways to act, moralism is about the setting up of moral rules – formulated from more or less the same standpoint – and about assuming that these will apply to everyone. Moralism thus has an authoritative element: the moralising actor gives herself interpretative prerogative, and the moral attitudes are expressed through the mechanism of either paying tribute or judging (Katz 1955: 289).

Ethics and moralism are two poles between which politics moves. But as Rose (1999: 192) points out, politics is often closer to moralism: 'It is all too easy for all this talk about ethics to become merely a recoding of strategies of social discipline and morality'. Not surprisingly, the same applies to urban planning. In Johansson and Khakee's (2008: 13) study of planners' view on ethics, it was found that a full forty-seven per cent do not consider planning a political activity. More than twenty per cent had a definite opinion that planning is *not* a political activity. Rather, and this I have already presented, they think of themselves as neutral experts. Johansson and Khakee (ibid.: 205) conclude that planners today 'hardly have anything to say about ethics and about how ethics is used in planning'.

This finding is supported by American architect Garth Rockcastle (2000), who says that few architects realise how omnipresent ethical issues are in the physical environment and in the hypothetical proposals on how the world should or could be. There is a widespread naivety, he says, and this is hardly a flattering picture (ibid.).

My point can be brought together like this: planners are good at moralism but worse at ethics. I have already emphasised the parallel between the planner and Apollo – the formative force. The parallel becomes relevant, again, in this context, where we consider the problem of ethics and its misfunction moralism, for moralism is nothing less than an Apollonian ethics. The concept of Apollonian ethics is Mary L. Coolidge's (1941), and it suits the planner's attitude well. The Apollonian and the Dionysian is a dualism that characterises the Greek soul (Vattimo 1997: 20). They are originally gods but can also be seen as forces or symbols where Apollo represents the dream and order, and Dionysus intoxication and wildness. The dialectical interplay between them characterises the sphere of art as well the whole human civilization. The various art forms are associated with the dominance of one of these forces. Architecture, for example, is Apollonian (Vattimo 1997: 24), and Apollo can be described as 'the force which civilizes [Dionysian] energies' (Hollingdale 2007: 17). Nietzsche (1999: §1) speaks of Apollo as a principle to rely on in a stormy sea. Apollo is the godly impersonation of the individual principle – *principium individuationis* – the one that says how the individual will create the liberating vision that makes her float gently on the ocean.

Apollo is the god of healing; the one who has the ability 'to remove disorder and to keep evil away' (Graf 2009: 101). 'Apollo is the form-giving force, who seeks to "grant repose to individual beings ... by drawing boundaries around them"' (Megill 1985: 38 including quote by Nietzsche). Apollo stands for moderation and conservation of individual boundaries, while Dionysus wants to blow these boundaries apart. We can see this clearly in Edith Södergran's (1984: 137) poem 'Dionysos':

> O Dionysos, Dionysos!
> above our heads we hear the thunder of your horses.
> Liberation, liberation
> sing the swift reins.
> O Dionysos, Dionysos,
> I clamber up onto your horses,
> with mad hands I hold fast to the chariot's wheels.

The Apollonian artist's primary medium is the picture – because it is primarily visual art that indulges in that which is ostensible. This is in line with Nietzsche's (1999: §9) idea that, '[e]verything that rises to the surface in dialogue, the Apolline part of Greek tragedy, appears simple, transparent, beautiful'. The Apollonian artist embodies an idea of humans as rational creatures. Since normative statements about how people ought to live are guided by perceptions of the nature of man, this view of humanity gives rise to a certain form of ethics: an Apollonian ethics. The life advocated is a life 'in harmony', and the image of man as rational 'has tended to an emphasis on an Apollonian rather than a Dionysian interpretation of good life' (Coolidge 1941: 458). Apollonian art is 'an art of "fair appearance", of fantasy and image; and it has always its "measured limitation" and "freedom from the wilder emotions"' (Coolidge 1941: 454 including quotes by Nietzsche). That some people prefer Apollonian ideals and others Dionysian is as natural as some are attracted to classical art and others romantic. And the planner, as Lefebvre has noted, is Apollonian: 'He despises drunkenness. ... [T]he Dionysian is a stranger to him. ... [W]hat pleases him most is to have everything pasteurized, everything hygienic and deodorized' (Lefebvre in Merrifield 2006: 90).

As architectural historian Francoise Choay (1997) has underscored, twentieth-century urban planning is influenced by Thomas More's *Utopia* from 1516; the arrangement of physical space is 'a way to represent and fix a particular moral order' (Harvey 2003: 161). More's book is an example of the kind of utopia that Harvey (ibid.: 160) calls '[u]topias of spatial form', in which the fixed spatial form excludes the temporality of social processes and thereby guarantees social stability. The Chicago School theorist Robert E. Park emphasised a link between 'a spatial pattern and a moral order' (ibid.), and there is no mistaking that functionalism is permeated by Apollonian-ethical reasoning. The manifest *acceptera*, which we have encountered several times before, is brimming with proclamations about what is good, beautiful, nice, reasonable, normal and necessary. And the following is a quote from a handbook of architectural drawing: 'The figures in a drawing should convey the nature of the activity in a space and be appropriate to the setting. The manner in which we draw them should answer the fundamental question: What activity should occur in this room or space?' (Ching 2003: 161, see also Vidler 2000: 7).

This seemingly neutral call, from expert to student, on how the student – when she herself becomes an expert – can/should use her instrument (the drawing), echoes of the superego's *Thou shalt!*, The handbook's authoritarian tone is all the more manifest in the following quote: 'Figures should be clothed appropriately' (Ching 2003: 161). As Lefebvre (1991: 361) writes: '[Architectural discourse] only too easily becomes ... a moral discourse on straight lines, on right angles and straightness in general'.

In the plans for Hammarby Sjöstad too, we find moralistic tendencies. The guaranteeing of a good quality of life, for example, is said to be central, and this may, for example, mean

> that you are tempted to be outside a lot; the air is clean and there is not much noise. This, I think, is extremely important. ... I do not think there is too much talk about sustainability, but I think we're talking about it in the wrong way. I would like to put a *reasonable lifestyle* more in focus. (Anonymous planner in Johansson and Khakee 2008: 196, my emphasis)

Thus, city planning is still imbued with what Jacobs (1992: 41) describes as 'puritanical and Utopian ideas of how people should spend their free time'. In Hammarby Sjöstad and Södra stationsområdet, one of the objectives was, as we know well by now, to create urbanity. However, in the planning documents, there is hostility towards genuine difference – the kind of difference that blows systems apart. For example, this hostility can be seen in the following statement by the director: 'At Södra station, we started with a pretty strict plan. The entire project was threatened by those who wanted to dissolve the plan. One must have even stricter conditions in a project of this size [Hammarby Sjöstad] or there will be total chaos' (Hultin et al. 1992: 22).

Moreover, the director sees Stockholm as unique in Europe in terms of the strong role that the city has in planning. When he was asked whether he thinks that this has meant that Stockholm has been more successful in urban construction than other major cities, he replies, 'I think so' (ibid.: 25). Planning's tendency to moralism – the desire to control people's behaviour – is reflected in its codification of space. The planning of space is, in fact, a detailed expert engineering of lifestyles and activities that are considered 'reasonable'. In this context, it is easy to agree with Marcus's (2000b: 19) bold thesis that architecture and planning has very little to do with urbanity. This view is also expressed by Lefebvre (1996: 207), who calls Le Corbusier 'a good architect but a catastrophic urbanist'. Here we can remember what Nietzsche (1986a: §31) wrote as well: 'Only very naive people are capable of believing that the nature of man could be transformed into a purely logical one; but if there should be degrees of approximation to this objective, what would not have to be lost if this course were taken!'

The goal of 'creating urbanity' may be new, but the mindset is the same. The planners say they reject modernist functional separation, but as Taylor (C. 2003: 168) notes: '[J]ust saying that you reject [something] is not necessarily climbing out of the picture that embeds it. You also have to explore and bring to awareness how that picture holds you captive'.

If we are to believe Lefebvre (1991: 382), the planner's conceived or instrumental space is conditioned by a logic that cannot harbour any qualitative difference. Conceived difference is already reduced since the various elements are already parts of one and the same thought, one intellectual manoeuvre. Or, as Arendt (1998: 287) insightfully notes: '[W]herever we search for that which we are not, we encounter only the patterns of our own minds'. Conceived difference is implicit in all planning documents, even if the planners themselves express a desire to create diversity, for example. Differences – when consciously imagined – are merely induced and thus minimal. Minimal or induced difference is difference that exists within a system, a system which is generated according to a specific rule. This rule characterises the system in question. We only have to think about the numbers in a numerical system or variations within a specific fashion. The latter variations are only induced, because they are stipulated by the fashion itself (Lefebvre 1991: 372). Difference in colour or design between houses in a residential suburb, is another example of minimal or induced difference. Illustrating these same limits in thought, an advertisement for Järvastaden, a new residential area outside of Stockholm, states that 'the environment is diverse with both multi-family and semi-detached houses and houses' ('Solna – the City of the Future' 2010: 41).

In contrast to this kind of minimal difference, Lefebvre (1991: 372) argues, is maximal, or produced, difference – a difference that requires 'the shattering of a system; it is born of an explosion'. Urban space, as I concluded in the previous chapter, is a space marked by difference, a place where variation or diversity is maximised. Lived, urban space is dialectical; it represents '[a] life without concepts'. Bureaucratic systematisation, however, is an activity organised by 'concepts without life' (ibid.) – the very antithesis of difference, and thus – one might say – to the urban. In this light, the task of planning for urbanity stands out as a paradox. For already Aristotle acknowledged that the city, by its very nature, is a multitude (Nordström 2008: 225f).[8]

The zoning idea of functionalism permeates the planning of Hammarby Sjöstad and Södra stationsområdet. Nothing seems left to chance: '[A]ll land has a thought-out function and design' (Detaljplan för kvarteret Kölnan 2003: 9). Even the spaces where people are to meet and enjoy themselves are designated. In a drawing, a set of steps in a park are presented as 'a popular place to dwell on' and the park as 'a natural gathering place for various events (concerts, performances of various kinds, etc.)' (*Södra Stationsområdet* 1984: 25). In Hammarby Sjöstad, the spaces where services, activities, meeting places and places for recreation should be located are marked. 'City life', as one of the planners puts it, is concentrated in the main thoroughfare (*BoStad02* 2002: 23). Even the parks and the many paths (*stråk*) are broken down by their different character: 'Large scale along Hammarbyleden, intimate and small scale along Sickla Kanal' (ibid.). The green space will provide meeting places and thereby 'replace ancient venues such as the church and the square' (ibid.: 64).

The fact that the architects have a moralistic attitude is probably a result of their training in drawing houses – intended for private life. We have already seen that the architects entered urban planning relatively late, at the beginning of the twentieth century. When they were faced with the task of planning entire neighbourhoods or cities, this undertaking was – and still is – handled in the same way as if the task were to build a house (Hillier and Hanson 1984: 19ff, Marcus 2000b: 16ff). Consequently, (public) streets, squares and parks are treated as if they were an interior (see for ex. Sitte 2005: 417; 421). Which activities are to be carried out where are determined in advance, 'in the same way that a schedule disciplines time, urban planning disciplines space' (Franzén 1982: 18). Planning, roughly put, controls two aspects of living space. *What functions should this area have?* and *where should these functions be located?* The different rooms or spaces are signals that seem to speak to us: Eat here! Sleep here! Play here! Every space has its function – its own.

> Everything is clear and intelligible. Everything is trivial. Everything is closure and materialized system. The text of the town is totally legible, as impoverished as it is clear, despite the architects' efforts to vary the lines. Surprise? Possibilities? From this place, which should have been the home of all that is possible, they have vanished without a trace. (Lefebvre 1995: 119)

So it is that social values are reproduced and differences are minimised. To illustrate how urban planning today is based on the principles of house planning, let us look at some examples. In an ad the municipality of Södertälje writes

---

8   In relation to this discussion about minimal and maximal differences, see Gunder and Hillier's (2009: 115–33) critique of the concept of multi-culturalism – a master signifier of contemporary Western planning discourse.

about the planning of the Södertalje city centre: 'Each park has its own distinct character. These include fine parks, activity parks, recreation and sports parks, recreation parks for walks, play and games' ('Hållbar stadsutveckling' 2009: 16). An article about Minneberg also reads like a housing plan: 'The dense plan is well organised, which is necessary if we are going to have enough land. There is no waste' (Brunnberg 1987: 4).

A third example reveals itself in the program for Södra stationsområdet (1984: 2): 'Transportation systems for pedestrian and car traffic in the new area are separated mainly to reduce risks and interferences'. The streets are classified according to their function, and each type will have its own name: 'main streets', 'local streets', 'landing streets', 'dead-end streets' and 'loading streets' (ibid.: 18).

That house planning is generally a detailed business is not particularly surprising. The individual, or group of individuals, that inhabits a private house (or apartment) tends to reproduce existing activities; they have breakfast at the kitchen table, work at the desk, hang their coat in the hall, sleep in the bedroom and so on. Furthermore, there is only a limited number of people who use the same house in question, which means that all (adult) members of the household are often able to come to an agreement as to what they want to do and where. But when this morally rectifying attitude is directed towards public space – or that which is meant to function as public space – it takes on a new, power-laden dimension. Behind the physical shape of the room is an ideology of each thing in its place. When this ideology is translated to material form it counteracts change and resistance to the prevailing ideology in that it encourages the reproduction of already proposed activities. So, in this way, people are forced to abide by the politicians and experts, in the same way that children are forced to obey their parents' ideas about what to do, when and where.

The architects relate to cities as if they were houses – a conclusion for which we find support when Habraken (2005) gives his view of the architectural profession in his book *Palladio's Children*. Architects of today are expected to consider the context, too, that is, the social and physical environment in which the building is located. Habraken (ibid.: 153) calls this 'the field'. But these considerations are not made, he writes: 'We [architects] devote years to learning to shape architectural form but barely skim the surface of the fields to which our architecture will contribute' (ibid.: 151). The roots of this tendency can be traced to architecture's heritage, more specifically to the Renaissance architect Palladio, whose drawings does not indicate any context: 'We see neither the landscape nor topography in the representation of the villas' (ibid.: 9).

> Architecture, from Palladianism onwards, has largely been a matter of exquisite signature objects. ... We still live with the ambiguity of this legacy. Architects up to the present day habitually provide minimal information about site or context ... Architectural photographers, editors and authors routinely keep us in the dark about surrounding everyday environment. (ibid.: 10)

So, given the above argument, we have now come a little closer to an understanding of why some urban areas are disurban[9] although the intention is to create urbanity. Above all, I have pointed out that the architect treats the city as if it were a house, which means that she not only seeks control over the form of space but also over its function(s).

The question of functions has, on the whole, been on the lips of planners since the breakthrough of modernism. The identification of functions has simplified the discussion of the city. But here we must remember that it is only with respect to tangible things that we can be sure that we are talking about the same thing. Therefore, it is not enough to talk about functions. These must be translated into things. So it is that the different life functions – dwelling, work, recreation and transport – in the name of communication and clarity – are operationalised into forms, into things. In the planners' analyses, it is not only dwelling that is distinguished from recreation and traffic (which by definition excludes sitting in your apartment by the window listening to the traffic on the street below as a form of recreation), dwelling is also translated into an object: the house. Similarly, *friytor* (open spaces) – this frequently used word in urban planning – are there to meet the need for recreation, or leisure time. People work, sleep and transit from one place to another, but they also recuperate and seek amusement, the analysis goes. And an effective way to manifest your benevolent intentions as a planner is to mark out a space where this can take place.

Reification

> The speaker who anchors himself in existing things is understood by everybody ...
> It is obviously easier to agree that we are talking about the same object, if that
> object is a concrete thing which stems from the realm of the sensible rather than
> an abstract relation that comes from the world of the intelligible. (Olsson 1980a:
> 68b, see also 2007: 89)

In the planning of Hammarby Sjöstad, urbanity appears to be a function alongside, or added to, the four functions identified by the functionalists. 'It's about functionality, not just forms', one of the architects says (Hultin et al. 1992). But as I pointed out above, functions are translated to forms: dwelling to houses, work to office buildings, recreation to green areas. 'Through a series of euphemisms people's life activities become things and objects of planning, means for overall planning policy objectives', writes planning theorist Susanne Nordström (2008: 198). Similarly; urban attributes are operationalised to roofing materials and façade colours. One of the architects says, '[T]he unique Stockholmian colour scale in warm yellow and red colours of plaster has been deliberately used to mark a unity with the historic city' (*BoStad02* 2002: 69). At

---

9   This is Bill Hillier's (2007: 144) concept, and in Chapter 6 I will return to it.

one point the project got a rebuff from the Urban Planning Committee on the grounds that it did not meet the Committee's vision of urbanity and urban life. The measures that were undertaken in response to this are described by the architects: 'The buildings ... were reworked so that the previously open slits of light are replaced by sealed glass and balconies while the top floors of the buildings are built together. This provides closed facades while "urban windows" still let light into the yards' (ibid.: 31). Here, the phenomenon of urbanity is translated into something tangible: a form.

Reification can be illustrated by another example. Silverdal is a new area outside Stockholm, built after the garden city ideal: 'In Silverdal a settlement is created that gives the whole area an impression of an idyllic small town. A living idyll where large green spaces create opportunities for social interaction' (www. silverdal.se 2009-03-06). In an article in *Dagens Nyheter*, the reporter notes that the big green commons adjacent to the residential buildings is empty, whereby a resident responds: '[I] think we Swedes are bad at making use of common areas in residential areas. We must get better at going out!' (Fresk Aspegren 2007: 5). Here we see that what the detailed plan marks out as 'the main public space of the garden city; the commons' (Detaljplan för Margreteborg 2000), as a place for social interaction, in reality, is an empty surface with grass. This surface can also be seen as a reminder that '[t]here is no such thing as obligatory play, play on command' (Bauman 1994: 143).

Plans of this type, however, are something to show to the politicians, for they are explicit signs of social concern. Where cars will drive and where people are going to sleep is relatively easy to identify in a plan, but where do people hang out and enjoy themselves? The city is not only a place for work, sleep and transportation! We had better reserve space for this other need too! A pamphlet for the Silverdal Square reads:

> By the benches, the planted pines and the flowering cherry trees, the neighbours get together ... Between the buildings, north of Silverdal Road, we create a shared courtyard with green space, shrubs and small trees. A gathering place with a calmer character designed with seating and a barbecue area for the adults and play areas ... for the little ones. (Projektbroschyr för Silverdals Torg)

So it is that political benevolence and Apollonian ethics, communication and reification are intimately linked. Once again we can recall Lefebvre's story about Mourenx. He uses many positively charged words to describe the town: Mourenx is 'well-planned', 'well-lit' and 'properly built' and the overall plan has 'a certain attractiveness' (Lefebvre 1995: 118). The contrast is striking when he uses the word 'terrified' to describe his feelings when visiting the area.

In the planning of Hammarby Sjöstad the benevolence takes the following expression: 'Residential open spaces in neighbourhoods with yards and parks should be available within 50–300 meters from the home, be sunlit and have a good local climate, be designed for play, relaxation and socialising. Surface measurement is 50 m²/apartment, when exploitation is high 25 m²/apartment' (Detaljplan för Sickla Kaj 1999: 11). But what exactly is an 'open space'?

> The open spaces [*friytorna*] can be classified into three types, namely 1) the land areas of the houses including landscaped footpaths, play and planting areas in the residential block, 2) the central park areas of the areas, consisting of intensely cultivated parks ... 3) the natural and recreational areas of the blocks ... Within all three types specially designed and equipped open spaces for play are required.
> (*Increased requirements for space in the urban environment* 1965: 28)

In recent years, there have been attempts to update the meaning of the concept of open space. For example, in *The Sociotope Map* (*Sociotopkartan* 2002: 14), signed by Mats Pemer, director of urban planning in Stockholm, aims to 'identify parks and open spaces [in Stockholm] from the social and cultural point of view'. Ultimately, the aim is to create a complement to biotope maps as a basis for planning decisions. Here you can read that the concept of 'open space refers to undeveloped land and water, which are not used for transport or terminal purposes' (ibid.). In the survey there is a distinction between the objects themselves – the open spaces – and people's values. 'An object must be identified. Then it is up to the subjects (stakeholders/users) to relate. In this case the object is open spaces in the inner city, and then you must identify them before evaluation can take place' (ibid.).

In order to systematically identify the open spaces in the city, they are typologised under four main categories: large open spaces, individual open spaces, built areas, transport and terminal areas. Individual open space means 'undeveloped land which is between 0.5 and 50 acres in an urban area. In dense urban environments it is parks, beaches, piers, esplanades, pedestrian streets and squares' (ibid.). The identification of open spaces is presented via schematic maps, which are meant to be used as a basis for planning and user scores. To summarise the planning process, first the open spaces are identified and defined, and then they are valued. In other words, the implicit assumption is that identification and valuing are different things, that definitions are value-free.

The Sociotope Map is often portrayed as a good example of how planning since the 1960s and 70s has 'softened', in a positive sense, and become 'more humane'. It represents an ambition to take into account more aspects of the city than the 'hard' technical ones. Basically, however, practice is unchanged: city life is disintegrated and reified. 'For bridges to connect, there must first be a separation' as Olsson (1984: 75) writes. Reification is often as unnoticeable as it is inevitable; the planner has to produce visible results: 'The only things that count are those which can be counted, and the only things that can be counted are those which we directly or indirectly can touch' (Olsson 1980c: 12, see also Ramirez 1995: 127). As evident by the name, 'The *Socio*tope Map' is intended to highlight the social qualities of the city. But the name – 'The Sociotope *Map*' – also testifies to reification, for what is a map if not a translation from story to picture, from process to form (see Olsson 2007)?

Behind the notion of functions in the city, are ideas about the *needs* of man. Therefore, let us examine this idea.

Need – Desire

Need = The word originates from the old English word *nied*, which means 'necessity, compulsion, duty', originally 'violence, force' from the pre-Germanic word *nauthis*, probably akin to the old Prussian *nautin* 'need' and perhaps the Slavic *nazda*, Russian *nuzda* and Polish *nedza* 'misery, distress' from the proto-Indo-European *nau-* 'death, to be exhausted'. The more common old English word for 'need, necessity, want' was ðearf, linked by the idea of 'trouble, pain'. The two could be put together, *nieððearf* 'need, necessity, compulsion, thing needed'. (*Online Etymology Dictionary* 2009-08-11, my summary)

Desire = The English word *desire* comes from the old French word *desirer*, from Latin *desiderare* meaning 'long for, wish for' or originally probably 'await what the stars will bring' from the phrase *de sidere,* 'from the stars'. (Ibid.)

Why did Woolf refer to the need for a pencil when she took to the streets of London? And why do planners so often talk about people's needs? If we look at the etymological meaning of the word and compare it with that of desire, we see, first, that desire seems to have almost poetic connotations, whereas need is associated with compulsion and necessity. One conclusion we can draw is that (the satisfaction of) needs is necessary for survival; it indicates something we have to have. If our needs are not met, we cannot live; this leads to misery, exhaustion and/ or death: 'A need can be defined as something that is bad for you if left unmet' (von Wright 1986: 140). We see no signs of this aspect of base necessity or desperation in the definition of desire. Rather, desire seems to denote something beyond the everyday, beyond the essential; it is something we can 'treat ourselves to' when we our needs have been met. I can only desire, that is, wish something from the stars (*de sidere*), if I have food in my stomach and clothes on my body. Here we see a connection in purpose (or, rather, lack of purpose) between desire and play: 'Play is "unnecessary", it is grounded in neither physical necessity nor moral duty' (Asplund 1987: 63).

As Lefebvre has already noted, the planner ignores desire; for her there are only needs (Merrifield 2006: 90). The following statement from *acceptera* illustrates this: 'The feeling of comfort in a home depends to a great extent on how well a dwelling can satisfy the needs of those living there in terms of practical functions' (Asplund et al. 2008: 237). Functionalism not only represses desire but also creativity and political action (Baum 2008). Architecture and planning is, as Denis Hollier (1989: 3) puts it, 'the system of systems'. Its hallmark is systematisation – something that results in the displacement of 'anything resembling play, exteriority, or alterity' (ibid.).

The spokesmen for the functionalist ideology defended Le Corbusier's idea of the house as a machine with these words: 'All he is saying is that a dwelling should function effectively for its intended needs – and who could disagree with that?' (Asplund et al. 2008: 335f). In the General Plan for Stockholm from 1952, we learn that planning in many ways is about defining the needs of the urban residents. In the one-and-a-half-page-long section on conceptual determinations, the word *need* is used no less than fifteen times (*Generalplan för Stockholm* 1952: 112).

But why need and not desire? Besides the fact that planning is an activity performed by Homo Faber, one explanation is a reliance on visual perception; the fact that planners primarily take into account that which we can see. One of the meanings of the word need is 'thing needed'; need primarily addresses material things – it can be translated to food, shelter, oxygen molecules, green surfaces (i.e. grass) and so on – that is, it can be fixed to a particular solution. Desire, however, cannot be reified. There is no solution to the problem of desire. The difference between need and desire could also be described as a question of objectivity and subjectivity (while not necessarily mutually exclusive). While the ability to identify the needs of others is something that can be taught and learned (medical school is an obvious example), desire is something that remains hidden to everyone but the one who harbours it (and not seldom, of course, to her as well).

Imagine that you have just found out that you have to move from your apartment. You are now in need of a new home. You put up an ad and receive immediate response from someone who has an apartment to rent out. You find out where it is and go there to look at it, but you feel uneasy; you experience discomfort as you walk around in this place, so you decline the offer. Why in the world did you do that? You were in need of an apartment and your need was about to be met! This seemingly irrational behaviour is completely rational in light of Heidegger's (1977) philosophy. As he emphasises, the realm of the home, the dwelling, reaches beyond the apartment, the actual dwelling unit. The apartment is a thing that exists – independent of whether it is occupied or not. Dwelling, however, is as separated from man as life itself. To dwell is more than to sleep and eat in a concrete place; to dwell is to be a human being on earth. This reminds us that today's perfunctory equation between dwelling and housing is a mistake termed 'reification'. Here we see what happens when the original meaning of a word (in this case, dwell) is forgotten and replaced by something more superficial.

While a need often has a clear goal – food or clothing, for example – this is rarely, or never, the case with desire. We often imagine that needs must lead somewhere; they must, so to speak, 'land' somewhere, so that they can be met and moved out of the way. Bradley Macdonald (1999: 28) interprets Marx:

> [H]umans as 'sensuous' beings are always striving toward what they desire but never fully attaining their goal … our existence is always 'conditioned and limited', and we are thus in a constant condition of 'suffering' as we attempt to make our desires real through objectification.

As previously stated, need is something fundamental; if we do not meet a need, we will die. But applying the same reasoning to desire becomes problematic because desire – like urbanity – does not allow itself to be (fully) anchored in material things. Here we can recall Woolf's pencil – the official and concrete goal of her wandering the streets of London. But to think that it was for the sake of a pencil she walked through the city that winter's evening would be to empty both her and London from what make them what they are. In other words, 'The mere existence of a desired object is never enough to count as the gratification of a desire' (Kenny 1963: 112).

In Hammarby Sjöstad efforts have been made to include art works which 'will engage and enhance the experience of the external environment' (*BoStad02* 2002: 66). Parks, or 'green spaces', are intended to be 'public landscapes and attractive environments with strolling paths for people' (ibid.: 64). But this rendition of the external environment ignores the idea that an intersection with traffic flowing in from all sides, where car horns are blaring – for some – can give pleasure, and that people may long for jostling with other people on shaded pavement. Woolf, for example, loved to see the buses run up and down Southampton Row (Moorcroft Wilson 1987: 107). But a modernist-influenced urban planner does not take into account this perspective. For her assumption seems to be more in line with what architectural historian Alan Colquhoun (2002: 152) summarises as one of modernism's more or less explicit messages: '[C]ultivation of the spirit and the body takes place in parkland'.

The singer and song writer Frida Hyvönen, in her song 'London!', touches on a theme that connects her with Woolf. Here, I am not thinking of the commonality that both write about London, or that both are women; rather, they both seem to require something inaccessible and cold, something – well, almost unfriendly. 'London!', Hyvönen (2008) sings, 'the way you hate me is better than love and I'm down on my knees / London! The way you're trying to get rid of me makes me weak in the knees'. To Hyvönen, London is both pleasure and pain; harmony and conflict. The painful aspect is indeed an essential part of the pleasure it gives; to experience passion, to be passionate, is not only associated with pleasure but also involves suffering. Karl Marx, who is generally not a source of insights on desire since he put material needs at the forefront of his ideas, does, however, have something important to add on the subject when he says that man is 'a *suffering* being, and because he feels his suffering, he is a *passionate* being' (in Macdonald 1999: 28).

Woolf portrays the area of Richmond – a small town outside London where she lived for periods of time – as 'soft'. Bloomsbury in central London, however, she described as 'fierce and scornful and stonyhearted' – but beautiful (Moorcroft Wilson 1987: 107). In Bloomsbury, Woolf 'felt herself for the first time fully alive … Bloomsbury had "bite", even if it hurt!' (ibid.: 46f). Its beauty lay in its vitality, 'for it seemed to her pulsing with life' (ibid.). In Woolf's own words (2008: 180), 'We walk home from theatres, through the entrails of London. Why do I love it so much? … for it is stony hearted, and callous'.

Overall, the above examples all challenge the planners' insistence on harmony, order and beauty in their traditional and narrow meanings. As evident in the following extract from an interview with the planners behind Hammarby Sjöstad, they have sought to eliminate the city's negative aspects altogether: '[Interviewer]: In big cities drugs and crime thrive, but also creativity and knowledge ... Can you weed out the bad sides and get a 'new type' of city? [Architect Hammarby Sjöstad]: We cannot eliminate crime. But regarding planning qualities one must seek to answer yes' (Hultin et al., 1992: 26).

Brown (1991: 190) has questioned the often perfunctory division between pleasure and pain as well as the idea that you can achieve pleasure by eliminating pain. We encounter a more realistic picture of man in the psycho-analytical, the conflicted, the Dionysian: 'This world was, is, and always will be, ever living fire', he writes, and continues: 'It will never be a safe place, it will never be a pastoral scene of peace and pleasure' (ibid.). Sennett (2008: 96f) has also criticised the idea that the free and enjoyable aspects of life can be separated from the painful and the conflicted. 'Buried in this hunger for preplanning along machinelike lines is the desire to avoid pain', he writes; to create an environment that is conflict-free (ibid.: 98). Planning expresses a fear of losing control.

When we try to understand the difference between need and desire, it's helpful to think of Homo Faber and Homo Ludens – the two different attitudes I discussed in the previous chapter. Homo Faber always has a goal behind what she does; everything has or should have a function, a purpose. That which meets needs, she understands. *Flânerie* is, as we have previously highlighted, the ultimate form of play, and play does not have a goal beyond itself. As Bauman (1993: 170) has noted, 'play may make us more healthy, but more often than not its impact is the very opposite of what medical men would describe as health'. Play is not about survival; '[a] being that is at play is a being that goes beyond the task of self-preservation and self-reproduction, that has not got the perpetuation of itself as its only goal' (ibid.).

The happiness calculations of utilitarianism are based on a black and white picture of life as consisting of, on the one hand, desire, on the other hand, pain (Hylland Eriksen 2008: 187). The goal of both the individual and society is considered to be that of maximising pleasure and minimising pain. But this is an overly rigid picture: 'Every pleasure is connected with pain', as Marcuse (1968b: 174) says – a contention that in turn leads to the conclusion that there rarely exists any 'pure', 'unqualified' or 'true' kinds of pleasure. At least not when it comes to social life: 'Unmixed pleasure is to be had only in those things which are most removed from the social life process', Marcuse (ibid.: 175) continues and refers to the 'pure' kind of pleasure mentioned by Plato. According to Plato, it is possible to experience pure pleasure, but only when it comes to non-organic objects. That is, pure pleasure is to be found 'in lines, sounds, and colours that are beautiful in themselves, in other words, enjoyment released from all painful desire and restricted to inorganic objects' (Marcuse 1968b: 174). Is it not this kind of pleasure that the architect is seeking? I am inclined to answer yes. But as Marcuse writes (ibid.), 'This enjoyment is obviously too empty to be happiness'.

It is not just the planners' visions of a conflict-free world that Woolf's and Hyvönen's texts challenge but also the feminist idea that relationships should be symmetrical and equal. Both writers desire London, but London – on its part – seems rather indifferent to them. In fact, and paradoxically, this is what makes their feelings so strong. For Hyvönen, it is the way in which London is trying to 'get rid of' her that makes her weak in the knees. Here, I refer to a question that Nehring (2009) poses, here formulated by Wigorts Yngvesson (2009): 'What if passion is not or should not be equal or easily accessible? What if passion also carries dangers, darkness, fear and struggle for power?'

Freud noted that many of our words have diametrically opposed meanings. The Latin word *sacer*, for example, means both 'sacred' and 'accursed' (Brown 1991: 197). A sacred act must involve violence, a breach of a limit. Therefore, human culture can be seen as an incessant effort to accommodate both Eros and Thanatos, both the Love God and the Death God (ibid.). And now: If pleasure and pain in reality are close to each other, if they presuppose each other, it is easy to understand why I felt a sense of discomfort in Hammarby Sjöstad, where everything is created in the name of harmony, beauty and convenience. So it is that good intentions are turned on their head. Hammarby Sjöstad manipulates; it flirts with its perfection and seems to speak to me: *See – am I not beautiful? Don't you love me? Don't I offer you everything you want? Because I know exactly who you are and what you need!* Behind the plan's statement that the green spaces are 'attractive environments' where people can meet (*BoStad02* 2002: 64) is, in fact, the planners' attempt to categorise not only the area's different parts but also you and me. Here, Bauman's (1993: 11) words provide an important generalisation on the topic: '[T]he [moral] impulse to care for the Other, when taken to its extreme, leads to the annihilation of the autonomy of the Other, to domination and oppression'.

As I stated in the beginning of the previous chapter, I started from the idea that the *flâneur* is a fundamentally timeless figure. Her grazing ground – to borrow Bauman's term (1994: 147) – may have changed and the supply of appropriate grazing grounds decreased since the late nineteenth century, but her desire for the urban has by all accounts not diminished – if anything, it has increased. The urban experience still has, and will always have, 'existential relevance', to borrow an expression from Johannisson (1997: 12f).

Both the drive to emphasise the *flâneur*'s desire for the urban as a timeless theme and the drive to define the essence of the urban are neither new nor unchallenged. And to refer to nineteenth-century Paris as the ideal type of urbanity is sometimes considered a sign of sentimentality or of 'slum romantisation'. Critics include Moa Tunström (2009), human geographer, who has examined contemporary constructions of ideals and problems in Swedish discussions on urban planning. Her argument is that we do not have to 'mourn the loss' of a real, traditional city or public space. Instead, we should 'open up to new influences' and 'fill the strong key concept [of the city] with alternative meanings' (ibid.: back cover). But – and this is my question back to Tunström – what if there is a *real* loss and a *real* sense of mourning? For those individuals that express it, I mean. Tunström's criticism makes me think of a well-meaning parent who tells her love-grieving teenager to get her act together and forget the object of her love all with the sober justification, 'You don't *need* a boyfriend – you have so many friends!'

Richard Sennett is one of the so-called mourners of the urban. As he points out in the preface to *The Uses of Disorder*, his arguments are sometimes dismissed as 'romantic', but he insists that the urban is something that plays a significant role in human life. The urban experience must be kept strong and vibrant, he holds, because it is intimately connected with freedom (Sennett 2008: xiii). More specifically, he writes,

> I am not arguing that we return to the old ways of city life when times were hard; rather, I have tried to show how the emergence of a new city life in an era of abundance and prosperity has eclipsed something of the essence of urban life – its diversity and possibilities for complex experience. (Ibid.: 81f)[10]

In an interview, Tunström (in Granath 2009) says that she finds it 'a little odd' that the urban ideal of today is to try to recreate the conditions that characterise the nineteenth-century city – conditions 'which perhaps were functional and necessary at the time ... [b]ut which do not have the same function and needs today'. What is more, she even doubts whether there is anything at all in the nineteenth-century city that is worth idealising: 'Most Swedish cities at this time were characterised by major class differences, poor sanitation and crowding', writes the interviewer, summarising her argument (Granath 2009). In Tunström's own words (in ibid.): 'We want to have apartments with lots of space, which is difficult to reconcile with the small scale. We have advanced communication technology that decreases the need for public meeting places. We have refrigeration and thus we do not need to go shopping every day'. In short, our needs are no longer the same as they were in the nineteenth century.

Tunström's line of argumentation makes me think of the report *Increased requirements for space in the urban environment* (1965) discussed earlier; that which asserts that the increase in economic prosperity has increased the amount of leisure time, which, in turn, has led to an increased demand for increased (!) land area in the form of open spaces, which, in turn, is interpreted as a sign that even more land area will be needed in the future. In other words, the experts behind the report reason from *is* to *ought*. In the interview quoted above, Tunström too transforms passive connections into active (see Fleck 1979: 10), starting from the

---

10   As Merrifield (2004: 937) shows in an article on the Situationists' relationship to Paris, a sentimental approach to a city's history does not necessarily exclude a desire for change: 'The Situationists were men and women of change. They were the ones who wanted to rebuild everything, but they also loved the past. They somehow wanted to go back to the future, wanted to reconstruct the best of the old world in the worst of the new, in its ruins'.

observation that people today *have* more living space, she makes the inference that people in general (or 'we', which is the word she uses) *want to* live like this. Her use of the word 'thus' in the statement 'We have refrigeration and thus we do not need to go shopping every day' demonstrates this (implicit) inference.

The use of the term 'thus' then makes me think of the manifest *acceptera*, whose title refers precisely to what the functionalists see as the necessity of accepting 'the reality that exists' (Asplund et al. 2008: 338). The message is that we live in a new era – an era that has no room for sentimentality:

> Changeability in the city environment – that is the logic. ... The way we feel
> about a certain monumental, or old, picturesque part of the city is natural. ... If
> it has to go, we will miss it like an old friend, even though we know that nature
> also ordains that our friend must in the end depart ... But no reasonable person,
> not even our archaeologists, merely wants to 'preserve' and 'avoid', wants to
> prevent the natural renewal of the city. (Ibid.: 330; 325)

This quote illustrates another example of planners' reasoning from *is* to *ought* – a rhetorical trick (whether intentionally or unintentionally used) that is never innocent. Since it must not be forgotten, let me repeat the following point: planning is a fundamentally benevolent activity. So is the focusing on human needs. Architect Goodman (1972: 52f) talks about his profession as 'the soft cops', but stresses that 'we do not think of ourselves as agents of the oppressors, yet we are not really that far from being the Albert Speers of our time'. This role often goes unrecognised, because architects are generally perceived to be, both by others and by themselves, 'more sophisticated, more educated, more socially conscious than the generals' (ibid.).

Freud argued that sexuality is something that constantly interferes with other human activities. It gives not only pleasure but also pain – very much, indeed. But – and this 'but' must not be forgotten – if we try to eliminate it, we will find ourselves in a state of tranquility and stillness; a state that resembles death. And the idea that life and death are inter-woven means that the fear of death and pain 'is likewise a fear of life' (King 1972: 159).

In urban planning today, the urban seems to be regarded as a(nother) function; a solution to a(nother) need – a need that planners can make sure is met by delineating space in their drawings. Since desire is difficult to link to things that can be seen, planners and other interested parties instead discuss the issue of needs. These needs, in turn, are reified into buildings, open spaces, pedestrian and cycle pathways. But the consideration of human needs is paradoxically one of the ways in which planners' benevolence becomes a dehumanising practice, for '[i]t is a Freudian axiom that the essence of man consists, not, as Descartes maintained, in thinking, but in desiring' (Brown 1959: 7).

Woolf was most satisfied when she was in the city – especially when she could walk. It seems as if it were life itself she wanted, but she also seemed to want to transcend the boundaries of her own personality and to momentarily escape, to become one with the environment. The difficulties of pinning down a specific object and linking it to the right to the city or the desire for urban is an important conclusion of this chapter. Kierkegaard remarked that 'one will never find consciousness by looking down a microscope at brain cells or anything else' (Laing 1967: 2, see also Cassirer 1972: 5). Similarly, one can argue that it is not entirely possible to reify urbanity as a phenomenon. The difficulty of this task becomes even clearer if we take into account the parallel between the urban and life itself. For what is life? 'To breathe, eat, work and procreate', one possible need-based answer reads. We can find parallels in the response to the question of what a city might be: it consists of houses, human bodies, pavements, buses, service establishments and so on. Described like this, a city is something that satisfies each of our different needs: protection from the weather, selling and buying goods and services and transportation, for example. Both Mourenx and Hammarby Sjöstad meet these needs; of this there is no doubt. But Plato knew that while satisfied needs are required in order to survive, desire is essential to live: '[N]o one desires drink, but good drink, nor food, but good food; for everyone, after all, desires good things; if then, thirst is a desire, it would be for good drink and for good whatever it is, and similarly with the other desires' (Plato 1991: §438).

The focusing on needs suggests that urban planners tend to (unconsciously) close their eyes to the totality of responsibility – that is, the fact that large-scale planning means taking responsibility not only for various human needs, but for (urban) life in its entirety. Needs and functions are chiselled out – all in the name of good intentions. The result is that the lifeworld is dissected: what is 'good' is separated from that which is 'bad', and the ultimate goal is an altogether happy human being in an altogether good city. However, in reality, the result is not 'more human environments' but 'alienation'. 'Life in paradise is safe but boring, and it turns us into sleepwalkers' writes anthropologist Thomas Hylland Eriksen and continues: 'Maybe you could say that the opposite of happiness is boredom?' (2008: 208).

José Luis Ramirez (1995), planning theorist and professor of rhetoric, has noted how urban planners more or less have lost a certain kind of knowledge, a wisdom or judgment that Aristotle termed phronēsis. Phronēsis is knowledge that is independent of fixed rules for the assessment of individual cases. In other words, it takes into account the context. This type of knowledge has been overlooked in modern society; it has been squeezed out by the dominance of the scientific method. However, it is an 'essential political virtue' in planning (Ramirez 1995: 379): 'Phronēsis is the ability to put our instrumental acts in a human context without letting the trees obscure the forest and the individual events repress meaning'.

An interesting parallel can be drawn between planners' and parents' responsibility. As moral philosopher Hans Jonas (1984: 101) points out, there are similarities between parental and political responsibility. The object of parental responsibility is '[t]he child as a whole and in all its possibilities, not only in its immediate needs'. He continues:

The bodily aspect comes first, of course, in the beginning perhaps solely; but then more and more is added, all that which falls under 'education' in the broadest sense: faculties, conduct, relation, character, knowledge, which have to be stimulated and guided in their development; and together with these also, if possible, happiness. In brief: the pure being as such, and then the best being of the child, is what parental care is about. (Ibid.)

Likewise, the object of political responsibility is the state as a whole – not merely its different parts or functions. And as for the city planner; she must see to the city as a whole, not only as its basic functions of dwelling, work, recreation and transportation. In short, the city must be made liveable, and just like raising a child, this is a challenge.

To connect directly back to psycho-analysis, the analysand seeks the analyst's help because she has long ignored the bigger picture; the balance between the id and the superego, desire and conscience, passion and duty, is disturbed. One of the consequences that can come from the repression of the desire dimension in favour of the need dimension is that we estrange ourselves from our experiences. And estrangement is another word for alienation (von Wright 1986: 31). Therefore, we now turn to this subject.

The Problem of Alienation – Part I

The failure of modern society lies in our alienation. (Wander 2007: ix)

Most often, we do not have any well-developed concepts for that which torments us. [For example] [v]ery few people have a well-thought-out concept of boredom. It is usually a blank label applied to everything that fails to grasp one's interest. Boredom is first and foremost something we live with, not so much something we think about systematically. (Svendsen 2005: 8)

Alienation is a type of neurosis. Alienation can partly be seen as a social problem, partly as an individual problem. Although the distinction may be relevant for scientific analysis, it is somewhat misleading, because society and the individual are two sides of the same coin. Still, it is in the body of the individual, the single one, where this condition is played out, and it bears a resemblance to what I have so far described as boredom.

But why not be content to speak of boredom? Why raise the issue of alienation? Isn't alienation a fairly obsolete problem? Svendsen (2005: 36) has expressed this view, and he is probably not alone in rejecting the concept of alienation. This rejection avoids alienation's political associations, even though recent discourse of boredom and melancholy are based on previous reflections on the subject (Goodstein 2004: 353). Alienation as a concept, we might say, has become out of fashion. However, this tells me that we ought to discuss it. Today's planners and architects are aware of the mistakes of their modernist predecessors; urban planning in the Western, post-war world, has spawned alienating environments – this they know well. As I highlighted when commenting on *The Sociotope Map*, it has become more or less standard procedure to apply a 'social' perspective in urban planning today. But since this is a psycho-analytically inspired critique, I keep a sceptical distance from planners' statements (like 'we have left modernism behind us') and instead try to get hold of the taken-for-granted rules behind them. And these rules are of a nature that encourages reification – a process that is closely associated with alienation (Goodstein 2004: 416).

The idea that an individual is alienated implies two things. First, there is a conflict between society and the individual; a part of the individual's desires must give way for a society to be possible at all. In psycho-analytic terms, it is only through sublimation and/or displacement of the individual's primary instincts that she can adapt socially (Freud 2002, Marcuse 1955, Brown 1959). Secondly, the concept implies that the individual must be alienated from something (Israel 1971: 11). So what is it that she has become alienated from? Or formulated into a more active question: What is it she has alienated herself from? The answer is her own experience, which in turn is strongly linked to the body, the body's (more or less unconscious) desires. In the case of urban planning, Homo Faber (the planner) represses Homo Ludens (the *flâneur*). From the perspective of the former, play – or *flânerie* – is redundant; it has no purpose outside of itself.

Alienation – like most neuroses – is a consequence of an imbalance between the forces in the human psyche. It is a result of an over-reaching repression of the body, of Homo Ludens' desire for play. As Nietzsche (1986a: §57) writes in a discussion on the topic of morality, 'Is it not clear that … man loves *something of himself*, an idea, a desire, an offspring, more than *something else of himself*, that he thus *divides* his nature and sacrifices one part of it to the other?' And he continues: 'In morality, man treats himself not as *individuum* but as *dividuum*' (ibid.).

This view of morality is in line with psycho-analysis (Freud 2002: 103), which sees many of society's moral demands as non-psychological (which, however, is not the same as saying that they should be eliminated). Weber (1994: 365) argues that one of the conditions for success in politics is that 'things must be emptied and made into matters-of-fact (*Versachlichung*), and the following must undergo spiritual proletarianisation, in order to achieve "discipline"'. Nietzsche, and later Foucault, found moralism problematic because it implies subjection to the codes, regulations and standards to which we are linked through fear and guilt (Rose 1999: 96). Consciousness is a field where different parts of the ego fight each other; the ego is the scene in which the moral life drama unfolds, where different and conflicting impulses are struggling against each other (Vattimo 1997: 70f).

Here we posit that the two basic conditions of alienation – the society/individual conflict and the repression of a part of the self – are interrelated. Basically, these are the same conflicts, for where is the individual/society conflict manifested if not in the individual, in her body? Although society has an objective existence in the form of urban areas, government buildings, schools and churches, the idea of society is not located anywhere else than in ourselves. Hence, with the terminology of psycho-analysis, we can translate the society/individual conflict as a conflict between the superego and the id.

Israel (1971: 12) notes that different theories of alienation suggest different types of solutions. The problem is the same – incompatible demands – but depending on where we put the emphasis, we see different solutions. If we see alienation as created by social processes, the problem concerns how to *change society*. On the other hand, if alienation is seen as caused by human behaviour, *social adjustment* becomes the solution. However, I reject the idea that there *is* a solution to the problem of incompatible demands; incompatibility means incompatibility, period. This is partly what distinguishes psycho-analysis from Marxism: where Marx sees a solution (total societal transformation), Freud sees no solution, but an incompatibility that we must learn to live with (Kalin 1974).[11] 'Psycho-analysis cannot tolerate happy endings; it casts them off the way the body's immunological system casts off transplanted organs. Throughout its history, attempts have been made to change the tragic character of psycho-analysis, and all have failed' (Malcolm 1981: 102). Or in the words of Johansson (2011: 154): 'Society's goal is a kind of happy, carefree and positive person, who rather sees opportunities than obstacles. ... [But] according to psycho-analysis ... there is no life worth the name that does not also involve some degree of mental suffering'.

This does not mean that things cannot improve. As already emphasised, the responsibility for making improvement efforts is ultimately something that belongs to the individual. This idea is also found in Sennett (2008: 107), who argues that the cause (if we for the moment allow ourselves to speak of a 'cause' without further problematisation) behind man's alienation can be found in man himself. The emotional poverty that characterises life in the suburbs is *voluntary*, he holds (ibid.). I would not go so far as to use the word voluntary, since it denies limitations and power asymmetries, but I do agree when Sennett says that it is all too easy to locate the roots of the problem 'at the impersonal, mechanical schemes that have created the economic frame, the abundance of the age' (ibid.). Man, in some sense, has a choice;[12] a responsibility to improve the balance between certainty and ambivalence, between the Apollonian and the Dionysian, if you will. With regard to the formation of the living environment of the city, this responsibility belongs to the planners, to those who in one way or another plays a formal role in the urban planning game.

Here I would like to clarify what type of (ideology) critique psycho-analysis is, and what it is not. First and foremost, it is not a moralistic critique (or, rather:

---

11   One important difference between Marxism and psycho-analysis lies in the fact that while the latter sees a conflict between individual and society, the former sees a conflict *within* society, namely, between existing classes (Israel 1971: 182).

12   Hylland Eriksen (2004: 134; 131) writes, 'When do we choose freely? The answer is: never. But the answer also is: We choose freely within the horizon of the opportunities we see. This horizon is created both objectively and subjectively. ... Belief in the free, individual choice is modern man's biggest life-long lie'.

criticism). To believe this would be a mistake, since it was not against intentional acts and conscious choices that Freud directed his analytical focus. Moralistic criticism is to point out to someone that they have violated a moral rule and broken society's norms on how to act, such as 'thou shalt not lie' or 'thou shalt not commit adultery'. As I explained in the introduction, such a critique is wasted if you share Freud's belief that no one really chooses to make herself miserable. However – and this is the crucial point – Freud holds the analysand *ethically* responsible. For as a result of her own mental activity, she leads an unhappy, limited life. This can be summarised with the help of Jonathan Lear (2005: 62f): 'Freud's criticism is not about *what* [the analysand] decides to do, but *how* she goes about living'.

The purpose of psycho-analysis is to free the analysand's mind from the inaccurate and often unconscious belief that she must continue to think and act in a certain way. For this reason, '[a]nalysis provides one with the greatest possible freedom regarding what one does' (Malcolm 1981: 103, see also Marcuse 1964: 162). It is ultimately the individual who must do the work that psycho-analysis demands: 'Abolition of repression [is] an individual rather than a social task' (King 1972: 159). In fact, work (*Arbeit*) is the essence of Freud's argument (Sjögren 2008: 27). Through relentless inner work we learn to view the outer world in light of the inner world; trading neurotic distortion for sound understanding. However, paradoxically, the freedom that an analysand is working towards is actually what she is hiding from, since with freedom comes responsibility: 'To experience oneself as compelled ... is often a defence against the fear of having to take responsibility for one's actions' (Sandell 1993: 3).

There is also another reason why Freud did not rely on moralistic rules on how to behave. Moralistic rules apply to everyone – they are formulated with regard to the collective. Ethical choices, however, must be made by each and every one of us; we are ultimately alone in this process. In other words, 'There is no advice that would be beneficial to all; everyone must discover for himself how he can achieve salvation' (Freud 2002: 26).

As I noted in Chapter 2, to talk about the eye and body when it comes to urban planning is a way to talk about conceived space and lived space, about the authority that architecture and planning exercises on the *flâneur*'s body, but also about the intellect's repression of the bodily, the sexual, the impassioned. '[A]bstract space ... denies the sensual and the sexual', Lefebvre (1991: 49) writes. The 'normal' rational human is a human cut off from her body – 'a half-crazed creature in a mad world'; a creature that is 'completely adjusted to [her] alienated social reality' (Laing 1967: 47; 119). Ultimately it is a question of society's repression of the individual and of the individual's (in this case the planner's) repression of herself (Brown 1959: 3). My argument, which is made in the spirit of Freud, Nietzsche and Lefebvre, is that this often overlooked power relation, in the long run, leads to alienation and that alienation is a key to understanding my immediate reaction on my first visit in Hammarby Sjöstad – a moment of insight that has taken years to develop into coherent ideas. As Brown's analysis (1959) shows, alienation is exacerbated by sublimation; the channelling of sexual energy into culture, art and beauty. However, and paradoxically, it is precisely art works in public space, beautiful forms and facades, that planners are investing in to make the urban environment 'more human'.

City planning is an activity in which the superego has run amok, falling into its own trap. Due to the superego's desire to avoid the irrational and the chaotic, it has more or less overdosed the rational and the orderly, so much that it can be diagnosed as neurotic. This insight – on a general level – is summarised by Laing (1967: 50): 'We live equally out of our bodies, and out of our minds' (see also Adorno and Horkheimer 1981: 242). For what other conclusion can we draw from Jacobs's verdict on the New Urbanism movement, the one that aims to restore the traditional, lively, European city: The urban areas created by New Urbanism are 'hopelessly suburban', she says and continues: 'They only create what they say they hate' (in Goldberger 2006, see also Harvey 2003: 169–73).

If we are to believe Adorno and Horkheimer (1981), it is the transformation of increased knowledge into stupidity that is the essential paradox of history. And Olsson (1991: 61) teaches us that this paradox is inherent in the logic of human action. But to demonstrate this paradox is a project that can provoke resistance; it is to talk about the taboo. Using Freud's and Nietzsche's works to look beneath the history of our decisions means partaking in the forbidden, and to communicate this experience is problematic because it shows an unflattering picture of ourselves. We generally find it easier to defend ourselves against threats from the outside than to accept that we are sometimes our own worst enemy (Freud 2002: 29f, Ricoeur 1970: 293). Accepting psycho-analysis is not an intellectual but affective challenge (Freud 2008: 267, see also Turkle 1981: 27). If the feelings of the listener are alienated, there is no basis for understanding.[13]

The risk of psycho-analysis is in what it reveals: 'When our eyes are open, and the fig leaf no longer conceals our nakedness, our present situation is experienced in its full concrete actuality as a tragic crisis' (Brown 1959: xii). The advent of psycho-analysis meant a relaxation of the clear boundary that existed in psychiatry between the (normal) doctor and the (sick) patient: 'Freud's theory makes it hard to draw such lines by insisting that if the psychiatrist knew himself better, he would find more points in common with the patient than he might have thought' (Turkle 1981: 28, see also Roazen 1979: 185). Hence, psycho-analysis meant a kind of Copernican revolution (Malcolm 1981: 22f).

Norman O. Brown is a thinker who combines Freud's theories with Nietzsche's radicalism. Described by historian Richard H. King (1972: 159) as 'a messenger from Freud to contemporary man', Brown (1959) argues that Freud *encourages*

---

13 Susan Sontag has interestingly noted that resistance to psycho-analytic ideas seems especially strong in Sweden. At a visit she was surprised by the fact that Swedes, who generally are so self-conscious, 'are remarkably unpsychological. Psychiatry ... in any of the forms that stem from Freud ... has never taken root here' (Daun 2005: 47). This is not entirely true. A careful mapping of the influence of psycho-analysis in Sweden has been made by Per Magnus Johansson in *Freuds psykoanalys* (four volumes in Swedish).

sublimation and the disciplining of the body, which can only lead to a worsening of the condition because then we end up being alienated from life and from our own bodies. Culture and the development of civilization rest on sublimation and are thus necessary and inevitable; however, this does not lead to a harmonious state but, rather, to neurosis, Brown holds.

Connecting these ideas to planning, the implicit goal of 'city-like' building is to avoid the alienation of suburbia. '[Hammarby Sjöstad] will not be confused with suburbia or an independent satellite community!' exclaims one of the architects (*BoStad02* 2002: 76). The contradiction between society and the individual is something that many experience but few of us put into words – not even to ourselves. For as the case with everything that is important and everything that comes really close to us, this conflict has been sealed with the silence of the taboo (Olsson 1980c: 17). Planning in a welfare state like Sweden means 'promoting a good living environment for all citizens and to promote human progress' (Strömgren 2007: 246); no wonder we are filled with guilt when we experience a discomfort even though everything around us is created to meet our needs! Or is the discomfort *because* everything should meet our needs? Here we can recall what Plato (1991: §420) says in *The Republic*: '[I]n founding the city we are not looking to the exceptional happiness of any one group among us but, as far as possible, that of the city as a whole'. But, again, the idea that a society isn't created to provide exceptional happiness is taboo; '[w]e refuse to recognize it at all', that is, the idea that the 'institutions that we ourselves have created [cannot] protect and benefit us all' (Freud 2002: 29).

The fact that our institutions cannot protect and benefit us all – is it because the planners are spiteful? As the reader by now has understood, this is not how I choose to see it because I am not looking for a scapegoat with evil intentions. Planners, like everyone else, are governed by a web of societal norms that they themselves may not even be conscious of. '[N]o one has done anything but followed one's own and one's culture's internalized reasoning and behavior rules' (Olsson 1980c: 20). Here we find ourselves again at Kant's and Nietzsche's subject-centred epistemology; it is in our understanding of the nature of the planners' actions that the problem rests. Speaking of the inability of our institutions to satisfy the individual, Freud (2002: 29f) notes that it is precisely this kind of suffering that we have been unsuccessful at preventing. And considering this, we can no longer hold back the suspicion that 'here too an element of unconquerable nature may be at work in the background – this time our own psyche' (ibid.).

Perspectivism, again, teaches us that what is good for me is not necessarily good for you, even if I act upon the belief that it is. Our experts, Lefebvre (1995: 118) writes, have their hearts in the right place. Aristotle gave insight into this idea in *Nichomachean Ethics* (2013 Book III, part 1), writing that 'it is for [the pleasant and noble objects] that all men do everything they do', but – 'of what he is doing a man might be ignorant'. And the philosopher Epictetus said that we should distinguish between situations that depend on us and those that do not depend on us, for we can only be held responsible for what we do with one hundred per cent awareness (Thom 1979a: 11). But as Thom (ibid.) points out, this division is too simplistic – unawareness of the consequences of our actions does not automatically excuse us from responsibility. The world is full of situations where we cannot be sure of the consequences of our actions. And he adds: 'Who has not, in offering an excuse, uttered words which in fact, worsened the blunder?' (ibid.: 11f).

In the next section, we make a closer encounter with the problem of sublimation – a mental activity that is related to the defence mechanism of repression (Brenner 1970: 91f) and which is helpful when it comes to understanding alienation and the neurosis of urban planning.

Animal Sublimans

> To approach a city, or even a city neighborhood, as if it were a larger architectural problem, capable of being given order by converting it into a disciplined work of art, is to make the mistake of attempting to substitute art for life. (Jacobs 1992: 373)

> Sublimations satisfy the instincts to the same degree as maps satisfy the desire to travel. (Brown 1959: 168)

The planner's world is a world of conventional logic, architectural beauty and artistic transcendence. Very little room is given to the body and to the dialectic. In Chapter 7 we will look closer at the question of logic and dialectics; for now, let me just stress that architecture is an art form that emphasises Apollonian form and visual order. Apollo urges us not to be too much, to respect boundaries, to fear authority figures, to bow to the divine (Brown 1959: 174). Therefore, Apollonian form is a form that denies matter; it is an immortal form that escapes death and the bodily. Architecture is an example of sublimation, a creation of symbols of symbols, a weaving of a flattering veil over life's ugliness. All of this makes the architect the ultimate example of an *animal sublimans* (Brown 1959: 167), a creature who, through her desire for transcendence, beauty and refinement, creates a distance from the body, from life. For philosopher Arthur Schopenhauer, for example, art and the contemplation of art works was a way to escape life; something that made it possible to escape the troubled life's will, the body's desires and pains, and to find peace outside time and space (Berg Eriksen 2005: 166). This is the role of sublimation.

The architect creates *symbols of* urbanity – not urbanity itself – and thereby frustrating what she says that she wants to create. We find traces of this argument in Jacobs (1992: 372): '[A]lthough art and life are inter-woven, they are not the same things. Confusion between them is, in part, why efforts at city design are so disappointing'. And the artistic process can be defined with the help of Berg Eriksen (2005: 166) as 'a disciplined, rigorous discernment of that which is *not* life. In relation to life's changing and literally endless entanglements, art is limited, symbolic and abstract'. Enlightening in this context is the fact that Dionysus is the god who traditionally embodies what has been lost (Seaford 2006: 146). To suffer from boredom, according to the poet Fernando Pessoa, is 'like having the drawbridge over the moat round the castle of our soul suddenly raised, so that there is no longer any connection between the castle and the surrounding land' (interpreted by Svendsen 2005: 44).

The urban is something that I, with the help of Woolf and Strindberg among others, so far have portrayed as a kind of synonym for life itself. And if architecture is about *symbolising* life – about creating a distance from and thus escaping life – it seems reasonable to assume that architecture has very little to do with urbanity. Rather, it is alienation-inducing. Yet, we must ask ourselves this: Isn't the role of art to act as a *cure* for the alienation of modern man? This was at least how the Romantic writer Friedrich Schiller saw it (Megill 1985: 13).[14] But, as we learn from Heidegger (1977: 34), art in the modern world has lost this function; art has become an object among others, subordinated to the will of man.

In modern society, man's relationship to art is sorted under aesthetics. That is to say, art has become 'yet another post-Cartesian science', to borrow Megill's (1985: 144) words. Increasingly confined into the realm of aesthetics, art is mainly an object, no longer allowed to appear in its entirety as a part of life and being (ibid.). Here we can recall what Carse (1986: §44) writes: 'Art is not art ... except as it leads to an engendering creativity in its beholders. Whoever takes possession of the objects of art has not taken possession of the art'. This could be an explanation as to why modern architecture does not prevent, but facilitates, alienation.

A related explanation is that architecture is an Apollonian art form that by definition draws lines, boundaries, and these separations cause alienation. The architect shapes the physical environment on the basis of her analysis of what kind of life should be lived in this environment; it is not only the rooms that are separated from each other but life activities as well. And separation is what alienation is all about. Perhaps it is more likely, then, that the art forms of Dionysus – that is, poetry, music and dance – can counteract alienation? According to philosopher Espen Hammer (2006: 101), this is at least what Schopenhauer and Bataille believed: 'By identifying with the music, one can reach a point where the self, the sense of being a separate individual, ceases and one believes that one has "become one" with the tunes'. In such situations, an excess takes place, which belongs in the domain of 'intoxication, sexuality and madness' (ibid.), but also – I would add – to the domain of the festival, of the urban.

---

14   In brief, Schiller argued that man has two fundamental drives: one sensuous and one related to the desire to delineate and give form. The first seeks perpetual change, the other uniformity and persistence. To prevent the first from intruding upon the ethical sphere, and the second upon the emotional, both must be kept in place, and this is done through a third drive: the drive for play. It is this drive that makes man a free being, and the home of this drive is *art* (Megill 1985: 13).

Sublimation is an activity that man has engaged in since the first cities were founded – an activity by which the soul has done away with the body. But what was once repressed does not disappear; it haunts us with an ever-increasing power, creating in the end a neurotic, anxiety-filled and alienated state. No wonder Freud said that civilization makes us discontent! We have created for ourselves an orderly, Apollonian world, which, like the dream, installs a veil between us and life. We keep life and the body at a distance – something that makes us socially adapted but unsatisfied, frustrated. To create 'more humane' cities, planners are engaging even more in sublimation and focus even more on the beauty apparent to the eye. If we are to believe Brown (1959: 307), this only worsens the condition. Jacobs (1992: 373) seems to share this view: 'The results impoverish life instead of enriching it', she writes. The solution, according to Brown (1959), must lie in an alternative to sublimation – in Apollo's opposite: Dionysus. Dionysus is a symbol of the ego – or rather the body ego, which, according to Freud (1995: 636f), is the original ego. This is the reality that psycho-analysis finds behind the veil. 'Dionysus is not dream but drunkenness; not life kept at a distance and seen through a veil but life complete and immediate … Dionysus does not observe the limit, but overflows' (Brown 1959: 175).

But to eliminate all repression and give in to the Dionysian altogether would neither be realistic nor desirable because then we face pure madness. According to Brown (1959: 175), the solution is not found in a synthesis of the Apollonian and the Dionysian. But how else can we live if not by reaching (or striving for) a balance between them, I wonder? To seek this balance is – briefly put – what both dialectics and psycho-analysis are about. The effort that these traditions (the dialectic and the psycho-analytic) are making to exceed conventionally sustained boundaries – whether in society or in the conceptual-cognitive sphere of logic –makes it possible to see them as opposites to a largely soul-less and bureaucratic contemporary culture. Jacobs's 'solution' to this problem, according to my interpretation, is in line with Brown's, but it also bears traces of the kind of approach represented by space syntax, to which we soon will turn Jacobs (1992: 375) writes,

> Instead of attempting to substitute art for life, city designers should return to a strategy ennobling both to art and to life: a strategy of illuminating and clarifying life and helping to explain to us its meanings and orders – in this case, helping to illuminate, clarify and explain the order of cities.

Evidently, Jacobs is not critical of planning per se. Rather, she puts her hope on a different type of design than that which she describes in the introduction to her book. In light of these ideas, let us refine our analysis of the activity of urban planning.

Is Planning Always Destructive to Urbanity?

> The failure of realized utopias of spatial form can just as reasonably be attributed to the processes mobilized to materialize them as to failures of spatial form *per se*. (Harvey 2003: 173)

> [T]here are cities, or parts of cities that are different from others by being architectural, and ... the reason they are different is that they are the products of individuals with a certain disposition that can be called architectural knowledge ... (Marcus 2000b: 16)

So far I have presented arguments that urban planning has a destructive impact on the urban; the planner's conceived space dominates the lived space of the *flâneur*. But this raises an important question: Does it mean that planning is always anti-urban? As Reuben Rose-Redwood (2006) has pointed out in an attempt to nuance Lefebvre's conceived-lived-space-dichotomy, there is no inherent contradiction between Cartesian, rational, conceived space, on the one hand, and lived, urban space, on the other: '[W]hile repressive in numerous ways [the production of abstract space] establishes the epistemological basis not only for state-centred disciplinary projects; it also provides a system of orientation, or frame of reference, for the "population at large"' (ibid.: 49f). Here we can take the example of the Manhattan grid from 1811. This greatly rationalised space with rectangular blocks and logical numbering has facilitated the most thriving urban life. Hence, it is not this type of planning and organising that seems threatening to urbanity – on the contrary. But this type of planning is different from that which we have hitherto discussed, the type advocated by those indoctrinated by functionalism and whose moralising attitude controls and adjusts what will happen in a particular space.

In order to further explain what I mean, I turn to architectural theorist Christopher Alexander's (1965) distinction between *natural* and *artificial* cities. Natural cities have arisen more or less spontaneously over many years. Artificial cities, however, have been deliberately created by planners. Manhattan, which I just mentioned, is an example of a natural city, while Brasilia can be classified as artificial. But wait a minute... Is not Manhattan exceptionally artificial with its rectangular grid, measured out by ruler and compass? Why, then, categorise it as natural? Because the content of the grid system has evolved gradually over many years. What the grid was to include – besides a capitalist society – was not involved in the plan (Ballon 2012, Marcus 2000b: 15, Bergman 1985, Andersson 2010a). It was simply not in the planners' interest to determine what types of activities that would take place where. So the difference between artificial and natural cities is to be found in the way they are planned – or, more precisely, in the planners' attitude or motive.

The creators of Brasilia can easily be pinpointed: Lúcio Costa designed the plan, Oscar Niemeyer most of the public buildings and Roberto Burle Marx was responsible for the landscape design. The grid constructors of Manhattan, however, are anonymous to most of us; their perspective differed from the aforementioned; they were not interested in micromanaging what would happen where. They did not – as Costa, Niemeyer and Burle Marx – set out to make an individual (artistic) imprint but to ensure that everyone who wanted and could afford to build a house or a business on Manhattan could do so. So they established boundaries – nothing more. In this regard, the Manhattan grid designers were like the *horistei* behind the ancient cities of Greece; *horistes* means 'the one who draws boundaries' (Marcus 2000b: 15). Planners like Costa, however, have a moral purpose with their plans; they want to control life in the city.

We can find another illustration of the difference between natural and artificial cities if we compare the inner and outer parts of Stockholm. The division is rough and does not take into account variations in the respective areas, but it serves its purpose for my particular points here. The knowledge of architecturally influenced urban planning, which started to spread around nineteen-hundred and which has given rise to the suburbs in Stockholm can be contrasted with the planning that dominated the latter half of the nineteenth century. Both the inner and the outer city is planned, but in different ways and for different purposes. Insights into the difference we get in the book *Den ekonomiska staden* (translates into *The Economic City*) by historian Hossein Sheiban (2002). In the nineteenth century, planning in Stockholm served primarily economic purposes, whereas planning from approximately the year 1900 onwards increasingly emphasised social goals. The aesthetic dimension also became more important, as the architects began to participate in planning.

The planners behind the inner parts of Stockholm can be likened to those who laid out the Manhattan grid. The main purpose of the Stockholm plan was to form a seamless system of transit that would facilitate 'movement' (rörelse) – a keyword in the late nineteenth-century urban-planning discussions (Sheiban 2002: 63). 'Movement' (*rörelsen*) referred to the circulation of money and supplies, consumers and producers, but it was also a generic term for all economic activity; it referred to the cycle of capital from investment to accumulation (ibid.: 48; 85).[15] The city laid out the city plan; it established boundaries between public streets, squares and quays, on the one hand, and private land, on the other. The implementation of the city plan was financed by selling pieces of land to private individuals and enterprises. For property developers to become interested there had to be connections (streets) to other parts of the city, or else one's property could not

---

15 Stockholm was not the only city whose structure was changed in order to facilitate the movement of pedestrians and horse carriages. As Penelope Corfield (1990: 147) notes, the cities in England during the eighteenth century were built according to this principle: 'A successful city life drew sustenance from good communications, so the residents and municipalities devoted much attention to sustaining access and mobility ... Numerous specialist occupations were developed to assist the flow of people and vehicles'. Twentieth-century planners (e.g. Le Corbusier) also wanted to facilitate 'movement' but with the intention of separating motor traffic from other kinds of traffic.

be reached by the 'movement', by capital. The street system in the inner parts of Stockholm, thus, was the artery of capital; it provided the various 'body parts' (properties) with 'oxygen' (consumers/producers). What can be called a side effect of this rigorous economical planning we witness today: well integrated and well used public space offering a wide range of activities and services. In other words: urbanity. Here we can remember geographer William William-Olsson's conclusion (1934: 34) that businesses do not seek out an area in the wider sense but 'particular streets'. Good locations for business, he noted, are sites that have good connections and good contact with the public. And this was exactly what the nineteenth-century urban planners wanted to create. Thus, the highly elusive urban atmosphere that is so sought after today – for various social and cultural and not only economic reasons – was an (unintended) side effect of a quite crude economic planning.

In contrast to the strict economic rationality of the nineteenth century, twentieth-century urban planning strove to 'promote a healthy environment for all citizens and to promote human progress' (Strömgren 2007: 246). As Sheiban (2002: 120ff) describes, more and more at the end of the nineteenth century, the aim began to be to protect the 'public interest' through regulations of various kinds. Again, we must consider the planner's viewpoint in order to understand the difference between nineteenth- and twentieth-century urban planning, in relation to that between natural and artificial cities. The planners behind Stockholm's inner city wanted to facilitate movement so that they could sell blocks of land to various property owners. Thus, they invited a variety of people and perspectives into the process of forming what will happen in the city. This type of planning by definition expresses a multitude of viewpoints, and what gives the city its eventual form are the building processes that start from the point of view of each and every one who participates in the building of the city('s content) (see Marcus 2000b: 15). Here we find the difference between a single building and a city.

> [B]y definition, a building must be the spatial articulation of one actor – even if this actor is not necessarily an individual person but a judicial person of some kind ... A city, on the other hand, is the spatial articulation of the actions of many actors, since we normally cannot identify any distinct individual actor as [in the case with the building], even though a perusal of history books will provide us with many aspirants – both tyrants and democrats – with such ambitions. (Marcus 2000b: 87)

Understanding the type of environment that this type of planning produces, we can use Marx's metaphor of the beehive or the spider web (see Merrifield 2006: 66). We can also look to Lefebvre's (1995: 116) analogy of the seashell:

> The thing is that men have two different ways of creating and producing, and as yet these have not intersected: spontaneous vitality, and abstraction. On the one hand, in pleasure and in play; on the other, in seriousness, patience and painful

consciousness, in toil. Might not the same be true of towns, those products of social living? (Lefebvre 1995: 125)

In the case of Stockholm, the focus of suburban twentieth-century planning has been on whole neighbourhoods at a time; planning has been large in scale and formulated from more or less one single viewpoint – the experts'. What determines the city's form and content in this case is the planners' view of the good city. The distribution of functions has thus been a conscious process – not something that has occurred more or less spontaneously over time by a variety of actors. This meticulous type of planning can be seen as a conscious desire to reproduce social values and to minimise differences. This, in turn, may be connected to the tendency of architects to treat the city as if it were a house, which serves the private life. And in some ways, the city is like a large house, the Renaissance architect Alberti claimed (Marcus 2000b: 198). But – as it reads when Marcus (ibid.) ends his book *Architectural Knowledge and Urban Form*: '[T]his is far from an innocent proposition'.

Chapter 4
The Impossible Profession

Our task now is to construct everyday life, to produce it, consciously to create it. ...
The new town is a challenge to men to create human life! ... But no one should say
that it's an easy task!

Henri Lefebvre

An assumption of this book is that the *flâneur* – not the planner – is the 'real'
expert on the urban. This is because she relates to this phenomenon in a concrete –
not abstract – way. The urban is the main focus of her awareness; it is her home,
her salvation. The *flâneur* lives and breathes the city; she takes it in in an unsorted
way with all her senses. In contrast, the planner – who faces the challenge to create
urbanity – by necessity has a different approach. As we saw in Chapter 2, her
perspective is visual and characterised by distance. The urban becomes something
abstract – an idea or an image for the mind's eye. And the architect translates this
idea into form before it is projected onto reality. So when I placed the planner's
perspective alongside that of the *flâneur*, it became clear that they differed
widely. While the *flâneur* appreciates the jumble of audio-visual impressions and
unexpected discoveries in crowded places, the planner puts emphasis on order,
harmony, beauty in form, friendly expanses and uninterrupted lines of sight.
Furthermore, to the *flâneur*, the potential danger of the city is part of its allure. The
planner, on the other hand, seeks to eliminate this element and create a peaceful
living environment characterised by stillness, light and greenery. This is hardly
surprising, I also noted, since the architect is part of a tradition that harbours and
cultivates precisely this kind of Apollonian attitude, and it does so in a largely
wordless, unconscious way.

The planner is the right arm of politics (Olsson 1985). She is to implement
politically formulated goals; to translate ideals into tangible reality. In fact,
being fundamentally political, planning is one of the three professions that Freud
(1976) characterised as impossible. That is, professions in which you can be sure
to achieve unsatisfactory results (the other two being education[1] and psycho-
analysis). This view finds support in a quote from the architect Ivar Tengbom
in 1911 (in Eriksson 2001: 172): 'There are so many interrelated factors to take
into account that the art of city planning stands out as the most demanding of all
the arts; it is the sum of all architectural experience and knowledge'.

---

1 For an interesting psycho-analytical reflection on education, with focus on
transference, see Finkel and Arney (1995).

In everyday speech, a profession is synonymous with occupation, but if we look at its more precise definition we see that profession refers to an occupation based on 'scientific knowledge and proven experience' (Lundequist 1991: 64). Its purpose is to offer society specialised services and sound advice. Urban planning is a profession (whether you are trained as an architect, a social scientist or an engineer). However, as the present study has shown, there is something rather arbitrary about planners' ideas of how to implement the goal of urbanity. First, there is confusion as to what the term urbanity, or city-like, really means. This frequently used word has, in fact, proved to be 'one of the popular clichés of planning rhetoric' (Svensson 2004: 77); it is used 'routinely and without thought in almost every planning project' (Lundström 2002: 4, see also Marcus 1998, Westin 2005a). Nevertheless, it is a beacon – not only for the majority of today's urban planning projects but also for the education of planners. The fact that 'city-like' is both undefined and widespread is a frequent target of criticism (see Marcus 1998). However, this is hardly surprising, for as Gunnar Fredriksson (1992) has pointed out in his analysis of the language of politics, preservation of ambiguities is the very prerequisite of political agreement. Planning, as Gunder and Hillier (2009: 2) write, is made up of 'empty signifiers'; that is, '"comfort terms" ... meaning everything and nothing'; ideas that mean 'all things to all people'.

Secondly, it seems that planners do not really know how to build in order to create urbanity (if we, for the moment, agree to the meaning of urbanity as a kind of function or atmosphere most often found in city environments built roughly before the twentieth century). Just agreeing on the elements of urbanity is a challenge. 'Urbanity means streets on four sides and closed blocks', one planner may say. 'We don't want to do this', says another. 'Many people think that it is varied content that creates urbanity. But this is wrong', says a third, arguing instead that 'it is all about street axes and clear place formations'. As we have seen, common solutions to the problem of trying to create urbanity have been to strive for density and to design buildings and public spaces so that they demonstrate a visual resemblance to the inner city. Materials and details of design are here seen as important tools in promoting an urban atmosphere. We have also seen how planners rename streets and places, ensuring that the project carries the word 'city' (Hammarby Sjö*stad* literally means Hammarby Lake *City*). In sum, we see here how the planners put their trust in various *symbols* when trying to implement the goal of creating urbanity (see also Jacobs 1992: 13).

To an outsider with a critical eye, this modus operandi, which is a form of manipulation, may indeed seem foolish and unwise. But even if the planners' ideas about what creates urbanity have more in common with wishful or magical thinking than with empirically grounded knowledge, we are hardly helped by categorising the ideas as delusions – at least not if we stop at this judgement. Again, if we want to find the key to the planners' mistakes, we need to look for it in their ways of reasoning; in their artistic-visual, Apollonian ethical outlook.[2]

---

2   That architects tend to regard themselves as artists is testified by Linn (1998: 48), Schorske (1981: 71), Sternudd (2007: 138) and Zumthor (2005: 19). There are, however,

Leone Battista Alberti, an artist who has had a great influence on architecture and urban planning (Choay 1997), declared that the task of the Renaissance artist was to create some kind of illusion. More precisely, the artist should

> draw with lines and paint in colors on a surface any given bodies, in such a way that at a fixed distance and with a certain determined position ... whatever you represent will *seem to* stand out in relief and exactly to resemble the bodies in question and in the same relief. (Alberti in Olsson 2007: 130f)

Good art should thus strive to be effective by being affective, seem real rather than be real (Olsson 2007: 131, see also Cassirer 2005: 141f). And Alberti was an artist who was not content with interpreting the world – he wanted to change it, too. In light of this insight, the planners' actions do not seem arbitrary. On the contrary; from the frame of reference of the Renaissance artist, it appears rational to trust the power of symbols when trying to invoke an atmosphere or a feeling – in this case, a vibrant urban atmosphere. But, wait! What about basing one's actions on scientific knowledge and proven experience, which we saw is the requirement of a profession? If the artistic dimension is allowed to play such a large role in the architecture and planning profession, and if the artistic sphere is a sphere where it is impossible to maintain any 'objectivity claims' (Cassirer 2005: 141), can we still speak of it as a profession – like, for example, the medical profession?

The status of architecture in society is dual. It is a 'social art'[3] meant for utility and social improvement as well as to promote beauty (Lundequist 1989: 91). It is both a profession and an art form. A profession, we know by now, needs to be based on science, and the task of science – on the most general level – is to describe and depict reality (Molander 1995: 125). But the other side of architecture – which spells art – is about 'showing personal expression and creating new realities' (ibid.).[4] When we refine the double meaning of architecture like this, we see that the latter aspect is hard to reconcile with the former.

'Social art' is a rather curious concept. Hence, it is not surprising to see that there, within the discipline of architecture, exists a kind of chasm between, on the

---

important differences between the artist's and the architect's modus operandi. As pointed out by Sölve Olsson (1989), the artist today (compared to the Middle Ages and the Renaissance) is often her own employer, while the architect is embedded in a context and must proceed from a concrete task, a given place and so on. Nonetheless, the following condition applies to both professions: 'That which is not manufacturing, but design, demands a personal decision; an assessment by one individual' (ibid.: 98).

3 *Nyttokonst* in Swedish, where *nytta* means 'utility' and *konst* means 'art'.

4 In this line of argumentation I rely on an unproblematised division between art and science, but when studied more closely, the boundary starts to erode. 'The sciences began in poetry; in poetry they will conclude', Megill (1985: 17) writes when referring to one of Nietzsche's predecessors, Schelling. For other arguments against a sharp division between the two knowledge spheres, see Berg Eriksen (2005: 325), Granström (2009), Hermodsson (1968: 15), Molander (1995), Olsson (2007) and Seip (1995).

one hand, artistically oriented practitioners, and on the other hand, theoretically oriented researchers. As Östnäs and Werne (1987) have noted, in Swedish architectural education, scientific thinking and systematic knowledge-building is de-prioritised in favour of professional training.[5] And this, of course, has its downsides: 'The lack of specialisation in *any* area of knowledge leads to an uncritical and superficial approach to knowledge in general, and not infrequently to a contempt for knowledge among the students' (ibid.: 27). The emphasis on artistic design encourages a release from external criteria and standards and stimulates instead the creation of one's 'own' criteria (although all individuals are influenced by role models/teachers – especially, it seems, students of architecture). The knowledge imparted to students is largely tacit and intuitive: 'Teaching is mixed with a development of taste, and in this process it is very difficult to separate one aspect from another – this applies to the discerning teacher as well' (Sternudd 2007: 150). As Habraken (2005: 1) puts it, 'We know, deep down, when form is good'. Silent, intuitive knowledge thus plays a critical role in professional practice, and this is why Lundequist (1991) calls the profession of architecture 'incomplete' (*ofullgången*).

But, someone might ask, isn't functionalism – the planning ideology that still characterises much of today's planning – scientifically based? In their manifesto from 1931, the functionalists speak warmly of the need to study cities scientifically, objectively, rationally (Asplund et al. 2008). Their faith in the ability of science to create a good life is well documented (see Franzén and Sandstedt 1993: 145): 'Go to the root of the problems; study the mathematics, statics, logic of urban planning' Åhrén (1928: 175) declares. But as Choay (1997), Hillier (1996: 65ff), Jacobs (1992) and Rådberg (1997) have argued, the claim that modernism is based on science is a myth. The empirical studies that back modernist design principles focus almost exclusively on the home and on housework. Moreover, attention was on how cities ought to function, not how they actually function. The kind of logical analysis made was a dissection of the problem of the city into four different categories: dwelling, work, recreation and transport, whereby these were used in the construction of new (versions of) cities. Science was primarily something the functionalists alluded to in order to gain support for their ideas. Logic was used as an effective rhetorical tool – a smokescreen, if you will – to hide a (much more arbitrary) artistic vision and a moralising ideology.

That the artistic perspective – not the scientific-theoretical – is most prevalent in the eduction of architects is hardly surprising when considering that it is the oldest. Architecture has been studied as an academic discipline since the Renaissance, and up to the end of the nineteenth century its nature has been more or less purely artistic. Thereafter, society's view of architecture and the architects' position was affected by rapid technological development. In Stockholm, architectural education was moved in 1877 from the Academy of Fine Arts to the

---

5   This, however, does not mean that professional training in Swedish architectural schools is satisfactory. On the contrary, if we are to believe Sternudd (2007: 151).

Royal Institute of Technology (KTH). It was believed that the architect's social status would increase if she (or, rather, he) was trained at a scientific institution (Östnäs and Werne 1987: 23). However, the move was not without controversies; the discussion of whether architecture belongs to the sphere of art or science continues to this day, and both words – art and science – currently appear on KTH's logotype.

Space Syntax – a Revolution?

Bill Hillier is a researcher who, since the 1970s, has been committed to developing the scientific perspective and making architecture into a complete profession. Together with his colleagues at the Bartlett School of Architecture in London, most notably, Julienne Hanson, he has developed the research paradigm of space syntax. What Hillier has done is to take note of the following: If architecture is an art, if it is a language that speaks to us humans, it is vague and polyphonic (Torsson 1995: 39). It speaks not only to the eye but also to the body. By their very existence buildings affect where we can and cannot go. And because people's movements are crucial for how cities function – in this case how cities are used – this is of great interest if we want to learn more about the relation between urban form and urban life, between space and society. For if we study this relationship, the message reads, we can become better at using architecture as a means to achieve social goals.

Here we can see that space syntax means a revolution. Architecture and planning will continue to act as an extension of politics – space syntax does not aim at changing this. What is new is the moving of focus from the eye to the body; from what the built environment signifies to what it does. Or, formulated in another way, focus is put on architecture's performative side rather than its representative side (Marcus and Koch 2005). For as we already have concluded, architecture since the Renaissance has focused on the visual. From their 'silent offices' (Lefebvre 1991: 6), the modernist architects describe their heavy concrete buildings as floating and likened their walls to membranes, as if the buildings did not have anything to do with physicality. As if they did not affect people in their daily lives. As if it was only through our eyes that architecture would evoke emotion.

Space syntax is a scientific paradigm rooted in a feeling. This feeling can be described as a sense of contradiction between what the eyes observe and what the body experiences. This is how Hillier (in Westin 2011: 232) describes his starting point:

> My starting point was in the 1960s when they were building visually very exciting housing estates. I thought it was the best architecture that had ever been, it was very exciting. And then when you went into the places, you got this terrible sense that life was not worth living. There is something completely

wrong here. And space syntax originated in trying to understand that. That feeling of 'Oh, my God! I can't bare this – this is wrong!'

Lars Marcus, Sweden's most prominent space syntax theorist, also started out with a feeling – a feeling of disappointment and confusion – when he in his doctoral thesis embarked on a study of how the new 'city-like' areas (really) work. His suspicion was that 'city-like' building 'was not what it was said to be, namely, a revival of traditional urban form and its qualities' (Marcus 2000b: 38).[6] If functionalists argued that the functional was the beautiful, it seems that today's architects – Marcus says (2000a) – think that the beautiful is the functional. And he continues: 'Both claims are nonsense and in equal measure threaten architects' credibility' (ibid.).

The theory of space syntax can be seen as a continuation of Jacobs's *The Death and Life of Great American Cities*, a book that seeks to clarify how cities actually work, not how they should work (although the methods used in space syntax are much more technologically advanced). And what is Jacobs's book if not an empiristic-emancipatory manifesto, an Enlightenment-inspired project with intent to expose the 'pseudo-science of city planning' (Jacobs 1992: 12)? Jacobs seems to be motivated by the same ideas as Marcus (2000a) when he writes, 'I simply believe that time has come to discuss the knowledge content of the profession'.

So it is that Hillier and his colleagues have spent the last four decades trying to clarify the relation between the form of the city, on the one hand, and the life of the city, on the other. Briefly put, the aim is to strengthen the knowledge of the performative phase in the architect's work, that is, how the form might function. Architects usually have very good knowledge of the generative phase – the phase where the architect uses her artistic creativity to come up with new solutions (Hillier 2007: 46). Here we can remember what I earlier referred to as the gap between drawing and building; it leaves the architect handicapped because there is no way for her to know how the building in question will be experienced in reality. Space syntax is the first architectural theory to seriously take on the challenge of bridging this gap, and thus – if you will – making the profession complete.

In Chapter 6 we will look more closely at space syntax, but first we need to construct an anchor for the urban.

---

6   Marcus himself does not dwell on the fact that his research is based on a feeling or a subjective experience – this is my reading. As shown by the quotation, he frames it more neutrally.

Chapter 5
Urbanity = ?

[T]he equality sign serves the same function as the anchors of a ship. It grounds our thoughts and actions and keeps them from drifting into obscurity. ... Nobody can do without the sign ... It is the basis of communication.

Gunnar Olsson

What surrounds us we endure better for giving it a name – and moving on.

E.M. Cioran

In the previous chapter, we saw that space syntax started out as a critique of conventional architectural practice. While the majority of practicing architects emphasise the visual-symbolic dimension of the built environment, space syntax means a focus on what the built environment does to the body, how it affects movement. In fact, Hillier's understanding of the urban is close to that of the *flâneur*, and for that matter Lefebvre's; it is in the (moving) crowd of people that the essence of urbanity is to be found – not in roofing materials or façade colours.

Despite these similarities, space syntax is by no means a poetic perspective. Nor (as I will explore in Chapter 7) does it bear any resemblance to Lefebvre's dialectical-Dionysian worldview – on the contrary; being a reaction to what is essentially viewed as artistic and/or political 'fudge' in post-war urban planning, it is a testimonial to the exact expressions of science, to Apollo. Space syntax theorists say we should not base our actions on speculations about how the material dimension will affect the social but instead use empirically based predictions. What forms give rise to urbanity and what forms counteract it? Put another way, what is the relation between the urban, on the one hand, and the buildings, streets and squares that make up the built environment we call the city?[1] The question holds relevance to this book, which explores the gap between the intention of creating urbanity, on the one hand, and the reality imbued with suburban boredom, on the other.

Taking forward the issue of urbanity's physical-spatial conditions means placing urbanity in a scheme of causal inference. To explain is the goal of science, and to explain involves specifying some kind of law, a kind of mediator between cause

---

1   This division between 'the urban' and 'the city' draws on Lefebvre (1996: 103) but is also used by Hillier (2008a) and Vaughan (2007). One important difference between Lefebvre and the latter two is how far they take this division. My use of it resembles that of Lefebvre; I see the division as a provisional arrangement.

and effect (Olsson 1980a: 166b, Liliequist 1997: 9, Giddens 1996, Gullberg 1986). But before we can do this, we must first define the concept of urbanity. An important part of defining is to sort out the ontological status of the phenomenon we want to study, or else we run the risk of screwing in a screw with a hammer. As philosopher Bertrand Russell (1946: 10) points out, the question whether life is 'divided into mind or matter, and, if so, what is mind and what is matter', is the basic philosophical question on which all science implicitly rests but which science itself cannot answer (see also Olsson 1980a: 23e, Gullberg 1986: 83).

So, what is 'urbanity'? Is it a thing? Is it something that exists out there, in the form of tangible objects that you and I can see and touch? Or is it a *not-thing*, an intangible? Is it something that primarily exists *between* people, and *between* people and things, and thus (only) subsists[2] in our consciousness; does it float around and cannot be captured in any other way than through language? Let us assume that the latter is true, that urbanity is a term that denotes the complex web of social relationships that can be summarised in the word urban life. In other words, we are dealing with a social and mental phenomenon – a feeling or an atmosphere – which, with Lefebvre's (1991: 101) help, can be described as an irreducible moment, as 'encounter, assembly, simultaneity'.

However, before we make this jump, we need to be careful categorising urbanity as a *not-thing*. For it gives the impression that it is an independent, transcendent being that floats around freely, regardless of material circumstances. In fact, the opposite is true; the urban is a delicate and fleeting quality that is highly dependent on the physical structure of the city. If the prerequisites for encounter, assembly and simultaneity fail, urban life escapes – modernist-planned cities have made us all too aware of this problem. The city can be described as a 'socio-material field of action', in that the physical environment allows or prevents certain human actions (Østerberg 1990; 2000).

Human geographical research often discusses 'the urban', but any clear definition is seldom given. This raises questions about the meaning of the word; what is its opposite and how is it related to 'the city'? Generally, urban geographers as well as urban sociologists since the 1970s tend to distance themselves from physical space (Franzén 1987: 389, Hetherington 1997: 184). Social scientists are interested in *the urban* – that is, the city as a complex system of human activities and interactions or the city as experience – while architectural theorists are studying *the city* – a collection of buildings connected through space (Nylund 2001, Madanipour 1996). Concisely, we can say that there seems to be both a social city and a physical city and that the various disciplines see the one through the lens of the other (Vaughan 2007).

David Harvey (1989), John R. Short (1984) and Edward Soja (2000) all take a macro-approach to the city with the overall goal of integrating the studies of the urban with a larger analysis of society. Interest in the morphological dimension of

---

2   I use the word 'subsist' as an opposite to 'exist' (see Olsson 1980a). Ideas and meanings subsist, i.e. they are not tangible, while things and signs exist – they are tangible.

the city was greater in geography before the 1970s, with William William-Olsson (1934) and Lennart Améen (1964) as Swedish examples. Economic geographer William-Olsson studied retail structure in Stockholm and he noted – among other things – that retail concentration in a city is controlled by two factors: population density and residents' income. As mentioned before, when he analysed the exact location of businesses, he found that businesses do not seek out an area in the wider sense; they seek out particular streets (William-Olsson 1934: 34). The inner differentiation of Stockholm is controlled by a competition for positions, and the location meant 'not only a coordinate on the map but a collection of a place's characteristics' (ibid.: 40). Two important place characteristics for businesses, he stated, are good connections (to other places) and good contact with the public (availability). As we will see, this is something that space syntax also acknowledges (although without reference to William-Olsson). Few geographers, however, have continued in William-Olsson's footsteps and studied the physical-morphological aspect of urban life.

Urban sociology also lacks developed theories about the material dimension of urbanity. For Simmel (1995), the first urban theorist of modern times, as well as for his successor Louis Wirth (1938), the question of the essence of urbanity in many respects was a question of what, or who, *the urban person* is. Wirth, who belonged to the Chicago school, did not do any in-depth analysis of the city's physical aspect (Franzén 1987: 389) but described the city as 'a relatively large, dense, and permanent settlement of socially heterogeneous individuals' (Wirth 1938: 8). Manuel Castells, too, avoids highlighting and spatially specifying the material structure (Franzén 1987: 389). The same can be said of R.E. Pahl (1975). And Lofland (1998), who has studied the public realm of cities, and who acknowledges the role of the built environment in social life, does not in any detailed way approach the question of how the layout of physical space affects the urban.

Today, there are signs of a chasm between the social sciences and architecture's theoretical urban studies – a chasm that can be seen in the fact that the former emphasises discursive and/or social relationality, and the latter, material relationality. A schematic summary of the different positions of this chasm can be portrayed like this: 'Technical-scientific urban analyses are deterministic, and ignore the fact that space is socially produced and that knowledge is socially constructed!' social scientists say. On the other hand, architects say, 'Social scientists never say anything that can be converted into actual planning practice!'

Although space syntax is a rapidly growing research paradigm, it has received relatively little attention from geography. Two of the exceptions are David Seamon and Edward Soja. Seamon (1994; 2004; 2007) has argued that Hillier's research complements the phenomenological knowledge of urban life-worlds studied in humanistic geography and vice versa – an idea that resonates in this book. Soja's analysis (2001) is more critical in nature and is, in some aspects, in line with the critique put forth in Chapters 6 and 7. Furthermore, space syntax was assigned an entry in the 2009 edition of *the Dictionary of Human Geography* (Gregory et al., 2009), which can be interpreted as a sign of a growing interest.[3]

The interest has been minimal from sociology as well.[4] '[S]ociology does not want to engage with the physical world. ... [I]t is afraid of determinism, of the idea of mechanisms', Hillier posits (in Westin 2011: 230). Pointedly, one could say that as much as space syntax researchers – with their rhetoric and their claims – attract city planners, they seem to alienate many social scientists and humanists (see Leach 1978: 386, Soja 2001). A broadly humanistic or anthropological story of man and his environment does – in principle – not allow any deterministic models, be they religious, social or biological (Johannisson 1997: 13). But here I would like to borrow the words of Peter Gould (1999: 101): '[R]esentment is not a mood conductive to clear and open thinking'. Therefore, the present study is an attempt at a hopefully cross-fertilising dialogue.

Back to Materiality

> [I]f in the last five years we have seen important work showing us specific ways beyond the transparency of language, I think it is now time to take those advances and move back to the world. (Rabinow 1985: 12)

> The truck never comes down the road, though we may find ourselves talking endlessly about the grounds for the possibility of our knowledge that it is coming. (Megill 1985: 83)

Social scientists' aloofness from physical space was, as already stated, in part a reaction to the quantitative revolution in geography in the 1950s and 1960s. In short, we can say that physical space is no longer considered to have any explanatory value in itself; space does not exist outside of or adjacent to society but is part of a society's social and economic processes and should therefore be studied as a process or a relationship (see e.g. Crang and Thrift 2000). The result of this development – which can be described as 'a socialization of spatial analysis' – was a relational concept of space (Gregory 2000: 769). The concept of relational space refers to the process or processes 'in which space is "folded into" social relations through practical activities' (ibid.). Or in Jens Tonboe's words (1985a: 14), 'We must not fetishize space. Only people act'.

Previously, space was described as neutral, uniform and universal, but this hides inequalities and differences in class, ethnicity, gender, sexual orientation and so on. So geographers in the 1970s began to turn their attention to themselves

---

3   Attempts at building bridges have been more common from the side of architecture; besides Hillier (2008a), one should mention Kärrholm (2004; 2010; 2012), Read (2004), Budiarto (2007) and Legeby (2010; 2013).

4   Prominent exceptions are Franzén (2009), Liebst (2011) and Löw (2012).

and, more specifically, to their own ways of conceptualising space. Significant for this reevaluation – which was more political than intellectual – was Marxist geography with Harvey (1973) in the lead but also feminist geography. Gillian Rose, for example, emphasised that the dualism of 'real, material, concrete space' and 'non-real, imagined, symbolic space' means the practice of 'normative power within a masculinist geographical imaginary' (in Gregory 2000: 771). Feminist geographers in general have argued that many traditional discourses of space deny pluralism (Agnew 2009: 16). This way of thinking has had a deep impact, which is evident in the following quote by sociologist Rob Shield (2006: 149), in which he formulates his interpretation of space:

> We need to know space as not just about relations and distance between elements but as social, produced 'order of difference' that can be heterogeneous in and of itself. 'Knowing space' is not enough ... We need to know about 'spacing' and the spatializations that are accomplished through everyday activities, representations and rituals.

This quote is representative of the so-called spatial turn in the social sciences, accelerated after 1991 – the year when Lefebvre's *La production de l'espace* from 1974 was translated.[5] Space, according to Lefebvre (1991: 83), 'is not a thing but rather a set of relations between things'. It is not so much space (as a noun) that is at the centre, as the creation of spatialities (as a verb) (see also Thrift 2006: 140f).

If I were to summarise the development described here, it has been about an expansion of a constructivist approach to the world and our knowledge of it – an insight that frames knowledge as a social product. Space is no longer seen as something objective, unproblematic and eternal – an understanding that has given rise to a growing number of studies concerned with the discursive, that is, how we talk about and understand the world. Language and theories are important because they emphasise certain aspects of reality and hide others; they work as systems of preclusion that establish historically and culturally contingent boundaries between the true and the false, normal and abnormal (Foucault 1993: 10f). The motivation behind these studies, it is said, is emancipation; a critique of power. However, I would like to problematise this with the use of some examples.

Social constructivism has contributed greatly to scientific research and has allowed for much power criticism (Berger and Luckmann 1967, Burr 2003), but as important as it is to question objectivity claims, it is equally important to acknowledge the limitations and paradoxical effects of this questioning activity. As human geographer Kenny Jansson (2009: 180) points out, much social constructivistic research throws out the baby with the bathwater. All that

---

5   Although Harvey and Soja had acknowledged Lefebvre's work before then (Dixon et al. 2008: 2554).

is material is placed within the discursive realm – a placing, which implicitly conveys a message that the tangible aspect of the world around us is irrelevant.[6]

Many urban-geographical and urban-sociological studies tend to neglect the fact that the human body is a materiality that cannot go through walls (Østerberg 2000: 32). Simonsen (1993), Pløger (1997) and Krange and Strandbu (1996), for example, can be said to argue that the city's physical design does not determine the residents' behaviour, that 'late modern people relate freely and creatively, partly reflexively, to their environment' (Østerberg 2000: 31). In one sense this might be true, but, nevertheless, this 'free approach', if you will, is conditional. The various situations we find ourselves in act as obscure but significant limits on what we can do; both the external environment and our own abilities restrict our choices. It is mainly when our actions are prevented in one way or another – whether the obstacle is 'inside' (sickness, fatigue, hunger and so on) or 'outside' (a street that ends, a fence and so on) – that we become aware of our bodies. Suddenly, we experience a limit to what we can do. And here we find the ultimate expression of the architect's power over the *flâneur*'s body; for the architectural ideas transformed into concrete structures virtually scream at us: WALK HERE! DO NOT WALK THERE! (Lefebvre 1995: 119).

An illustrative example of a study that focuses on the discursive and where the physical (urban) space – and hence neither the social nor the lived – is given any importance is Tunström's thesis (2009) *På spaning efter den goda staden* on the construction of ideals and problems in contemporary Swedish urban planning discourse. Tunström's goal is 'not to produce yet another statement about how "the good city" should like or be achieved, but to critically examine others' perspectives and put them in a larger perspective with the help of urban research and discourse analytic methods' (ibid.: 14). And Tunström does not fail her purpose; she does not formulate any definition of the concept of the city; rather, she calls for 'more voices, more ideals, more concepts and categories in order to talk about the city in many ways, to open up the discourse so that it includes several different ideals and experiences' (ibid.: 175).

Hence, it is not her ambition to fill the concept of the city with meaning. In fact, Tunström gives voice to a more general definition reluctancy; she directs criticism at (others') claims to say something universal about the urban. But what is the source of her reluctancy? We find one clue when she writes, 'There are always definitions or meanings that are overlooked, denied, forgotten or rejected' (ibid.) She also adds, '[The concept of urbanity] is not innocent in itself, nor innocently used' (ibid.: 174). To claim that a particular urban environment is more 'urban' or

---

6 The critique I develop in this section of what can be called a 'dematerialisation' of geography due to the 'cultural turn' (see Philo 2000) has relatives. As Anderson and Wylie (2009) have noted, since the beginning of the twenty-first century, calls for the 'rematerialisation' of the geography discipline abound (see ibid.: 318 for examples of recent published literature on the so-called material turn, or, *re*turn). For a problematisation, see ibid. and Kearnes (2003).

more 'traditional' than others, Tunström holds, is to take prerogative, to indirectly assert that 'everyone is like me' (ibid.: 175).

Herein, we find the motive behind her definition reluctancy, a motive closely linked to the idea of what it means to be a discourse analyst. To take this role is to take a 'critical' position, in the sense critical-detached, for this is how the critical researcher is portrayed by advocates of discourse analysis. In their widely-used textbook on discourse analysis, Marianne Winther Jørgensen and Louise Phillips (2000: 28) urge researchers to 'put parentheses around themselves and their own "knowledge" so that their own values do not overshadow the analysis', and to use 'specific tools' in order to 'make yourself a stranger' to the material.

But, again, what is it in the striving for (universal and exact) definitions that the social constructivist is so keen to avoid? My answer is this: she is afraid of being exclusionary; of being an authoritative voice, which denies the fact that people are different and hence have different understandings of what a city is. For as Tunström (2009: 174) discusses in the above-mentioned human geographical study, today's dominant urban discourse (the one that speaks of 'the city' in singular form, idealises the 'traditional' city and which sees the suburb as 'less urban' than the inner city) conveys 'elitism and a belief in universal values'.

Elitism. This word choice is interesting. It raises a question: In what way is it elitist to define the basic characteristics of a city (as in formulating an ideal type)? Can you relate in an elitist way to the city as a built environment; to its bricks and mortar? No, not really. Then, is the elitism directed at those who built the suburbs – the functionalists? This cannot be the case either, since the functionalists – if anyone – belonged to the so-called elite. No, the group of people whom Tunström wants to protect from elitism and give voice to is the people who live and work in the modernist-planned suburbs. For as she points out, the categorisation of the types urban versus non-urban implies a stigma that in the long run 'might affect not only the places in question but also … the people who live and work there' (Tunström 2010: 12).

The choice of the word elitism is interesting on another level as well. Tunström (2009: 174) uses the word in a negative sense, which makes me wonder about its opposite. What is its opposite? Populism? Maybe it is humbleness she is referring to, but if so, that idea has fallen out of sight. This question remains: Is populism something to strive for, or how are we to interpret this criticism of elitism and what should we do with it?

Discourse analysis as a method is important from a social-scientific perspective because it facilitates the deconstruction of common conceptual meanings and a questioning of political consensus. But – and this is my point – it is unfortunate if the insight into the social construction of knowledge is carried too far. It is first and foremost the state that demands that we pay heed to 'the truth'; universal values are usually used as a tool for authoritative control (Berg Eriksen 2005: 154). But this acknowledgement should not overshadow the reality that not all universal claims are tools for authoritative control. For example, what about ethical values (see Arendt 1990, Eagleton 1998)? I will not dwell on this issue for too long, but the following point should be made: If we now consider the question of universal values and the relative status of knowledge in this light, we quickly realise that the criticism of universal values (for example, the ethical principle of human beings' equal worth) paradoxically can strengthen – not subvert – authoritative power. And, furthermore, if we only take into account the discursive level, we waive the right to make any judgement of whether a statement can be considered more reasonable than another. All statements are necessarily equally true or equally preposterous – something that moral philosophers refer to as 'vulgar relativism' (Williams 1972: 20ff). Social constructivists take seriously Nietzsche's insight that God – that is, the truth – is dead. But the question of what happens if this insight is carried to its consequential extreme is answered by the writer G.K. Chesterton: 'When a man ceases to believe in God, he doesn't believe in nothing. He believes in anything' (in Nehring 2009: 14).

It is in this regard that the critical-constructivist approach runs the risk of being perverted. At worst, the approach acts as an inhibitor of reality descriptions, without which a genuine criticism of power cannot be formulated. A concrete example is the previously mentioned criticism of 'the suburbs'. As we have seen, Tunström (2009: 174) interprets this criticism as an expression of elitism and as something that stigmatises people who live and work in the suburbs. But what this elitism stamp contributes to, I argue, is a disarming of the criticism that tries to put words to the difference between what kind of life it is possible to lead in the physical morphology of a typical modernist-planned environment, on the one hand, and what kind of life that is supported by the morphology characteristic of most inner city environments, on the other. The elitism stamp seems to also vote against the criticism directed against the functionalist ideology behind the construction of the suburbs. When the discourse analyst remains faithful to her constructivist approach, she ignores the very reality that people – through their words and stories – are trying to describe.

After all, it is nowhere but in real life – as it appears for each individual in her particularity – that human beings experience injustice and oppression, joy and excitement. And this idea must also be applied to architecture: '[A]rchitecture forms a space that clearly has a bearing on the way people feel on a daily basis' (Bartetzky and Schalenberg 2009: 7). When only taking into account representations of the city, one tends to make the discursive all that there is; suggesting that the city only exists (or, rather, subsists) on a mental level. Hereby, it is both possible and easy to come to Tunström's (2009, back cover) conclusion; that is, to say that people do not have to 'mourn the loss' of a real, traditional city, and that they should instead 'open up to new influences and ... fill the strong key concepts with alternative meanings'. Against the backdrop of her discursive approach, the rejection of the sense of mourning seems rational, for what is there to mourn in a world that only consists of words? What we see here is how political correctness ('there is not *one* city but many') easily becomes an emotional correctness ('It makes no sense to mourn what you experience as the city's 'essence' for no such essence exists').[7]

---

7   Another example of how the constructivist critique – by consistently failing to recognise that which in some way is related to the physical, tangible reality – might hold back

The purpose of this discussion has not been to reject all constructivist research but, rather, to illustrate how constructivism can be counter-productive in its focus on plurality and difference. Overall, the discussion above has revolved around an eternal ethical problem: the tension between universalism and relativism. In geography, this problem has become even more manifest during the last decades with an increased interest in diversity and difference (D. Smith 1997). As McDowell (1995: 292) points out, in the wake of the feminist, post-structuralist, post-colonial, and Marxist critique of universalist knowledge claims, we face an important challenge: namely, '[to] establish ways of criticizing universalistic claims without completely surrendering to particularism' and – with Smith's words (D. 1997: 585) – to defend 'some universals against unreflective particularism'.

I do not doubt that the discourse analyst is interested in reality. Not infrequently, she is motivated by a wish to convey the experiences of marginalised groups in order to challenge authority. But since it is the discursive that is put into focus, and because it is the discursive that she says she is interested in, the discourse analyst implicitly and unconsciously transfers the social, lived level to the discursive-mental and vice versa. The discourse analytical approach does not allow any real concern for the realities that are being described, for what people's stories signify. This is problematic because '[f]or conflicts to be voiced, they must first be perceived, and this without subscribing to representation of space as generally conceived' (Lefebvre 1991: 365).

What I am presenting here is 'a point of critique, not criticism', to borrow Gould's expression (1999: 107). The disregarding of the critical content of people's stories is, ironically, a result of the discourse analyst's desire to do right, to be consistent, to not break the rules of her applied critical methodology. It has been asserted that choosing discourse analysis as a method necessarily means buying the 'full package' (see Winther Jørgensen and Phillips 2000: 10). The package includes 1) philosophical premises, 2) theoretical models, 3) methodological guidelines, and 4) specific techniques (ibid.). Whew! Here it is helpful to look at Gould's (1999: 107) ideas again: 'Any framework upon which the human (or physical or biological) world is projected has the capacity to trap thinking'.[8] It is partly my own experiences of discourse analysis that has made me aware of

---

reality descriptions and thus paralyse a different kind of emancipatory research, is described by Gould (1999: 142f). He discusses Rob Imrie's (1996) and J.B. Gleeson's (1996) critique of Reginald Golledge's (1993) paper 'Geography and the disabled', in which Golledge – who himself was blind – urges geographers to use their insights and practical imagination to help blind people in their daily lives. The critics' message was that a blind person is not handicapped compared to a person whose sight is intact – 'but simply marginalized and oppressed by socio-political processes' (Gould 1999: 142). Gould (ibid.: 143) answers by asking the critics whether they were aware that Golledge 'woke up one morning to find that the capillaries feeding the optic nerves had closed down and destroyed them?'.

8   Altogether, this makes me think of Paul Feyerabend's (2000: 25) point that science has never worked according to a rational method and, indeed, that it should not work according to a rational method. Science, he states (ibid.; see also Sennett 2009), is a fundamentally anarchistic activity. This position can be contrasted to discourse analysts

its problematic sides (Westin 2005b). It tied my hands when I wanted to say something substantial about the urban – something that could be a counterweight to the planners' depictions, which I felt was misleading. The approach is usually fruitful when it comes to scrutinising dominant conceptions of and in society, but its inherent inability to take seriously people's experiences highlights its problems as a critique of power and production of knowledge.

Lefebvre (1991: 7) was early (in the 1970s) to identify how the discursive approach unintentionally confuses the different dimensions of space. 'This school', Lefebvre writes, 'whose growing renown may have something to do with its growing dogmatism, is forever promoting the basic sophistry whereby the philosophico-epistemological notion of space is fetishised and the mental realm comes to envelop the social and physical ones' (ibid.: 5).

In sum, studies that evolved during geography's quantitative era depicted, as McDowell (1995: 284) points out, 'a landscape without power, poverty, or political struggles'. Today, the pendulum has swung, and the world painted by human geographers all too often resembles a landscape without physical barriers. A question worth pondering is that which Hillier (2008a: 223) asks: 'Is space completely amorphous, and so nothing, until given shape by social agency?' One problem with the constructivist-inspired view of space is that it simply prevents a range of questions – even obvious ones – from being asked. For example, what is the physical-morphological base of urbanity?

Urbanity – an Exact Definition

> Be it with our hands, be it with our mind, we can grasp only what endures. All that is evanescent – melting snow, fog rising from a meadow, fireworks, a smile – eludes us. (Harries 1973: 29)

> The urban is not a soul, a spirit, a philosophical entity … [It] cannot go without a practico-material base, a morphology. (Lefebvre 1996: 103)

In one of the opening quotes in this chapter, Olsson likens the equality sign – the basis for communication – to an anchor. The anchor, which forces the phenomenon we are discussing to stand still so that we can inspect it, can be constructed in different ways. However, what is crucial when pinpointing a meaning is that we are clear about what we are after (Dewey 2005: 305). So far, I have defined urbanity as a social and mental phenomenon, a quality that often eludes us in the same way that life itself does. To borrow someone else's expression from elsewhere, 'we need to flesh out the contours, surfaces, and lines of flight associated with this shadowy figure' (MacDonald 1999: 29). In the end, we can only experience

---

Jørgensen and Phillips' (2000: 30) idea that it is 'a stringent use of theory and method that legitimises scientifically produced knowledge'. Both are right, of course.

the world through a form (Seip 1995: 28, Torsson 1995: 33). But what kind of accuracy am I looking for?

To describe – as we saw Strindberg and Baudelaire did – the city as an 'electric generator', 'an immense reservoir of electrical energy', which one can plug into in order to retrieve existential energy, is one way to define urbanity. Maybe this rendering can help us understand what kind of phenomenon we are talking about by bringing to life a kind of identification; a sense of how the urban is *felt*. This kind of accuracy can be described as poetic accuracy. Accuracy to a poet or a writer means the ability to – in the mind/body of the reader – evoke an impression that is similar to the material that the author in question intends to describe. Accuracy in poetry and fiction can also be described as the ability to convey (private) emotions so that they seem universal. Furthermore, to say several things in the same sentence, or better still, with a single word, is a form of poetic precision, because reality and life – or whatever it is that one seeks to portray – are multifaceted phenomena. With the words of Huxley (1963: 12; 14), 'Human life is lived simultaneously on many levels and has many meanings ... The ambition of the literary artist is to speak about the ineffable, to communicate in words what words were never intended to convey'. Or, as Sander Gilman (1976: 17) writes when interpreting Nietzsche, 'The artist cannot become a scientist, a rigidly systematic thinker, for this mode of thought is destructive to the very nature of art ... [T]he role of art is to express the inner confusion of man confronted by humanity's drive for formal expression'.

Accuracy for a scientist, however, is something else. Her professional world consists not so much of diverse qualities as quantified regularities. To achieve the greatest possible precision she must simplify and strip away any opportunity for subjective interpretations, for arbitrariness. In other words, 'The scientist's aim ... is to say one thing, and only one thing, at a time' (Huxley 1963: 14). In other areas, definitions may suffice to be indiscriminate and arbitrary, but the scientist's concepts must be defined (Toulmin and Goodfield 1963: 251). What you and I are talking about should preferably lie before us on the table, so that we can be sure that we are talking about the same thing. Albert Einstein, for example, defined time as 'that which is measured by clocks' (in Granström 2009). Banal, certainly, but accurate and freed from metaphysical problems. On the opposite side of the spectrum, one could say, we find Balzac's fire metaphor, which we met earlier and with which he described the city of Paris. His rendering is certainly not scientific but poetic, and here I come to think of Prendergast's (1992: 56) insightful comment: '[O]ne thing that is certainly burnt [in Balzac's fire metaphor], ravaged by the intensities of the writing itself, is the project of a settled and coherent "scientific" representation of the city, undertaken from some serene point above and beyond, and hence untouched by, the frenzy of the scene represented'. Scientific representation, unlike poetic representation, is characterised by a distance to that which is depicted; a result of a treating of the research subject as a separate object.

If we now remind ourselves of the task that I presented in this chapter – to find how the city affects the urban – we understand that the phenomenon of urban life must be understood as operationalised into something tangible, something that can be captured; it must be conceptualised as something extensional that we can place in the scheme of causal inference belonging to conventional logic (Olsson 1980a: 24bff). In this case, it is not enough to state that the urban equals freedom or the sense of excitement and anticipation that the *flâneur* feels as she is walking along the street. Again, we need to be more (scientifically) accurate: 'The hallmark of [the schema of causal inference] is that statements about an empirical phenomenon are logically deduced from a set of statements about antecedent conditions and from a set of relevant scientific law statements' (ibid.).

The scheme, which can be used both for explanation and prediction, is based on Galileo Galilei's conviction that the language of nature is mathematics. This involves translating the phenomenon under study to a quantitative vocabulary, which in turn implies an ontological reductionism, since that which is not possible to count or be described in terms of either-or is excluded (ibid., Livingstone 1992: 325f). And since thinking in terms of causality assumes that *a* affects *b*, *a* must be clearly separated from *b*. Thus, we must force the sprawling concept of urbanity into precise categories of thinking, or, put another way, we need to construct an anchor that prevents its meaning from disappearing into the fog. And as already argued, the urban indeed has – like all social and mental phenomena – a material base (Lefebvre 1991: 403).

So, if we boil it down to something that we can count – in short, a *thing* – where does this take us? Here we have to use our eyes, because things can be seen. Consider, for example, the photographs below (Figures 5.1–5.5). Each photograph depicts street life in different cities at different times in history. The temporal and cultural contexts are thus different, and if one felt like dwelling on the differences between the city life of early twentieth-century Stockholm and that of twenty-first-century Paris, one could – of course – do that. But when the task is to identify a general, scientific, definition of urbanity, the aim should be to conduct the analysis on a level of abstraction that makes the similarities appear – regardless of the variation. So if we distance ourselves from the concrete details of the pictures and focus on the apparent similarities, what do we see?

At the most basic level we see many people in the same physical space. Or, more accurately, we see human bodies in the same physical space. Or, even more accurately, we see physical objects in the same physical space. As we will see, this is very much how Hillier operationalises the urban. In its most basic, objective form, he argues, urbanity is about used space, about co-presence.[9]

---

9   'Used space' (Hillier 1996: 170,) and 'co-presence' (Hillier in Westin 2011: 231). Others that have emphasised co-presence as the basis of urbanity, although formulated in different ways, are Grönlund (2005: 25), Whyte (1990: 9), Hannerz (1992: 203), Jacobs (1992: 150f). In sociology, Ervin Goffman (2005), whose work has been continued by Randall Collins (2005), was a pioneer in acknowledging the importance of co-presence for social phenomena and that interaction in public space is an embodied practice. However, being a sociologist, Goffman takes physical space for granted.

Figure 5.1   London, Oxford Street
Source: Author's photograph from 2008.

Figure 5.2   Stockholm, Kungsgatan 1909
Source: Photograph by Axel Malmström, City Museum Stockholm.

Figure 5.3   Boston, Newbury Street
Source: Author's photograph from 2008.

Figure 5.4   Stockholm, Götgatan
Source: Author's photograph from 2008.

Figure 5.5   Paris, Rue de Steinkerque
Source: Author's photograph from 2009.

For if we only take into account that which we can safely conclude and agree upon, we can say little more than this. In David Lowenthal's words (1975: 111), 'Looking down from a window, like Descartes, we say that we see men and women, when in fact we perceive no more than parts of hats and coats'.

What I have done in this chapter is to move from the identification of the urban as a *not-thing* into talking about it as a *thing*. This is not uncommon; all definitions imply elements of reification (Olsson 1984: 74). Right or wrong, I have hereby constructed an anchor for the forthcoming discussion of the space syntax theory. The material used in the next chapter is mostly texts written by two proponents of the theory: Bill Hillier and Lars Marcus. The discussion is also based on an interview I did with Professor Hillier in his office at Torrington Place, London, on a windy Good Friday in 2008.[10]

---

10   The interview is published in its entirety in *Space and Culture* in 2011 (14 (2), 227–37).

Chapter 6
The Theory of Space Syntax

Our most critical area of ignorance is about the relation of means to ends, that is, of the physical city to the functional city.

Bill Hillier

Cities are large physical objects animated and driven by human behaviour. By far the most interesting and difficult questions about them are about how the two connect: exactly how is the physical city linked to the human city?

Bill Hillier

The theory and method of space syntax was launched by Julienne Hanson and Bill Hillier (1984) in *The Social Logic of Space* and was developed by Hillier (1996) in *Space is the Machine*. Although further development of the subject since then has been enormous, these books – especially the latter – count as the paradigm's theoretical foundations (Hillier 2007: ix). In Scandinavia, research is being done at the Royal Institute of Technology (KTH) in Stockholm, led by Lars Marcus (2000b), whose dissertation draws on Hillier (1996). In the previous chapter, I discussed the concept of urbanity and argued for the need of a precise (scientific) definition if we are to investigate how this phenomenon is linked to the city – which is a central question for space syntax and one of the central questions of this book. Such definition I found in the expression *used space*, or *co-presence*, which is how space syntax theorists operationalise the urban.

We are thus already acquainted with space syntax, but in this chapter I will look at this theory more closely. The aim is to analyse the concept from a human-geographical and social-theoretical perspective, in order to discover its strengths and weaknesses. The space syntax technique can be applied to several different levels of analysis, but most often the focus is on districts and cities – a scale level that is more similar to urban geography than to traditional architectural theory; it is not urban design nor regional planning but, rather, something in between. The overarching question that the theory seeks to answer is this: '[W]hat is the influence of urban configuration on social life?' (Ratti 2004: 487). Or, in Hillier's (2008b: 30) own words,

> Originating in the last quarter of the twentieth century the aim of the space syntax movement was to bring together the study of the city as object with the study of social, economic, and cultural processes, and so, show these processes to be spatial in an architectural way, and allow us to bring together urban design with urban reflection and research.

While social-scientific theories tend to, as Hillier (2008a: 218) puts it, 'approach the society-environment relation "society first", in that the form of the environment is sought as the product of the spatial dimensions of social processes', space syntax wants to 'turn the question the other way round and, through "environment first" studies, look for evidence of social processes in the spatial forms of the built environment'. Social scientific spatial theorists, he claims, lack the precision required to clearly explain the relationship between the city's tangible and intangible dimensions: 'Social sciences tend to be weak not because they lack theories but because they lack regularities which theories can seek to explain and which therefore offer the prime test of theories. The first task in the quest for an analytic theory of architecture is therefore to seek regularities' (Hillier 1996: 5).

Space syntax is thus an analytic theory. But what does this mean? For starters – and this I have already touched upon – space syntax differs from previous architectural theories, which are partly normative, partly made up of ideas and concepts borrowed from other disciplines (Hillier 2007: 42; 2). Hence, the discipline of architecture had previously not developed its own deep understanding 'of the phenomenon of architecture and how it affects people's lives' (ibid.: 2). Space syntax is not another normative theory, Hillier writes (ibid.: 41), but an analytical – or in other words, truly scientific – theory of how the city *is*: 'Scientific theories help us act on the world, but only because they have first described the world independently of any view of how it should be' (ibid.).

Hillier distinguishes between weak and strong theories, where the first type notes how things relate 'on the surface'; these theories resemble more or less mundane statements such as 'the sun rises' (ibid.: 51f). However, strong theories, of which space syntax is an example, 'aim at a greater truth because they seek not to bring order to surface regularities but to show how those surface regularities arise from invariant necessities buried deep in the nature of things' (ibid.: 52). What, then, are the underlying regularities or constant necessities that space syntax seeks to explain? Hillier (ibid.: 7) answers: '[A]rchitectural theory is a matter of understanding architecture as a system of possibilities, and how these are restricted by laws which link this system of possibilities to the spatial potentialities of human life'.

Space syntax's main message, as well as its main point of critique of modernist architectural theories, is that we must take into account a crucial aspect in the form-function relationship – namely: spatial *configuration*. Configuration is a term that represents how individual urban spaces and places are connected (Hillier 1996: 1). Hillier directs harsh criticism towards modernist architectural and urban theories and calls them unscientific – even though modernists alluded to scientific reasoning (ibid.: 65). His message is that modernists were not wrong in formulating an architectural theory with the purpose of generating social impact through built form; it was just the approach that was flawed (ibid.). Also, modernists strove to shape a new kind of (moral) man and not 'merely' shape urban environments. Le Corbusier gave rise to modernism – a tradition that Hillier calls the machine paradigm – a paradigm that claimed to explain the relationship between form and function (ibid.: 376ff). But the theory lacked scientific basis and consequently failed to say what effects a particular design will generate when it is built (ibid.). The machine paradigm's mistake was that it did not handle the form-function relationships credibly (ibid.: 378f); it was based on the idea that physical objects have a direct impact on human behaviour, that there is a direct relationship between the building and the individual. According to this view, the built environment is a kind of backdrop to human activity and is assumed to have a symbolic impact on human behaviour. No such relationship between form and function exists, says Hillier. Or at least the relationship is not interesting (ibid.).

The focus of the machine paradigm was the building. However, at the centre of space syntax is not the building but space – or, rather, its configuration: '[W]hat space syntax has actually done ... is to bring to light space as a hidden variable in the city by showing its essentially configurational nature' (Hillier and Netto 2002: 13.8). It is this belief that has given name to the space syntax 'bible' *Space is the machine*. For it is not the building that is the machine, writes Hillier – it is space. Spatial configuration, which simply means 'relations taking into account other relations' (Hillier 1996: 1), cannot be seen with the naked eye since it is an underlying structure and since relationships are mental constructs. Therefore, it is 'lifted up to the surface' quantitatively by so-called axial maps, that is, graphic representations of the structure of urban space showing possible movement paths using straight lines (Hillier and Hanson 1984: 91): 'An 'axial map' is the least set of longest lines of direct movement that pass through all the public space of a settlement and make all connections' (Hillier 2002: 153). Hereby, spatial relationships are handled as empirical facts with predictable empirical effects (Hillier and Netto 2002: 13.7).

> There are relationships, then, between the formal describability of space and how people use it. These elementary relationships between the form of space and its use suggest that the proper way to formulate the relation is to say that space is given to us as a set of potentials, and that we exploit these potentials as individuals and collectivities in using space. It is this that makes the relation between space and function analysable, and to some extent predictable. (Hillier 2007: 115)

Space syntax analysis of the built environment is intended to provide a realistic description of how people move in urban environments. In particular, the theory introduces a new use of the concept of distance. Instead of defining distance in meters as a limiting factor, one assumes a distance that is measured in the number of street changes a pedestrian must make to get between two points ('Place Syntax Tool'). The result is an axial map.

Figure 6.1 (below) depicts a map of Rome, in which the conventional way of representing buildings in black and space in white has been reversed in order to draw attention to the spatial structure (the black-marked on the map)

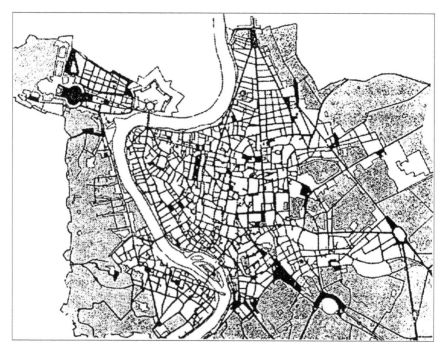

Figure 6.1   Map of Rome, created by Marios Pelekanos
Source: Hillier (2007: 115).

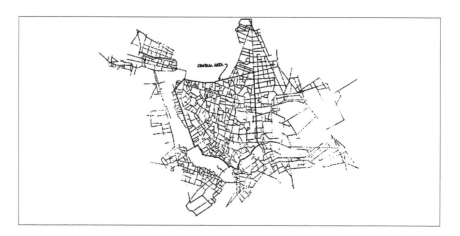

Figure 6.2   Axial map of Rome, created by Marios Pelekanos
Source: Hillier (2007: 115).

(Hillier 2007: 116). So, through this technique (reversal of colours), Hillier displays a new way of looking at the city, where space – not buildings – is central to how cities work. Figure 6.2 shows an axial map of Rome. These figures show different ways of looking at (urban) space. Seeing the city through different lenses can lead to new insights in our understanding of urbanity and the city: 'A spatial layout can thus be seen as offering different functional potentials' (ibid.). There are many questions that they can help to answer:

> What is it like to move around in it? Does it have potential to generate interaction? Can strangers understand it? and so on. All these questions are about the relationship of space as formal potentials to different aspects of function. A layout can thus be represented as a different kind of spatial system according to what aspects of function we are interested in. (Ibid.)

In addition to spatial configuration, the concept of movement is central. Buildings create spatial relationships, which affect the movement of people in the city. And this is important since pedestrian movement is assumed to be of essential importance for urban life (Hillier 1996: 170). Hillier (2002: 153) describes how we can visually see this relationship: 'The structure of the urban grid has independent and systematic effects on movement patterns, which can be captured by integration analysis of the axial map' (see also Hillier et al. 1993). An urban city is described as a 'movement economy', a mechanism for generating contact (Hillier 2007: 125ff). Therefore, spatial configuration is a source of knowledge about how the form of the city works in terms of how it is being used. The primary use is movement, but this in turn has a number of side effects in the form of shops, cafés and meetings, or 'the urban buzz' (ibid.: 126). If we can get better at analysing how spatial configuration controls movement in the city, we have come a long way in understanding what generates and what counteracts urban life; this is Hillier's basic argument. He writes, 'The urban grid through its influence on the movement economy is the fundamental source of the multi-functionality that gives life to cities' (Hillier 1996: 170). In sum, the urban structure governs what is called 'natural movement', the proportion of movement that is determined by the urban fabric and not by special 'magnets' such as certain shops, services or activities. A shop can attract people, but it cannot change a street's location in the structure as a whole. Shops and businesses are located at a certain place mainly because there is most movement there (ibid.: 168). This clearly shows how Hillier analyses the urban *through* the city, that he assumes that (physical) space 'comes first'.

> Physically, cities are stocks of buildings linked by space ... Functionally, they support economic, social, cultural and environmental processes. In effect, they are means-ends systems ... (Ibid.: 111)

This quote clearly shows how the space syntax theory is modelled after the natural sciences, according to which the world is understood as shaped by universal laws.

It also shows how Hillier implicitly assumes the scheme of causal inference (see Olsson 1980a: 24bff), supported by the fact that he is asking for the 'effects' of the built environment (see Hillier 2002: 153). For as Gullberg (1986: 7) writes, 'For there to be a question of effect, the relationship between a planning intervention and a possible effect must be causal'.

Generally speaking, natural science also typically has objects – not subjects or social relations – as its main focus of study (Skjervheim 1996: 5). This means that if space syntax is to investigate the built environment's social dimension, the latter must be operationalised into something physically tangible. When Marcus (2000c: 39) explains what is meant by the social dimension, he uses the Cartesian division between the two spheres of reality: *res extensa* and *res cogitans*. *Res extensa* is characterised – briefly – as having an extension in space; it is external and palpable. *Res cogitans*, on the other hand, represents an inner world, the mental aspect of man, whose characteristic is thinking (Skjervheim 1996: 59). Marcus (2000c: 39) thus points at two aspects of man: first, he is a physical body that exists and moves, and, second, he is a mental consciousness. While the first aspect gives rise to how the built environment works, the other gives the built environment meaning. In light of this, Marcus discusses two relationships between man and the built environment: first, between form and function, and, second, between form and meaning. As a natural consequence of the space syntax theory's neo-positivistic approach, Marcus focuses exclusively on the former relationship, implying that the human being is primarily regarded as a body. It is an artificial division, Marcus (ibid.) admits, but it is necessary since only the body dimension – unlike the meaning dimension – can be measured with quantitative techniques. Here I come to think of Huxley's (1963: 8, 14) words: '[T]he man of science does his best to ignore the worlds revealed by his own and other people's more private experiences ... At its most perfectly pure, scientific language ceases to be a matter of words and turns into mathematics'.

Numeric language is the instrument of measurement, and it plays a fundamental role in the rationalisation efforts of planning because it is well suited for predictions (Nordström 2008: 86, see also Johannisson 1988, Wide 2005). Gottfried Wilhelm Leibniz, the epochal mathematician, saw exact calculation as a prerequisite not only for knowledge but for a better world and a better life (Liedman 2008). This is how Marcus (2000b: 45) conveys the benefits of precise mathematical language:

> Describing a phenomenon in the world, for example a moving car, in a mathematical, or a quantitative way, saying that it moves at 80 km/h for example, has great advantages. Because this is a very abstract and even reductive description it is able to capture something universal rather than individual in the moving car, that is something of principal importance, which can be compared to other phenomena of a similar kind.

Hillier too argues for the need to distinguish between what is physical and what is social, in order to make it possible to investigate the impact of urban space on urban life. The purpose of the separation is not to deny the social aspect of space; on the contrary, 'it [is] only by extracting space from its embedding and treating it as a thing in itself that we are able to bring to light its configurational properties, and it turns out to be these that link space back to society' (Hillier and Netto 2002: 13.6).[1] Or, as he has put it elsewhere: '[I]f we wish to understand [cities] we must learn to see them as "things made of space", governed by spatial laws whose effects but not whose nature can be guided by human agency' (Hillier 2007: 262).

In the section that follows, I develop the way in which space syntax could enrich social scientific studies of the city.

Useful Terminology

> The concepts are not as rich as reality, but they do allow a discussion of it.
> (B. Eriksson 2007: 57)

One of the merits of space syntax, from an urban studies perspective, is that it offers a vocabulary that makes it possible to talk about different types of urban environments. Within the social-scientific field of urban studies, 'urban areas' are often equated with 'city areas' in general, but we are looking for a clearer specification of which types of city areas are urban because not all city areas are urban in the sense of having a vibrant city life. Within social scientific research on segregation, the term 'residential area' (*bostadsområde* in Swedish) is frequently used, and/or neighbourhood (*grannskap*). The latter is defined by Howard Hallman (1984: 13) as 'a limited territory within a larger, urban area, where people interact socially'. Another example can be found in Petra Sundlöf's (2008: 19) human geographical thesis on the subject of segregation:

> [The neighbourhood] can be likened to a district in a big city or a neighbourhood within a city district. The size of the neighbourhood is thus smaller than a municipality, but larger than, say, a block. The neighbourhood serves as an arena for social interaction between people, and it is here that individuals form their social identity.

The term 'neighbourhood' is then equated with 'residential area', whereupon the latter is used consistently. Any further details with regard to the areas' physical characteristics are not given – something that is representative of the research tradition in which the above-cited study is included. Most commonly, the concept is

---

1   Hillier has later formulated what seems like a rebuttal to this argument. In Westin (2011: 235) he says: 'I think that the critical thing here is that space is not one thing and society another. You have to understand that space is built into everything that people do, everything they do happen in space'. The occasions when he expresses a view on space as 'an objective entity in itself' (Hillier 1993: 15) are nevertheless recurring (see also Kärrholm 2004: 160).

defined with regard to administrative boundaries. This is not theoretically motivated but a consequence of the availability of index data (see Bergsten 2010: 183). When the physical aspect is brought up, it is often operationalised into a question of tenure, types of housing and apartment sizes (see Bergsten and Holmqvist 2007: 50; 52).

The purpose of this section is to concretise the aforementioned argument that there are reasons to define the urban as a socio-spatial phenomenon and to name its opposite. I agree with Marcus (1998: 2) when he writes that without more precise descriptions of the phenomenon we call 'cities', we give way to great arbitrariness; we are simply not able to see how one built environment differs from others. Why is it, for example, that some neighbourhoods are more attractive than others for business owners and/or residents? What are the main reasons why wealthy individuals often choose to live in certain neighbourhoods and avoid others?

It is questions like these that the segregation-oriented research seeks to answer. Segregation is a complex problem which involves geographers, political scientists and sociologists (Bråmå 2006, Magnusson 2001). However, as noted in the previous chapter, these disciplines tend to put the 'city' itself aside (Franzén 1987: 389). Researchers on segregation – as well as social-scientific researchers on the city in general – would have much to gain from taking into account the physical design of the areas that they study when analysing what the factors influence the segregation process (Carpenter and Peponis 2010, Vaughan 2007). What is it that makes a downtown apartment so much more sought-after than an apartment in a modernist Million Programme suburb? Why is it, really, that some areas have become 'problematic'? As architectural theorist Ann Legeby (2010; 2013) argues, sociology and geography have for a long time focused on *residential* segregation, so much that the fields have neglected the role of public space in social segregation.[2]

As mentioned earlier, the physical structure both facilitates and prevents human actions (Østerberg 1990; 2000). In fact, many of the 'problem areas' studied by segregation researchers often have a physical structure that is modernistic and highly movement-segregating. In Stockholm, as in many other Swedish cities, urban life – with some exceptions – is more or less only achieved in the inner city. 'The labour of the *flâneur* is pleasurable, but it is not easy. And it cannot be performed just anywhere', Bauman (1993: 174f) reminds us, and identifies the arcades of nineteenth-century Paris as *the* home of the *flâneur*. The arcades were cramped and crowded; people came here to linger, 'to *be in*, not just *pass through*' (ibid.: 175). This does not reflect the atmosphere on the outer edges of Stockholm: 'The way the suburbs were planned and built leads to a city form of distinction – its sprawling principle has produced radically different social conditions from that offered by the inner city' (Lilja 2006: 116). This fact seems to have motivated Franzén (1982: 17) when he wrote: 'The city we live in is hardly a city'. Street

---

2   Two interesting studies on how the morphology of areas with modernist housing estates affects different aspects of urban life, in comparison to older urban environments, are Hanson (2000) and Klasander (2004). Both draw on empirical studies (London and Gothenburg, respectively).

life has deliberately been obliterated, and conflicts between different functions and activities have been avoided at all costs (Franzén 1982: 16, Sennett 2008). A person who longs to take part in the urban diversity of life, who wants to be anonymous among strangers and experience the feeling of excitement, freedom or safety that can come out of it, would probably not – if she had a choice – move to an area where this experience of city living is not possible.

The most typical kind of built environment in Stockholm is suburban; it is where the largest part of the population lives (Lilja 2006: 113). Against this backdrop, one could describe the twentieth-century urbanisation process as non-urban:

> The northerners who in the 1960s moved to the 'big city' never really came to any city. Rather, they were placed in residential villages (often consisting of tall apartment buildings) with a few shops, post offices, schools and daycares ... A back-country resident who were forced to move to the suburbs became more peripheral in relation to workplaces, communities and decision-makers than in the small village he or she came from. (Söderlind 1998: 75)

Asplund (1991: 59) formulates an even sharper criticism against modernist urban planning: 'Anyone who finds that he has chosen a sprawled and impoverished city ..., has made a disastrous choice. He is forced to live a humiliating life and has become miserably betrayed by the pseudo-science of urban planning'.

Since the introduction of architectural knowledge into urban planning in the early twentieth century, the morphological basis for urbanity has not been sustained (Marcus 2000b). A space syntax analysis, which shows how integrated streets are in relation to the urban structure in general (Hillier and Hanson 1984: 108f), could serve as an interesting complement to the materials traditionally used in human-geographic segregation studies.

One of the effects of not defining the concept of the urban any more than as a synonym to the city is that the opposite of the urban automatically becomes the city's opposite, which traditionally has been the countryside. Sociologists Tönnies (1957), Simmel (1995) and Wirth (1938) all contrasted the city to the countryside. Today, when urbanisation and industrialisation have come so far, this dichotomy is in many respects outdated, which means we need other concepts that better capture the situation (Andersson 1987: 37–51, Asplund 1991: 41, Franzén 1987: 388, Lefebvre 1996: 158, Østerberg 2000: 27). Still, the urban-rural dichotomy is more or less taken for granted.

When I at times have asked students in urban-geographical studies what they consider to be the opposite of 'the urban', they more often than not respond 'the rural'. But frequently this response is often followed by a facial expression that reveals doubt. It is as if they respond, and only afterwards begin to think (an order of events by no means restricted to students). When they want to revise and nuance their response, it becomes clear how often they lack a vocabulary that would help them to refine their analysis. Therefore, I usually tell them about the concept of disurbanism: '"Disurbanism" is intended to convey the reverse

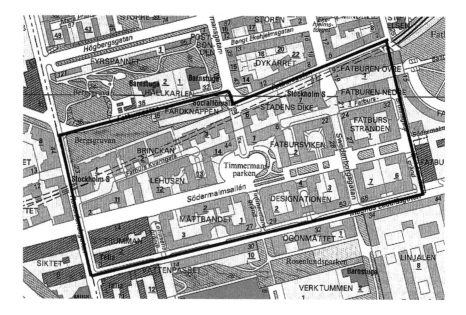

Figure 6.3   Map of Södra Stationsområdet
Source: Marcus (2000b: 131).

of the urban spatial techniques we have identified: the breaking of the relation
between buildings and public space, the breaking of the relation between scales
of movement and the breaking of the interface between inhabitant and stranger'
(Hillier 2007: 144). When pedestrian movement is spread out, opportunities for
urban life are minimised (ibid.: 147). One conclusion Hillier draws is that '[i]t is
not density that undermines the sense of well-being and safety in urban spaces,
but sparseness ... not the "unplanned chaos" of the deformed grid, but its planned
fragmentation' (ibid.). Södra stationsområdet, as Marcus (2000b: 133) has shown,
is an example of a disurban environment, where different types of traffic are
separated from each other. The area consists mostly of walking paths, many of
which seem inaccessible for those not familiar with the area or even to those who
know exactly where to go. Overall, this means that the utilisation rate decreases
– as evidenced by the axial map's many short-term lines (Figure 6.4).

Hillier's concept of disurbanism (or disurbanity, which is the term I prefer[3]), puts a
label on a type of urban environment that many before him have touched upon but not
had a name for. For example, Jacobs (1992) warns us of urban areas that, in the absence of
a public space that enables contact, are more or less empty of life. And as we saw earlier,

---

3   The reason is that the *-ism* ending often implies a movement or thought tradition
(e.g. modernism), while the *-ity* ending refers to a concrete, lived reality (e.g. modernity)
(see Eriksson 2001: 21f).

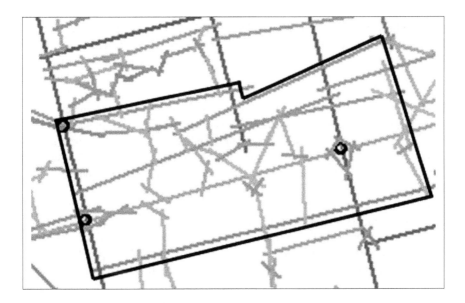

Figure 6.4   Axial map of the same area
Source: Marcus (2000b: 132).

**Figure 6.5   An example of a disurban environment where movement is
            dispersed. Södermalmsallén, Stockholm**
Source: Author's photograph from 2008.

Asplund (1991: 59) stresses that the individual's choice to settle in the city is 'disastrous' if she ends up in an area that lacks both the advantages of the countryside and those of the city. In the works of Lefebvre, urbanity's opposite is an urban environment where silence reigns, where political mobilisation has been hampered by an urban planning that has dispersed people; these areas are 'neither town or country' (Lefebvre 1996: 207). The list of attempts to capture the urban's opposite goes on, but the above researchers make it clear that it is useful to rethink and identify this idea. The terminology of the urban and the disurban is also a welcome step away from an undifferentiated and prejudicial use of *förorten* (the suburbs) and *innerstaden* (the inner city) (see Molina 2007: 15). In reality, there are urban areas in what are normally referred to as the suburbs, in the same way that there are islands of disurbanity in the inner city.

But is disurbanity really urbanity's opposite? These terms are probably not so much binary opposites but, rather, a kind of continuum in which urban environments may exhibit more or less urban features. Instead of equating disurbanity with not-urbanity, one could see it as a particular type of urbanity. For example, Marcus (2000b) makes a useful distinction between what he calls *architectural urbanity* and *general urbanity*. Characteristic of the former is a high degree of specificity in form and reproductivity in its function. Since public spaces in areas of *architectural urbanity* have been planned more or less in detail, they only encourage the reproduction of a number of preconceived activities (ibid.: 138; 190ff). *General urbanity*, on the other hand, means a high degree of potentiality; that is, the physical structure opens up for changes over time by not prescribing different functions to different places. Furthermore, areas of *general urbanity* are well integrated with the surrounding city and they are well used by different kinds of people (locals as well as visitors, for example). As for their way of functioning, these areas are productive, which means that they are generally suitable for economic activities because their physical structure supports exchanges of various kinds – economic as well as ideological (ibid.: 125; 138).

In sum, the theory of space syntax offers a number of concepts that the social-scientific urban researcher could use in analyses of how 'neighbourhoods' create and discourage opportunities for individuals or groups of individuals. After this discussion of some of the potentialities of space syntax, I will now proceed to argue why the theory also leaves me unsatisfied.

Measuring the Social

> [Mathematical descriptions] can ... form the basis of a scientifically stringent theory, since such a theory is concerned with the principles of the tangible world. (Marcus 2000b: 44)

> While illuminating those aspects of reality that exist, [quantitative techniques] leave the other aspects obfuscated and distorted. (Olsson 1980: 45b)

As is clear from the quotes above, saying that space syntax theory has merits is as true as saying that it is problematic. Again, creating an understanding is a balancing act between certainty and ambivalence; what you gain in precision you lose in breadth and vice versa. This is true of all definitions since they inevitably highlight certain aspects of reality and obfuscate others. Reductions are necessary, but – as Lefebvre (1991: 105) underscores – they have to be 'quickly followed by the gradual restoration of what has … been temporarily set aside for the sake of analysis'. It is to this form of 'restoration' that we shall devote this section and the next.

One of the most obvious problems of space syntax is that it is a (natural) scientific theory seeking to answer questions related to the social world. In order to measure aspects of the social world scientifically, these must first be operationalised into quantitative processes before they are mathematically related to the quantity of things that make up urban form (see Marcus 2000b: 44f). I previously noted that the social sciences – briefly put – study subjects and social relations, while the natural sciences study objects. In other words, the former study subsisting phenomena and the latter, existing phenomena. Moreover, social scientists are themselves a part of what they study (the constantly fluctuating phenomenon of society), while this is not true for natural scientists. Furthermore, natural scientific investigations involve procedures of extensionality, which means that the intentionality aspect of man as a social being is excluded (MacIntyre 2007: 83, Israel 1971: 343, Laing 1967: 53).

The difference becomes clear if we look at how geographers and architectural theorists define space. Briefly put, geographers tend to emphasise the social, political and mental aspects of space, while architects generally treat space as an absolute object, with a physical-geometrical extension (see Colquhoun 1989: 224). 'Space is not a scientific object', states Lefebvre (in Soja 1980: 210) – one of the main sources of inspiration for the perspective on space that has dominated the discipline of geography for the past decades. The architectural view applies to space syntax; space, as we have seen, is given an autonomy that allows it to be analysed on its own terms; it is made into a scientific object. This view is at once abstract and concrete (Kärrholm 2004: 17ff): Concrete since space is seen as something material, as a thing with a certain shape and dimension but abstract since space is taken out of context – onto the drawing board or the computer screen, disconnected from man and his experience (ibid.).

Hillier opposes a division between the natural and the social sciences: 'For me, it is not even a question', he says (in Westin 2011: 233). But I insist: this distinction is important, as it encourages us to reflect on what reasoning rules we use. 'Know thyself!', as Socrates exhorted the earliest philosophers (in Barrett 1962: 4). In short, a scientific approach to knowledge involves the belief that what is not possible to reify does not exist. Or at least we cannot say anything universal about it; it is only in regard to countable *things* that we can achieve the goal of science – that is, absolute and certain knowledge (MacMurray 1957: 36). However, this a view of man as a billiard ball, to use Laing's (1967: 53) metaphor. 'All modern science is … founded on the postulate of the mindlessness of things.

If this postulate appears rather well founded in physics ... it is not so in biology (nor *a fortiori* in the social sciences)' (Thom 1979a: 19).

Space syntax's ambition to try to explain the relationship between the city's tangible and intangible dimensions is an ambition coloured by positivism; a school that has traditionally attempted to translate long-lived philosophical problems – such as the relationship between *res extensa* and *res cogitans* – into an empirical language that can be comprehended (Livingstone 1992: 319). A challenging task, to say the least. This is acknowledged by Hillier (2007: 138), who writes, '[T]he very idea of "architectural determinism" – that buildings can have systematic effects on human behaviour, individually or collectively – seems to lead directly into the quagmire of mind-body problems which have plagued philosophy for centuries'.

In philosophy there is an established tradition that argues that the social sphere cannot be studied with the same methods as those used in the natural sciences.[4] This position involves a critique of the orthodox view of what social science is or should be: a copy of the natural sciences (see Giddens 1996). One reason why the positivist claim 'if A, then B' is not so suitable for understanding human processes is spelled: improvisation. This fundamentally human phenomenon is something that de Certeau (1984: 98) points to when he likens the walker with Charlie Chaplin, '[who] multiplies the possibilities of his cane: he does other things with the same thing and he goes beyond the limits that the determinants of the object set on its utilization'. This improvisational aspect, which makes man 'the most unpredictable of animals' (Kalin 1974: 114), is disregarded if one considers man as *res extensa*. The path I choose to walk today is not the path I choose to walk tomorrow: 'If bodies are objects or things, they are like no others', writes Elizabeth Grosz (1994: xi) and continues: 'Bodies are not inert; they function interactively and productively. They act and react. They generate what is new, surprising, unpredictable'. Or in the words of Arthur Koestler (1967: 202), 'By the very act of denying the existence of the ghost in the machine[5] – of mind dependent on, but also responsible for, the actions of the body – we incur the risk of turning it into a very nasty, malevolent ghost'.

As an illustration of the improvisational aspect and of how the perception of the external environment, in combination with the internal state of mind, in a relatively unconscious and unpredictable way affects how we move around in the city, we can return to Strindberg. In the short story *Deranged Sensations*, Strindberg (2008) – who seems to have been of a very delicate disposition – describes his arrival in Paris, or, more specifically, Versailles. After a long and tumultuous train ride, he decides to visit the castle and walks along the Avenue Saint-Cloud, but finds 'the

---

4   For example, Cassirer (1972), MacIntyre (2007), Skjervheim (1996) and Taylor (1985). Social scientists who share this view are, e.g., Flyvbjerg (2001), Giddens (1996), Israel (1971), Ollman (2003) and Olsson (1980a).

5   'The ghost in the machine' is an expression that Koestler borrows from Gilbert Ryle – a philosopher with 'strong behaviourist leanings' and who later came to use another metaphor for the human mind; a horse in a locomotive (Koestler 1967: 202).

inordinately broad avenue boring' (ibid.: 123). He continues: '[U]nconsciously, I end up on the path to the side, where the tree trunks soon press in upon me and the cross-vaulting tweaks me like pincers. Halfway along, I sink down on a bench'. As this quote illustrates, our behaviour is a function of our experience, and of the relationship between behaviour and experience, natural science knows nothing, Laing (1967: 17) posits. It is not an objective problem that we can put under the microscope. There is no logic to explain it; 'no developed method of understanding its nature' (ibid.).

One of the ideas behind space syntax is that if we generate enough knowledge about the configurational aspect of the constructed environment, it is possible to predict the social effects of architectural form (Hillier 1996: 378, Marcus 2000c: 39). '[O]ur objectives are clearly instrumental – we want to explain exactly what causes certain effects, so that we can develop tools possible to utilise in future practice' (Marcus 2000b: 44). Or, as Hillier explains, 'Any theory about how we should act to produce a certain outcome in the world must logically depend on some prior conception of how the world is and how it will respond to our manipulations' (Hillier 2007: 42). He also writes, 'By changing the design of a building or complex, we do change outcomes. There is, after all, some kind of mechanism between the built world and people' (Hillier 1996: 390f). The choice of words in these quotes reveals a view of man as a kind of stimulus-response mechanism (Livingstone 1992: 338), which, in turn, reminds us of the tendency of behaviourism to emphasise the causal role that external stimuli have on human behaviour. The words and expressions used by space syntax researchers ('response', 'manipulation', 'objectivity' and 'prediction') are a direct legacy of behaviourism – the psychological tradition that is modelled after the natural sciences and associated with the names Clark Hull, B.F. Skinner, Edward Thorndike, Edward Tolman and John Watson. Behaviourism is imbued with the idea that human behaviour is considered as an environmental product, and behaviourists tend to limit themselves to the study of phenomena that are quantitatively measurable. A distinction is made between man as an internal, subjective world and man as an outer, objective world, and the focus is on the latter. In Watson's words (in Koestler 1967: 5), '[T]he time has come when psychology must discard all reference to consciousness ... Its sole task is the prediction and control of behaviour; and introspection can form no part of its method'.

Although we humans at one level *are* stimulus-response mechanisms (for example, if we want to leave a room and there is only one exit, we use this exit), this is not our entire nature. As Kalin (1974: 114) writes, it is 'implausible to suggest that man, the most complex of the organisms, can be studied on the model of a computer whose output (conditioned responses) correlates neatly with its input (external stimuli)'. According to Hillier and his colleagues, the functional aspect of the city is a product of its form, which affects human behaviour (movement). What we miss when applying a behaviouristic approach is the fact that our behaviour is affected by internal stimuli as well; the thought aspect affects the body aspect and vice versa (Merleau-Ponty 2002, Sigurdsson 2006). If we perceive a certain environment as frightening, we go a roundabout way, that is, that which we consciously or unconsciously perceive affects how and where we move our bodies (see e.g. Frers 2007: 26). The quote from Strindberg's *Deranged Sensations* illustrates this idea clearly. More examples could be given, but the point I want to make can be summarised as follows: man's intentional aspect very much affects the city's functional aspect.

What I have done here is to draw attention to what many before me have noted: human intentionality and variability. Behaviourism is a loaded term: it has endured much criticism since its introduction in the early twentieth century; it has even been pronounced dead (see Smith 1986: 333). Among other ideas, my critique of space syntax ties in with the critique of the era of spatial science in geography; its 'determinism, economism, and abstraction [that] seemed to abolish human intentionality, culture, and man himself' (Ley 1981: 250). But what is the point of expressing this criticism once again? Isn't this pushing an open door? To this objection, which had been raised many times before, we might repeat what Asplund (1979: 264) has replied: '[I]f behaviourism is an open door, it is extraordinarily busy'. Behaviourism is a form of understanding that permeates much of our technological civilization. Its goal is 'the measurement of behavior by quantitative methods, and the control of behavior by the manipulation of stimuli' (Koestler 1967: 8). To refrain from criticising this tradition just because it has been criticised so many times before would be to refrain from questioning a chief aspect of the society we live in.

In its most general form, space syntax is a science of prediction and control of social processes. In other words, it is a technology. Here, I adopt a definition of technology as instrumentality; it is about the applying of means to achieve ends (Heidegger 1977: 5). Proponents would perhaps oppose the description that space syntax is about designing more effective strategies for the prediction and control of human behaviour, as this task is often negatively associated with modernist social engineering. And although social engineering today can be considered 'softened' because it takes into account human intentionality (see Montello 2007), its philosophical foundations remain the same. If the objective is explanation and/or prediction, which requires certainty, one must take note of what can be measured; of man as *res extensa*. That is, one must consider man as an object.

Hillier's idea is not his private or original idea – he only expresses a principle of the Enlightenment that has become part of the social order (see MacIntyre 2007: 84). Behaviourism is a doctrine so embedded in both science and politics that it is barely recognisable. Its hallmark – then as well as now – is its control interest.[6]

> An increasing number of activities in today's society need to be evidence-based,
> which means that there should be a scientifically established connection between

---

6   A control system is, as Asplund (1979: 269) points out, closely related to, but not identical to, a technology. In other words: all technologies are control systems, but all control systems are not necessarily technologies.

cause and effect, actions and results, which, in turn, means that activities where such relationships cannot be established run the risk of being classified as unnecessary, sloppy, even dangerous; in any event ineffective and therefore uneconomic. (Rosenberg 2009)

Using scientific or other organised knowledge for practical purposes – that is, instrumental rationality – is the very definition of technology but also of planning (Weber 1994). Instrumental rationality means that actions are aimed at a goal so that this goal is reached in the most efficient and economical way. Characteristically, this behaviour is based on some form of empirical knowledge – usually mathematics or logic. '[P]lanning, as a *technique*, represents instrumental rational action and is considered to be indifferent to goals imbedded in a social philosophy' (Israel 1971: 311). Or in Marcuse's (1968: 223f) words:

> Not only the application of technology but technology itself is domination (of nature and men) – methodical, scientific, calculated, calculating control. Specific purposes and interests of domination are not foisted upon technology 'subsequently' and from the outside; they enter the very construction of the technical apparatus. Technology is always a historical-social *project* …

One possible explanation for the viability of behaviourism is that it is nourished both within and outside academia. First, it embodies a positivist understanding that produces clear results, and second, it constitutes an effective instrument for the state. In the words of R.J. Johnston (1989: 62), 'Empirical science is presented in the ideology of most modern societies as a powerful tool in the promotion of societal well-being. Against this, some argue that it can be used by powerful groups within a society to promote their particular interests; it gives them greater ability to control'.

It should now be clear that it is wrong to say that science is not an ideologically driven activity. To assert that one is 'only' considering human behaviour in a 'neutral' and 'objective' manner – that one only regards man as *res extensa* – is to endorse the treating of man as an object. And this is an ethical decision, whether acknowledged or not. And the ultimate consequence of such an ethical stance is a manipulative social technology (Israel 1980: 20).

Before we go any further, I want to address the criticism that architectural theorist Mattias Kärrholm (2004: 158–63) directs towards space syntax because it can be placed within the behavioural-critical tradition drawn on above. He writes this:

> If you see space syntax as a method for predicting movement, you soon realise that the options decrease, as the individuals who move around in the system have a purpose with their movements, and as the other social factors, such as rules or conventions, affect movement (traffic signs, travel to and from work, etc.) (Ibid.: 159)

For this reason, Kärrholm (ibid.: 159f) argues that it is clear that 'there is seldom a general, universal relationship between the built environment and real movement'. Where people choose to go depends not only on material divisions of urban space but also on territorial divisions – an argument which, incidentally, is in line with Linda McDowell's (1999: 148ff) argument that aspects such as gender, ethnicity, class, age and sexual orientation in more or less significant ways impact on how people move in the city. Kärrholm (2004: 160) emphasises that 'the spatial structures do not have any explanatory value in themselves, but that their importance is dependent on a specific context and the situation in which the structures are traced'. Here, Laing's (1967: 21) comments are again useful: 'My experience and my action occur in a social field of reciprocal influence and interaction'.

Hillier occasionally admits that cultural and social factors do have a bearing on the formation of concrete space. However, he regards them as subordinate to concrete space. The distinction he uses is that between long and short models (see Hillier 2007: 193ff). As Kärrholm (2004: 162) points out, this theorisation is relatively unsophisticated and only gives a rudimentary answer to the complex question of how spatial codes and power aspects affect movement; Hillier's concepts of long and short models enhance his Cartesian view of space; they become 'a kind of formula for how well the relationship between cause and effect falls out'. Overall, Kärrholm's argument is that, within the theory of space syntax in particular and within architectural theory in general, there is a lack of a more detailed rendering of the link between configuration/movement and territorialisations of space. This is why he develops 'territorial and power genealogical input to the classic question about form and function' (ibid.: 299).[7] What Kärrholm does, basically, is to implicitly draw attention to the inference problem – a problem well known in geography and the one to which we now turn.

Space Syntax and the Problem of Inference

> [C]ertainty is in spatial form. Ambiguity is in human action. (Olsson 1974: 53)

> Human geography is concerned with the co-relation of society and space. However, every device that has been used to express the co-relation of social space breaks down. (Doel 2003: 140)

Space syntax offers, as we have seen, insights into prerequisites for 'used space' – an essential aspect of the phenomenon of urbanity. In particular, the theory

---

7   According to Kärrholm (2010: 252), 'one of the most important challenges for space syntax research is to integrate and contextualise the outcomes of space syntax research in a wider theoretical discussion on society and space'. His own suggestion for a possible starting point for such a meta-theory is Torsten Hägerstrand's last book *Tillvaroväven* (translating into something like *The Weave of Existence*), posthumously published in 2009 (ibid.).

presents evidence that used space requires a certain spatial configuration. To claim that urbanity assumes used space and that used space, in turn, requires a certain spatial configuration is to physically-spatially define the urban. It means making inferences from process to form. But is it also possible – as Hillier seems to do – to say that a certain spatial configuration generates used space and that used space is more or less the same as urbanity? In other words, is it possible to make inferences in the opposite direction, from form to process?

As already emphasised, this is an essentially human geographical problem – with a corresponding epistemological history. In short, one can say that the optimism for solving the problem was strong in spatial science in the 1950s and 60s – an optimism that came to an abrupt end in 1968 (Olsson 2002: 252; 1974: 52, see also Johnston 1997).[8] At this time, geographers had made new insights into the relation between theoretical-mathematical statements and social reality – insights summarised by Olsson (2002: 252): 'Although it is sometimes possible to reason from process to form, moving in the opposite direction is never appropriate; even though two plus two normally equals four, four can equal anything, including two plus two'.[9] The point can be expressed differently, borrowing from Nassim Nicholas Taleb (2007: 53): 'All zoogles are boogles. You saw a boogle. Is it a zoogle? Not necessarily, since not all boogles are zoogles'.

That space syntax analyses can bring confusion rather than clarity is something that Carlo Ratti (2004) has shown. For example, he points to the 'unacceptable situation' where one single urban configuration produces two conflicting outcomes when analysed with space syntax tools (Ratti 2004: 487).[10] However, it is interesting that Ratti – despite his acknowledgement of anomalies and contradictions – does not seem to doubt quantitative techniques in explaining and predicting social outcomes of physical forms; on the contrary, the problem can indeed be solved – if only computer technology improves: '[N]ew algorithms might allow a deeper understanding of urban texture [that] would contribute to answering the fascinating question which space syntax has helped to frame: what is the influence of urban configuration on social life' (ibid.).

---

8   In geography in recent years, there has been an increased interest in mathematics and geometry, although in a different form than during the era of spatial science. The focus is no longer on 'the mathematics of geography', to borrow Elden's (2008: 2645) expression, but rather on 'the geography of mathematics'. Or in Simonsen's (2004: 1336) words, '[T]he kind of geometry put forward in the new metaphorization is very different from the one known from spatial analysis. It is much more unstable, messy, nonlinear, and open-ended'.

9   Although it is a stretch to say that four can equal anything, four can indeed equal an almost infinite number of mathematical relationships. Here I do not only think of $1 + 3$ or $2 + 2$, or even $1,5 + 2,5$, but also $0,0001 + 3,9999$, $0,0002 + 3,9998$ and so on.

10   According to Ratti, this is due to the reductive nature of the basis for space syntax analyses: the axial map. This strictly topological representation excludes all metric information. This is untenable, Ratti (2004: 490) says, since metric information is hardly irrelevant when pedestrians choose their routes. For a rebuttal of Ratti, see Hillier and Penn (2004).

A similar optimism is shown by Daniel Montello (2007), environmental psychologist with an interest in space syntax. Between the lines in the following quote, there lies a trust in the strength of closed experiments and in their ability to eliminate the ambivalence that characterises all forms of 'causal circularity':

> Problems of causal circularity or ambiguity when applying space syntax to extant places will be disentangled with research on created environments, real or virtual. Manipulating actual built environments is possible, but quite difficult and expensive (except for modest environments built inside large rooms), so the possibility of studying space syntax and other aspects of environmental psychology with virtual environments has great appeal and has attracted quite a bit of attention. Some research on space syntax with virtual environments has already been done …, but much more is called for. (Montello 2007: 8)

As Gullberg (1986) has highlighted, when faced with the difficulties of evaluating the 'effects' of planning initiatives, many researchers try to close the system, that is, to make empirical studies in a limited area in space and time. In other words, they attempt to mould research to fit the scientific standards, with dubious results: 'Conventional scientific wisdom raises the experiment as *the* method to gain knowledge of causal relations' (ibid.: 93). 'But', he continues (ibid.: 145), 'the quest for closure of an un-closable system steers the theoretical and methodological efforts in a futile direction'. The very idea of the experiment is based on the assumption that the results produced in a particular here-now can be transferred to a not-here and a not-now, that inferences can be made from one event to multiple events and from multiple events to all events. Cassirer (1956: 41) calls this assumption 'questionable and precarious', for the making of such inferences results not so much in an extension of the time-spatial realm (from a here-now to a not-here and a not-now), but in a complete abolishment of this realm. The progress made in an experiment has not taken place in the here-and-now in which we live, but in another dimension – a theoretical one. It is this change of dimension that characterises the formulation of scientific laws (Cassirer 1956: 41f). The most problematic aspect of this process – and the criticism I here present concerns induction-generated knowledge in general – is that it is backward-learning. The problem is old, as summarised by Taleb (2007: 40): 'How can we know the future, given knowledge of the past; or, more generally, how can we figure out properties of the (infinite) unknown based on the (finite) known?'

The discovery of the inference problem shook the foundations of the geography discipline, as it beat against its main claims: that spatial analysis leads to knowledge of human behaviour (see Barnes 2004: 589).[11] Olsson (1984: 82) reflects on these

---

11   It should be said that the inference problem is not only relevant to the discipline of geography; it is a general problem that can appear in different contexts. Let me give an example from medicine. In medicine, when trying to discover kidney problems, ultrasound studies are performed. But – and this I noted during a pedagogical consultation visit at

ideas when looking back on what he and other quantitative geographers had been engaged in:

> What I and some others were searching for was the truth of human spatial interaction. Our ambition was to catch that truth in the most precise net we knew, that is to translate statistical observations into the clear and non-ambiguous language of causal relations ... We were after the kind of 'truth' that is necessary for the construction of an optimal world.

And he continues: '[R]eality was more evasive than our naïve minds had been taught to believe'.

As we have seen, proponents of space syntax are optimistic about the task of deriving a social process from a material form – provided that the road goes through spatial configuration. This idea, among others, emerged during my (SW) conversation with Hillier (BH) (Westin 2011: 234f):

> SW: [I]s it then possible to draw the conclusion that it is possible to predict the outcome of a certain form? If we want to, let us say, create an urban atmosphere, to create urbanity, is it possible to – through the form – create that?
>
> BH: Yes. Yes, you can do that.
>
> SW: If you have the knowledge.
>
> BH: Yes, if you have the knowledge it is not even difficult.

Marcus (2000b: 52), however, expresses some hesitation on the matter:

> [S]peaking about the cause and effects regarding the relationship form-function earlier, we said that built form was the cause and functional outcome was the effect. On reflection, this is absurd, as it would entail that we, for example through building certain spatial forms, like an 'urban grid', would be able to generate certain social outcomes, like an 'urban city life', in the middle of a desert. What is active obviously are people and their actions; in the end it is people who give meanings and functions to built form, and the latter can only create opportunities in one or the other direction.

In some of Hillier's statements, too, one can discern a hesitation when it comes to raising space syntax analyses to the rank of resolute theses. For example, he cautions, 'Space syntax gives a partial and incomplete view of the relations between human beings and their created environments' (Hillier 2005: 12). Still,

---

Uppsala University Hospital the 5th of February 2010 – medical students are taught early that the information you get from an ultrasound is only morphological. 'This is how it looks', the teacher said, while insisting on the inappropriateness of using this information to draw conclusions about the kidney's function.

reservations of this kind run the risk of being overshadowed by expressions like cause-effect (Marcus 2000b: 44), mechanisms (Hillier 2007: 139), spatial laws (Hillier 2002: 154), and evidence-based design (Hillier and Sahbaz 2008, Stonor and Stutz 2004). As philosopher of science Carl G. Hempel (1942: 41; 1966: §5.3) teaches us, if you speak about laws, the problem can, strictly speaking, not be a matter of probabilism, but determinism.[12] For what is a law if it can only be applied sometimes? And, correspondingly, if you speak about probabilism, Hempel (ibid.) underscores, it can hardly be a question of a general law. Let us look at an example:

> [I]f Tommy comes down with the measles two weeks after his brother, and if he has not been in the company of other persons having the measles, we accept the explanation that he caught the disease from his brother. Now, there is a general hypothesis underlying this explanation; but it can hardly be said to be a general law to the effect that any person who has not had the measles before will get them without fail if he stays in the company of somebody else who has the measles; that a contagion will occur can be asserted only with a high probability. (Hempel 1942: 41)

Although not all scientific explanations are based on laws of a strictly universal type (Hempel 1966: §5.4), it seems somewhat confusing to, as Hillier (e.g. 2007: 7) does, to talk about spatial laws while rejecting the idea that these laws would be deterministic; then the concept of *law* is deprived of its specific characteristics. This also applies to the reverse argument; accepting determinism while rejecting the idea of laws. As Hempel (1942: 46, emphasis removed) concludes, '[T]he use of the notions of determination and of dependence in the empirical sciences,

---

12   A parallel can be drawn to Marxism and the question whether it is economically deterministic or not. A relatively common interpretation is that Marx saw a deterministic relationship between the economic element and history. However, this is a misconception (Israel 1971: 339, Ollman 2003: 70f). In 1890, Friedrich Engels (in Israel 1971: 339) wrote the following to a friend: 'According to the materialist conception of history, the *ultimately* determining element in history is the production and reproduction of real life. More than this neither Marx nor I have ever asserted. Hence if somebody twists this into saying that the economic element is the *only* determining one, he transforms that proposition into a meaningless, abstract, senseless phrase'. However, Engels argues that he and Marx are likely to be blamed for the misconception of economic determinism: '[W]e had not always the time, the place or the opportunity to allow the other elements involved in the interaction to come into their rights' (ibid.). Perhaps space syntax, like Marxism, is being perceived as more spatial deterministic than its developers had in mind? What you want to say and what others think that you are saying are, as we all know, not always the same. And no technology is free from sociological and psychological aspects. Gustaf Östberg (2005: 235) has noted how technicians – in their heads – often transform probabilistic statements to deterministic ones. But when communicating this observation to the technicians themselves, he was met with opposition. To conclude this discussion, let me just say that the boundary between probabilism and determinism is not always clear.

including history, involves reference to general laws ... [T]o speak of empirical determination independently of any reference to general laws means to use a metaphor without cognitive content'.

If we look at what Hillier mean by the term spatial laws, we realise that he refers to laws that apply *sometimes*:

> The concept of spatial 'laws' is critical ... so we must explain what this means. Spatial 'laws', in the sense the term is used here, does not refer to universal human behaviours ... but to *'if-then' laws* that say that if we place an object here or there within a spatial system then certain predictable consequences follow for the ambient spatial configuration. Such effects are quite independent of human will or intention, but can be used by human beings to achieve spatial and indeed social effects. Human beings are *bound by* these laws in the sense that they form a system of possibilities and limits within which they evolve their spatial strategies. However, human agents *decide independently* what their strategies should be. Like language, the laws are then at once a constraining framework and a system of possibilities to be exploited by individuals. (Hillier 2002: 154, my emphasis)

He also says:

> Architecture is *law governed* but it is *not determinate*. What is governed by the laws is not the form of individual buildings but the field of possibility within which the choice of form is made. This means that the impact of these laws on the passage from problem statement to solution is not direct but indirect. It lies deep in the spatial and physical forms of buildings ... (Hillier 2007: 7, my emphasis)

As we see, it seems as if Hillier wants to soften the law concept by saying that the laws he is talking about are not 'of a deterministic kind' (Hillier 2007: 22). At the same time, as we saw earlier, he says that space syntax aims at elucidating the city's underlying regularities. And if you talk about regularities, you – again according to conventional theory of science – indirectly assume that they are governed under general laws.[13] In the words of Hempel and Oppenheim (1948: 136),

> [T]he explanation of a general regularity consists in subsuming it under another, more comprehensive regularity, under a more general law ... [T]he validity of Galileo's law for the free fall of bodies near the earth's surface can be explained by deducing it from a more comprehensive set of laws, namely Newton's laws of motion and his law of gravitation ... .

---

13   On the difficulties in separating causal relations from correlation relations, see Gullberg (1986: 89f).

That there, behind the regularities generated by the built environment, lies some kind of law, is shown in the following two quotes by Hillier (2007: 67; 338): 'Examining the space-time regularities of the phenomena generated by abstract artefacts, we cannot fail to note one overwhelming consistency; that they seem to be governed by pattern laws of some kind', and, 'The relation between spatial and social forms is not contingent, but follows patterns which are so consistent that we can hardly doubt that they have the nature of laws'.

Space syntax's main finding is that 'the structure of the urban grid considered purely as a spatial configuration is itself the most powerful single determinant of urban movement, both pedestrian and vehicular' (Hillier 2007: 113). '[T]his relation is fundamental and lawful', Hillier says (ibid.) and continues: 'Urbanity, we suggest, is not so mysterious. Good space is used space. ... [H]ow the urban system is put together spatially is the source of everything else' (Hillier 1996: 169f). Hillier can be likened to Socrates, who claims to know how to 'correct the world by knowledge, guide life by science, and actually confine the individual within a limited sphere of solvable problems' (Nietzsche in Megill 1985: 56). The rhetoric that he uses is not unlike that of the functionalists. Åhrén (1928: 174), for example, called for '[e]xact problems, exact solutions' in urban development and argued that it is 'strange that an area of human activity, where the conditions are very much rationally comprehensible and measurable, to this day has escaped to become science'.

Here, it seems appropriate to consider Olsson's (1977: 356) reminder: '[I]n the minds of modern man the concept of logic has assumed the position which once was occupied by God himself'. Against the almost religious faith in what space syntax can tell us, it should be said that the task of generating used space may be solvable, but used space is – as we have seen – merely one prerequisite for urbanity; it does not guarantee it. What about the other conditions? For example, how can you – through urban form – create or predict the social and cultural diversity of urbanity? When it comes to clarifying the relationship between built form and social diversity, even the most advanced spatial analysis falls short. The premise 'used space' does not say which people use the space. For example, many of the spaces of today's gentrified areas have a relatively low social and cultural diversity – despite their being well-used.

However, my point is not that space syntax theorists deny this difficulty (see e.g. Marcus 2000b: 77ff; 2010b). My point is that the application of quantitative methods – methods that by definition reduce social factors to measurable units – requires that we act as if this difficulty can be overcome. This, however, is not necessarily a bad thing.

Science is a negotiable entity (Livingstone 1992: 307). Knowledge, in general, is as self-referential as its own language (Olsson 2008). This is especially evident when it comes to how space syntax advocates and social scientific theorists look at the question of 'what comes first?' Is it – crudely put – space or social processes? According to Hillier (2007: 140), it is the urban structure that constitutes 'the fundamental source of the multi-functionality that gives life to cities', which is why he '[is] trying to detect society through space, in contrast with most commentaries on society and space which typically look at society and try to detect its output in space' (Hillier and Netto 2002: 13.3). 'Space precedes function' is the summarised message of space syntax (Klarqvist 1993: 12). Although social scientists sometimes express the desire to study the outcomes of social, economic and political processes in space – which is a kind of reverse determinism – a recognition of the interaction that exists between the social and the spatial is more common; in other words, a recognition of a dialectical relationship between the material environment and the immaterial social structures (Tonboe 1985b). 'The spatial structure partly reflects and partly determines the social structure', sociologist R.E. Pahl (1975: 147) writes. Others that express this idea include Harvey (1989), Castells (1977) and Soja (1980), but also Simonsen (1993) and Pløger (1997). All of these urban theorists reject the idea that space can be studied in its own right, that space has an explanatory value in itself when it comes to understanding social processes. For example, if we look at human geographer Per Gunnar Røe's (2007) study of the emergence of so-called mini-cities of Oslo's suburbs, we see that he explains this not by referring to space but to socio-cultural processes and practices. These 'mini cities' often show greater diversity than the segregated western parts of Oslo's city proper. As for the underlying forces behind this, he points to cultural factors, changes in cultural policy and the new practices and materialities linked to these. Overall, the study points to how a range of factors, especially the residents' practices, can affect urbanity's existence or non-existence. What you see depends on where you stand – the geographical inference problem in a nutshell.

Space Syntax – a Conclusion

> The entire apparatus of knowledge is an apparatus for abstraction and simplification – directed not at knowledge but at taking possession of things ... [W]ith 'concepts' [one takes possession] of the 'things' that constitute the process. (Nietzsche 1968: §503)

> 'Something' always survives or endures – 'something' that is not a thing. (Lefebvre 1991: 403)

As shown in this chapter, my main objection to space syntax is that it *overlooks* the inference problem and that it *overlooks* the fact that the social dimension of built form – urban life – is difficult to grasp using a (natural) scientific approach. The ceaseless auto-correlation that exists between the material and the social makes it impossible to explain cause and effect in the processes that mould and characterise (urban) space. There are simply too many variables that elude us (Bergman and Mannheimer 1974: 331). Some phenomena we can be more or less good at predicting, but the fact remains that 'predictability does not entail explicability'

(MacIntyre 2007: 103). Referring to space syntax as 'evidence-based design' is debatable, since it implies a view of the future as being 'obvious to the mind or eye', using the etymological meaning of the Latin word *evidens* (www.askoxford. com 2009-06-21). The term 'evidence-based design' provides a semblance of certainty, of 'deductive certainty' rather than 'near-certainty' or 'high probability' (see Hempel 1966: §5.4).

Having said this, it is also possible, even desirable, to use a different word and say that space syntax *defies* – not *overlooks* – the inference problem and that it *defies* the fact that we cannot grasp the essentially ungraspable. For without categories and definitions, both thought and action are confused (Nietzsche 1968: §521, Lefebvre 1995: 121). In Olsson's words (1980a: 11e; 121b), 'As in other instances of the human condition, tragedy captures the pattern. We are damned if we do and damned if we don't … [T]o argue that something cannot be achieved fully is not the same as to advocate fatalistic inactivity'.

What I want to say is that space syntax' problem, paradoxically enough, is also its strength – a conclusion reminiscent of Aristotle's point that what one cannot do perfectly, one must do as well as one can (Olsson 2007: xii). As Shakespeare's Hamlet teaches us, understanding kills action; action requires that you are wrapped in an illusion (Nietzsche 1999: §7). Too much modesty cramps initiative (Russell 1946: 855). It may also be that social scientists – like city planners – have to assume that the city in some respects is a cause-effect system, whose syntax can be clarified.[14] Although we cannot explain the relationship between urban form and urban life, we can at least increase our ability to make good predictions.

The advantages of a fixed anchor like Hillier's – to reconnect with Olsson's metaphor in the beginning of Chapter 5 – is clarity and transparency; urbanity is given a form, and form is the sensory path to knowledge (Torsson 1995: 3, Seip 1995: 28). As Hillier points out, 'co-presence' is not a social phenomenon in itself; it is the basis of social phenomena (Hillier et al. 1993, Westin 2011: 231). Although written in another context, the words of urban theorist Deniz Altay (2007: 71) fit well in this context: 'When people leave [public space], there is nothing left'. Hillier offers a dissection instrument with greater precision than those used by geographers or sociologists in analyses of how the city's physical structure affects the urban. The downside is that Hillier, in consequence and by definition, excludes urbanity's non-tangible – yes, social – aspects. Co-presence

---

14   A parallel can be drawn to football/soccer and the statistician Roland Loy's analyses of football games. Loy has analysed around 3000 games, and he uses the insights to overthrow common myths like, for example, the idea that crosses lead to goals: 'Crosses are perhaps the most meaningless thing there is in football … Football is not explained by one single parameter; there are thousands of factors that work together', and these must be studied statistically and objectively (in Hein and Thomma 2006: 6). However, the idea that players and coaches can learn how to act according to that which is statistically most efficient is naive, since football is a human and thus not an altogether rational activity (see Bar-Eli et al. 2007).

– which is what space syntax can make probabilistic predictions about – is, as we just learned, not a social phenomenon in itself. '[C]o-presence ... is just co-presence of bodies', Hillier says (in Westin 2011: 231) and continues: '[I]f you ask a social scientist "where does sociology begin?", they would say "with human interaction" It seems to me, ... what space does is to create co-presence. It does not create interaction; it creates co-presence – that is all it does'.

So, co-presence is not social in itself. In contrast, it makes up the foundation of social interaction (if we by social interaction refer to interactions in physical space – not over the phone or the Internet). And it is with social interaction that the social 'begins'. As Hillier points out, social scientists tend to begin their analysis with social interaction. One of them is Björn Eriksson (2007: 33), a sociologist, who in his book *Social interaktion* (translates into *Social Interaction*) argues that 'social interaction is the basis ... on which all other social phenomena rests'. And indeed; if social interaction is seen as the foundation for the social, for society, for culture, would not social scientists do well – as Eriksson does – to begin their analysis there, at social interaction? To this question, my answer is no. Otherwise we commit the mistake that is so common among social scientists (even among geographers): namely, regarding the social as a more or less independent, transcendent being. Social interaction does not arise out of nothing or in some kind of vacuum. The urban 'cannot go without a practico-material base', Lefebvre (1996: 103) writes, but was criticised later by Hillier (in Westin 2011: 232) for not following up on his claim: 'Lefebvre never went beyond that. He kept on repeating that, he stayed at the level of philosophy and feelings'.

Hillier is the one who has seriously taken up the challenge to go to the bottom of society's physical-morphological base, and, hence, he has probably pushed this problem considerably farther than what Lefebvre himself had wanted. For Hillier does not stop at Lefebvre's second warning; that is, if one is to distinguish between the 'city' and the 'urban' – the city's physical and social morphology – you have to manage this distinction 'with the greatest care, by avoiding separation as well as confusion' (Lefebvre 1996: 103). One could formulate the differentiation like this: While Lefebvre, as well as most of his followers, first and foremost seeks to avoid *separation*, Hillier and researchers of space syntax do what they can to thwart *confusion* (Westin 2010).

If we now return to Hillier's claim that co-presence is not the same as social interaction, we can problematise this with Erikson's (2007B) concept of *samhandlingskrets* (translates into something like a *sphere of joint action*). A *sphere of joint action* is the framework in which interaction takes place, such as when two people stand in front of each other talking. Within such a circuit you *must* respond; a default response is also a response. This would mean that if, for example, I find myself on a street with strangers and one of them confronts me, that is, claims my attention through words, gestures and the like, a *sphere of joint action* automatically occurs – regardless whether I want it or not. For me to get out of the *sphere of joint action* created between the stranger and me (if we assume this is what I want), I must act dismissively – either verbally or by using body language. If this does not work, I have to walk away – until we no longer can see each other; until we no longer find ourselves in the same physical space.[15] Consequently, even if co-presence is not the same as interaction, co-presence is likely to give rise to a *sphere of joint action* and thus interaction.

Regardless of where the social begins, we could conclude that the urban is something that, in reality, is *within* us as well as *between* us and the socio-physical environment that we encounter in the city. One could formulate the urban as residing in our meeting with the external environment – the buildings, people, sounds and smells. In other words, 'space is no more without us than within us', as Henri Bergson writes (in Jay 1994: 194). He also writes: 'Realism and idealism both go too far … it is a mistake to reduce matter to the perception which we have of it, a mistake also to make of it a thing' (Bergson 2004: vii). When it comes to specifying the urban any further, we face nothing less than a predicament, and what characterises the predicament is that it is unsolvable. If we want to (literally) grasp the phenomenon of urbanity, we are compelled to squeeze out all that which makes it social; and from a social scientific perspective, the social dimension – of course – is the very essence of urbanity. In the beginning of Chapter 5, we read Cioran's words that we endure that which is around us better if we give it a name. He continues: 'But to embrace a thing by a definition, however arbitrary … is to reject that thing, to render it insipid and superfluous, to annihilate it' (Cioran 2012: 7).

What began as a quest for certainty turned into a source of ambivalence; that which we finally catch when we grasp our study object too hard is nothing more than a form without content; a body without a soul; co-presence – not urbanity. We can no longer close our eyes to the consequences of this statement; namely, that space syntax does not measure what it purports to measure: the built environment's social dimension. In an effort to clarify the relationship between the social and the physical, it assumes that these aspects are independent of each other. This independence is the very condition for the use of statistical correlations (Israel 1980: 111); when we translate concepts (for example 'urbanity') to measurable variables (co-presence), we assume their mutual independence.

Here we can recall the words of one of space syntax's earliest critics, anthropologist Edmund Leach (1978: 387). He writes, 'When [Hillier et al. 1978a] turn from topology to sociology … they reveal a level of naivety that is unacceptable'. Leach too, directs criticism towards Hillier's lack of understanding of, or disregard for, the inference problem. He turns against the message he reads between the lines in Hillier et al. (1978a), namely that 'an analysis of the syntax of a settlement pattern will tell us something about the social structure that was peculiar to the society that devised that settlement pattern in the first place'

---

15 Here, we can remember Strindberg's narrator in *Alone*, who carefully and intuitively chose which way he was to go on his walks: '[I]f something is not quite right, I see only enemies looking scornfully at me. Sometimes the hatred emanating from them is so strong I have to turn back' (Strindberg 1998: 171).

(Leach 1978: 397). This he comments on as follows: 'If this is what they intend to say then I must disagree most vigorously … [E]ven if one could be sure of what the generative syntactic rules have been, one cannot infer anything at all about the society that makes use of the resultant settlement' (ibid.).

From the completed arguments in this chapter, we can now answer the initial question of what urbanity is. It is a *thing/not-thing*, something both tangible and non-tangible (Lefebvre 1991: 402). As the commodity was for Marx (Castree 1996: 356), urbanity can be described as a concrete abstraction, no more an immediate tangibility than a metaphysical essence, no more a question of buildings and human bodies than a question of relations and memories: 'Each … material underpinning has a form, a function, a structure – properties that are necessary but not sufficient to define it' (Lefebvre 1991: 403).[16] The definition is a paradox since it includes its opposite; urbanity is both *thing* and *not-thing* at the same time. The urban turned out to be a bat; sometimes a mouse, sometimes a bird; sometimes an existing empirical immediacy, sometimes a subsisting object of thought. At the same time, it is neither. 'In the struggle between ultimates, no one wins' (Olsson 1980: 77b). But what does this mean? The statement that the urban both exists and subsists is in itself not very provocative. However, what we have done is to identify the ontological status of the urban. And since the definition is dialectical, with its terms of both/and, it ought to be clear how problematic it is to try to capture the phenomenon with the conventional logic of either-or.

> The dialectical relations of existence and subsistence are tremendously important not the least because we tend to ignore them. … Asking 'How much do you love me?' and receiving the answer '1132' is … neither a question nor an answer, but a category mistake reflective of our own myths of communication, fetishism, and reification. (Olsson 1980a: 23e)

If we take this criticism seriously, thinking in terms of cause and effect in itself appears questionable since it assumes a separation between the city's social and physical dimensions. As we have seen, this is a basic assumption of space syntax. This criticism, a meta-criticism, may seem unfair, partly because all planning in one way or another assumes that we can achieve social goals through manipulating physical form, and partly because space syntax is far from alone in trying to grasp social phenomena in a (natural) scientific way. In fact, the latter is something that many social scientists explicitly or implicitly do (Asplund 2002, MacIntyre 2007,

---

16   As Łukasz Stanek (2011: 76) writes, Lefebvre's thesis of space as a concrete abstraction is stated several times in *The Production of Space* (Lefebvre 1991: 15, 86, 100, 341). However, as Stanek adds, this thesis is under-researched by Lefebvre's interpreters, even if it has been noticed by most of them: Stuart Elden (2004), Mark Gottdiener (1985), David Harvey (1989), Christian Schmid (2005) and Rob Shields (1999) – in particular Harvey and Schmid. For an investigation of the Hegelian and Marxist genealogies of the concept of space as a concrete abstraction, see Stanek (2011).

Sobel 1995).[17] Nevertheless, or, rather, precisely because of this, the question is a relevant subject of scientific discussion.

If that which I have explored is correct – that is, if Lefebvre (1991: 26) is right that '(social) space is a (social) product' – it ought to be impossible to 'make sense of the relationship between form and function' (Hillier 1996: 8). But to criticise space syntax theorists for focusing on the *thing* aspect of urbanity is not the same as arguing that this aspect is not important when trying to understand life in the city. The French playwright Alfred Jarry (2005) argued that there is neither night nor day, that life is continuous. Everything, really, is one and the same; days and nights are equally obscure. Despite an abundance of daylight and man's sharp vision, he is in fact blind – 'immersed in pitch darkness, unable to even imagine what life is all about' (Glas 2005: 157). Despite this belief – or, more correctly, because of it – Jarry chose to name his book *Days and Nights*. For without these pendulum movements, we cannot understand that life is lived continuously, without disruptions (Jarry 2005: 83). Disintegration is a prerequisite for any understanding at all to be possible, which is why a dialectical approach can never be a total contrast to conventional logic but, rather, a complement; a disruption of its stability. The city-urban distinction but also other distinctions made in this book – between vision and reality, individual and society, Apollo and Dionysus, the superego and the id – are both real and artificial. We need them and science needs them, which is why this book both criticises and reproduces them.

By exploring both the *thing* aspect and the *not-thing* aspect of urbanity, I have, in this chapter, tried to illustrate the impossibility of separating these dimensions without compromising its full meaning when defining the concept. In doing so, it is now hopefully clear that although certainty and transparency is the traditional goal of science, it is sometimes necessary to allow a certain degree of ambiguity in the terms we use to describe the world. If certainty becomes an end in itself, we risk ending up in a situation where we do not know anything at all, for the world does not always fit into our categories. In the words of Stephen Gale (1972: 299), '"Ambiguity of interpretation or function" is not always the mark of an unscientific language; it can also be the mark of language of science which seeks to express and incorporate a rich scope of meaning'.

But let us look at the concept of *thing/not-thing* again. There is a third, unspoken, element, which is expressed by the slash /. The slash, symbolising a relation, is the character that both holds together and separates the two parts of a whole (Olsson 1980b: 10). *Thing/not-thing* or *city/life*. In reflection, is it not this third element that space syntax wants to cast light on? The answer, I would argue, is both yes and no. On one hand, space syntax seeks to explain the relationship

---

17   Particularly social scientific studies that are concerned 'with the *actual occurrence* of human ideas or human behavior … usually follow the value-system of positivistic metascience', to borrow Israel's (1971: 344) formulation. These differ from critical theoretical studies, which study social phenomena 'from the point of view of whether they are true, right, and just' (ibid.).

between urban form and urban life, between urbanity's *thing* aspect and its *not-thing* aspect, if you will. It aims to do this by investigating spatial configuration and how it affects movement. Why, then, is the answer also no? Because the slash is the dialectical sign of internal relations – the kind of relations that are banned in conventional logic because everything is related to everything else and nothing can be untangled (ibid.; Ollman 2003). It seems that space syntax theorists would not conceptualise urbanity's third, unspoken element with a slash but with a hyphen (*thing-not-thing*, or *city-life*) – that is, the sign representing the search for explanations and/or predictions (depending on which direction you make inferences), the sign of conventional logic. Condensed, here we find the difference between social scientists like Harvey, Lefebvre and Olsson, and architectural theorists like Hillier and Marcus. What we also find is the more general difference between what is called the philosophy of internal relations, on the one hand, and the philosophy of external relations, on the other. In the next chapter I elaborate on this difference.

Although space syntax is a mathematical approach, it would be misleading to claim that it is all about quantities. The parallel to geography's quantitative revolution[18] is inevitable: '[I]t was not the numbers that were important', Gould (1999: 86) writes when describing this revolution, 'but a whole new way of looking at things'. This new way of seeing was a scientific wiewpoint, which, with the help of mathematician and philosopher Alfred North Whitehead, can be defined as 'to see what is general in what is particular and what is permanent in what is transitory' (in ibid.). Space syntax graphic axial maps can be interpreted as a rhetorical tool, which allows us to – figuratively speaking – go below the surface of the city and discover the underlying principles behind its organisation. For as Hillier writes, 'The extraordinary thing about cities is not that they are so different but that they are so alike' (in Marcus 2008: 135).

This is also where space syntax's most crucial – indeed, revolutionary – contribution is to be found. To urban-planning discussions, space syntax contributes to a shift in focus from architectural style, aesthetics and symbolism, to what can is *between* the buildings. '[T]he superficial appearance of the environment is nearly completely ignored by space syntax, including surface colors, textures, and patterns ... Space syntax says little or nothing about properties of layout other than

---

18   Soja (2001: 1.1) has also made this parallel: 'Thinking about the topic of Space and Society in the context of this Space Syntax Symposium [in Atlanta 2001] stirs memories of my first academic appointment in the Department of Geography at Northwestern University, in Evanston, Illinois. ... When I first joined the department in 1965 ... it was considered the most advanced center in the country for teaching and research in the new quantitative and theoretical geography that was rapidly transforming the discipline'. Despite these similarities there are many differences between the era of spatial science in geography and space syntax. For example, the methods that characterises the latter are more pragmatic and more closely related to specific local contexts than the mathematic models that were used within geography during the 1960s (ibid.: 1.2).

connectivity' (Montello 2007: 8; 7). Unlike many practicing architects, who often surrender completely to the *thing* aspect and who, in the spirit of Palladio, focus on individual houses and places (Habraken 2005), space syntax aims at illuminating the bridge that connects stones and people. Instead of trusting more or less unfounded speculations about what kind of forms generate urban life, space syntax offers tools to investigate, at the very least, which forms that counteract urbanity. And, it must be added, the realisation that urbanity is about co-presence, rather than 'city-like' roofing materials is promising – at least if one considers the issue from the point of view of the *flâneur* or the pulse addict, the ocnophil or the Sunday hater, who cherishes the crowd and its promise of capricious moments of friction.

When contemplating Marcus's (2010a) statement that 'society begins with people sharing space rather than values', it becomes rather obvious that space syntax has its place within a Jane Jacobean tradition of thinking about cities. For as Asplund (1991: 59) has noted, Jacobs's quest was 'to keep Gesellschaft intact'. Jacobs (1992) and Hillier (1996) may both be ideologues, but the ideology they advocate is an ideology of urbanity. They do not want to steer people away from each other in different insulating compartments; rather, they want to encourage clashes, collisions and exchange of ideas, activities that in the broad sense can help to transcend boundaries. In this respect – and this is one of my conclusions – one could say that space syntax is a helper not only of Apollo but of Dionysus, too.

To social-scientific urban studies, space syntax's theoretical contribution includes a (re)focusing on the city's material dimension. For even if the built environment by no means determines how people interact with each other, it unmistakably opens up as well as shuts down opportunities for social interaction. This fact has been neglected in humanistic inspired human geography.

> In retrieving man from virtual oblivion in positivist science, humanists have tended to celebrate the restoration [of man] perhaps too much. As a result values, meanings, consciousness, creativity, and reflection may well have been overstated, while context, constraint, and social stratification have been underdeveloped ... (Ley 1981: 252)

In conclusion, the aim of my critique of space syntax has not been to 'falsify for the sake of rejection' but rather to 'falsify for the sake of creative understanding', to borrow a formulation from Olsson (1980a: 18b). Or in the words of poet Elisabeth Hermodsson (1968: 14), 'To critically review – instead of forever chanting – the principles of science, does not, of course, mean a disapproval of science in general'. My intention in discussing the dialectical-philosophical approach has not been to reach a final definition of urbanity nor to replace scientific precision with a kind of post-modern 'delight in ambiguity', to borrow David Livingstone's words (1992: 343). Rather, I have sought a deeper understanding of the urban as a socio-spatial phenomenon as well as of the reasoning rules with which we try to capture it.

My critique is reminiscent of the critique that Stephen Gale (1972) directs at Harvey's (1969) *Explanation in Geography* – a critique that Harvey (1972: 324) came to call a 'counter-philosophy'. The comparison is motivated by the many similarities that exist between Harvey's *Explanation in Geography* (1969) and Hillier's *Space is the Machine* (1996). At a fundamental level, these books are very similar.[19] The most obvious similarity is the fact that both stand out as the first in the history of their respective disciplines to have introduced a thorough discussion of scientific theory and methodology. Both show a confidence in scientific methods, and they have a more or less monolithic view of science. Science is equal to natural science – positivism, mathematics and logic – and there is no reason why society cannot be studied in the same way as nature. In addition, they both express the idea that a scientific perspective is independent of subjective distortions and is therefore neutral and strictly objective. In order to capture the complexity of human spatial behaviour, it is almost a necessity, the argument posits, to use precise quantitative techniques and models. The development of a rigorous scientific theory is further regarded as a prerequisite for the development of an independent scientific discipline worthy of the name. Additionally, both Harvey (1969) and Hillier (1996) embody something that Robert D. Sack (1974) has termed 'the spatial separatist theme'; that is, 'the thought that it is possible to identify, separate, and evaluate the effects of the *spatial*, either as an independent phenomenon, or as a property of events examined through spatial analysis' (ibid.: 1). Last but not least, it should be mentioned that both Harvey (1969) and Hillier (1996) occasionally question the reasonableness of their own arguments. They nonetheless return to their original positions; positions where they argue that – *in principle* – there ought to exist laws that explain geographical and architectural phenomena (see Gale 1972: 295). Gale (1972: 297) writes, 'Harvey is indeed a sober critic; but he is a critic with a point of view which has not itself been subject to the same sort of criticism'. The same, I think, can be said about Hillier (1996).

When it comes to understanding the city, the urban and the relations between them, it seems that architectural theorists are looking to solve one puzzle, while dialectical social scientists are seeking to solve another. The former emphasises certainty, the latter ambivalence. However, most often the respective camps do not clarify the underlying rules that govern their thinking. So it is that some are talking about apples and some about oranges, while everyone believe that everyone else is talking about the same thing. As Soja (2001: 1.6) has noted, 'Sharing a common spatial language does not always lead to a common understanding' (see also Marcus et al. 2013).

Here we could stop and conclude that it is precisely because of this that everyone might as well continue on the track that each discipline has created; we live in incommensurable realms of thought and cannot learn from each other. In fact, the opposite is true. For by now we know that it is only in light of another's

---

19 Even though Hillier's book was published 27 years after Harvey's. Space syntax can – from a geographer's point of view – appear almost anachronistic; it saw the light of day at a time when the critique of the quantitative revolution in geography had spread on many fronts.

reasoning rules that we can get a clearer picture of our own. As Plato knew, to have knowledge is to know one's geometry (Olsson 2007: 103). Therefore, before moving on to the next chapter, I let Cassirer speak (2005: 146):

> [A] 'critical' philosophy must seek a more general perspective that can free us from the obligation to appoint any single form of knowledge to the universal and only possible, thereby prescribing to any of these various '*isms*'. This philosophy must look to the *totality* of the possible forms of knowledge and the relationship between its individual elements – a relationship that can be determined only when we understand each element in its specific character.

Chapter 7
Logic – Dialectics

[I]n the case of human beings, we produce our lives *knowingly* and self-consciously, making us special, gifted animals … smarter, right?

Andy Merrifield

SCHOOLMASTER: *(To the OFFICER.)* Now, my boy, can you tell how much two times two is? … OFFICER: *(Rises, depressed.)* Two – times two – just a minute – makes two – twos. … And I can prove that by analogy, the highest form of proof! Listen! – One times one is one, therefore two times two is two. For what applies to one must apply to the other! SCHOOLMASTER: According to the rules of logic your proof is quite correct, but the answer is wrong! OFFICER: What is right according to the rules of logic *cannot* be wrong! Let's prove it. One goes into one one time, therefore two goes into two two times. SCHOOLMASTER: Correct – according to the rules of analogy. But then how much is one times three? OFFICER: Three! SCHOOLMASTER: Consequently two times three is also three. OFFICER: *(Considering.)* No, that can't be right – or is it? *(Sits down in despair.)* No, I'm not mature yet. … SCHOOLMASTER: According to the rules of logic that is quite correct. … OFFICER: Then logic is insane. SCHOOLMASTER: It would certainly seem so. But if logic is insane, then the whole world is insane, and why in hell should I sit here teaching you insanities!

August Strindberg, A Dream Play

After examining the planner's perspective in Chapter 2, I continued to Chapter 3 where I likened urban planning to the superego – the guardian of morals and the instance in psychic life whose Apollonian orientation represses the individual, the body and the Dionysian. The architect's artistic-visual approach puts strong emphasis on how the built environment appears to the eye. And as the eye can only perceive that which has a form, the architect is looking to delineate and stabilise, to replace the formless with form, chaos with order. The designed is the beautiful, the beautiful is the designed – such is the architect's belief; a designed environment bestows safety and harmony. Overall, when examining the planners' statements about Hammarby Sjöstad, it becomes clear that these qualities are seen as important for life in the city. Furthermore, the fact that the architects primarily are taught to design individual houses and the fact that this perspective is applied more or less unreflectedly to public space too, means that each space in a planned urban area is given a specific function – something which further strengthens the Apollonian-ethical, or, moralistic, tendencies of urban planning.

The theory of space syntax, however, we learned in Chapters 4, 5 and 6, is a scientific perspective that does not imply any moralistic notions of what is beautiful or what counts as reasonable lifestyles. Nor do space syntax theorists show any interest in the representative, or symbolic, dimension of the built environment. Instead, they take note of what the environment does to our body, to people's movements, and thereby define not what buildings look like but how the space between them is configured and – consequently – used. Since I so far in my analysis have found that urbanity to a large extent is a question of people's movements in the streets – or, co-presence in public space – it is reasonable to assume that the space syntax perspective is that which comes nearest to grasping the essence of urbanity. Hence, space syntax is the theory that is probably best equipped to lay bare the physical-spatial conditions of the urban, and, consequently, to bridge the gap between vision and reality in urban planning.

But in the previous chapter it became clear that the space syntax theorist, too, is controlled by a superego: a scientific superego. The demand of conventional logic for quantifiability requires a displacement – or an eviction – of urbanity's immaterial dimension. Furthermore, for it to be possible to unravel the connections between the physical and social dimensions of society, these entities must first be dismantled. In order to detect linkages there must first be a separation, a narrowing of the scope, which says this-is-this and that-is-that. In other words, not only artistically oriented practitioners of architecture but scientists as well aim at delineation and stabilisation; at creating form.

To comprehend is an Apollonian project in which the act of form-giving is fundamental (Megill 1985: 216). Generally, the concept of form describes the contours, the marking of boundaries; form equals external borders of areas or volumes (Lefebvre 1991: 148). Logic – whose main characteristic is thinking in terms of either-or – is preoccupied with concepts that fall entirely outside of each other's boundaries. In fact, it is a product of geometry and follows, as Russell (1946: 823) writes, 'the direction of materiality'. It is not only architecture that bears the symbol of Apollo; the Apollonian is also 'the light of theoretical learning' (Megill 1985: 54). What we see here is that architecture and logic are related, their common denominator being the desire to achieve coherence, order and form. In fact, one could even say that logic *is* architecture or, more accurately, a will to architecture (Karatani 1995). When Neil Smith (1979: 356) writes about geography's quantitative era, he calls it '[a] search for order'. Along the same lines, Zumthor (2005: 21) describes the profession of architecture: 'To a large degree, designing is based on understanding and establishing systems of order'.

In this chapter I take note of the fact that planning is always based on the same ideology or form of reasoning: conventional logic (Olsson 1980a, Nordström 2008). Consequently, it is based on the philosophy of external relations. In short, the perspective of planning implies reification, disintegration and a view of reality as possible to exhaust as well as to manipulate. Logic as an epistemological system thus has ethical implications, which is why the chapter addresses some of these.

For those not previously familiar with the philosophy of external relations, it may sound obscure and like something that does not concern the pragmatic social scientist. In fact, the opposite is true. For what we are dealing with is nothing less than the most common perception of reality in the Western world, a way of seeing practiced by most people – scientists and laymen alike. Briefly, the philosophy holds that there are things and then there are relations, and neither of these categories can include the other (Ollman 2003: 69). '[A] convenient fiction' as Riviere puts it (in Brown 1968: 147).

The (more or less direct) message from the space syntax theorist to the practitioner of urban planning, to do such-and-such and not such-and-such, represents thinking in terms of cause and effect, a setting (*stellen*) upon the real, to borrow Heidegger's term (1977: 167). The term indicates a perspective on the world as a network of calculable forces, which, if we only get to know them, can be set so that the world is created to meet our needs. When we look at the city through this lens, it seems that the problem of the vision-reality gap can be solved with the help of objective, empirical-scientific knowledge about how the world out there works. What is needed is knowledge of the relation between the means, which planners have at their disposal, and the social processes that they want to attain. Although knowledge about the relation between the physical and social dimensions of the city is indeed relevant, this approach is problematic.

One of the arguments in this book is that urbanity by all accounts is a dialectical phenomenon that, in the benevolent hands of the planners, is turned into one or more concrete thing(s). Dwelling becomes apartments, urbanity becomes 'city-like' roofing materials and desire is translated into the more manageable notion of need. A phenomenon that is largely felt (the presence of other people in a crowd) and heard (the noise from the traffic and from other people's voices) is translated into (silent) forms, whose beauty is available only to the aesthetically trained eye. The essence of urbanity is both immaterial and material, but in the name of communication, and for the sake of clarity, the planners alleviate its paradoxical nature by cutting off the confusing tail of its circular reasoning. What remains is urbanity's concrete, visible dimension – a dimension that lends itself to plans and drawings, presented to the politicians who have formulated the aim of 'city-like' building. Things are no longer both/and but a manageable either-or – a state particularly evident when there is a delineated area reserved for each activity or function. When studying plans, we learn, for example, that 'recreation' should take place in open spaces and only in open spaces. This will minimise the risk of confusing overlaps, and order will be created. In other words, the goal can be clearly expressed: 'Organise coldly, coarsely, radically' as Åhrén (1928: 175) wrote.

In light of this reasoning, which says something about the practitioners' approach to the task of creating urbanity, the interpretation formulated by space syntax theorists seems more dynamic and insightful. The understanding of urbanity as movement and co-presence – of people, activities and ideas – simply appears more realistic, more accurate. But since space syntax theorists also dislike ambiguity, they too surrender to the *thing* aspect; the strict logic of mathematics forces all apostles of science to exclude everything that is not possible to delineate and quantify. And so it is that urbanity – again – becomes a *thing*; this time, it is the co-presence of bodies. In turn, co-presence is treated as something that is linked to – and, by definition, separated from – another thing: urban space. This is because the aim is to clarify how the latter affects the former. And implicit in all studies of how one thing affects another thing are ideas about how these things are related. According to space syntax theorists, this relation is external. In other words, implied is the philosophy of external relations – a natural consequence of the fact that space syntax adheres to the rules of conventional logic, which hold that x is x and not at the same time y and that the respective identities of x and y are preserved regardless of context. But, as we learn from Olsson (1980a: 8b), '[N]obody can understand the full meaning of a theory and a set of data without first having grasped the fundamentals of the chosen mode of discourse ... [S]implifying intricate philosophical issues into operational problems is the most common mistake of institutionalized scientists and bureaucratized funding agencies'. With the intention to take this idea seriously, I will now take a closer look at the philosophy of external relations.

External and Internal Relations

> The relations between parts of a system which possesses no truly separate parts can only be internal relations. (Ollman 1969: 436)

Central to a discussion of logic is the philosophy of external relations. Its opposite is the philosophy of internal relations – the philosophy of dialectics – and the difference is greater than what one might think because the logician asks questions that, from a dialectical perspective, are not even possible. Even the most fundamental and taken-for-granted idea of cause and effect (in science and in the Western world in general) does not have any place in the world of dialectical understanding. The idea of cause-effect implies exteriority.

> The exterior is that which is not the matter ... A thing is not affected by that which is on the outside; that is, it remains the same regardless of what is outside of it. The *exterior* or *outer* relationship between two things ... exists when each one of them can be considered separately, independently of the other, and it exists as it is, regardless of what the other is or is not. (Østerberg 1966: 9)

Overall, the difference between the philosophy of external relations and the philosophy of internal relations is the key reason to why many misinterpret Marx. Where a majority of researchers see *things*, Marx sees *relations*, and where others see relations as external connections between two or more separate and independent things, Marx sees relations that are immanent to the things themselves and the things themselves as immanent to one another (Ollman 2003). The result is often confusion; when Marx writes about apples, the reader thinks of oranges and believes that oranges are what Marx has in mind, too. An example of (the basic principle of) such a misunderstanding is when Hillier (2008a) discusses and criticises social-scientific urban theorists' approach to the space-society relation (he names this 'the spatiality paradigm'). When he claims that these theorists look at society – not space – 'first', he actually tells more about his own reasoning rules than those of the theorists he speaks about. In fact, many of them – especially Harvey, Lefebvre and Soja – have a dialectically inspired perspective on the world. And according to this world view, it is in principle not possible to say that something 'comes first' since that would imply that the phenomena in question exist separately from each other.

> When we speak of man and space, it sounds as though man stood on one side, space on the other. Yet space is not something that faces man. It is neither an external object nor an inner experience. It is not that there are men, and over and above them *space*; for when I say 'a man', and in saying this word think of a being who exists in a human manner – that is, who dwells – then by the name 'man', I already name the stay within the fourfold among things. (Heidegger 1993: 358)

But since Hillier has a logical way of looking at the world, he does what everyone else with a logical mindset does; he almost automatically starts to search for causality. And once you take on this quest, either one or the other side 'wins'; something always comes first (Ollman 2003: 27). However, this is not something that Hillier makes explicit, but, as pointed out by Ramirez (2003: 59), '[t]hat which is rhetorically interesting is not what is being said but, above all, that which is taken for granted'. If Hillier were to openly explore (all of) his assumptions, his arguments would not be as powerful, since he would then reveal that his knowledge is context-dependent and therefore not universal. In other words, his argument is valid within the specific form of reasoning named logic but not within dialectics – the form of understanding that characterises the spatiality paradigm (see Hillier 2008a). In fact, neither Lefebvre nor (the dialectical) Harvey puts anything 'first' – neither space nor society. But sometimes it seems as if this is what they are doing, in part because they are not fully consistent. Not even Marx was consistent on this point. This is natural because if dialecticians were to be absolutely true to their philosophy that everything is connected and nothing can be broken out, they would not be able to abstract any factor at all. They would be silent or remain in the sphere of poetry and art.

The difference between the two forms of reasoning can be expressed with the following analogy. Where the logician sees a number of pearls hanging on a thread, the dialectician sees a pearl necklace. In the first case, each pearl is independent from each other. They are also independent of the thread, because the pearls can be defined without it. When they exist one by one, or side by side, they remain what they are – nothing more and nothing less. The pearls are held together in the manner in which a statistical correlation joins two variables. When we see a pearl necklace, however, the identity of each individual pearl changes. The pearls now form a whole, and the necklace is what it is thanks to both the pearls and the thread together; the necklace can only be defined by the relation between the pearls and between the pearls and the thread. In the first case, the relation is external; in the other, it is internal (Israel 1980: 112). Taking these ideas back to the original idea, logic is an 'exteriorised way of thinking' (Østerberg 1966: 15ff), in that it considers the relations as external linkages between separate objects or processes. The dialectician sees an internal relation between man and space, which means that space cannot be understood apart from man and vice versa. Here we can remember Heidegger's arguments about the sphere of the dwelling; it extends beyond the apartment or house. Dwelling does not – as the apartment or the house – exist in addition to man but as a part of his being.

It can sometimes seem that Hillier advocates a philosophy of internal relations, especially when he refers to the urban structure as a kind of totality whose parts are interconnected: 'Places are not local things. They are moments in large-scale things, the large-scale things we call cities. Places do not make cities. It is cities that make places. The distinction is vital. We cannot make places without understanding cities' (Hillier 1996: 151). To reinforce his message Hillier uses the concept of 'moments', which is interesting because this is exactly what Marx uses when he talks about the different parts of a whole. As Ollman (2003: 66) notes, '[By referring to [some part or instance of a process] as a "moment"] he ... underscores its character as a temporally stable part of a larger and ongoing process'. Similarly, Hillier's use of the word 'moment' reflects an epistemology that favours motion rather than stability, so that stability – whenever it appears to us – is regarded as temporary or only apparent. The following comment by Marcus (2000c: 37) about the difference between the space syntax perspective and the practitioners' perspective reinforces the idea that Hillier may be a dialectician, after all: 'What configurative descriptions do, as opposed to traditional architectural descriptions, is that they focus on the relations of the parts in an architectural system, rather than the parts themselves, and even, as Hillier puts it, on the relations among relations in such system'.

Does this mean that space syntax implies a philosophy of internal relations in its approach to the urban structure and its (individual) places? Again, compared to many practicing architects and planners – who often focus on individual sites and places – Hillier seems like the great dialectician. But if we examine the issue more closely, we notice that he applies this philosophy only sometimes. When it comes to space and society, for example, or the urban and the city, *connections* are emphasised rather than *relations*. Or, in Marx's native language, German; *Beziehungs*, not *Verhältnisse* (Ollman 2003: 27). Relations between different places in the city are internal, but the link, or the connection, between space and society is external – this is the indirect message of space syntax. As we saw in Chapter 6, the separation of space from society is a prerequisite for any space syntax analysis to be possible at all.

Hillier's argument for the importance of distinguishing between the physical and the social is exactly this: it is necessary if you want to explore the impact of urban form on urban life. And indeed, this division is essential, because each synthesis is preceded by analysis; each urban planning project is preceded by ideas about how the different parts of the city and its life are related. Scientific analysis can only work on separate elements; we can only carefully observe one thing at a time, and this thing, in turn, must 1) have a form, 2) stand still, and 3) stay the same. In other words, the observed object 'is what it is, closed around itself, without any reference to anything but itself' (Østerberg 1966: 10). The purpose of this separation procedure, according to Hillier, is not to deny the social aspect of space; on the contrary, the separation is necessary in order to study how the physical dimension (of urbanity) affects the social dimension. But from a dialectical perspective this is an unreasonable task; to insist that there are relations (connections) between space and society is like saying that space exists side by side with society, in its own sphere (see Ollman 2003: 26).

Overall, it appears as if the space syntax theorist suggests that reality contains both internal and external relations. If we are to believe Ollman (ibid.: 177) this is merely a nuanced version of the philosophy of external relations since all proponents of this philosophy believe that there is a certain amount of internal relations in the world. Hillier's theoretical statements suggest a view of the world as consisting of a series of totalities or wholes in which internal relations exist, but that these wholes are connected through external relations. This is not the spirit of the philosophy of internal relations, which perceives everything in reality as internally related. Hillier's statements raise questions: How does he draw the line around the different 'wholes'? Where does space end and society begin? These questions are in fact only variations of the basic philosophical question – unanswerable by science – of what is mind and what is matter (Russell 1946: 10).

The reason why I turned to space syntax in the first place is because I was looking for an answer to how the city affects the urban. And this, in turn, would mean a bridging of the gap between intention and outcome in 'city-like' building. However, I later found the theory to be problematic because – as the analysis in Chapter 6 showed – the relation through which the urban is linked to the city is an essential part of the urban itself. The urban is a *thing/not-thing*, which means that nothing can be broken apart. If we separate the process from the form, nothing is left of urbanity. If urbanity is anything, it is a relation, a *Verhältnis* – represented by the slash /. I have previously likened the essence of the urban to that of Marx's commodity, but it can also be likened to his concepts of capital, value and labour. For all of these can be understood as relations – 'containing in themselves, as integral elements of what they are, those parts with which we tend to see them externally tied' (Ollman 2003: 25). If we are to believe Soja (2001: 1.4), it is precisely space syntax's ascription of autonomy to space that is its main problem. Hillier's desire to separate, Soja (ibid.: 1.3) states, is simply an example of what Whitehead (2011: 72) called 'The Fallacy of Misplaced Concreteness', that is, the error of mistaking the abstract for the concrete.

Olsson (1977: 356) has warned against the creation of a society that mirrors the techniques by which we measure it, a society that echoes of the language we use to talk about it: 'Instead of implementing plans which will aid man in his striving for becoming, we are entangled in so-called descriptive, objective and analytic techniques, which will produce just the opposite'. Therefore, let us proceed with our analysis of logical thinking.

The Disintegrating Logic

The quote by Strindberg (2000: 116–18) in the beginning of this chapter is taken from his drama *A Dream Play* and has seemingly nothing to do with geography. However, the message it conveys can serve as a condensation of the lessons of the quantitative revolution – a revolution that would move the discipline 'from the dark ages of its ideographic past to the dazzling promise of a nomothetic future' (Barnes 2006: 34, see also Entrikin 1977: 211, Gould 1999: 84–100, Livingstone 1992: 304–46, Olsson 1984; 2002, Soja 2001: 1.1).

In this revolution, positivism played the lead role; it was considered to be 'the light that would guide us ever onwards' (Scott in Barnes 2004: 583f). But since social reality proved more elusive than was previously thought, confidence turned into (self-)doubt. What was discovered was that logic, whose ultimate language is mathematics, is ill-suited to deal with the qualitative changes and subsisting phenomena that social scientists are interested in (Olsson 1980a: 22b; 1984: 82, see also Gale 1972).

The connection between logic and architecture implied in the beginning of this chapter is reinforced if we look at what architecture really means. With the help of Christopher Alexander (1970: 55ff) and Hillier (1996: 49) we can define architecture as theoretical knowledge applied to building. Or in the words of Louis Kahn: 'Architecture is the thoughtful making of space' (in Frederick 2007: 8). Architecture is different from traditional or vernacular construction, which is more or less about replicating what others have done in the past without using any consciously formulated rules or principles (Alexander 1970: 46). To design, however, is to invent, to consciously look for a new solution to each problem (Zumthor 2005: 22). Architecture is thus a careful deliberation; the actual construction is preceded by reflection and analysis. Therefore, we could summarise that while traditional construction primarily is about making, architecture is about thinking. Furthermore, architecture and planning are based on the idea that careful deliberation is what will lead to the best possible outcome. This idea is based on a trust in the ability of man to be aware of the factors that may affect the consequences of his actions; that he, with the help of reason, can gain visibility and control over cause-effect relations and, thus, of society.

All this may seem obvious and relatively unproblematic. Of course planners need to think before they act and of course the result will improve the more theoretical knowledge they have about whatever problem they are facing. For what else should they do? *Not* think? Think illogically? Not analyse but 'just do'? These questions may seem ludicrous, but my point is that the aura of objectivity that characterises the logical perspective warrants closer examination.

For example, let us look at what the word *analysis* means. The word can be traced to the sixteenth century and is defined as 'to break up', 'to disintegrate'; 'a resolution of anything complex into simple elements' (*Online Etymology Dictionary* 2009-12-06). Østerberg (1966: 10) gives a more detailed explanation: 'An analysis ... involves examining a whole by determining the parts with which it is composed as well as the relations between these parts. As a consequence, we have also determined the whole because we are now able to put together the disintegrated parts in a certain way'.

When the whole has been dismembered and the pieces have been studied separately, they must be put together again. Here we can think of a disassembled clock. To put the pieces together again we must know how the clock works, and this requires knowledge of how the different parts are related. When we put the pieces together again we apply our knowledge from the analysis, thereby creating a synthesis. Therefore, we can say that the analysis implies to 'loosen up a whole in its parts, but to do it in a thoughtful way, so that we understand what we are doing' (ibid.: 11). So what the planners must do before they take on the task of constructing an urban environment is to break the code to the syntax of urbanity. That is to say, first they need to decompose, then to assemble. This is known as thinking analytically or logically – regardless of what object we direct our thinking at. In medicine, for example, 'anatomization takes place so that, in lieu of a formerly complete "body", a new "body" of knowledge and understanding can be created. As the physical body is fragmented, so the body of understanding is held to be shaped and formed' (Sawday 1995: 2).

Logic was born in antiquity (Lefebvre 1995: 120, Barrett 1962: 78, 99) and comes from the word *logos,* which means reason and/or numbers (Russell 1946: 313, *Online Etymology Dictionary* 2009-12-06). *Lo'gos* is to consider carefully (Heidegger 1977: 8). Logic is thus the language of reason. Basically, logic – like geometry – is a form of rhetoric, but over time it has gained such a high status that it is considered natural or God-given (Olsson 2007: 97). *Logos* does not only have one counterpart in Swedish; besides *förnuft* (reason) it can mean *ord* (word) too, confirming its origin in rhetoric. We can even trace the connection back to the Bible (John 1: 1): 'In the beginning was the Word, and the Word was with God, and the Word was God'. Logic is not about anything other than our own mental constructions, constructions that 'cannot exist except through the existence of reason' (Russell 1946: 495). In its most general sense, logic is

> concerned with the form of abstract structures, and is involved the moment we make pictures of reality and then seek to manipulate these pictures so that we may look further into reality itself. It is the business of logic to invent purely artificial structures of elements and relations. Sometimes one of these structures is close enough to a real situation to be allowed to represent it. And then because

the logic is so tightly drawn, we gain insight into the reality which was previously withheld from us. (Alexander 1970: 8)

In this book logic is regarded as a form of ideology, as a way to interpret the world. It is a will to architecture; to organisation and systematisation (Karatani 1995). To tackle a problem logically means to cut it up into manageable parts, to give formless and hence incalculable problems a form and then to construct an internal map of reality so that it becomes possible to navigate. Take, for example, the city as a socio-material system: '[A]ll factors in city changes are interrelated with all other factors. Nevertheless, it is possible and useful to look at each of these forces in its own right' (Jacobs 1992: 242).

Space syntax theorists share this Jane-Jacobean view. The analytical approach is advocated on a basic level even by the modernist-influenced planners, whom they criticise. The report *Increased requirements for space in the urban environment* (1965: 7) that we discussed in Chapter 3, for example, states, 'In order to assess the need for space in an urban area, one must have a clear picture of how the city is composed. It is not certain that the different areas of the city were developed in parallel, so the parts must be studied separately'. So, what unites both urban planning professionals and their critics is the following way of reasoning: first analysis (disintegration) and then synthesis (composition). I have already put forth that disintegration of the world is indispensable, since no categorisation means no communication. This is evident in many ways, including if we look at the Swedish expression for 'to divide': *att dela*. *Att dela* means not only 'to divide' but also 'to share'. The duality of this word is apparent in the following sentence: *Vi måste dela för att kunna dela* ('We must divide in order to share'). Within our context, to divide the world into smaller pieces is necessary if we are to share our experiences and knowledge of it. Space syntax makes use of the most effective and precise sharing tool available: mathematics. In mathematics, as in logic, there are no grey areas.

Anyone who has seen a child destroy a tower of blocks knows that it is generally quite easy to decompose something. Knowing how to assemble the parts together again is often more difficult. This is true for urban planners, for it is almost impossible for them to get immediate and clear feedback on whether their design solutions are 'right'; on whether their efforts to analyse and synthesise 'worked'. The situation is different in traditional building, where novices learn from their mentors by being corrected more or less as soon as they have done something wrong; 'No, not that way, this way' (Alexander 1970: 63). No attempt is made to justify (in an abstract-theoretical way) exactly what the 'right' way is. This is the very meaning of the concept of tradition.

As already noted, architecture differs from traditional construction, where the need to create new solutions was small. Instead, traditional builders more or less unreflectively did as they had always done, which meant that construction was based on so-called proven experience. Assessment of whether something works could only be based on direct experience, and this is what hampers architects; they cannot escape the gap between drawing and building. Architectural skill, by definition, means thinking in new ways, freeing oneself from past design solutions. Thus, the situation contrasts with traditional building, and this is interesting, because when abandoning old solutions, the architect has to learn to argue why *this way* is good and why *that way* is bad. In other words, design principles are created, principles that encourage the architect to advocate for a particular form and avoid others. In this way an architectural canon is established, and a new kind of tradition has been created – even though it is a paradoxical one, since its main message is to break with tradition. Once the principles guiding what is good and bad design are formulated, the architectural profession can be effectively taught and new architects can be formed. In other words, '[I]t can now be learned – because it has been given form' (Alexander 1970: 63, emphasis removed).

How these principles are taught has been observed by Dana Cuff (1992) and Catharina Sternudd (2007). Both point to how students of architecture are trained to having certain taste and that the principles taught are arbitrary. Architectural education is largely organised in the form of project work (alone or in groups) and these projects are then assessed by the teacher. In the assessment sessions, the students are taught what is right and what is wrong – while they rarely get any reasons as to why. Teachers convey their own (or: their 'own') views in a way that is both evasive/unclear and objective/truth-like (Sternudd 2007: 151). Innovation is a virtue, which – again – is paradoxical if we think about how students are indoctrinated by the teachers with what is good and bad design. And if we are to believe Alexander (1970: 63) but also Marcus (2000b), it is when the architectural profession has created its own principles that the negative effects of the architects' reflective and deliberating approach start to show. But why is it so?

The source of the problem, according to Alexander (1970), is the individual. Or, rather, it is the demands placed on her as well as her inability to live up to these requirements. Let me elaborate: in traditional construction, the individual is relatively unimportant – she is 'only an agent' doing the best she can. Little is required of her except to learn how others have done this work before. She does not need to invent any new forms but only to make small changes in the old if it turns out that something does not work. Architectural construction is different. Here the individual is central. The architect's awareness of her individuality as an architect has important implications for the design process. Any type of form will now be connected to the individual – to the individual's ability to theorise and deliberate. With the architect's awareness of herself as an architect comes the desire to break away from tradition and to make an impression. As I have already pointed out, to deviate from tradition is seen as a virtue. This means huge demands on the individual – demands that are more or less impossible to live up to. It is thus a pessimistic picture that Alexander paints (1970: 59), for as he points out, it is unlikely that a single person, let's say after five hours at her drawing board, will reinvent design solutions that are better than those that took centuries to develop. The task is simply 'beyond the average designer' (ibid.). Quite evidently, here we find a large part of the explanation for the tendency of architecture to generate failed projects. If a culture relies on individuals to produce innovative solutions that work, and the individual cannot live up to this, there is no need to say much more; failure lurks around the corner. It is simply an immanent part of the architectural profession to take big risks. But the problem lies not so much in the inadequacy of the individual as in her attempt to overcome this inadequacy. Every architect who has faced a complicated design problem is aware of the complexity of her task. To carry out the task she uses strategies that simplify data and make it manageable.

To illustrate the complexity that a design problem implies and how great the need for guiding principles is, we can turn to Alexander's example (1970: 60) of the teapot. Suppose the task is to design a teapot. Then we need to take into account the following twenty-one requirements:

> It must not be too small. It must not be hard to pick up when it is hot. It must not be easy to let go of by mistake. It must not be hard to store in the kitchen. It must not be hard to get the water out of. It must pour cleanly. It must not let the water in it cool too quickly. The material it is made of must not cost too much. It must be able to withstand the temperature of boiling water. It must not be too hard to clean on the outside. It must not be a shape which is too hard to machine. It must not be a shape which is unsuitable for whatever reasonably priced metal it is made of. It must not be too hard to assemble, since this costs man-hours of labor. It must not corrode in steamy kitchens. Its inside must not be too difficult to keep free of scale. It must not be hard to fill with water. It must not be uneconomical to heat small quantities of water in, when it is not full. It must not appeal to such a minority that it cannot be manufactured in an appropriate way because of its small demand. It must not be so tricky to hold that accidents occur when children or invalids try to use it. It must not be able to boil dry and burn out without warning. It must not be unstable on the stove while it is boiling. (Ibid.)

Given that most people lack the cognitive capacity to have all of these requirements in their heads at the same time, we must start by simplifying. As philosopher A.J. Ayer (1971: 79) observes, '[O]ur intellects are unequal to the task of carrying out very abstract processes of reasoning without the assistance of intuition'. What do we do in this situation? To begin with, we can shorten the list; make a classification of things to consider. In the case of the teapot, we may divide it into 1) safety, 2) appearance, 3) capacity, and 4) economic demands. If we were in a hurry or if we just wanted to simplify further, we may make even simpler classifications: 1) its function, and 2) its economy. Now, the twenty-one demands have been reduced to two, and the problem has suddenly gone from being 'highly amorphous and diffuse' to manageable (Alexander 1970: 61).

The sheer length of the above quote gives us an idea of the many requirements that a teapot designer must take into account. Consider then the task of designing a house! Or to plan a city! It was this difficulty that brought architects together in a 1933 congress in Athens under the theme 'The Functional City'. To help planners to come to terms with what they saw as the chaotic situation in the cities, they formulated four basic functions, which we at this point in the book are well acquainted with: dwelling, work, recreation and transportation. The guidelines were formulated in the Athens Charter, which was to become the basic planning document of the international architectural organisation *Congrés International d'Architecture Modernes* (CIAM) (Franzén and Sandstedt 1993: 142ff, Rådberg 1997: 56f; 1998: 121). Through planning, whose foundation is scientific analysis, the city could now systematically be broken down into its basic functions so that order and transparency would be created (Franzén and Sandstedt 1993: 143).

Athens was at this time what might be called 'a truth spot' (see Barnes 2004: 582). The Congress and its publications produced an 'objective' picture of what the city is and how it should be approached. The chaotic situation had been given a form and become manageable. The planning measures to be taken would all be in accordance with these categories (Franzén and Sandstedt 1993: 143). Rådberg (1988: 122), however, has questioned the commonly painted picture that the core of functionalism is its call for a full separation of functions by referring to the fact that, in the Athens Charter, there is no such call. The conclusion is hasty, he says; the scheme of analysis does not require that the different functions are separated – they are just tools, helping aids in the analysis procedure. The very concept of functionalism is derived from the conviction that the ideal solution, the ideal city, arises from an analysis of the *function* or, in other words, the problem to be solved (Rådberg 1997: 11).

Rådberg's point can be summarised as follows: We can distinguish things in our head without necessarily separating them 'in real life'. This idea is widespread; we face it, for example, in today's planning efforts for urbanity and functional mix, where it takes on the following expression: First disintegrate (in our heads), then put together into a whole (in practice). However, the idea is problematic because here we are committing what philosopher William James pointed out as one of the errors of logic: the disregarding of the boundary between different spheres (see Olsson 2007: 183). Whether there in the Athens Charter exists any explicit requirement to separate the functions is irrelevant. The mere presence of a scheme of analysis is enough, as it shows us how to think about the city. As Israel (1980: 20) has pointed out, if you see something as composed of different parts, you begin to treat it accordingly. 'Each concept, at the time of its invention no more than a concise way of grasping many issues, quickly becomes a precept' (Alexander 1970: 70). Once the division is made and is circulating in a given thought collective, it easily transforms into conceptual dogmatism – a dogmatism that is difficult to ignore and to question. The scheme of analysis will have its own life; it ends up in the taken-for-granted, in the box of 'that which has always been' or simply 'that which *is*' – meaning 'that which *is* according to nature/ science/logic/God'. In the words of Alexander (1970: 70): 'The concepts control [the architect's] perception of fit and misfit – until in the end he sees nothing but deviations from his conceptual dogmas, and loses not only the urge but even the mental opportunity to frame his problems more appropriately'.

So, it is of less importance whether the Athens charter explicitly advocates a separation of functions as long as it encourages a separation of functions in the planner's mind. We only need to look at an urban planning document today to see that these functions still form the core of urban planning – even if the 'function' of urbanity, of 'mix', has been added. The purpose of the functionalists' scheme of analysis was to enable a change in the world in order to make it better, but you could also see it from a more pessimistic (and realistic?) standpoint: what the functionalists really did was to bring man back 'into the prison of his own mind, into the limitations of patterns he himself created', to borrow Hannah Arendt's words (1998: 288). And this is how Arnold Bartetzky and Marc Schaleberg (2009: 11) comment on the consequences of CIAM's urban planning principles: 'The results ... were countless disintegrated cities, dismal and monotonous, which appear almost inhuman today. The CIAM modernists, however, all laid claim to promoting the cause of the dwellers' happiness effectively and were convinced that they knew the single best way of achieving this aim'.

Here we can refer back to Alexander's (1970: 56) pessimistic critique of architecture. The root of the collective failures of architecture, he holds, is the architect's awareness of herself as a generator of solutions. It is the act of theorisation and deliberation itself that has become pathological. The planner bites off more than she can chew, to put it simply, when she thinks that she – more or less merely by using her intuition – can dissect and then assemble such a complex socio-material system that a city is. To conceal this inadequacy – not so much from others as from herself – the architect develops and emphasises her individuality as an artist (ibid.: 10f). In a famous article 'The city is not a tree', Alexander (1965) shows how planners tend to reduce urban complex structures to simple tree structures. The reason is that the tree structure is simpler and easier to visualise than the so-called semi-lattice structures, namely the complex structures in which various elements form units that overlap each other. The strategy has been widely applied in twentieth-century urban planning (Karatani 1995: 29). As Alexander (1965: 61) concludes, this reduction is devastating to any social organisation, for it leads to sectoral breakdown and isolation: 'In a society, dissociation is anarchy. In a person, dissociation is the mark of schizophrenia and impending suicide'.

It is important to remember that Alexander (1970) does not criticise rationality and logical analysis per se; on the contrary, what he criticises is *supposedly* rational and *supposedly* logical thinking. Overall, this is what makes him interesting for this study, in which I criticise the planner who believes that she has control over her task but, in fact, makes gross oversimplifications that are based on inherited principles of how to proceed – principles that are often arbitrary in the first place.

> Whether we like it or not, however rational we should like to be, there is a factor of judgement in the choice and use of a logical system which we cannot avoid. Logical pictures, like any others, are made by simplification and selection. It is up to us to see which simplifications we wish to make, which aspects to select as significant, which picture to adopt. And this decision is logically arbitrary. However reasonable and sound the picture is internally, the choice of a picture must be, in the end, irrational. (Alexander 1970: 194)

This makes me think of Taleb's (2007: 156) general remark that '[p]lans fail because of what [can be] called tunnelling, the neglect of sources of uncertainty outside the plan itself'.

If we now return to space syntax, we can say that this theory represents an attempt to increase the planner's abilities to handle complex systems. I have already noted that the axial map can be interpreted as a rhetorical tool that encourages us to – figuratively speaking – go below the surface of the city and discover the underlying principles behind its spatial organisation. In this regard, these maps can be seen as a realisation of what Alexander (1970: 6) called for – namely: to reduce the gap between the designer's low (but normal) cognitive capacity, on the one hand, and her highly difficult task, on the other. Through mathematical techniques of analysis, space syntax enhances, so to speak, the planner's mental capacity, just like machines did with human physical capability during the industrial revolution. For man has limitations – both physical and cognitive; the example of the teapot is one illustration of this.

It is no wonder that architects (still) focus very much on individual sites and – when, for example, given the task of designing a lively, well-used area or square – try to enhance the quality of this particular site; they cannot in the same mental manoeuvre understand how a place is related to other places in the city and how this particular location in the larger morphological structure will affect its usage. Instead, architects do the best they can to attract people to the site by, for example, constructing beautiful stone walkways, benches with an interesting design, or perhaps designing a 'welcoming' facade of an adjoining building. At the same time, the site may have a position in the city's structure that does not allow it to be used as a passageway, which means that it is rarely used. So it is that the 'ultimate' meeting place in the architect's mind – the one that is said to have 'every chance of succeeding' – is left empty (see e.g. Keller 2006).

The Humpty Dumpty Problem

> Humpty Dumpty sate on a wall, Humpti Dumpti [*sic!*] had a great fall; Threescore men and threescore more, Cannot place Humpty dumpty as he was before. (Ritson 1810: 36)

> One of the most highly developed skills in contemporary Western civilization is dissection: the split-up of problems into their smallest possible components. We are good at it. So good, we often forget to put the pieces back together again. (Toffler 1984: xi)

To repeat: (scientific) analysis means to explore a whole by determining its parts and observing how they are related. But here it is important to distinguish between situations where the whole is given and those where it is not (Østerberg 1966: 10). With this in mind, how should we categorise the situation that the planners find themselves in when faced with the task of planning a city or an area within the city? Is the whole then given? That is, is it obvious? What does 'obvious' mean, exactly?

The word *obvious* comes from Latin *obvius* which refers to something that is 'in the way, presents itself readily' (*Online Etymology Dictionary* 2010-03-20). *Ob* means 'against' and *viu* means 'way'. Hence, that which is given is something that lies before us, in our way and in our view. In philosopher Roger Bacon's words, '[W]e can understand nothing fully unless its form is presented before our eyes' (in Olsson 2007: 130). If we were to answer yes to the question of whether the whole is given to the city planner, we would convey a view of the planner as a being who is able to uncover the essence of the city; she has the syntax of urbanity neatly laid out on the table in front of her, and it has spoken to her and said, 'This is how I work!'. This is the knowledge ideal on which ancient as well as modern science rests (von Wright 1986: 24f). But from Nietzsche and Chapter 1 in this book, we learned that the world itself is quiet; its voice is our own voice.

If the question whether the whole is given had been posed to a clockmaker, the answer would have been yes; her whole – the clock – is *ob vius* to her; her task is merely to put the parts together again. A clock is a type of machine. When there are no more components left on the table, we can assume that all parts are in place. If the clock does not work, we can either see if we have lost a few parts on the floor, or we can rearrange them to see if it works better then. However, when it comes to the planner and the city, the answer is no; the whole is not *ob vius*. First, a city is much larger than a clock. Second, it is a socio-spatial system – or, rather, a socio-mental-spatial system – and all social and biological systems are open, which means they change with time. As Gullberg (1986: 148) notes, 'Because of the relative instability of open systems it is ... not possible to pre-determine what mechanisms will be effective'. And in Alvin Toffler's (1984: xv) words,

> [W]hile some parts of the universe may operate like machines, these are closed systems, and closed systems, at best, form only a small part of the physical universe. Most phenomena of interest to us are, in fact, *open* systems, exchanging energy or matter (and, one might add, information) with their environment. Surely biological and social systems are open, which means that the attempt to understand them in mechanistic terms is doomed to failure.

In opposition to Hillier's claim, I would like to say that the city is not a machine.[1] This statement is a statement of philosophy of science; it does not deny that the city might still be *perceived* as a machine. For example, Woolf uses the metaphor

---

1   In his master dissertation, 'Is space a machine? Aspects of Bill Hillier's configuration theory', Kärrholm (1999: 95) formulates a similar criticism: 'If the metaphor of the machine is applicable at all, we must see space only as part of the machine. [...] It is important to emphasise that regardless of the degree to which space impacts different functions, this impact is only partial'.

in her depictions of London[2] and – as we saw in Chapter 2 – Strindberg likened the city to an electric generator.

While the city planner can see what she perceives to be parts of the city, the city as a whole remains concealed from her view. We can make an omelette out of eggs, but we can't make eggs from an omelette. This problem has a name: the Humpty Dumpty problem (Ollman 2003: 156). Nevertheless, it is the planner's job to sculpt the whole – that is, the city of the future. Her task is to construct an image of this city so that it becomes *ob vius*. Only then she can assess where the parts are to be installed. Tellingly, the word utopia means 'no place'; utopia is what is not here, nor anywhere. The planner must use her imaginative ability if she is to make the intangible, formless and absent future present – both in terms of what we can see (maps, drawings, 3D animations) and touch (models), as well as the time *right now*. In short, the city must be treated as a machine – as 'a spatio-temporal coherence of motion calculable in some way or other in advance' (Heidegger 1977: 169). And once we have begun to doubt that it is a machine, we need to put our blinders up. The realisation that most of reality is not stable and orderly but, rather, changing and procedural must at all costs be challenged, ignored, defied. The Dionysian man who takes formlessness and the indefinite life of open systems seriously runs the risk of being paralysed by his own powerlessness.

> Dionysiac man is similar to Hamlet: both have gazed into the true essence of things, they have *acquired knowledge* and they find action repulsive, for their actions can do nothing to change the eternal essence of things; they regard it as laughable or shameful that they should be expected to set to rights a world so out of joint. Knowledge kills action; action requires one to be shrouded in a veil of illusion – this is the lesson of Hamlet … (Nietzsche 1999: §7)

Jacobs (1993: xviii) considers it 'urgent that human beings understand as much as we can about city ecology – starting at any point in city processes'. This view is undeniably shared by space syntax theorists – so much that they, in their zeal for clarity, consciously or unconsciously ignore the fact that the city is an open, not closed, system. One can also – as we did in the conclusion to Chapter 6 – put it in positive terms and say that they behave like good scientists when putting an

---

2   'London was like a workshop. London was like a machine. We were all being shot backwards and forwards on this plain foundation to make some pattern. The British Museum was another department of the factory. The swing-doors swung open; and there one stood under the vast dome', Woolf (2005b: 579) writes in *A Room of One's Own*. She returns to the metaphor later, on page 587f: 'Lamps were being lit and an indescribable change had come over London since the morning hour. It was as if the great machine after labouring all day had made with our help a few yards of something very exciting and beautiful – a fiery fabric flashing with red eyes, a tawny monster roaring with hot breath. Even the wind seemed flung like a flag as it lashed the houses and rattled the hoardings'.

Apollonian veil over reality. For it should be clear by now that the Dionysian man would be an exceptionally poor planner. The Apollonian man, however, is quite different; he is the god of prophecy (Nietzsche 1999: §1), the formative force, the light of theoretical learning (Megill 1985: 38ff). He sheds light on people, putting a flattering veil over the brutal and confusing reality, the full burden of which we cannot stomach. Apollo plays an important role in civilised society; it was he who made the Greeks civilised and separated them from the barbarians. Every society, every culture requires its delusion; the urban planning collective is no exception. And what is the illusion called in this case if not the law of causality?

Cause-Effect

> [T]he planner's activity [is imbued] with a clear acceptance of unilateral statements of cause-effect transformed into commands wrapped in statutory participation. Do this; then you will achieve that! (Olsson 1990: 84, see also Gullberg 1986: 4)

Logic, Nietzsche knew, rests on conventions. In other words, 'Logic is to treat different things as if they were the same in order to create coherence and order' (Berg Eriksen 2005: 154). It is the will to power – the other side of the will to truth – that operates in the desire to fix things in the world. Behind logic is a desire to establish duration in the impermanent; certainty is valued higher than uncertainty; truth higher than illusion (Nietzsche 1997: 2f). Impermanence creates in us a sense of powerlessness – it is for this reason that the will to power hates everything that changes, turns and passes away (Berg Eriksen 2005: 155). Positivism is based on a freezing of the intangible into something material here and now and has therefore been called the ideology of the present (Olsson 1980c: 18).

In this light space syntax and its promise of evidence-based design appears as every state's dream. Thanks to its basis in science, it creates a relatively stable foundation in planning decision processes. According to Tim Stonor and Chris Stutz (2004: 5), representatives of the consulting firm Space Syntax Limited, space syntax aims to predict the effects of different interventions in the city's physical environment. This will make it possible to produce design results that match the client's – in this case the British government's – intentions (ibid.).

By now it should be clear that space syntax – its theoretical as well as its applied side – is based on the principle of cause and effect. As Nietzsche (1968: §497) has pointed out, the law of causality is the most widespread of all taken-for-granted 'truths'. But in Nietzsche's own rhetorical question of whether this makes it a truth, he exclaims: 'What a conclusion! No, truths are illusions about which we have forgotten that this is what they are' (Nietzsche 1982a: 47; see also Sleinis 1999: 72). But why then, one might ask, is this rule so prevalent in our thinking? It is partly a result of habit, partly of mental limitation, his response seems to suggest. 'As soon as we are shown something old in the new, we are calmed. The supposed instinct for causality is only fear of the unfamiliar and the attempt to discover something familiar in it – a search, not for causes, but for the familiar' (Nietzsche 1968: §551). He also writes:

> Cause and effect: there is probably never such duality; in truth a continuum faces us, from which we isolate a few pieces, just as we always perceive a movement only as isolated points … An intellect that saw cause and effect as a continuum, not, as we do, as arbitrary division and dismemberment – that saw the stream of the event – would reject the concept of cause and effect and deny determinedness. (Nietzsche 2001: §112)

As pointed out by Kern (2004), Sennett (2009) and Taleb (2007: 132), causality is strongly linked to the human tendency to think in stories, in narratives. Causality, says Kern (2004: 1), is 'a centrepiece of the inquiring human mind', a basic impulse through which we try to give actions meaning in terms of their consequences. Thinking in terms of cause and effect is a way to think critically and to create context – it is 'a tool for social understanding' (Sennett 2009). This tool also helps us to think ahead, to think strategically, by projecting onto the future the possible consequences of a given action.

But just as planning can be destructive (as well), our tendency to think in logical chains of cause-effect not only helps but also hinders our understanding, both of the social world and of ourselves. This is something that psycho-analysis has seized upon. For as van Zuylen says (2005: 54), 'the patient of psycho-analysis … is considered on the way to recovery as soon as he or she relinquishes coherence and forsakes all narrative ordering principle'. To present a story – as a writer, as a researcher on urban planning, or privately as an individual – is to cover up, to create contexts, to make understandable. And one of the most common and effective tools in this work of concealment is the idea of cause-effect: '[W]e continue to project into the future as if we were good at it, using tools and methods that exclude rare events. Prediction is firmly institutionalized in our world. We are suckers for those who help us navigate uncertainty' (Taleb 2007: 135).

According to Nietzsche (1968: §551–2), the concept of cause-effect is rooted in linguistics rather than in reality.[3] And it is dangerous too – because it requires sacrifice. When the world does not fit into our categories (or rather: in spite of the world not fitting into our categories), we all too often continue to give the formless a form, to make the invisible visible and the unmeasurable measurable. The 'ghost' in the machine called man is reduced away (Koestler 1967), the urban is separated from the city, the sense of community or lively atmosphere is separated from (and then translated back again into) physical space and so on. The danger, however,

---

3   Nietzsche was neither first nor last in highlighting the fictitious nature of causality. One of the earliest was probably Hume; his radical critique of causality is often considered as the origin of modern philosophy (Arendt 1998: 312). For a cultural historical study of causality, see Kern (2004).

lies not in the simplifications per se – because without them we would not be able to communicate, let alone to pursue the goals of science. No, the danger arises if (or, rather, when) we, in our eagerness, forget what we have sacrificed, and if/when we equate our abstractions with reality. This leads us to the next section.

Thinking/Acting – "the Chiasm"

> Conceptual thought can ... be regarded as good, as performing an entirely necessary and essential function. But it also has a negative side, for people forget that the structure of concepts is entirely man-made ... [T]hey take it to be a portrayal of reality itself. (Megill 1985: 52)

> We speak of nature and forget to include ourselves: we ourselves are nature, *quand même* [*after all*] – . It follows that nature is something quite different from what we think of when we speak its name. (Nietzsche 1986b: §327)

> All the sciences are themselves a part of the system which they study. (Boulding in Smith 1979: 360)

So far I have emphasised that architecture is about thinking, not doing. This is a simplification, and as with all simplifications, it can be misleading. For example, it seems to imply that thoughts and actions are different things. I have already highlighted the difficulty of maintaining the distinction between analytic and normative statements. In fact, the distinction between them is a modern invention. Ancient scientists, as von Wright (1986: 26) points out, did not distinguish between laws in the sense of regulations or standards for how to behave, on the one hand, and laws describing regularities in natural processes, on the other. So, no wonder we get confused when trying to separate them. The difficulty of separating also holds for the thought-action concept(s). At the core of this book are thoughts – not actions. Does this mean that I think actions in urban planning are unimportant? The question is wrongly put because thoughts and actions are, in fact, so intertwined that they cannot easily be separated (Olsson 1980a: 3–20b). Laing (1967: 117) expresses the relationship like this: 'As we experience the world, so we act'. He continues, 'We conduct ourselves in the light of our view of what is the case and what is not the case'. The reason why I study planners' conceived space is precisely because it has practical consequences; these ideas are closely linked to issues of knowledge and power – and, thus, to ethics. In the words of Marcuse, '[I]f man has learned to see and know what really is, he will act in accordance with truth. Epistemology is itself ethics, and ethics is epistemology' (in Olsson 1980a: 4b).

I have previously pointed out that space syntax theorists are more thorough in their logical analysis than the functionalist and artistically trained planner; that is, the practitioner, whose understanding of the city is of a more intuitive-speculative and *supposedly* scientific nature. It is against this backdrop that I would characterise the space syntax perspective as more honest. Its proclaimers seem – like the good scientists they are – to be aware of the fact that '[t]heories do not describe particular realities' (Hillier et al. 1978b).

But how should we interpret that space syntax theorists call their design 'evidence-based'? Is that not a promise that they can predict how plans will turn out *in reality*? If the answer is yes, Hillier is inconsistent (theories do *not* describe particular realities, we just read). If the answer is no, we can no longer escape this question: What, then, are these predictions good for? The fact that the predictions are produced in a hypothetical, theoretical, abstract space is no secret, nor is it any secret that the analytical language makes it possible to talk about the city. But what about the predicted effects? Do they also belong to the theoretical-abstract spatial dimension? Or is it not – ultimately – in lived space that they are and will be experienced? Is there anyone at all who, after this rather confusing discussion, can vindicate a strict division between theory and reality?[4] In Lefebvre's words (1995: 125), 'Mathematicians are trying to measure the perceivable and the concrete; it seems they have reached their goal – and then suddenly concrete reality vanishes; the gap seemed to be narrowing, but up close it appears wider than ever'.

But assume that I am wrong; assume that the space syntax theorist does know the difference between what is theoretical and what is real. Even then, it is still important to ask what happens when the technique ends up in the hands of politicians and planners, who do not reflect upon and, thus, do not recognise this difference. What politicians and planners want are clear answers – preferably in the form of 'evidence' – to the question of what effects their plans will generate (*in reality*). The discussion might look like this: 'Need help to create urbanity? Contact a space-syntax consultant!' Behind the term 'evidence-based design' there is a reassuring aura of objectivity and rigor that should make any planner happy. Indeed, as Hermodsson (1968: 14) concludes: 'There is a deep respect for science – a respect that sometimes takes the form of a faith'. Or in the words of philosopher Alf Ahlberg (1958), 'Science tends ... to do away with the sense of awe with which people look at a world that is strange to them, by making believe that they can understand and predict the course of natural phenomena and even, to some extent, control them'.

Thinking about the relation between theory and reality, another philosopher, Ayer (1971: 78), has pointed out that it is 'natural' for us to think of geometry, for example, as the study of physical space, and, consequently, assuming that geometrical statements have actual content. However, this is a misconception: 'A geometry is not in itself about physical space; in itself it cannot be said to be 'about' anything. But we can use a geometry to reason about physical space. ...

---

4   I have already made parallels between my critique of space syntax and Gale's (1972) critique of Harvey (1969). This is a point where the parallels become evident. As Gale (1972: 308) points out, Harvey's reasoning displays 'a confusion ... between models and reality'.

[Geometry] is therefore a purely logical system, and its propositions are purely analytical propositions' (ibid.).

And one thing that characterises all analytic statements – as the space-syntax-generated statements are examples of – is that they can never be judged true or false. Therefore, it is meaningless to ask whether they describe reality. In fact, analytic statements are tautologies. They cannot be refuted because they do not refer to empirical reality; they only express our decision to talk about the idea in a certain way. What we can and should ask, Ayer (ibid.) claims, is whether they are useful or not at a given time, whether they can be applied to a given empirical situation.

Again, planners are the extended arm of politics. The politician enlists the help of the planner, the planner enlists the help of a scientist and the scientist, in turn, consults the computer. Somewhere along this chain, there is a danger of confusion between the abstract and the concrete, the general and the particular, theory and reality, *and,* above all, of forgetting what the original task was. What was it that the politicians asked for again? Oh, yes – 'urbanity'; an attractive, vibrant big-city atmosphere where citizens and visitors will thrive. But nothing is said about the means by which the goal is supposed to be reached. At best, the 'evidence-based design' of space syntax may generate many bodies in the same space – not necessarily urbanity.

As I stated earlier, the planner inhabits partly a conceived (professional) world and partly a lived (private) world. It is when these worlds get mixed up – when the conceived realm is taken for the lived and the visualisation models of the city are taken for the city itself – that alienation waits around the corner. And here, again, we see that epistemological statements have ethical implications.

One central ambition behind the development of space syntax is to paint an informed picture of the implications of planning projects. Here, I recall Marcus's words (2000b: 44): '[O]ur objectives are clearly instrumental – we want to explain exactly what causes certain effects, so that we can develop tools that are possible to utilise in future practice'. If we interpret this statement in the light of Jonas's (1984: 27) moral philosophy, we find that this is 'the first duty' of an ethics of the future (see also Merton 1968: 623). An ethics of the future implies 'visualizing the long-range effects of technological enterprise' (Jonas 1984: 27). With the development of modern science, the consequences of our knowledge have gotten bigger and bigger. It is thus essential, Jonas asserts, that we gain as much knowledge as we can about the potential consequences of our actions.

Can we hereby characterise the space syntax perspective as *ethical*? In light of what we just learned from Jonas it does indeed seem reasonable to do so. However, to stop at this would be to underestimate the complexity of ethical concerns. For as Jonas (1984: 7f) points out, it is not enough to make good predictions; we must also humbly acknowledge the limited nature of our knowledge. And here – again – we are faced with a contradiction. A responsible approach to the future requires that we know *and* that we recognise that which we do not know: '[R]ecognition of ignorance becomes the obverse of the duty to know and thus part of the ethics' (ibid.: 8). Judging by the fact that advocates of space syntax call their services 'evidence-based design', this humbleness is nowhere to be seen. Rather, the message seems to be: 'God is alive!'[5] As Olsson (1980a: 29e) astutely observes, '[M]ost of us refuse to accept [the Nietzschean challenge that God is dead]. Instead we continue to turn one concept of God into another. One of these incarnations is clearly the progressive god of Scientific Reasoning. And that creature is just as demanding of sacrifices as all other gods'.

The balancing act between knowing and not knowing is difficult but crucial. Perhaps we can say that genuine knowledge – which is closer to wisdom than instrumental know-how – includes both knowing and not-knowing, both certainty and ambivalence. Knowing is not only knowing the facts but also reflecting on these 'facts' *and* on ourselves as knowing subjects, as (imperfect) homo *sapiens* (remembering that *homo sapiens* is Latin for 'wise man'). Here, we can recall Heidegger's distinction between calculative thinking, on the one hand, and recollective thinking, on the other, where the former can be partly conceived of as a flight from the latter (Megill 1984: 178). Psycho-analysis is often referred to as the most effective (although not very time-effective) road to self-knowledge; by reflecting on our way of reasoning and its shortcomings, we might reduce the risk of making ourselves miserable. As both Laing (1967) and MacIntyre (2007: ix) have pointed out, modernity is an obstacle to self-knowledge. One way to overcome this obstacle is to look back at history to get a better look at contemporary values. Have our values really changed, or are we making the same mistakes over and over again?

While it may be desirable that planners paint pictures of the potential effects of their planning measures, this can also be problematic. In Chapter 6 I drew a general parallel between space syntax and behaviourism – the school of thought that seeks to develop more effective strategies for prediction, control and manipulation of human behaviour. Space syntax is a positivistic theory based on empiricism, whose goal is to explain the world (the city) through observation and calculation. This type of science can be criticised for reproducing a conservative ideology, an ideology that takes society and the world's way of functioning for granted and then uses this knowledge to manipulate and control development in a desired direction (Johnston 1989: 63). In other words, we can question the value neutrality of the space syntax approach by demonstrating that there – in practice – is no strict division between *is* and *ought*, between knowledge and valuation, between science and politics. The difference is obscured, for example, when we consider the fact that space syntax is an instrument. It bears repeating: The present book is, in its most basic form, a challenge to the idea of the city planner as a 'neutral expert'. This applies to space syntax advocates as well, although the space-syntax-inspired

---

5   Nietzsche's claim that God is dead is – contrary to what one may think – not a metaphysical statement on God's existence. Rather, it summarises the results of what he calls the self-abolition of morality (Vattimo 1997: 81f). Nietzsche's whole philosophy is based on the discovery of the fact (or suspicion) that man's belief in truth is (only) a belief (ibid.).

planner usually has far more empirical support behind her design solutions than the more conventional modernist/artistic practitioner.

Marcuse (in Israel 1971: 110) has pointed out that modern technology itself – not only its application – is a way of exerting power; 'methodical, scientific, calculating and calculated power'. In this light, space syntax researchers, too, become ideologues and practitioners of power. They can be said to belong to 'a scientific priest class, untouched by our earthly political considerations, gathering data and charting the future for everyone' (Goodman 1972: 199). Facts are 'only' facts as long as they are not used: '[A]s soon as they're put together to support or reject a particular position, the facts become part of that position' (ibid., see also MacIntyre 2007: 57f). Or in Israel's words (1971: 311), 'So science and technology serve not only as productive forces but also as a means of social domination. Whereas science had an emancipating effect during, for example, the period of the Renaissance – when it freed man from the power of dogmatic social forces – this is not so today when science and technology are tending to become means of social dominance'.

Modern science – the thought tradition that distinguishes between descriptive and prescriptive statements – has released scientists from the implications of ethics and responsibility. As Hermodsson (1968: 15) has pointed out, it is only the politicians and the military men that are regarded as guilty when the results of science are misused. Scientists are innocent; they merely uncover pure facts. If we – inspired by Jonas's (1984: 27) ethics of responsibility – equal responsibility in the urban planning profession to gathering as much knowledge as you can about the impact of urban planning measures, we are faced with a paradox. For experts, Asplund (1979: 83) points out, are 'not actionable. They are the officials of truth. And truth just *is* – no one is responsible for it'. The most reliable expert is the most anonymous one; in our civilization an expression like 'personal expertise' is a contradiction in terms (ibid., see also Brenner 1988: 9). So it is that planners – these 'neutral experts' – are released from responsibility.

Now we can turn the question around: Does this mean that space syntax can be characterised as manipulative and therefore *unethical*? Again, let us not jump to conclusions, especially not on ethical matters. In contemporary society the empirical sciences have a high position because, basically, they offer tools for the control of society and of the future. The empirical sciences are usually contrasted with the critical sciences, whose intention is to challenge what is regarded as 'truth' and to emancipate people from dominant and oppressing ideologies. 'Critical social science is subversive and potentially even revolutionary', Johnston (1989: 63) states. But in fact, the distinction between knowledge that is manipulative and ideology-preserving, on the one hand, and knowledge that is emancipatory, on the other, is highly arbitrary. From one point of view, space syntax looks like the former kind of knowledge, for example, because of its kinship with behaviourism. But empiricism can also be liberating (Johnston 1989: 63). And I have already drawn attention to this dimension of space syntax – in particular in Chapter 4 when I described this theory as an important step away from the arbitrariness and moralism that has characterised and still characterises urban planning. However, from a critical social scientific perspective this subversive potential of space syntax analyses is easily overlooked; it tends to be overshadowed by behaviouristic terminology and a more or less naive assurance of value neutrality.

To clarify what I mean when I say that space syntax in general can be emancipatory, we can return to the concept of disurbanity. Disurban environments – and this is my interpretation – can be seen as a result of state domination, of measures designed to create and retain control over the citizens. For as Foucault (2004) has taught us, the material-spatial aspect of society is an effective tool for establishing desirable means of communications and exchanges, or perhaps more importantly, for interrupting undesirable ones. The state's ultimate goal is to create obedient citizens who submit to its rule (Weber 1994: 311) and in order to achieve this, the state has to find a way to manipulate the human psyche. The Swedish functionalists unabashedly expressed their ambitions to create a new and better type of human being (Asplund et al. 2008). But since humans are not so easily manipulated, the functionalists – like all skilled planners – went *indirectly* to their target; that is, they directed their actions not to the psyches of people but to their bodies. Furthermore, it is generally easier to control a *thing* than a *not-thing*. So by manipulating urban form one can spread out people's movement and thus prevent people from meeting. The result of these control measures we can now not only experience or witness, but also – thanks to space syntax – put into words (or, rather, a word): disurbanity. This is just one example of how space syntax can help us explore the power-laden relation between space and society, between politicians and planning professionals and citizens.

Earlier I highlighted the planner's Apollonian character. The planner – unlike the Dionysian man – cannot be content with simply contemplating the world's complexity since it would lead to resignation and paralysis. 'Who, with the exact vision of his nullity, would try to be effective and to turn himself into a savior?' Cioran (2012: 6) rhetorically asks. The planner must 'show some muscle' and produce visible results by adding an Apollonian veil, a form, onto the city's incalculability and formlessness so that it will appear like a manageable set of cause-effect relationships. In turn, this means that targeted measures not only will appear as possible but also desirable. Moreover, the planner would not easily accept Sennett's (2008: 100) conclusion that planners 'are bound always in the end to be out of control' (see also Gunder and Hillier 2009: 23–38). No, instead the planner embraces the lesson of Hamlet: 'knowledge kills action' (Nietzsche 1999: §7).

However, the planners' audacity – if you will – seems to turn into resignation when it comes to taking responsibility. As Merton (1968: 622) has pointed out, scientists and engineers are indoctrinated with a sense of limited ethical responsibility. This is a consequence of the high degree of specialisation that characterises modern society, not excluding urban planning, where the road from assignment to implementation usually is long and winding. At the same time the consequences of our knowledge have become increasingly dire (Jonas 1984). It is hard to not see how paradoxical this is.

The paradox can be summarised like this: More and more advanced technologies (knowledge) have led to ever-more perplexing and serious consequences. However, the distance between action and consequence has increased, which has reduced the sense of responsibility. The paradox is inherent in the bureaucratic system itself. For the system to work effectively, each individual has her own limited remit. In addition, in order to justify her place in the system, she has to produce visible results. Carrying out her duties, the individual may perceive herself as an instrument, as an object of other's will, of the system's will. Accordingly, the responsibility lies elsewhere.

What this suggests is that in planning there is an interesting interplay between activity and passivity, action and resignation; between the planner as a subject and the planner as an object. How are we then to summarise the insights we are starting to get a glimpse of? Although logic – the primary tool of science and planning – is seemingly directed at the world, it contains implicit assumptions about the science-producing and planning person herself.

If you allow me to simplify, the planner's actions are directed at the world, at the things and people that surrounds her. However, the world also includes the planner. Thus, she acts not only on the world but on herself as well (see Laing 1967: 31). As moral philosopher Alasdair MacIntyre (2007: 68) points out, it has long been a sociological insight that the bureaucratic system puts humans in a manipulative relationship with each other. This is an important point, especially if we want to understand the book's central issue: contra-finality. MacIntyre's insight is relevant to our discussion of logic as well. Logical thinking shows itself in the planner's or scientist's tendencies to disintegrate the problems she faces. If the problem is society or the city in a broad sense, it is precisely this that is subject to disintegration. The entire modern society is largely a product of the Enlightenment belief in analytical-logical thinking, where humankind is seen as facing a world full of objects. But if man views the world as an object and he himself is a part of this world, this means that he also sees himself as an object. The bureaucratic system, for example, is designed as an efficient machine to handle the problems that can arise when people live side by side in society. But because we ourselves are what constitute this system, we objectify ourselves.

Hence, there is feedback here: as we see the world, we see ourselves. For planning, this means the following: What the planner does when she divides the city in various functions is to divide life into various activities. In fact the main reason for her interest in the city in the first place is because it is her living space. On the surface it seems as if the planner handles technical-physical things – things that may seem like decomposable machines dictated by the cause-effect principle. But what she really disintegrates is life itself, or: herself.

In the introduction I suggested that the individual – in a broad sense – is responsible. The aim is not to express voluntaristic ideas that humans are free to act as they want, as if there were no restrictions. Rather, the aim is to challenge the widespread idea that planner 'only does her duty'; that she is merely a cog in a machine. Here we should remember that even though the bureaucratic machinery transforms the planner into a cog, the planner herself has to allow it to happen. In some sense she makes herself into a cog. Thus, it is not the machine that robs her of her spontaneity and judgment – she sets it aside herself (Carse 1986: §84). When, or if, the planner excuses any action by saying that she only did what she was told, she indirectly says that she is an object that is only acting in accordance with other's will. She hereby perceives herself not as a decision-making subject but as a more or less powerless pawn, incapable of acting differently. Basically, this is a chimera because even the failure to do something – in this case, for example, not doing your duty – is also an action. Humans are sometimes subjects, sometimes objects – but never just one or the other (Israel 1980: 203, see also Sigurdsson 2006: 319). The status of an object is closely linked to playing a role in a game, and as I have previously stated, planning is like a game that the planner agrees to play.

However, as Carse (1986: §13) has pointed out, there is a discrepancy between the actual freedom to 'step off the field of play at any time' and the perceived necessity to continue. The subject's veiling of the self – that is, putting on the costume of an object – is an integral part of the game in question. The planner must take her role as a planner with a certain degree of seriousness; she must identify herself as a planner and play the role in a way that convinces both her and others that she *is* the role she plays. It is the nature of acting, Carse (1986: §13) concludes, that 'we are not to see this woman as Ophelia, but Ophelia as this woman'. That the actor keeps her own person apart from the role is one of the requirements of acting. It is nevertheless important to ask 'whether we are willing to lift the veil and openly acknowledge, if only to ourselves, that we have freely chosen to face the world through a mask' (ibid.). Having said this I would like to note that my point here is not that it is wrong or unethical to play a role. Rather, my point is that the veiling of the self is a contradictory act – 'a free suspension of our freedom' (ibid.).

Bauman (1993: 183) argues along these lines as well; the state has a 'soporific effect' on moral conscience, he says:

> True, its awesome powers allow the bringing of succour to distant sufferers which could not be helped by a less resourceful assistance. But bringing succour is now the *state's* responsibility, and so are the decisions about relative importance of needs and the needy. Once more, the moral subject is put to sleep. He is saved now from moral agony, but his moral vigilance, and moral competence, get rustier by the day. They will not be of much use if (or when) the state decides to put its now uncontested moral authority to immoral uses.

Coupled with the fact that humans are both subjects and objects, is the fact that they are both unpredictable and predictable. According to MacIntyre (2007: 103ff) this fact can be linked to social sciences' need for generalisations. In order to live, we must be able to engage in long-term projects, such as marriage, building a house, planning a trip and so on. But life's unpredictability makes our plans and projects vulnerable. All humans, in one way or the other, make plans – in itself an attempt to make the natural and the social world as predictable as possible. But while we want/expect the environment to be predictable, we ourselves strive to be as unpredictable as possible. For being unpredictable (to others) means being free; we are in control. We want to be masters of our own lives, not just part of other people's plans and projects. Here it's important to remember that power is something that is in constant motion (see e.g. Olsson 2007: 245). Overall, both of these quests – that is, to make the world predictable and to make ourselves unpredictable – are completely necessary. And in urban planning, the main task is all about the former. To borrow a formulation from Taleb (2007: 57), '[U]nderstanding how to act under conditions of incomplete information is the highest and most urgent human pursuit'.

I have previously noted that science as well as modern urban planning presupposes that we humans are able to predict the effects of events and actions and thus control our environment. In other words, this says something about the planner herself; the planner believes she is in control. And there is no doubt that this is a highly flattering picture. And if we are to believe Charles Taylor (1985), it is precisely here – in the image of the self – that the lure of science resides. Natural science's implicit picture of human nature is that we are free, disconnected, independent operators. There are signs of this in space syntax; it reduces humans to things whose motion is conditioned by the physical environment. As Soja (2001: 1.2) has written, it was this aspect of force – the fact that the method itself decides what can and should be studied – that led him and others to reject the approach that characterised the quantitative revolution in geography. Space syntax implies a respect for the natural environment, for the fact that we are subordinate to it. We cannot walk through walls; we have to go around them, so we are not completely free agents. But beyond this, space syntax seems to assume that we can do basically whatever we want; take the most logical route home and so on. The natural scientific approach makes it difficult to take into account how people's movements are influenced by factors beyond the purely physical. Humans appear here as relatively untouched by various hazards, moods and power structures.

The ethical dimension of science is only implicit; it is often shadowed by the epistemological dimension. Many advocates of a scientific perspective of the social world are aware of the epistemological problems arising from it. However, they are more comfortable with the image of man that this perspective implies. Challenging naturalism is challenging a highly flattering picture of the self as a free actor, who stands in a causal relationship with the world and who therefore can easily gain control over the effects of events and actions. If we are to challenge naturalism, we need to challenge this view of the self, and that can be difficult on a personal level.

In this context it may be interesting to note a language habit. Israel (1971: 280) notes,

When we talk about 'the human factor' and its influence, we often imply that man introduces an irrational element into a perfect and mechanically well performing system. Take, as example, the notion that an airplane accident was due to the 'human factor'. Human behavior thus is identified as *irrational*, whereas robotlike functioning is conceived of as *rational*, as predictable behavior. … [I]t is interesting to note that this expression is used when one tries to explain lack of functioning. The concept 'human' has in this connection a negative connotation: the goal is the elimination of the disturbing 'human factor' or to prevent its influence, so that a mechanical system can function in a perfect way.

That science offers a sense of purity and freedom has also been noted by Bernard Williams (2002: 143). He says: 'In itself, [natural science] offers liberation from humanity, rather than expressing liberation for humanity'. The reason is very much the same as the one put forth by Taylor: that the content of science transcends humanity. Yes, science transcends human affairs in general; its content is intended to be a representation of reality as it 'is' – cleaned of human idiosyncrasies. But in what way does science offer a sense of freedom? One answer is that it portrays humans as free from other people's will. However, freedom from others' wills is not total freedom: 'To be free, in the most basic, traditional, intelligible sense, is not to be subject to another's will. It does not consist of being free from all obstacles' (ibid.).

Overall, this discussion sheds light on the seductive pull of space syntax. This theory implies an idea of us humans as free and relatively uncomplicated. But, as I pointed out earlier, space syntax does not only have a seductive effect; it can be off-putting as well –to social scientists and humanists. Here, too, the explanation is found in the non-explicit view of man as *res extensa*. Perspectivism, indeed.

Russell (1946: 823) is one of those who perceive science's implied image of humans as anything but flattering. Logic and mathematics, he says, 'do not represent a positive spiritual effort, but a mere somnambulism, in which the will is suspended, and the mind is no longer active'. Here we can recall our discussion of the bureaucratic system's tendency to transform the individual into a cog in a machine. And the image of man implied by behaviourism is that he is one-dimensional and predictable – a stimulus-response mechanism (Kalin 1974: 114, Livingstone 1992: 338). We can now say that science's image of the self is far from univocal. Humans are partly free (from other people's will and from the bounds of mankind, in general), partly unfree (our behaviour is possible to predict and manipulate). And, thus, it is important not to forget what Ludwig von Bertalanffy, a critic of behaviourism, wrote: 'When the intellectual élite, the thinkers and leaders, see in man nothing but an overgrown rat, then it is time to be alarmed' (in Koestler 1967 : 353).

To make a short detour, the criticism I have here directed at the (natural) scientific perspective can be directed to the social-constructivist discourse-analytical approach as well. The only difference is that, in this latter case, it is the physical – not the social or mental – limits that are neglected. In other words, discourse analysis also presents a flattering picture of man; he comes across as a soaring spirit with the ability to speak and write – seemingly indifferent to his physical environment. In Arendt's (1998: 9) words,

> [M]en, no matter what they do, are always conditioned beings. Whatever enters the human world of its own accord or is drawn into it by human effort becomes part of the human condition. The impact of the world's reality upon human existence is felt and received as a conditioning force. The objectivity of the world – its object- or thing-character – and the human condition supplement each other; because human existence is conditioned existence, it would be impossible without things, and things would be a heap of unrelated articles, a non-world, if they were not the conditions of human existence.

The discussion has led us to a problem that can be summarised in what Merleau-Ponty (1968) called the Chiasm,[6] the intertwining. This word captures the intertwining between vision and the visible, between the phenomenal (experiencing) body and the objective (visible) body. The Chiasm can be briefly described as follows: the hand that touches objects can itself be touched and is therefore (also) an object among others. Sight is not independent of sensation – they overlap. It is the same body that both sees and touches. In contrast to the widespread message of Cartesianism that vision equals the (disembodied) intellect, Merleau-Ponty pointed to the Chiasm and replied: no, vision is not disembodied, because observers cannot be external to the world which they observe (Sigurdsson 2006: 319). '[M]y hand, while it is felt from within, is also accessible from without, itself tangible, for my other hand, for example, if it takes its place among the things it touches, is in a sense one of them, opens finally upon a tangible being of which it is also a part' (Merleau-Ponty 1968: 133).

What we can take with us from the above discussion of the ethical dimension of science is precisely this: the Chiasm. It summarises the realisation that when we act, we act not only on the world but also on ourselves. And as thought and action are interwoven, I include attempts to understand in the definition of actions. Seeing something as an object means upholding the idea that one should treat it as an object as well (Israel 1980: 20). This becomes clear if we look at the word *grasp* (*begripa* in Swedish), which means to understand but also to hold, grip, clench (*gripa*). It implies that understanding is an act, not unlike the physical act of literally grabbing something by the hand. The reverse is also true; if we see the world as socially constructed and not physically tangible, we renounce any practical action in this world.

From the Chiasm we learn that when the urban planner disintegrates and reifies the world in her logical analyses, she does this to herself as well, since she is part

---

6 *Chiasm* is an anglicised form of the Latin word *chiasmus* or *chiasma*. *Chiasmus*, in turn, is related to Greek *khiasmos*, which means 'a placing crosswise, diagonal arrangement'. *Chiasma* means 'a crossing' in medical Latin and the concept is used in the study of cells (*Online Etymology Dictionary* 2013-06-07).

of the world that she analyses.[7] Or to borrow Olsson's words (2007: xi), '[T]he social engineers may well find themselves not in the heavens to which they aspire but in the dungeons they have designed for the others' (see also Olsson 1993, Carse 1986: §84, Nyman 1989: 10). In other words, the Chiasm says something important about the relation between means and ends – an issue central to all planning and the focus of the next section.

Means/Ends

From the outset, modern urban planning has justified its existence with the idea that it is a means to achieve ends (see e.g. Banfield 1959). Here, we must remember that the planner's second name is Homo Faber, a working human being who is constantly producing and using instruments to produce. Everything that Homo Faber does, she does for an end purpose. The idea of planning as a means is widespread. Let us look at an example of how this view can be supported. Urban researcher Lisbeth Söderqvist (2008: 182f) defines social engineering – which is another word for planning – as a method and nothing else. She backs this by saying that the engineers – the practitioners of this 'art' – were not the ones who formulated the ends; they merely identified problems and stated rational solutions to these problems:

> [S]ocial engineering denotes politicians/experts/architects or other groups that use technical terms when dealing with social problems ... Scientific method and rational solutions are considered to be the tools that are suitable for creating a good society. It is the latter that is the goal, of course, not the method itself. (Söderqvist 2008: 182)

---

7   That Hillier (2007: 307) seems to have acknowledged the problem of the Chiasm (although he does not use this term) is evident at a certain point in *Space is the Machine*, where he writes, 'We should see ourselves not as things, perhaps, but as processes. The common-sense definition of individuals as things, and even of things in general, seems after all to be illusory, the result of a naïve perception of the world'. But, thereafter he asks (apparently and understandably frustrated): 'But where does it end? Is all "flux and change", and are all assertions of the "thingness" of the world just temporary fixations? Or can we save the idea of thingness by a more careful definition?' So, Hillier realises the problem of seeing human beings as things, but he still wants to 'save the idea of thingness'. When attempting to save this idea, he uses a metaphor (a swarm of mosquitos and a box), but the discussion is too long to be related here. However, the point is that the swarm has configurational persistencies, and that it is this fact that motivates our calling it a thing – despite the fact that it is in constant motion and that its movement is ostensibly aleatoric. He writes, 'From here, it clearly works for less difficult cases such as human beings. If it has configurational persistencies, we might say, then it's a thing' (ibid.: 308). My immediate objection is his referring to 'cases such as human beings' as 'less difficult'.

Söderqvist (2008: 301) repeats her message later on: 'The tools are not to be confused with the objectives'. This view of planning as a largely apolitical and neutral activity is – as already stated – widespread. 'The good society' is the goal (which the politicians formulate); engineering is only a means to achieve this and the means is designed and implemented by neutral experts. 'Of course'.

While I am being critical of this definition of planning, it is warranted to ask if the reproducing of the means-ends division – which we see in Söderqvist's text – is merely an expression of a will to describe how things 'are'. This division was and is, after all, posited by the social engineers themselves. But to reproduce this 'fact' means a passive acceptance of the reality described by these experts. Characteristic of Homo Faber's attitude is 'a trust in the all-comprehensive range of the means-end category' (Arendt 1998: 305). In fact, and ironically, Söderqvist's insistence that means and ends are different things can be seen as an indication that they really are interwoven. Why else forcefully deny it (see Zupančič 2012)? Let us examine this possibility more closely.

The conventional view that means and ends are two different things is highly reasonable, for we are, after all, using two different words. Moreover, the end is usually seen as preceding the means, since the end is usually formulated first, and only after, the means to achieve it are chosen. But the distinction between what counts as ends and what counts as means is not always obvious. For in another sense, the means precedes the end because the means is used to achieve the end. To borrow an example from everyday life: if my end is to clean a wall, I will likely use detergent. I may reach my end; the wall becomes clean and I will be happy. But I may well use a detergent that is too strong, and which makes the wall corrode. In that case, I would not reach my end; the means I have chosen has come to dominate the end (Wide 2005: 17).

One important message of this chapter is that means and ends are not separate. If we have decided on a means, such as quantification, we have indirectly decided on an end, reification, because to calculate without reifying is impossible (Olsson 1980a: 130b). A reifying attitude towards the world means that you are treating the world as an object. In Weber's words (1994: 364),

> The specific means of *legitimate violence per se* in the hands of human associations is what gives all the ethical problems of politics their particular character. Anyone who makes a pact with the means of violence, for whatever purpose – and every politician does this – is at the mercy of its specific consequences.

Urban planning, again, was originally a solution to a problem, a means to an end. This view was adopted specifically by the functionalists, according to whom planning is 'the only way to really master' the activity of city building, and to whom planning stands out as that which will 'lead to the best possible outcome' (Åhrén 1928: 175). The director of the Hammarby Sjöstad project shares this view and thus exhibits a great faith in planning: 'Edge cities, chaos, non-places, and a grid structure have been said to be a true expression of our time. The

Hammarby Sjöstad project represents the opposite. It reflects a belief in that the city requires planning' (Inghe-Hagström 1997: 32). So, the city needs strong planning if we are to achieve what is the opposite of chaos. Hammarby Sjöstad represents this, and it is presented as something positive. This is also true for Södra Stationsområdet. In the following quote, the director comments on the cooperation with the Spanish architect Ricardo Bofill, who drew the so-called Bofill arc at Fatbursparken. The planning director says, 'The cooperation with Bofill has ... brought obvious qualities to the project. ... Bofill, for his part, is obviously happy to be getting the opportunity to implement a project in a planned urban environment, not just a separate monument in an otherwise chaotic city district' (Inghe-Hagström 1987: 33).

At one point I took on the task of sorting out what planners were referring to as ends respectively means in their statements about Hammarby Sjöstad and Södra Stationsområdet. I quickly ran into difficulties. At first I thought the fault was mine; I was not a sufficiently clear-sighted and consistent interpreter of the planners' statements. Maybe I ought to use some sort of table and sort the statements in separate columns? One for 'ends' and another for 'means'. If I could only be systematic enough, I would probably get to the bottom of it, I thought. In other words, I reasoned in accordance with the 'old-fashioned logicians, – the sheep and goat separators', to use William James' expression (in Olsson 2007: 183).

In time, however, I began to see the difficulty of separating them as interesting in itself. It seems that what was actually intended as a means – planning and control – for the planners had become an end in itself. This shift from means to ends is apparent in the following quote: 'The main idea with the plan was to stop the ongoing spontaneous transformation of the old harbour area to an area of speculation-driven expansion of office buildings' (Inghe-Hagström 1997: 32). Another document states that the 'essential purpose' of the Hammarby Sjöstad project is 'to continue the planning for this large urban project', and to see that the ongoing spontaneous development is stopped (*BoStad02* 2002: 18f). So, the paradoxical and tautological conclusion is that the end of planning is... planning. Or, in other words: the goal of what the planner is doing is to reach her goal.

Marcuse has reflected on this by discussing Weber's concept of formal rationality (in Israel 1971: 168; 110). To act rationally was originally a means in the production processes of modern society, but over time, acting rationally has become an end in itself, and this tendency has spread and penetrated all sectors of society so deeply that it is difficult to detect. Formal rationality has, in fact, become a part of a value system, the ideology of natural science. But due to the illusion of science as value-free, this is rarely recognised as an ideology but as a given.

The stated end of creating urbanity thus co-exists with other, unspoken ends: gaining and maintaining control and avoiding chaos. And suddenly it seems understandable why Hammarby Sjöstad lacks many of the characteristics associated with urbanity. If the goal is a rich city life, and disintegration is the means, we run the risk of disappointing ourselves, since the actual result is likely to carry traces of this disintegration. And so is it that the end we had in mind, like a rainbow, has moved on when we arrive.

John Dewey is one of those who have noted that the end pursued can never be separated from the means by which one seeks to achieve the end; the end will always embody the means (Martin 2002: 241). Let me make this more concrete: Dewey criticised the Soviet revolutionary and Marxist Leon Trotsky for advocating a means – revolution – as a way to achieve the end of a socialist, democratic and peaceful society. This means that Trotsky, like Stalin, 'would achieve the end of a revolution embodying the means used to achieve it: terror, coercion, control. Such means used would result in a dictatorial society rather than a democratic one (ibid.: 421). In other words, if you use violence as a means, violence – when the revolution has been completed – will continue. The modern human being is 'the whore of reason', to borrow the Swedish writer Jan Myrdal's words (in Olsson 1980a: 130b). And Olsson (ibid.) notes that 'those who determine public policy have forgotten that all moral codes agree that every act has a duty to acquire good with good and that the employed means are more important than the imputed ends'. This argument we can see in Lefebvre's (1995: 121) writings, too: '[M]eans [are becoming] more important than ends'. And he continues: 'And everything is subsiding into boredom'.

Here I come to think of an anecdote that geographer David Ley told me about Jane Jacobs.[8] Jacobs spoke to a group of planners in North America sometime in the 1990s. Her ideas had had a major impact there, and her status was almost heroic. In her speech, she laid out – as she usually did – a critical perspective on urban planning. Suddenly someone interrupted her with the words: 'Please do not criticise us – we all follow your ideas!' This is a fascinating story, a reminder of the danger of ignoring the frames or conditions of an idea, while more or less unreflectingly utilising its perceived message and applying it in a new context. At worst, this new context counteracts the original message, which is not only lost but perverted into something new, the consequences of which we may not even realise. This is a risk that all so-called critical ideas run when they undergo some form of institutionalisation; a process that is both a consequence and a cause of the idea being interpreted literally, while thinking itself – the thinking that generated the idea in the first place – is put in the background. Overall, this makes me think of Nietzsche (1992: 6), who wrote that '[o]ne repays a teacher badly if one remains only a pupil'.

In light of this anecdote, the following observation by Goldberger (2006) seems to make sense: 'In the twenty-first century, the danger is not with those who oppose Jane Jacobs, but with those who claim to follow her'. During the over fifty years since Jacobs presented her radical ideas, they have moved from a marginal to a dominant position. Previously, it was relatively easy to identify who were the proponents of so-called anti-urban ideas; they were the 'car people', Jacobs (1993:

---

8   During a meeting at Ley's office at UBC, Vancouver, 26 October, 2009, which I am grateful for.

xii) explains, and most planners and architects belonged in this category. And, as we saw in the introduction, Lofland (1998: 208) concludes that 'the postwar agents of transformation knew exactly what they were doing'; they wanted to create a different, less 'chaotic' city. The 'foot people', on the other hand, cherished this 'chaos' and wanted to preserve it, to let it thrive. Today, these roles are not so simple; Jacobs's pro-urban ideas have been (rhetorically) appropriated by planners and architects, and have become a new orthodoxy, often without the advocates of the idea reflecting on it. A planner who defends Jacobs's diversity ideals and has them as a goal may not realise that the means she uses to reach it – means, which to a large extent are of the same meticulous nature that the functionalists used – may come to characterise the result.[9] Here, once again, I think of Nietzsche (1992: 100, emphasis removed), who writes, '[T]he harm the good do is the most harmful harm'.

An action is ethically justifiable only if it treats human beings as human beings and not as things or means to an end (Arendt 1998: 155). Urban planners and space syntax researcher use, as I have already noted, analytical techniques that force them to eliminate all ambivalence. This practice – which characterises bureaucrats and scientists alike – involves reification (Israel 1971, Ollman 2003, Olsson 1980a). But the dehumanisation embedded in this practice is not meant to be callous; on the contrary, it is the consequences of the actor's good intentions. Weber (1994: 365) has thought about this:

> Anyone wishing to practise politics of any kind, and especially anyone who wishes to make a profession of politics, has to be conscious of [its] ethical paradoxes and of his responsibility for what may become of *himself* under pressure from them. He is becoming involved ... with the diabolical powers that lurk in all violence.

Politics is about identifying problems that require collective solutions, but – as we are well aware of by now – means and ends are very much interwoven (Martin 2002: 422). Philosophy, on the other hand, is the criticising of the methods with which we humans try to achieve our goals: '*How* we think will lead to *what* we think, and what we do' (ibid.: 423). The risk of confusion increases if we – as the good logicians we often are – think in absolute terms. The result is often paradoxical, as in Hammarby Sjöstad, where the planners decided to close down the various businesses that were in the area in order to achieve the goal of mixed uses and businesses.[10]

---

9   For more reflections on Jacobs and her legacy, see Page and Mennel (2011) and Harvey (2003: 164).

10   'To carry out the transformation from industrial and harbour area into a district with both homes and businesses, many businesses have been forced to evacuate and move to new areas of land and premises' (*BoStad02* 2002: 45). Thörn (2013) gives an even more striking example of this.

In this context, it may be illustrative to distinguish between so-called intrinsic values – those that are valuable in themselves – and instrumental values, that is, those that are beneficial for helping us achieve what we want. The doctors Frank Lindblad and Carl Lindgren (2009: 73) use these concepts in their book *Välfärdslandets gåta* (translates into *The Enigma of the Welfare State*) about the powerful side effects of the welfare state. Health, they say, is something that has both intrinsic and instrumental value. That is to say: it is positive both to have health and to work to achieve this. If the latter is taken too far, however, it turns into so-called health craze. Pursuing health may require such a large amount of psychic energy that it impacts negatively on one's health. In these cases, contra-finality is a reality. Faced with children's and young people's health, society's reaction is to produce even more expert and authority information on hazards and risks in order to reduce or eliminate ill health. In other words, the solution is 'more of the same' (ibid.: 166). As shown in this book, we can see a similar tendency in urban planning. If planning so far has not led us to the goal of collective and individual happiness, let us plan more – and preferably with a stronger and more fine-tuned hand; let us refine the technology of modern urban planning so that it takes us where we want to go.

The difficulty of maintaining a distinction between means and ends is built into all consistent utilitarianism. Utilitarianism is the planner's, or Homo Faber's, philosophy par excellence. Its overall goal is to maximise utility (*utilitas* in Latin). Take the example of a chair. The chair is an end for the carpenter, for her work. But the chair, which to the carpenter was an end, is a means to someone else; it may be used to rest or to sit down and write. So, the carpenter's end is actually to produce a means because if the chair would be useless in the literal sense, the carpenter would not have achieved her goal. Ends and means are – when talking about utility – a ceaseless chain, where each end is destined to be short-lived and transformed into means to other ends (Arendt 1998: 153f).

The utilitarian can answer the question why this and that is done – the answer is always 'it maximises utility'. But when she is asked to justify 'why utility?', she immediately encounters a problem. If we are to believe Arendt (1998: 154), this is due to the inherent inability of utilitarianism to understand the difference between the useful and the meaningful, between that which we linguistically express with the words 'in order to' and that which we express with 'for the sake of'.[11] Homo Faber does everything 'in order to' something else. Everything she does is – or is thought to be – useful. But is it meaningful? It is rare that the question even arises – which says that the prevailing view is that the useful is the meaningful. It is as nonsensical to say that we are striving for utility because it is useful as it is to say that we plan in order to plan. Yet this form of reasoning is evident in contemporary urban planning. City planners – those who do things 'in order to' –

---

11   Here it is interesting to look at Woolf's (2008: 11) choice of words in one of her diaries: 'I decided to go to London, for the sake of hearing the Strand roar'. To use 'in order to' instead, in this sentence, would have been grammatically correct, too.

are themselves incapable of understanding the 'meaningful', for the meaningful, as Arendt (1998: 154) says, must be permanent and not lose its status of being meaningful whether it is achieved or not. An example of a meaningful activity that lacks an end is play. Play, as we have already concluded, serves no useful purpose. Still, according to the psycho-analytical tradition, play is what makes life worth living; it is fundamental for psychological health (Winnicott 1989). Here we can recall Woolf's short story *Street Haunting: A London Adventure* because it can, as pointed out by Selboe (2003: 185), be seen as a parody of society – a society characterised by utility. The fact that Woolf uses the word *excuse* in the quote about the pencil 'quite clearly shows that it [buying a pencil] is a stand-in motive' (ibid.). Additionally, Woolf's short story highlights the subversive qualities of *flânerie*: 'The city is full of speed and ambition, but the act of *flânerie* is in itself inefficient and useless', Selboe (ibid.) emphasises.[12] In fact, many of our actions in life qualify as useless in the strict meaning of the word: 'When called to justify itself in terms of the function it serves, play reveals its utter and irremediable *redundancy*' (Bauman 1993: 170). Coupled with play is eroticism, and eroticism, Asplund (1987: 68) reminds us, is 'redundancy'.

The goals of the utilitarian, however, are different; as soon as they are achieved, they cease to be an end. They are instead turned into an object among other objects – among which utilitarians can choose as their means to achieve other, new ends. Take, for example, the functionalist city; this was the functionalists' end. Today, these environments are no longer an end; rather, they are a part of the means with which planners today are looking to achieve new ends.

Let us now talk about an idea that is crucial to a discussion of ethical issues in general: Do we, when we are talking, use singular or plural; that is, are we referring to the individual or the collective? I have previously highlighted the fundamental conflict that exists between the individual and society. This becomes clear if we look at utilitarianism – the value system that explicitly or implicitly permeates much of today's planning and policy. This is a form of teleological ethics, also called consequential ethics, which means that the assessment of an action is made with respect to its consequences. Thus, central to utilitarianism is the effort to foresee the consequences of actions. The end (*telos* is Greek for end, purpose or goal) is to achieve the greatest possible utility for the greatest possible number of people. That the measures taken will have a negative impact on *some* individuals is more or less expected. 'Their' unhappiness is part of the plan, of the means: 'Utilitarianism's insistence on the greatest good for the greatest number systematically denies the rights of the minority' (Silverstone 2007: 145, see also Hylland Eriksen 2008: 187). However, it is the end that is important; the end justifies the means.

---

12   Today, in an increasingly neoliberalised Sweden, there are signs that the concept of the *flaneur* has been kidnapped by politicians and urban developers who want to spur 'growth'. '*Flaneur*' is used as a euphemism for 'consumer'. In other words: the *flaneur* is seen as a most useful cog in the capitalistic urban machinery.

Thus, a defence of a utilitarian basis for society's quest for justice assumes that we stay on the plural level. If, however, we view planning from the singular level, as we mostly do in this book, utilitarianism becomes problematic, for the negative side-effects of utilitarian-motivated planning measures are ultimately experienced by the individual, in her body. It is on the basis of this insight that Marcuse (1968b: 166) notes that 'general happiness apart from the happiness of individuals is a meaningless phrase'. Statistically speaking, the terms 'happiness' and 'suffering' are abstract and meaningless. It is in the lived reality – that cannot be experienced by anything other than the individual – that these concepts are filled with meaning.

What, then, is utilitarianism's counterpart? Which philosophy would take the side of the individual and only the individual? If we turn to Marcuse (1968b: 166f) for help, he suggests that the answer is hedonism: 'Hedonism advocates happiness equally for all individuals ... For hedonism, happiness remains something exclusively subjective. The particular interest of the individual, just as it is, is affirmed as the true interest and is justified against every and all community'. However, we soon understand that hedonism – which sees happiness and usefulness as something entirely subjective – is utterly unthinkable as a societal ideology. Because for society to function without falling apart into anarchy, the majority of people have to accept the dominant ideology of the ruling elite (ibid.). An ethical theory must, in one way or another, be applicable to everything; it must be universal (Johansson and Khakee 2008: 34). Utilitarianism is such a theory: '[A] society is structured – through, for example, its educational institutions – to further that ideology, and attitudes, interests and goals are influenced accordingly' (Johnston 1989: 49). Since hedonism opposes the idea that the individual can accept or incorporate someone else's opinion in any way, it cannot be much more than a hypothetical alternative to utilitarianism. Nevertheless, it is an interesting thought experiment.

We have utilitarianism and society, we have hedonism and the individual and then we have the insurmountable discrepancy between them. This brings us back to the problem of alienation, because alienation is a word to describe a discrepancy – between social ideals and social reality, between the ways in which the ideals of society are formulated and the ways in which those ideals are put into practice (Israel 1971: 151).

The Problem of Alienation – Part II

> Specialization is the price we pay for the advancement of knowledge. A price, because the path of specialization leads away from the ordinary and concrete acts of understanding in terms of which man actually lives his day-to-day life. (Barrett 1962: 6f)

Modern scientific knowledge is the product of specialisation. 'The spirit of science rules its parts, not the whole.' (Nietzsche 1986a: §6, emphasis removed). And specialisation, we learn from Barrett's words above, has a price. This price is a rather high one, it seems, because specialisation means 'the death and dismemberment of what is being analysed' (Lefebvre 1995: 121). When the lived space of the urban, which – like life in general – is lived on many levels, is disintegrated, it follows that the world comes to us in the form of a Meccano or Lego set; broken up into thousands of mini-worlds (ibid.). One consequence of this dismemberment is alienation. I have previously identified alienation as estrangement, as a result of repression. Homo Faber represses Homo Ludens; the intellect seeks to free itself from the body. Alienation basically means that the whole is broken up into a number of components whose interrelations no longer can be ascertained. It is the shattering of man and his activities into many parts (Ollman 1976: 135).

Alienation can only be understood as the absence of non-alienation – where each state acts as a reference point for the other (Ollman 1976: 131). To Jean-Jacques Rousseau, who did not develop any specific theory of alienation but who reflected on the subject, the concept meant 'detachment' (Israel 1971: 21), which demonstrates that we are dealing with a division, with some sort of gap. This gap is perceived by the individual, and it is in the individual that this gap takes its expression. Being a gap, a breach, alienation is something that (quietly) baffles us with its elusiveness, partly because a gap by definition is invisible and intangible, and partly because that against which it is measured – an ideal or a non-alienated state – also escapes clear delineation. Put another way, both alienation and the ideal against which it is measured are of a specific ontological status. In short, they subsist in our heads.

Therefore, if I experience a discrepancy between the planners' ideal of urbanity and actual reality, it is inevitably *my interpretation* of this ideal that I compare reality against. For we now know that the idea might be one thing in my head and another in yours, and I have previously put forth that solipsism is my epistemological starting point for this investigation. What we are dealing with is simply social science's often overlooked dilemma; namely, that many of our key research objects are not objects at all. Community, freedom, justice, knowledge, development, safety, identity, urbanity and so on are all largely subsisting phenomena that are (partly or wholly) intangible. Furthermore, the interpretation of the ideal of urbanity is emotionally affected; I *feel* that I am alienated as I walk around in Hammarby Sjöstad. The planners' words echo in my head – 'This is urbanity, this is a rich city life, this is an attractive environment to live in' – and they chafe against my experience. The non-alienated state in this case is the festival, the busy urban street, which can be exemplified by Götgatan on Södermalm in Stockholm (see Figure 5.4). To some extent, this state is similar to the state of Dionysian intoxication (see Graf 1993: 143f).

A common 'solution' to the dilemma of social science (that we can never be sure that the concepts we use to describe social phenomena have the same meaning for you as they have for me) is to ignore the difference between subsistence and existence. This is to ally with certainty (Olsson 1980a: 68b), and it is also to ignore what makes social science *social*.

The thinker who is traditionally associated with the concept of alienation is Marx, and, as Ollman (1976: 131) writes, he saw it as a consequence of capitalism: 'The theory of alienation is the intellectual construct in which Marx displays the devastating effect of capitalist production on human beings, on their physical and mental states and on the social processes of which they are a part'. But the concept's long and multi-faceted history tells us that the problem – in its most general form – is a discrepancy between the collective and the individual, between vision and reality, and that alienation can occur regardless of social condition, in capitalist as well as socialist societies, democratic as well as totalitarian (Israel 1971: 151). In Marx's theory of alienation it is the worker who experiences a discrepancy between her own idea of ideal work and the actual work – determined by historical conditions: 'The worker himself has an emotionally influenced perception of his work and experiences a discrepancy. Since his labor does not fulfil basic needs in his "ideal" personality, he *feels* alienated' (Israel 1971: 263). For Marx, the non-alienated life is the life that man lives under communism (Ollman 1976: 132).

Although one generally speaks of two different perspectives on alienation – either you see it as a sociological-psychological problem or as an ontological-ethical problem (Israel 1971: 10) – I think we do well in avoiding too sharp of a separation between these two views. Seeing alienation as a constitutive element of all human existence does not refute the fact that the problem can worsen under certain sociological and/or psychological conditions. As long as there is more than one person on earth, and as long as they are grouped in some form of collective, there is a possibility – or a risk – of alienation; that is, of a gap between how the collective world (ideally) ought to work and how it is (actually) experienced by the individual. For example: the gap between the political ideal of justice for all and individual experiences of injustice. Perhaps it was this realisation that prompted William Blake to state: 'One Law for the Lion and Ox is Oppression' (in Kaufmann 1974: 257).

As Seaford (2006: 146) has highlighted, alienation can be seen as '[o]ne aspect of the development of humankind'. And political scientist Wolfgang Abendroth has said that 'social institutions – social-economic conditions, ... political organizations (e.g., the state) and legal norms, but also political theorems – raise themselves as independent powers above those human beings who have created them' (in Israel 1971: 269). The question is this: How can man – who is able to create something as complex as modern society – perceive society as something that exists independently of himself and his activities?

Proponents of functionalism assured that planning is what leads to the best possible results (Åhrén 1928: 175). The best for whom? Society? The individual? For both, of course! The planner's mission is to ensure that society functions properly for both society and individual. But we also know that this is formulated in an Enlightenment spirit of how planning *should* work – an idea that is problematised by Marcuse (1968b: 167):

> The idea of reason aims at universality, at a society in which the antagonistic
> interests of 'empirical' individuals are canceled. To this community, however,
> the real fulfillment of individuals and their happiness remains alien and external;
> they must be sacrificed. There is no harmony between the general and the
> particular interest, or between reason and happiness.

Alienation is a consequence of this bias; it proves, if you will, that things are not
as the social engineers intended. Marx used the term alienation to refer to a state –
any state – which is 'away from' or 'less than' non-alienation. Marx speaks of
alienation as a mistake, an error, as something that should not be. Although Marx
examines capitalism from different vantage points, it is usually the producer he
thinks about when he speaks of man's alienation (Ollman 1976: 132). Alienation
provides a vantage point from which it is possible to understand human beings –
a point of view that emphasises the practical collapse which has occurred in the
interconnection of the elements that characterise them. All the characteristics
that distinguish man from other living beings – qualities that Marx understood
as relations – have changed, have become something else. In order to discuss
alienation, social psychologist Klaus Ottomeyer (1978: 13) declares, 'one must
have an informed idea of what people are really alienated from'. In Marx' words:
'What requires explanation is not the *unity* of living and active human beings
with the natural, inorganic conditions of their metabolism, with nature, and
therefore their appropriation of nature ... What we must explain is the *separation*
of these inorganic conditions of human existence from this active existence' (in
Ollman 1976: 133).

Theories of alienation are thus driven by the idea that something essential
has been broken in two. According to Marx, man has been separated from the
material world, from his own products. He no longer has any control over what he
produces (Ollman 1976: 133). But it is not only his products that he is separated
from; because of competition and class contempt, he is separated from his fellow
human beings, too. And, ultimately, what all these divisions have done is to
deprive man from everything that makes him human. Here, then, it makes sense
that Lefebvre (1995: 120) called analytical thinking 'the evil genius of abstraction
and separation'. The stripped naked, deprived and alienated person has become
an *abstraction*. But what does this mean? Ollman explains (1976: 134): 'At its
simplest, "abstraction" refers to the type of purity that is achieved in emptiness.
Its opposite is a set of meaningful particulars by which people know something to
be one of a kind'.

And all these particularities in the human world involve internal relations; they
are connected with the social whole, and the social whole is always expressed in
each particularity. And because we do not understand the ways in which the social
whole is present in every particularity, the particularity seems to be independent
of the social whole, and it becomes an abstraction. When a particularity becomes
an abstraction, it is no longer itself. What make a particularity unique is its internal
relations to other particularities, but we lose sight of this idea when we stare at the

superficial similarities that this particularity shares with other abstractions. And it is on the basis of these similarities – generalised as classes or types – that the alienated individual tries to understand her world. Thus, the alienated human being is an abstraction because she has lost contact with human particularity (ibid.).

In an alienated society, the basic elements of what it means to be human are understood as being independent of each other, as units that appear to be something other than what they really are. The whole is broken up into a number of parts and the inter-relationships can no longer be ascertained. This is the concept of alienation – whether the part being studied is man, his activities, his products or his ideas. In Ollman's (1976: 135) words, 'The same separation and distortion is evident in each'.

The Dynamic Dialectics

> Paradox = 'statement contrary to common belief or expectation', from Latin *paradoxum* 'paradox, statement seemingly absurd yet really true', from Greek *paradoxon*, noun use of neuter of adjective *paradoxos* 'contrary to expectation, incredible', from *para-* 'contrary to' + *doxa* 'opinion' (*Online Etymology Dictionary* 2013-04-04)

What, then, is the alternative to the disintegration and reification of conventional logic? The answer is dialectics, the form of thinking that starts off with the whole, that takes this whole for granted and that sees all relations as internal parts of each particularity and not as external connections between them (Ollman 2003: 156). Dialectics helps us to see 'the bigger picture'. It represents a counterpoint to conventional scientific analysis that often fails to see the forest because of the trees. The conventional view of the whole is a closed circle. A dialectical understanding of the big picture is that it is never completed, never closed (Ollman 2003: 55). A whole is – to the dialectician – something that we are not able to see; we will never and can never get a hold of it. What is it, then? Is it nothing and everything at the same time? No, a whole – from a dialectical point of view – is defined as interdependence.

While conventional logic is characterised by an either-or way of looking at the world, dialectics is characterised by a both/and, and it is expressed by the slash /. Dialectical concepts thus have double meanings; they are paradoxes in the truest sense, in that they include opposites. The urban, as we saw in Chapter 6, is both a *thing* and a *not-thing*, like Marx's concept of value. So how can we define value? It is something invisible but nevertheless real. Can we explain value by referring to notes and coins? The answer is no because even if a note actualises the value, it is not the same as value – a note is in itself just a piece of paper (Castree 1996: 356). The slash represents that which both separates and unites; form/process, city/ life, society/individual. Friedrich Hegel created his dialectics for a purpose; he wanted to understand history and life as well as the qualitative changes and elusive phenomena that these subjects include (Olsson 1980a: 22b, Ollman 2003: 158). Within geography, in the 1970s, dialectics became an alternative to the positivist worldview that had dominated the discipline during the quantitative era,but which had been proven ill-suited to understand the changing processes that are essential to the social realm (Dixon et al., 2008, Smith 1979, Soja 2001). Logics – the basis for positivism – is based on Leibniz's principle of identity or mathematical equivalence; the same word always has the same meaning; number eight is always number eight; you remain who you are and I remain who I am. Overall, this characterises our expectations of what scientific concepts should do: they ought to provide a sense of certainty – not ambiguity. If they do not follow this pattern but, rather – as Marx' dialectical concepts – sometimes appears as mice, sometimes birds – we are surprised, confused, puzzled (see Olsson 1980a: 66b; 2002: 255). As Eagleton (2005: 193) writes: 'There is something challengingly counter-intuitive about [dialectics] for us heirs of the Enlightenment'.

Israel (1971: 330–32) has pointed out that dialectical theories are non-reifying since they presuppose a dialectical relationship between man and his environment, between the social and the physical, between form and process. But is dialectics really an *alternative* to logic?[13] That, of course, depends on what you want to do, but the important thing to remember in a study of planning like the present one is that dialectics can never be used for predictions – a fact that explains its uselessness in the eyes of the 'doer'; the action-oriented planner, or the searcher for evidence-based design theories. In Ollman's words (1976: 59), 'When used for predictions, the dialectic can never be shown wrong, only foolish and worthless'.

Here it is interesting to recall Harvey's treatment and partial dismissal of Gale's (1972) criticism of Harvey's 'positivist manifesto'[14] *Explanation in Geography*. According to Harvey (1972: 326), Gale occupies a position that is largely 'impotent'. Furthermore, he describes Gale's points of rejection of positivism as 'counter-revolutionary in that they becloud, obscure, and obfuscate the reality we seek to understand' (ibid.). Harvey makes an important point here. For as I pointed out in Chapter 5, the critical social scientist's rejection of objective statements about the physical, concrete world not only prevents reality descriptions but also stops certain questions from being asked (and – consequently – answered). In other words, going too far in any direction is problematic. To forcefully deny distinctions, which a 'true' dialectician ideally would do, 'is to sound more like a monist than a dialectician', to borrow Eagleton's words (2005: 191).

It is important to discuss dialectics if one wants to shed light on the differences in perspective that often exist between how social scientists and architectural theorists understand the city and the urban. Hereby, we can get to know ourselves as knowledge-seeking beings. The chasm was already mentioned in Chapter 6; while the space syntax theorist sees a hyphen between the words city

---

13   For a discussion on the role that dialectics might play in geographical studies, see Sheppard (2008) and Elden (2008).

14   This label is mine.

and life in the term 'city life' (city-life), the dialectician sees a slash (city/life). The hyphen represents a *connection* (between two separate things), while the slash symbolises interdependence, a dialectical *relation* between continuously changing things/processes. Since the logical approach can only focus on one thing at a time, the different parts of city life are studied in turn, and – to borrow Ollman's words (2003: 18) – 'their mutual interaction [is] often mistaken for causality'.

The dialectician is sceptical about too rigorous and systematic disintegration since it fragments wholes and regards relations between entities and phenomena as external to what they are: 'Meaning is not in things but in between them; in the iridescence, the interplay; in the interconnections; at the intersections, at the crossroads', Brown (1968: 247) states. Ultimately, as Russell (1946: 760) writes, 'there are not as many as two things in the world; therefore the Whole, considered as a unity, is alone real'. He elaborates:

> First we say: 'Reality is an uncle'. This is the thesis. But the existence of an uncle implies that of a nephew. Since nothing really exists except the Absolute, and we are now committed to the existence of a nephew, we must conclude: 'The Absolute is a nephew'. This is the antithesis. But there is the same objection to this as to the view that the Absolute is an uncle; therefore we are driven to the view that the Absolute is the whole composed of uncle and nephew. This is the synthesis. But this synthesis is still unsatisfactory, because a man can be an uncle only if he has a brother or sister who is a parent of the nephew. Hence we are driven to enlarge our universe to include the brother or sister, with his wife or her husband. (Russell 1946: 759)

So it reads when Russell discusses Hegelian dialectics. The conclusion is that the premise of dialectical thought is that 'nothing can be really true unless it is about Reality as a whole' (ibid.). If we apply this insight to the question of the city and the urban, we find that statements about the urban as a social and mental phenomenon cannot be made without acknowledging the city as a physical phenomenon and vice versa. Russell (1946: 780) again: 'Since everything, except the Whole, has relations to outside things, it follows that nothing quite true can be said about separate things, and that in fact only the Whole is real'. Here I come to think of a poem – 'Jag är ett vimmel av dig' (translates loosely into something like 'I am a crowd of you') by Sandro Key-Åberg (in Wästberg 1995: 98). It begins as follows:

> My love
> where do you begin
> where do you end;
> you,
> the one who is constantly moving through my world[15]

---

15   'Älskade, var börjar du, var upphör du i mig, du som ständigt rör dig genom min livsnejd'.

Here we see that the dialectic is the poetic; the poetic is the dialectic. Moreover, the poet and the dialectician have the same purpose: to create *awareness* – nothing else. This applies to the psycho-analyst, too; having a dialectical worldview she sees man not as one but as several; 'a corporate body; incorporated, a corporation' (Brown 1968: 147). Relationships in the social world are internal:

> We tend to think of any one individual in isolation; it is a convenient fiction. We may isolate him physically, as in the analytic room; in two minutes we find that he has brought his world in with him ... That self, that life of one's own ... so casually taken for granted, is a composite structure which has been and is being formed and built up since the day of our birth out of countless never-ending influences and exchanges between ourselves and others ... These other persons are in fact therefore parts of ourselves. (Riviere in Brown 1968: 147)

To apply a dialectical approach means starting with the big picture, the system, or at least as much of the big picture as we understand, and then we proceed to examine the parts in order to see where they fit and how they work – which will hopefully lead to a richer understanding of the big picture (Ollman 2003). Logical analysis, however, begins with a small part, and then it tries to reconstruct the larger whole through establishing connections between this part and other parts. Starting with a supposedly independent part requires a separation, with its corresponding distortion of meaning that no post-mending can overcome.

> Something will be missing, something will be out of place, and, without any standard by which to judge, neither will be recognized. ... As with Humpty Dumpty, who after the fall could never be put together again, a system whose functioning parts have been treated as independent of one another at the start can never be reestablished in its integrity. (Ollman 2003: 14)

In this chapter, I have discussed and compared two basic forms of understanding: logic and dialectics. The comparison was motivated by the book's main research tool – perspectivism, which, originally, was chosen for its potential to deepen understanding. The problem called for it; whenever we experience a discrepancy between the image of reality that we have in our head, on the one hand, and the reality that we experience through our body, on the other, perspectivism can be illuminating. In other words, when you experience a chafing feeling between how you, as an individual, feel, and what the institutions and representatives of society say you should feel. And now, as we have come full circle, we are approaching the end of the journey.

Conclusion
Planned, All Too Planned

On all sides we hear talk about the housing shortage, and with good reason. Nor is there just talk; there is action too. We try to fill the need by providing houses, by promoting the building of houses, planning the whole architectural enterprise. However hard and bitter, however hampering and threatening the lack of houses remains, the *proper plight of dwelling* does not lie merely in a lack of houses. ... The proper dwelling plight lies in this, that mortals ever search anew for the essence of dwelling, that they *must ever learn to dwell.*

Martin Heidegger

Technocrats, unaware of what goes on in their own mind and in their working concepts, profoundly misjudging what is going on (and what is not) in their blind field, end up minutely organizing a repressive space.

Henri Lefebvre

You, the reader, know where we started, but where have we ended up? The starting point for the study was an experience of a problem in the world – a problem I referred to as the gap between vision and reality in urban planning. In order to transform the experience into understanding, I turned to the philosophy of perspectivism and established two fixed points between which I continuously alternated. One was called the body of the *flâneur*, and this represented my own perspective, and the other I named the eye of the architect, a point that represents the planner in general. In other words, I have interpreted the vision-reality gap as a gap between so-called expert statements about what constitutes a vibrant, urban environment, on the one hand, and what I felt was, in actuality, an environment pervaded by boredom, on the other. In the chapters that followed, this problem was extended, which meant that the original family name – the vision-reality gap – found new names: society-individual, eye-body, Homo Faber-Homo Ludens, philobatism-ocnophilia, need-desire, Apollo-Dionysus, superego-id, form-process and, in the most recent chapter, logic-dialectics. Along the way, it became increasingly clear that my starting point – whose worth and seriousness I was initially unsure of – turned out to be anything but trivial: it opened the door to a fundamental sociological-psychological but also ontological-ethical problem: alienation. Alienation is estrangement and embedded in the aforementioned opposites is a problem of repression; an uneven power relation where one represses the other. This problem can be summarised as follows:

The eye represses hearing and the body's other senses / Homo Faber sees, as a result of her own thinking, no point in Homo Luden's lust for play / The Apollonian planner has a perspective that focuses on clearly defined and translatable needs and, hence, represses the Dionysian force that is the *flâneur*'s desire / The expert's world of abstract, specialised analyses, materialised in the form of drawings and models, does not and cannot take into account the layman's experience of the completed building / Society's interest is in the well-being of the collective – not the individual / *Animal sublimans* is looking for beauty, transcendence and freedom from pain and anxiety, therefore creating a distance from the body; from sexuality, from life / The ideology of the straight line that belongs to the modernist architect represses the aimless wanderings of the *flâneur* / The philobat's longing for friendly expanses represses the ocnophil's desire to be held by objects / The either-or of logic represses dialectics' both/and / The superego's strict demands for moral conduct repress the id's desire for instant (sexual) gratification / Form is generally ranked higher than formlessness since understanding, vision and communication – these basic and related human activities – require that things are reified; given form.

In light of the psycho-analytical tradition, I have identified the problem of alienation and hence the book's main problem as a constitutive element of all human existence. Repression is a necessity; its purpose is to avoid suffering. But it is also true that repression – especially when it is severe and/or prolonged – causes suffering and ultimately neurosis.

To further summarise the argument and connect it to the backdrop of the book – the current attempt to create urban atmospheres in Sweden – we can say that it is a paradox to create urbanity. This is because planning (in its current form) and urbanity – in essence – are opposites. Planning is basically a quest to make the world – or life – *flat* (*flat* is *plan* in Swedish), to freeze the present, to make things out of processes and to transform ambivalence into certainty. Planners say that the environments they create are urban, but what they actually do is to construct buildings and open spaces. Here we can remind ourselves of the essence of Freud's criticism of civilization – summarised by Johansson (2011: 155):

> Despite the advancement of science and economic development, it seems that people are finding it increasingly difficult to find meaning in our late modern social conditions. The Enlightenment and the production of new valuable knowledge bring nothing immediate or obvious in terms of people's abilities to find a satisfying life. Desire and passion – that which seems to be the prerequisites for a life that is not merely emptiness and superficiality – do not present themselves automatically.

The paradox is that the planners themselves claim that they think. They analyse, make calculations and draw logical conclusions. Compared to traditional building, architecture, in short, means thinking – not doing. How can planning improve the lives of people? And how can we do this through careful calculation?[1] Such is the benevolent question of planning. But there is a difference between thinking and *thinking*. The thinking that characterises planning – but also conventional planning critique – very often stops at the content but seldom questions its form, its reasoning rules. And so it is that the planner rushes from one project to another, avoiding the question why she so often obstructs her own course.

Meanwhile, social scientists have, for quite some time now, theorised about the urban. Since the 1970s, in the name of social constructivism and the critique of oppressive norms and power structures, social-scientific researchers on the urban have, in brief, argued that (urban) space is socially produced and, thus, without physical boundaries. Dionysus has reigned at the expense of Apollo and this 'new' discourse on space has resulted in the conclusion that urbanity can be basically anything. In turn, this idea has led to the silencing of a range of issues – including that of urbanity's material prerequisites. But, as Lefebvre (1996: 103) knew, to understand the urban, we must think not only of its social morphology but also its material, although we should not forget that this division is temporary, always risky. From this perspective, the architectural theory of space syntax stands out, since it re-establishes the Apollonian element in our knowledge of the urban.

To shed further light on the book's main problem, we can look at what Asplund (1987) has to say about what he calls abstract sociality. The spread of abstract sociality, he argues, 'seems to have culminated in our days' (ibid.: 170). But this social phenomenon is not new; it was detected as early as the eighteenth century. However, it was only during the nineteenth century, with the emergence of sociology, that it became an object of scientific inquiry. Sociology, as developed by Émile Durkheim, is nothing more than 'the abstract study of abstract sociality' (ibid.: 154). Abstract sociality has concrete sociality as its counterpart. In modern society, both these forms of sociality exist, and both put a mark on the individual. The individual can be described as the point at which both of these ways of being meet. The following excerpt from Asplund (1987: 170) explores what I have laid out:

> Let us say that Sven Svensson is a carpenter, married, father of two and a Social Democrat [a political party affiliation]. Moreover, he is an abstract social being and is now and then understood as such by himself and others. He is both a real person and an abstract social being, and it is this ambiguity or duplicity that is perhaps the most important feature of historical development. The ambiguity can be experienced very strongly in the situation that I find myself in right now as a lecturer. I stand before you, both as myself and as an abstract social being. My abstract double is nevertheless not a creature that … I feel myself to be … whenever I stand in a classroom, but the double is my constant companion. This is the case for all of us.

---

1   I have already defined the meaning of calculation as 'to compute, to estimate by mathematical means'. It also means 'to plan, devise' (*Online Etymology Dictionary* 2013-04-22).

In abstract sociality all of us play a role. This role has nothing to do with me or you as a person: 'As soon as I perceive myself as a role, I have gone from perceiving myself as a real person to perceiving myself as an abstract social being' (ibid.: 174). Furthermore, abstract social creatures have no body; they do not bleed, they do not feel. Abstract sociality is clean and empty. But – and this is what I want to get at – the political decisions that are made by abstract social beings (read: planners) have implications for the concrete individual. Specifically, they resonate in the actual body of the individual. In other words, '[p]olitical decisions in Stockholm eventually give rise to individual physical symptoms in Tomelilla [a small town in Sweden]', Asplund's (ibid.: 177) example reads. However, I would go a step further and say the decisions made by the politician and abstract social creature *x* may sooner or later cause individual physical symptoms in the concrete person *x*, not only in *y*. We simply cannot do away with our role-playing double; we cannot remove it 'as if it were an overcoat' (ibid.: 178).

Asplund's reasoning about the duality that characterises the individual in modern society relates to the conclusion in the previous chapter that humans are both subjects and objects – never just one or the other. We can also think of the psycho-analytical view of the adult as a being who always holds traces of the child she once was. Perhaps the key to the problem of alienation is a general imbalance between these different forms of socialities or, put another way, between humans as objects and humans as subjects.

The imbalance is experienced by the individual, but as dialectics teaches us, we must not stop our analysis here. Alienation is an ongoing social – not primarily individual – *process*. According to Asplund (1987: 139–78), it is this imbalance that lies behind what is today known as nervous exhaustion or 'burnout' (*utbrändhet*). The imbalance can be characterised as the advantage of abstract sociality over concrete sociality. This argument is summarised by Johannisson (2009: 237): 'The state [of a nervous exhausted person] is not related to the individual's fatigue, not the work itself and cannot be remedied with rest ... Instead, it is located in the social sphere ... The state is caused by a lack of social interaction. ... Nervous exhaustion is not fatigue, but alienation'.

Asplund (1987), who is a social psychologist, defines alienation as a *parting* of some kind – an estrangement from something that previously *has been* or something that *is* below the surface, from something that has fallen out of sight and whose absence we do not experience (or at least do not necessarily notice) until the process has gone too far and the state of alienation/neurosis is a reality.

* * *

In what remains I will look at what this 'something' might refer to. Related to the problem of alienation and estrangement in modern society is the question of meaning. The question of meaning – or rather the lack of meaning – is, in turn, linked to the problem of boredom. In Chapter 2, I pointed out that both Woolf and Lefebvre led a struggle – a struggle against boredom. This is how Svendsen (2005: 35; 30) describes boredom:

[B]oredom is not a question of work or freedom but of meaning. ... Human beings are addicted to meaning. We all have a great problem: Our lives must have some sort of content. We cannot bear to live our lives without some sort of content that we can see as constituting a meaning. Meaninglessness is boring. And boredom can be described metaphorically as meaning withdrawal. Boredom can be understood as a discomfort which communicates that the need for meaning is not satisfied.

The fact that we humans are 'equipped with a burning need for meaning' is also emphasised by Hylland Eriksen (2008: 220). Meaning is an elusive concept, but the type of meaning I am looking for is inextricably associated with meaning *for someone* (see ibid.: 35). Svendsen refers to his colleague Peter Wessel Zapffe, who writes, 'That an action or a life fragment has meaning means that it invokes in us a most specific sensation that is not easily reworked into a thought' (in ibid.). Thus, we can now say that meaning – not surprisingly – is something subjective, related to the individual's emotional experience.

Here, I would like to revisit the discussion on recreation and open spaces in Chapter 3. In this discussion, we saw that the experts behind the report *Increased requirements for space in the urban environment* (1965) argued that open spaces, or recreational spaces (*friytor* in Swedish, plural form of *friyta*, literally 'free surface'), must expand in size, as people have gotten more free time (*fritid*). If we interpret the word *friyta* as well as *fritid* literally, we see the linguistic parallels to the word *frihet* – the Swedish word for freedom (*fri* means 'free'). Here, it is interesting to ask: What kind of freedom is implied in these concepts? Let us look at what Svendsen (2005: 35) has to say about free time:

What sort of freedom are we talking about? A freedom from work? In that case, it is work that provides a negative definition of freedom. Are we freer in our free time than during our time at work? We undeniably have a slightly different role, for while we are producers in our working hours, we are mainly consumers in our free time. However, one is not necessarily freer in the one role than in the other, and the one role is not necessarily more meaningful than the other. As mentioned before, boredom is not a question of work or freedom but of meaning.

Consequently, as Svendsen seems to point out, an individual can be insufferably bored in her free time (and, thus, in recreational space, too). The conclusion may seem trivial since there are few who would argue that people always enjoy their free time. But since we are engaged in a critique of urban planning, the point deserves to be made. Hammarby Sjöstad is known as a neighbourhood where much emphasis has been put on beautifying public spaces in order to make them attractive. *Here people will be happy* – such is the intention. Therefore, the planners have landscaped park paths, plants and trees and installed permanent artwork and sculptures. In other words, planners have created open, recreational spaces where people can spend their free time. In light of this, I would like to sharpen my argument a bit further and liken Hammarby Sjöstad to a party that is a bit over-planned: enjoyable – but very boring. And '[t]he strange thing about this form of boredom', Svendsen informs (2005: 120), 'is that [we] are unable to identify exactly what [we are] bored with'. He continues: 'Even though the party [is] pleasant and entertaining, it [is] completely empty' (ibid.).

This emptiness I would generally describe as a consequence of the fact that everything in Hammarby Sjöstad seems to be finished. And the fact that everything is finished can, in turn, be traced to the planners' perception of urban planning as a 'finite game', to use Carse's expression (1986). That is, urban planning is regarded as an activity with an obvious beginning and an obvious end. In fact, the party turned out not to be a party at all; the meticulous planning that had preceded it stifled all forms of spontaneity and turned it into a ritual. This is how the director of Hammarby Sjöstad reasons: 'A lesson from Södra Stationsområdet is that we ..., at an early stage, ought to start a discussion about the end result' (in Hultin et al. 1992: 22). He also says: 'The shanty town [Figure C.1] remained until 1998 when it was demolished to make way for the new buildings in Hammarby Sjöstad ... A new era in the history of Lugnet,[2] Södra Hammarbyhamnen and Sickla Udde has begun' (*BoStad02* 2002: 12f).

This is a functionalist way of reasoning. According to this thinking, exact city planning is 'the only way to really master the activity and lead to the best possible result' (Åhrén 1928: 175). What these seemingly innocent statements lay bare is a vision of urban planning as a finite activity – an activity whose overall aim is to be completed: '[Finite observers] are looking for closure, for the ways in which players can bring matters to a conclusion and finish whatever remains unfinished', Carse writes (1986: §69). The same applies to finite observers' relations to art: they look at it and make an object of it (ibid.). This, I think, is a possible reason as to why the large-scale investment in artistic decoration in Hammarby Sjöstad has not necessarily helped to make the area 'lively'.

As we saw in Chapter 3, architects approach the city as if it were a house; they see public space as an interior, where different locations are assigned with different functions. Thus, the different places become signals. In Lefebvre's words (1995: 119), 'Everything is clear and intelligible ... Everything is closure and materialized system. The text of the town is totally legible'.

If we once again look at what Svendsen (2005: 31f) has to say, we see that the emptiness of meaning – the essence of boredom – is due to the fact that 'all objects and actions come to us fully coded', while humans – who are not only a product of the Enlightenment but also of Romanticism – insist on *personal* meaning, 'a meaning that we ourselves realize'. '[W]e are not as a matter of course completely at home in the interpreted world', Svendsen (ibid.) writes, referring to Rilke. And he continues, 'Man is a world-forming being, a being that actively constitutes his own world, but when everything is always already fully coded, the active

---

2   Lugnet was the name of the shanty town. See Skoglund and Eklund (1997) for a documentation of Lugnet before demolition.

Figure C.1   The shanty town Lugnet in 1996, two years before demolition, at the location where Hammarby Sjöstad was built

Source: Photograph by Per Skoglund.

Figure C.2   Designed form and, hence, order in Hammarby Sjöstad after the demolition of Lugnet

Source: Author's photograph from 2009.

constituting of the world is made superfluous, and we lose friction in relation to the world'. And if there is anything that urban planning since its birth has tried to eliminate, it is friction; between different activities, between different areas of life, and – perhaps most importantly – between bodies. The following is a quote from *acceptera*: 'One thing is certain, however, which is that comfort vanishes if a home is not suitably organized to allow life to be lived with the minimum of friction' (Asplund et al. 2008: 244).[3]

Against this backdrop, space syntax – whose proponents seem to encourage, not discourage, friction – seems to imply a revolution. It is in itself fascinating that Hillier's scientifically substantiated definition of the urban in some respects coincides with the poetic understanding of the *flâneur*: Urbanity's essence is nothing more and nothing less than *many bodies in the same physical space*, Hillier asserts. Similarly, but differently, Baudelaire (1995: 9) talks about the crowd: The crowd is for the *flâneur* 'as the air is that of birds and water of fishes ... [A]n immense reservoir of electrical energy'.

As already noted, the perspective of the space syntax theorists differs from that of most practicing urban planners. In Chapters 4 and 6 we saw that space syntax means a change of focus from the buildings to the space between them, and that its interest is first and foremost what architecture does to the body and not what it signals to the eyes. The perspective of space syntax advocates differs in another way, too; it seems to regard city building as an infinite – not finite – game. At least this is how I interpret Hillier's (2007: 193) reasoning about what he terms *rituals* and *parties*. Certain spatial configurations support rituals, and act – briefly put – as courtrooms. Others encourage parties and can be likened to funfairs (ibid.: 304).

> A ritual is a ... social event [in which] all that happens is governed by rules, and a ritual typically generates a precise system of spatial relationships and movements through time ... A party is a[n] event [whose] object is to generate new relationships by shuffling them in space ... In a [ritual], space is adapted to support the rules, and behavioural rules must also support it. In a [party], space evolves to structure, and often to maximize, encounter density. (Hillier 2007: 5)

We find equivalents of Hillier's concepts rituals and parties in Marcus's (2000b: 190ff) concepts of *architectural urbanity* and *general urbanity*, which we met in Chapter 6. These types of urbanity function differently; they exhibit a reproductive versus a productive functionality. With these concepts, Marcus wants to illustrate that during the twentieth century, urban planning has given rise to architectural urbanity with a reproductive functionality, that is, a type of urbanity that involves the reproduction of already established activities and values (you walk here, you drive there, you play here and so on). As a result of this highly moralistic (but/and benevolent) governance of life in the (future) city, urban planning during the twentieth century has almost exclusively encouraged rituals – not parties.

---

3   For a versatile study of the concept and metaphor of friction, see Åkerman (1998).

Here, I will let Carse (1986:§35) speak: 'Society is a manifestation of power. It is theatrical, having an established script. Deviations from the script are evident at once. Deviation is antisocietal'.

As Marcus (2000b: 193) underlines, this is not to say that parties are better than rituals; society needs both, but – and this is his point – 'if it is true that there is a preference for urban form with a reproductive functionality in the twentieth century, this may imply that the need for urban form with a more productive functionality is not satisfied and, further, that this may be a loss for society in general'.

This – I would say – is the main message of Marcus's book – a message that is highly relevant for critical studies on urban life and urban planning. Yet, it has been largely neglected in social-scientific research. In this book, I have tried to interpret and give a broader critical and philosophical meaning to this argument, which Marcus arrives at through applying the quantitative theory and method of space syntax. As a result of this cross-fertilisation, we can now conclude that the problem that Marcus generally refers to as a 'loss', but which he does not investigate further, is, in fact, a growing *alienation*, a loss of social interaction, of personal meaning. Put differently, it is a qualitative loss whose result is that the *flâneur*, or Homo Ludens (the second name that she got in Chapter 2), has been made homeless.

Now, one question remains to be answered: Is it not *meaning* that the architecture in Hammarby Sjöstad offers its residents? Architecture is (partly) an art – this we have already concluded. And art, in general, aims, to give the world beauty and meaning. But – again – the answer depends on how we interpret the concept of meaning. We can find clues to what we mean in our grammatical expressions. For example, to say that something *has* a meaning is one thing; to say that it *is* meaningful is another. The type of meaning that the architects offer the residents differs from the type of meaning that the residents themselves attach to their life and to their world. In some respects, walking around in Hammarby Sjöstad means to practically wade in meaning; behind almost every detail, every material, every colour, is an idea – an idea of what associations that particular detail, material or colour will arouse in the beholder. A certain type of facade will remind the viewer of the inner city, and so on. But this is not personal meaning and therefore not the kind of meaning I am looking for. In Hylland Eriksen's words (2008: 219): 'The question "What is the meaning of life?" is ... wrongly put, because it presumes that life has a meaning beyond itself. ... [L]ife does not *have* meaning, life *is* meaning'.

Here we can recall that while the conventional scientific viewpoint is that man is primarily a thinking creature that *has* a body, the phenomenological insight says that he *is* a body (Sigurdsson 2006: 308). The activity of building houses and planning cities may *have* a meaning; constructing them is essential to protect ourselves from the cold and other conditions – yes, to survive. But as this book underscores, there is a difference between surviving and living, between need and desire, between building and dwelling. Dwelling – like life – is an infinite game that falls outside Homo Faber's mental horizon because Homo Faber does everything 'in order to', not 'for the sake of'. To live is an infinite game that does not have any other goal but to continue living. Similarly, one can say that living has no goal – because what would that be apart from dying?

Grammatically, the words 'to live' and 'to dwell' belong to the category of intransitive verbs, that is, verbs that are not constructed with an object. Man lives; man dwells – full stop. In contrast, 'to build' is a transitive verb, and characteristic of these is that they are usually accompanied by one or more objects (one builds a house, one builds a porch and so on). Again, to live *has* no meaning; it *is* meaning. It is this clarification that Heidegger (1993: 349) makes when he describes the etymological roots of the phrase 'Ich bin' (I am). The old German word *bin* (is) belongs to *bauen*, which originally meant 'to *dwell*'. Therefore, to say 'I dwell' is merely another way of saying 'I am'.

To dwell is to live, and we do not only live in our house or apartment but outside of it, too. It is an infinite game, in which finite games – like building a house or a porch – can be included. Infinite games can, thus, include finite (we saw how Virginia Woolf set up 'goals' for her walks), but finite games by definition exclude infinite games. There are several finite games but only one infinite. This understanding can be deepened if we recall the difference between need and desire. Borrowing from Carse (1986: §61), we can formulate it so that the satisfaction of our desire 'is never an achievement, but an act in a continuing relationship ... Its lack of satisfaction is never a failure, but only a matter to be taken on into further play'.

The fact that planners so consistently and so often talk about needs (which, in contrast to desires, can be met) can be interpreted as yet another sign of their understanding of planning as something that can and must be completed. Discussing Södra Stationsområdet, for example, the planning director states: 'The whole project was basically planned in one go' (Inghe-Hagström 1987: 33). The city, or the district within the city, is thought of as one large building that must be completed already at the planners' drawing boards. In other words, in the foreground is the construction of space, of concrete objects like buildings and roads, while the planners seem to forget that the city is also a place for the infinite game of dwelling – which may include the finite game of building (something) but which still encompasses more than that. Thus, planners become fixated on the concrete result of an action, rather than on the act itself (Marcus 2000b: 83, Ramirez 1995: 117ff, Carse 1986: §93).

Now that I have named my research problem as a problem of alienation – a problem that is the result of a way of reasoning about urban development (and thus about urban life) as a finite game, one important point remains to be said. Or rather, the argument has been made earlier in the book, but it should be emphasised here, in an abbreviated form. The argument is that people in general, and the planner in particular, are not only objects – cogs in a bureaucratic machine – but also ethically responsible subjects, beings with a certain acting space. I have formulated a critique of urban planning, but not a critique that depicts planners as a group of more or less power-ridden oppressors of other, more marginalised, groups. Had this been the case, the 'solution' to unjust or contra-final planning would have been to replace this group of planners with another, 'better' group. As the psycho-analytical perspective helps us understand, man is a creature not only capable of, but very much inclined to, repressing himself. He is able to – metaphorically speaking – arrive at a place that is diametrically different from the one he originally aspired to. Human, all too human, if we are to believe Nietzsche (1986a: §57), for '[i]n morality man treats himself not as *individuum* but as *dividuum*' – that is, as divided, in constant conflict with himself.

* * *

To plan, to try to predict events in the social and the natural world, to try to manipulate them to fit (what we think are) our purposes is a human trait. But it is also a human trait to seek freedom, to wish to escape other people's attempts at categorisation and manipulation. To this duality, logic – the conventional reasoning rule of the Western world – is relatively blind. And so it is that planning as a sphere of building – Homo Faber's abiding-place par excellence – alienates man from his world of experience, from the world in which Homo Ludens dwells. Or, rather, he alienates himself.

Even if the disjointing to some extent is an inevitable aspect of the fact that man is a social being, a member of civilization, psycho-analytical introspection contributes to a relaxation – and, henceforth, also a correction – of the imbalance between rituals and parties, between the planned and the unplanned, between the Apollonian and the Dionysian. A balance may be what we are searching for in modern society, whether we know it or not.

References

Abrahamsson, C. 2008. *Topoi/Graphein* Doctoral thesis. Dept. of Social and Economic Geography, Uppsala University.

Adorno, T.W. and Horkheimer, M. 1981. [1947] *Upplysningens dialektik. Filosofiska fragment* [*Dialectic of Enlightenment*] translated from German by L. Bjurman and C-H Wijkmark. Gothenburg: Röda Bokförlaget.

Agnew, J. 2009. Place. In *Handbook of Geographical Knowledge* edited by J. Agnew and D. Livingstone. London: Sage.

Ahlberg, A. 1958. Religion och logik. *Svenska Dagbladet* 10 April.

Åhrén, U. 1928. Synpunkter på stadsbyggandet. Byggmästaren häfte 32, Allmänna upplagan 22, 173–5.

Åkerman, N. (ed.) 1998. *The Necessity of Friction* Boulder CO: Westview Press.

Alexander, C. 1965. The City is Not a Tree. *Architectural Forum* April, 58–62.

Alexander, C. 1970. *Notes on the Synthesis of Form*. Fifth Printing Cambridge: Harvard University Press.

Altay, D. 2007. Urban Spaces Re-Defined in Daily Practices – 'Minibar', Ankara. In *Encountering Urban Places* edited by L. Frers and L. Meier. Aldershot: Ashgate.

Améen, L. 1964. *Stadsbebyggelse och domänstruktur. Svensk stadsutveckling i relation till ägoförhållanden och administrativa gränser*. Lund: Carl Bloms.

Améen, L. and Lewan, N. 1970. *Bebyggelse och samhällsplanering*. Stockholm: Kungliga Boktryckeriet.

Andersen, S. 1997. *Som dig själv. En inledning i etik* translated from Danish by P.L. Månsson. Nora: Nya Doxa.

Anderson, B. and Wiley, J. 2009. On Geography and Materiality. *Environment and Planning A*, 41 (2), 318–35.

Anderson, K. and Smith, S.J. 2001. Editorial: Emotional Geographies. *Transactions of the Institute of British Geographers*, New Series, 26 (1), 7–10.

Andersson, E. 2009a. Arkitekt efterlyser debatt. *Svenska Dagbladet*, 3 Dec.

Andersson, E. 2009b. Stockholm får tätare stadsbild. *Svenska Dagbladet*, 3 Dec.

Andersson, E. 2009c. Klartecken för Tors torn. *Svenska Dagbladet*, 12 Dec.

Andersson, O. 2010a. Manhattans vitalitet uppstod på gatunivå. *Svenska Dagbladet* Under strecket, 9 Feb.

Andersson, O. 2010b. En stelnad och senil modernism: Kommentar Slussen. *Svenska Dagbladet*, 17 Feb.

Andersson, R. 1987. *Den svenska urbaniseringen. Kontextualisering av begrepp och processer* Doctoral thesis, Geografiska regionstudier 18, Uppsala University.

Andersson Wij, T. 2004. *Stjärnorna i oss.* Music album. Sweden: Metronom/ Warner Music.

Appleyard, D., Lynch, K. and Myer, J. 1967. View from the Road. In *Environmental Perception and Behavior* edited by D. Lowenthal. Chicago: Public Litho Service, Inc., 75–88.

Arendt, H. 1990. Philosophy and Politics. *Social Research* 57 (1), 73–103.

Arendt, H. 1998. [1958] *The Human Condition* USA: University of Chicago Press.

Aristotle. 2013. [350 BC] *The Nichomachean Ethics.* Public Domain English, translated from Greek by W.D. Ross: http://people.bu.edu/wwildman/ WeirdWildWeb/courses/wphil/readings/wphil_rdg09_nichomacheanethics_ entire.htm 2013-02-11.

Armstrong, A.C. 1907. Individual and Social Ethics. *The Journal of Philosophy, Psychology and Scientific Methods* 4 (5), 119–22.

Arnstberg, K-O and Bergström, I. 2001. *Åtta postulat om planering av staden som livsmiljö* Stockholm: Formas.

Asplund, G., Gahn, W., Markelius, S., Paulsson, G., Sundahl, E. and Åhrén, U. 1980. [1931] *acceptera* Arlöv: Berlings.

Asplund, G., et al. 2008. [1931] *acceptera* translated from Swedish by D. Jones. In *Modern Swedish Design: Three Founding Texts* edited by L. Creagh, H. Kåberg, and B. Miller Lane. New York: MoMA.

Asplund, J. 1970. *Om undran inför samhället* Lund: Argos.

Asplund, J. 1979. *Teorier om framtiden* Stockholm: Liber.

Asplund, J. 1987. *Det sociala livets elementära former* Gothenburg: Korpen.

Asplund, J. 1991. *Essä om Gemeinschaft och Gesellschaft* Gothenburg: Korpen.

Asplund, J. 2002. *Avhandlingens språkdräkt* Gothenburg: Korpen.

Ayer, A.J. 1971. *Language, Truth and Logic* Harmondsworth: Penguin.

Balint, E. 1959E. Distance in Space and Time. In *Thrills and Regressions* edited by M. Balint. New York: International Universities Press.

Balint, M. 1955. Friendly Expanses; Horrid Empty Spaces. *The International Journal of Psycho-analysis* 36(4–5), 225–41.

Balint, M. (ed.) 1959M. *Thrills and Regressions* New York: International Universities Press.

Balint, M. 1979. *The Basic Fault. Therapeutic Aspects of Regression* Evanston: Northwestern University Press.

Ballon, H. (ed.). 2012. *The Greatest Grid: The. Masterplan of Manhattan, 1811–2011* New York: Columbia University Press.

Banfield, E.C. 1959. Ends and Means in Planning. *International Social Science Journal* XI (3).

Bar-Eli, M., Azar, O.H., Ritov, I., Keidar-Levin, Y. and Schein, G., 2007. Action Bias among Elite Soccer Goalkeepers: The case of penalty kicks. *Journal of Economic Psychology* 28, 606–21.

Barnes, T. 2004. Placing Ideas: Genius loci, heterotopia and geography's quantitative revolution. *Progress in Human Geography* 28 (5), 565–95.

Barnes, T. 2006. Between Deduction and Dialectics: David Harvey on Knowledge. In *David Harvey. A Critical Reader* edited by N. Castree and D. Gregory. London and New York: Blackwell.

Barrett, W. 1962. *Irrational Man. A Study in Existential Philosophy* New York: Doubleday Anchor Books.

Bartetzky, A. and Schalenberg, M. (eds) 2009. *Urban Planning and the Pursuit of Happiness. European variations on a universal theme (18th–21st Centuries)* Berlin: Jovis Verlag.

Bartyzel, M. 2007. Henry Bean Fights Back Against the 'Noise' of Car Alarms: http://www.cinematical.com/2007/10/23/henry-bean-fights-back-against-the-noise-of-car-alarms/ 2009-12-03.

Baudelaire, C. 1995. [1863] *The Painter of Modern Life and Other Essays* translated from French by J. Maine. London: Phaidon Press.

Baum, K. 2008. Against Architecture. *Art Lies. A Contemporary Art Quarterly* 'Urban Myths' Issue 58.

Bauman, Z. 1994. Desert Spectacular. In *The Flâneur* edited by K. Tester, London: Routledge.

Bauman, Z. 1993. *Postmodern Ethics* Oxford and Cambridge: Blackwell.

Bean, H. 2007. *Noise* Film.

Beaujeu-Garnier, J. 1976. [1971] *Methods and Perspectives in Geography* translated from French by J. Bray. London and New York: Longman.

Bender, M. 1999. Virginia Woolf's London. NYSL Travels, The New York www.nysoclib.org/travels/woolf.html 2009-03-19.

Benjamin, W. 1999. [1935] *The Arcades Project* translated from German by H. Eiland and K. McLaughlin. Cambridge MA and London: The Belknap of Harvard University Press.

Berg Eriksen, T. 2005. *Nietzsche och det moderna* translated from Norwegian by S. Andersson. Stockholm: Atlantis.

Bergdahl, E. and Rönn, M. 2001. Planering för funktionsintegrering – problem och utgångspunkter. CERUM Working Paper 30: 2001.

Berger, P.L. and Luckmann T. 1967. *The Social Construction of Reality. A Treatise in the Sociology of Knowledge* London: Penguin.

Bergman, B. 1974. Stadsbygget som politisk strategi. Henri Lefebvre och stadens befrielse. *Ord och Bild* 6, 83, 318–28.

Bergman, B. 1980. *Han ville staden – en arkitekturhistoria* Stockholm: Bokomotiv.

Bergman, B. 1985. *Manhattan också!* Lund: Institutionen för byggnadsfunktionslära, Lund University.

Bergman, B. and Mannheimer, O. 1974. Det samhälleliga rummet. Ett samtal med Henri Lefebvre. *Ord och Bild* 6, 83, 329–34.

Bergson, H. 2004. [1896] *Matter and Memory* translated from French by N.M. Paul and W. Scott Palmer. New York: Dover.

Bergsten, Z. 2010. *Bättre framtidsutsikter? Blandade bostadsområden och grannskapseffekter. En analys av visioner och effekter av blandat boende* Doctoral thesis, Geografiska regionstudier 85, Uppsala University.

Bergsten, Z. and Holmqvist, E. 2007. Blanda olika befolkningsgrupper – fortfarande en målsättning? Research report 2007:1, IBF, Uppsala University.

Berman, M. 1983. [1982] *All That Is Solid Melts into Air. The Experience of Modernity* London: Verso.

Bloom, A. 1987. *The Closing of the American Mind* New York: Simon and Schuster.

Bondi, L., Davidson J. and Smith M. (eds) 2005. *Emotional Geographies* Aldershot: Ashgate.

Bonnier, J. 1997. En möjlig relation till solitären J.A. In *Seendets pendel. Festskrift till Johan Asplund* edited by F. Oddner and B. Isenberg. Stockholm/ Stehag: Symposion.

BoStad02 2002. Programskrift för Hammarby Sjöstad.

Boye, K. 1994. *Complete Poems* translated from Swedish by D. McDuff. Newcastle: Bloodaxe Books.

Boyer, C.M. 1997. *Dreaming the Rational City. The Myth of American City Planning* Cambridge MA: MIT Press.

Bradley, K. 2009. *Just Environments. Politicising Sustainable Urban Development.* Doctoral thesis, KTH, Stockholm.

Bradley, K., Broms Wessel, O. and Tunström, M. 2004. Stadsplanering saknar naturlagar. *Dagens Nyheter* 5 Nov.

Bråmå, Å. 2006. *Studies in the Dynamics of Residential Segregation* Doctoral thesis, Geografiska regionstudier 67, Uppsala University.

Brenner, C. 1970. [1955] *Psykoanalysens grunder* [*Elementary Textbook of Psychoanalysis*] translated from English by M. Kihlbom. Stockholm: Prisma.

Brenner, C. 1988. [1982] *Psykiska konflikter* [*The Mind in Conflict*] translated from English by L. Bryngelson. Stockholm: Natur och Kultur.

Brooks, D. 2010. Children of the '70s. *The New York Times*, 17 May.

Brosseau, M. 1994. Geography's Literature. *Progress in Human Geography* 18 (3), 333–53.

Brown, N.O. 1959. *Life against Death: The Psycho-analytic Meaning of History* Middletown CT: Wesleyan University Press.

Brown, N.O. 1968. *Love's Body* New York: Vintage Books.

Brown, N.O. 1991. *Apocalypse and/or Metamorphosis* Berkeley: University of California Press.

Brown, R.H. 1992. *Society as Text. Essays on Rhetoric, Reason and Reality* Chicago IL: The University of Chicago Press.

Brunnberg, H. 1987. Minneberg Stockholm. Brunnberggruppen. *Arkitektur* Tema: Stadsbygge. 1, p. 4.

Buck-Morss, S. 1986. The *Flâneur*, the Sandwichman and the Whore: The politics of loitering. *New German Critique* 39, 99–140.

Budiarto, L. 2007. Senses of Place: Understanding urban location as an organisation of places *Proceedings, 6th International Space Syntax Symposium*, Istanbul.

Burr, V. 2003. *Social Constructionism* Andra utgåvan London: Routledge.

Butler, T. 2006. A Walk of Art: The potential of the sound walk as practice in cultural geography *Social and Cultural Geography* 7 (6), 890–908.

Caldenby, C., Johansson, P.M. and Linton, J. 2012. Planerandets Paradoxer. Intervju med Sara Westin. *Arche. Tidskrift för psykoanalys, humaniora och arkitektur* No. 40–41, 90–129.

Callard, F. 2006. 'The sensation of infinite vastness'; or, the Emergence of Agoraphobia in the late 19th century *Environment and Planning D: Society and Space* 24, 873–89.

Carpenter, A. and Peponis, J. 2010. Poverty and Connectivity: Crossing the tracks *The Journal of Space Syntax: Architecture, Urbanism, Society* 1 (1), 108–20.

Carse, J.P. 1986. *Finite and Infinite Games: A Vision of Life as Play and Possibility* New York: The Free Press.

Carter, P. 2002. *Repressed Spaces. The Poetics of Agoraphobia* London: Reaktion Books.

Cassirer, E. 1956. *Determinism and Indeterminism in Modern Physics. Historical and Systematic Studies of the Problem of Causality* translated from German by T. Benfey. New Haven CT: Yale University Press.

Cassirer, E. 1972. [1944] *An Essay on Man. An introduction to a philosophy of human culture* New Haven CT: Yale University Press.

Cassirer, E. 2005. [1939] *Axel Hägerström. En studie i samtida svensk filosofi* translated from German by J. Jakobsson. Stockholm: Thales.

Castells, M. 1977. [1972] *The Urban Question. A Marxist Approach* translated from French by A. Sheridan. London: Arnold.

Castree, N. 1996. Birds, Mice and Geography: Marxisms and dialectics. *Transactions of the Institute of British Geographers*, New Series, 21 (2), 342–62.

Cederström, J. 1985. Kaos eller skönhet? *Form* 9, 15–16.

Certeau, M. de, 1984. [1980] *The Practice of Everyday Life* translated from French by S. Rendall. Berkeley and Los Angeles: University of California Press.

Ching, F.D.K 2003. *Architectural Graphics* 4th edn New York: Wiley and Sons.

Choay, F. 1997. [1980] *The Rule and the Model. On the Theory of Architecture and Urbanism* translated from French by D. Bratton. Cambridge MA and London: MIT Press.

Cioran, E.M. 2012. [1949] *A Short History of Decay* translated from French by R. Howard. New York: Arcade Publishing.

Collins, R. 2005. *Interaction Ritual Chains* Princeton NJ: Princeton University Press.

Colquhoun, A. 1989. *Modernity and the Classical Tradition. Architectural Essays 1980–1987* Cambridge MA and London: MIT Press.

Colquhoun, A. 2002. *Modern Architecture.* Oxford History of Art. Oxford and New York: Oxford University Press.

Coolidge, M.L. 1941. Ethics – Apollonian and Dionysian. *The Journal of Philosophy* 38 (17), 449–65.

Corfield, P.J. 1990. Walking the City Streets. The Urban Oddyssey in Eighteenth-Century England *Journal of Urban History* 16 (2), 132–74.

Cosgrove, D. 2008. *Geography and Vision. Seeing, Imagining and Representing the World* London and New York: I.B. Tauris and Co.

Crang, M. 2003. The Hair in the Gate: Visuality and Geographical Knowledge *Antipode*, 35 (2), 238–43.

Crang, M. and Thrift, N. 2000. *Thinking Space* London: Routledge.

Crary, J. 1992. *Techniques of the Observer. On Vision and Modernity in the Nineteenth Century* An October Book, Cambridge MA and London: MIT Press.

Crosby, A.W. 1999. [1996] *Att mäta verkligheten. Europa 1250 – 1600 [The Measure of Reality. Quantification and Western Society, 1250–1600]* translated from English by M. Eklöf and L. Mutén. Stockholm: SNS Förlag.

Cuff, D. 1992. *Architecture: The Story of Practice* Cambridge MA and London: MIT Press.

Cuff, D. 2000. The Design Professions. In *Design Professionals and the Built Environment* edited by P. Knox and P. Ozolins. Chichester UK: Wiley and Sons.

Czarniawska, B. 2009. The Platonists meet the Sophists once again. In *Feelings and Business. Essays in Honor of Claes Gustafsson* edited by M. Lindahl and A. Rehn. Stockholm: Santérus Förlag.

Daston, L. and Galison, P. 2007. *Objectivity* New York: Zone Books.

Daun, Å. 2005. *En stuga på sjätte våningen. Svensk mentalitet i en mångkulturell värld* Stockholm/Stehag: Symposion.

Davidoff, P. 1996. Advocacy and Pluralism in Planning. In *Readings in Planning Theory* 2nd edn edited by S. Campbell and S.J. Fanstein. Oxford: Blackwell, 210–23.

Davidson, J. 2003. *Phobic Geographies: The Phenomenology and Spatiality of Identity* Aldershot: Ashgate.

Davidson, J. 2010. Phobias and Safekeeping: Emotions, Selves and Spaces. In *The SAGE Handbook of Social Geographies* edited by S.J Smith et al. London: SAGE.

Davidson, J. and Milligan, C. 2004. Embodying Emotion Sensing Space: Introducing emotional geographies *Social and Cultural Geography* 5 (4), 523–32.

Dear, M. 1986. Planning and Postmodernism. *Environment and Planning D: Society and Space* 4 (2), 367–84.

DeKoven, M. 2003. Psycho-analysis and Sixties Utopianism *Journal for the Psycho-analysis of Culture and Society* 8 (2).

Deleuze, G. 2006. [1962] *Nietzsche and Philosophy* translated from French by H. Tomlinson. New York: Columbia University Press.

Descartes, R. 1988. *Selected Philosophical Writings* translated from French by J. Cottingham, R. Stoothoff and D. Murdoch. Cambridge: Cambridge University Press.

'Det nya Stockholm' 2006. Ad from Stockholms stad Markkontoret. Distributed by *Dagens Nyheter* 2006-03-17.

Detaljplan för kvarteret Kölnan, 2003. Hammarby Sjöstad Dp 2001-00820-54 Stockholm's Office for City Planning.

Detaljplan för Margreteborg, 2000. Helenelund, Sollentuna kommun. Stockholm's Office for City Planning.

Detaljplan för Sickla Kaj m.m., 1999. Hammarby Sjöstad DP 1997-01274-54 Stockholm's Office for City Planning.

Dewey, J. 2005. *Art as Experience* New York: Penguin Group.

Dixon, D.P., Woodward, K. and Jones III, JP. 2008. On the Other Hand ... Dialectics, Guest editorial *Environment and Planning A*, 40, 2549–61.

Doel, M. 2003. Gunnar Olsson's Transformers: The art and politics of rendering the co-relation of society and space in monochrome and technicolor *Antipode*, 35 (1), 140–67.

Driver, F. 2003. On Geography as a Visual Discipline *Antipode*, 35 (2), 227–31.

Dyrssen, C. 1995 *Musikens rum*. Doctoral thesis. Gothenburg: Chalmers, Bo Ejeby Förlag.

Eagleton, T. 1990. *The Ideology of Aesthetics* Oxford: Blackwell.

Eagleton, T. 1998. A Short History of Rhetoric. In *Rhetoric in an Antifoundational World* edited by M. Bernard-Donals and R. Glejzer. New Haven CT: Yale University Press.

Eagleton, T. 2005 [1997] David Harvey. In *Figures of Dissent: Critical Essays on Fish, Spivak, Žižek and Others*. London and New York: Verso, 189-195.

Ekelöf, G. 1949. *Färjesång* Stockholm: Bonnier.

Elden, S. 2004. *Understanding Henri Lefebvre: Theory and the Possible.* London: Continuum.

Elden, S. 2008. Dialectics and the Measure of the World. *Environment and Planning A* 40 (11), 2641–51.

Emerson, R.W. 1841. *Self-Reliance* from *Essays: First Series.* http://www. emersoncentral.com/selfreliance.htm 2013-10-06.

Entrikin, N.J. 1977. Geography's Spatial Perspective and the Philosophy of Ernst Cassirer *Canadian Geographer* XXI, 3, 209–22.

Epstein Nord, D. 1995. *Walking the Victorian Streets. Women, Representation, and the City* London: Cornell University Press.

Eriksson, B. 2007B. *Social Interaktion. Flöden, Positioner, Värden* Sverige: Liber.

Eriksson, E. 2001. *Den moderna staden tar form. Arkitektur och debatt 1910–35* Stockholm: Ordfront.

Eriksson, E. (ed.) 2003. *Stockholms stränder. Från industri till bostäder* Stockholm: Ordfront/S:t Erik.

Eriksson, K. 2007K. Ljudets etnologi *Kulturella Perspektiv*, 4, 25–33.

Eriksson, M. 2010. Vägande kritik från vänster *Svenska Dagbladet* 3 Feb.

Esherick, J. 1984. The Professions of Architecture. *Journal of Architectural Education*, 38.

Evans, R. 2003. *Translations from Drawing to Building and Other Essays* London: Architectural Association.

Fainstein, S. 2010. *The Just City*. Ithaca NY: Cornell University Press.

Farinelli, F. 1992. I segni del mondo: Imagine cartografica e discorso geografico in etá moderna Firenze: La Nuova Italia.

Ferlin, N. 1933. *Barfotabarn* Stockholm: Bonnier.

Feyerabend, P. 2000. [1975] *Mot metodtvånget. Utkast till en anarkistisk vetenskapsteori* [*Against Method: Outline of an Anarchist Theory of Knowledge*] translated from English by T. Brante and C. Hansson. Lund: Arkiv förlag.

Finkel, D.L. and Arney, W.R. 1995. The Paradox of a Personal Pedagogy: Freud's concept of transference. In *Educating for Freedom. The Paradox of Pedagogy* edited by D.L.Finkel and W.R. Arney. New Brunswick NJ: Rutgers University Press, 55–83.

Fleck, L. 1979. [1935] *Genesis and Development of a Scientific Fact* translated from German by F. Bradley and T.J. Trenn. Chicago IL: The University of Chicago Press.

Flyvbjerg, B. 1996. The Dark Side of Planning: Rationality and realrationalitat. In *Explorations in Planning Theory* edited by Mandelbaum et al. New Brunswick NJ: Center for Urban Policy Research.

Flyvbjerg, B. 1998. [1991] *Rationality and Power. Democracy in practice* translated from Danish by S. Sampson. Chicago IL: The University of Chicago Press.

Flyvbjerg, B. 2001. *Making Social Science Matter* Cambridge: Cambridge University Press.

Fogh Kirkeby, O. 2000. *Management Philosophy. A Radical-Normative Perspective* Berlin, Heidelberg: Springer-Verlag.

Forester, J. and Krumholtz, N. 1990. *Making Equity Planning Work* Philadelphia PA: Temple University Press.

Foucault, M. 1984. On the Genealogy of Ethics: An Overview of Work in Progress. In *The Foucault Reader* edited by P. Rabinow. New York: Pantheon Books.

Foucault, M. 1993. [1971] *Diskursens ordning* [*The Discourse on Language*] translated from French by M. Rosengren. Stockholm/ Stehag: Symposion.

Foucault, M. 2004. [1975] *Övervakning och straff: fängelsets födelse* [*Discipline and Punish: The Birth of the Prison*] translated from French by C.G. Bjurström. Lund: Arkiv förlag/A-Z förlag.

Franzén, M. 1982. Gatans disciplinering. *Häften för Kritiska Studier* 5/1982.

Franzén, M. 1987. Staden som livsvärld och system – mellan ångest och helhet av maxima. In *Den sociologiska fantasin – teorier om samhället* edited by U. Bergryd. Simrishamn: Grafo Tryck AB.

Franzén, M. 2004. Preface to Jane Jacobs [1961] *Den amerikanska storstadens liv och förfall* [*The Death and Life of Great American Cities*] translated by C. Hjukström. Gothenburg: Daidalos.

Franzén, M. 2009. Matters of Urban Segregation. In *Proceedings of the 7th International Space Syntax Symposium* edited by L. Marcus, D. Koch and J. Steen. Stockholm: KTH, 105:1–105:2.

Franzén, M. and Sandstedt, E. 1993. *Välfärdsstat och byggande – Om efterkrigstidens nya stadsmönster i Sverige* Lund: Studentlitteratur.

Frederick, M. 2007. *101 Things I Learned in Architecture School* Cambridge MA: MIT Press.

Fredriksson, G. 1992. *Det politiska språket* Sjunde upplagan Stockholm: Tidens Förlag.

Frers, L. 2007. Perception, Aesthetics, and Envelopment – Encountering Space and Materiality. In *Encountering Urban Places* edited by L. Frers and L. Meier. Aldershot: Ashgate.

Fresk Aspegren, A-K. 2007. Nära city och skogen. *Dagens Nyheter* 21 Sept.

Freud, S. 1953. [1907] Creative Writers and Daydreaming. Translated from German by J. Strachey. In *Standard Edition of the Complete Psychological Works of Sigmund Freud.* London: Hogarth Press.

Freud, S. 1970. [1924] *A General Introduction to Psycho-Analysis* translated from German by J. Riviere. New York: Pocket Books, Liveright Publishing Corporation.

Freud, S. 1976. [1937] Analysis Terminable and Interminable. Translated from German by J. Strachey. In *Standard Edition of the Complete Psychological Works of Sigmund Freud* Vol. 23. New York: Norton, 211–53.

Freud, S. 1989. [1909, 1910] *Five Lectures on Psycho-Analysis* translated from German and edited by J. Strachey. New York and London: Norton.

Freud, S. 1995. [1923] The Ego and the Id. Translated from German by J. Riviere in *The Freud Reader* edited by P. Gay. Great Britain: Vintage Original.

Freud, S. 2002. [1930] *Civilization and its Discontents* translated from German by D. McLintock. London: Penguin.

Freud, S. 2008. [1917] *En svårighet för psykoanalysen [A Difficulty in the Path of Psycho-Analysis]* translated from German by L.W. Freij. In *Samhälle och Religion. Samlade skrifter av Sigmund Freud Band X* edited by C. Craaford, L. Sjögren and B. Warren. Stockholm: Natur och Kultur.

Frisby, D. 1994. The *Flâneur* in Social Theory. In *The Flâneur* edited by K. Tester. London: Routledge.

Gale, S. 1972. On the Heterodoxy of Explanation: A review of David Harvey's *Explanation in Geography. Geographical Analysis* IV (3), 285–322.

Gavalda, A. 2007. [2004] *Hunting and Gathering* translated from French by A. Anderson. London: Vintage Books.

Geertz, C. 1995. *After the Fact: Two countries, four decades, one anthropologist* Cambridge MA: Harvard University Press.

Gehl, J. 1991. Jakten på den goda staden. Translated from Danish by L. Hogdal. *Arkitektur* 9, 28–33.

Gelernter, M. 1995. *Sources of Architectural Form. A Critical History of Western Design Theory* Manchester: Manchester University Press.

Generalplan för Stockholm. 1952. The Town Planning Office of the City of Stockholm.

Gestaltningsprogram för Kvarnbergsplan, 2005. Huddinge Kommun.

Gibson, J.J. 1950. *The Perception of the Visual World* Cambridge MA: The Riverside Press.

Gibson, J.J. 1969. [1966] *Våra sinnen som perceptuella system* [*The Senses Considered as Perceptual Systems*] translated from English by L. Eriksson. Stockholm: J. Beckmans bokförlag AB.

Giddens, A. 1996. What is Social Science? In *In Defense of Sociology. Essays, Interpretations and Rejoinders* Cambridge: Polity.

Gilman, S.L. 1976. *Nietzschean Parody. An introduction to reading Nietzsche* Bonn: Bouvier Verlag Herbert Grundmann.

Glas, P. 2005. Afterword in Alfred Jarrys *Dagarna och nätterna. En desertörs roman* [*Days and Nights: Novel of a Deserter*] [1897] translated from French by I. Gadd and Y. Lindberg. Lund: Bakhåll.

Gleber, A. 1999. *The Art of Taking a Walk. Flânerie, Literature, and Film in Weimar Culture* Princeton NJ: Princeton University Press.

Gleeson, B.J. 1996. A Geography for Disabled People? *Transactions of the Institute of British Geographers* 21, 387–96.

Goffman, E. 2005. *Interaction Ritual. Essays in face-to-face behaviour.* Introduction by J. Best. New Brunswick NY: Transaction Publishers.

Goldberger, P. 2006. Uncommon Sense. *The American Scholar* http://www.theamericanscholar.org/uncommon-sense/ 2009-11-19.

Golledge, R. 1993. Geography and the Disabled: A Survey with Special Reference to the Vision Impaired and Blind Populations. *Transactions of the Institute of British Geographers* 18 (1), 63–85.

Goodman, R. 1972. *After the Planners* Harmondsworth: Penguin.

Goodstein, E.S. 2004. *Experience without Qualities: Boredom and Modernity* Stanford CA: Stanford University Press.

Gordon, L. 2006. *Virginia Woolf. A Writer's Life* revised edn London: Virago Press.

Gottdiener, M. 1985. *The Social Production of Urban Space* Austin: University of Texas Press.

Gould, P. 1999. *Becoming a Geographer* New York: Syracuse University Press.

Gould, T. 1963. *Platonic Love* Westport, CT: Greenwood Press.

Graf, F. 1993. *Greek Mythology. An Introduction* translated from German by T. Marier. Baltimore MD: Johns Hopkins University Press.

Graf, F. 2009. *Apollo* New York: Routledge.

Granath, J. 2009. Har 1800-talets stadsideal någon plats i vår tid? *Planera, Bygga Bo* 5, Boverket.

Grange, K. 2013. Shaping Acting Space: In search of a new political awareness among local authority planners. *Planning Theory* 12 (3), 225–43

Granström, H. 2009. För prövade fysiker återstår endast poesin *Svenska Dagbladet* Under strecket, 4 March.

Grant, D.P. 2000. The Nature of Design and Planning. In *Design Professionals and the Built Environment* edited by P. Knox and P. Ozolins. UK: Wiley and Sons.

Greenberg, V.D. 1994. 'A Piece of Logical Thread ... ' Freud and Physics. In *Reading Freud's Reading* edited by S.L. Gilman et al. New York and London: New York University Press.

Gregory, D. 1994. *Geographical Imaginations* Oxford: Blackwell.

Gregory, D. 2000. Human Geography and Space. In *The Dictionary of Human Geography* 4th edn edited by R.J. Johnston, D. Gregory, G. Pratt and M. Watts. Oxford: Blackwell, 767–73.

Gregory, D. et al. (eds) 2009. *The Dictionary of Human Geography* 5th edn. Chichester: Wiley-Blackwell.

Grigor, M. 2008. *Infinite Space. The Architecture of John Lautner* Documentary film. The Googie Company.

Groat, L. 2000. A Conceptual Framework for Understanding the Designer's Role: Technician, Artist or Cultivator? In *Design Professionals and the Built Environment* edited by P. Knox and P. Ozolins. Chichester: Wiley and Sons.

Grönlund, B. 1995. Planmönstren och det urbana. En kommentar till Björn Klarqvists 'Staden som helhet' *Nordic Journal of Architectural Research* 8 (3), 88–96.

Grosz, E. 1994. *Volatile Bodies. Toward a Corporeal Feminism* Bloomington and Indianapolis: Indiana University Press.

Guillén, C. 1971. On the Concept and Metaphor of Perspective. In *Literature as System* Princeton NJ: Princeton University Press.

Gullberg, A. 1986. *Det fängslande planeringstänkandet och sökandet efter en utväg* Stockholm: Plana.

Gullbring, L. 2002. Svenska stadsplanerare Aleksander Wolodarski: Samhället har ett ansvar. *Aktuella Byggen* 6, 18–22.

Gunder, M. and Hillier, J. 2009. *Planning in Ten Words or Less. A Lacanian Entanglement with Spatial Planning.* Farnham: Ashgate.

Habraken, N.J. 2005. *Palladio's Children* edited by J. Teicher. New York: Taylor and Francis.

Hadley-Kamptz, I. 2002. Att planera en stad *Dagens Nyheter* 28 May.

Hägerstrand, T. 1986. Den geografiska traditionens kärnområde. Bilaga 1 *Svensk geografisk årsbok* 62 (38), 38–43.

Hall, P. 1988. *Cities of Tomorrow* London: Blackwell.

Hall, T. 1998. *Urban Geography* London: Routledge.

'Hållbar stadsutveckling' 2009. Ad from Mediaplanet No. 4, Sept. Distributed by *Svenska Dagbladet*.

Hallman, H.W. 1984. *Neighborhoods: Their place in urban life* Beverly Hills, CA: Sage Publications.

Hammer, E. 2006. [2004] *Melankoli. En filosofisk essä* translated from Norwegian by C. Hjukström. Gothenburg: Daidalos.

Hannerz, U. 1992. *Cultural Complexity: Studies in the Social Organization of Meaning* New York: Columbia University Press.

Hanson, J. 2000. Urban Transformations: A history of design ideas. *URBAN DESIGN International*, 5, 97–122.

Haraway, D.J. 1991. *Simians, Cyborgs, and Women. The Reinvention of Nature.* New York: Routledge.

Harries, K. 1973. Descartes, Perspective, and the Angelic Eye. *Yale French Studies* No. 49, Science, Language, and the Perspective Mind: Studies in Literature and Thought from Campanella to Bayle, 28–42.

Harvey, D. 1969. *Explanation in Geography* London: Edward Arnold.

Harvey, D. 1972. On Obfuscation in Geography: A comment on Gale's heterodoxy *Geographical Analysis* IV (3), 323–30.

Harvey, D. 1973. *Social Justice and the City* London: Edward Arnold.

Harvey, D. 1989. *The Urban Experience* Baltimore MD: Johns Hopkins University Press.

Harvey, D. 2003. *Spaces of Hope* Edinburgh: Edinburgh University Press.

Healey, P. 1992. Planning through debate. *Town Planning Review* 63 (1), 146–63.

Healey, P. 1996. The Communicative Turn in Planning Theory and its Implications for Spatial Strategy Formation. In *Readings in Planning Theory* 2nd edn edited by C. Scott and S.J. Fanstein. Oxford: Blackwell, 237–55.

Hedfors, P. 2003. *Site Soundscapes: Landscape architecture in the light of sound* Doctoral thesis, Acta 407, SLU.

Heidegger, M. 1977. [1954] *The Question Concerning Technology and Other Essays* translated from German by W. Lovitt. New York: Harper Perennial.

Heidegger, M. 1993. [1951] Building, Dwelling, Thinking. Translated from German by A. Hofstadter in *Martin Heidegger: Basic Writings* edited by D.F. Krell. London: Routledge, 347–63.

Heil, J. 1983. *Perception and Cognition* Berkeley and Los Angeles: University of California Press.

Hein, T. and Thomma, N. 2006. Forskningen gör mos av alla fotbollsmyter *Dagens Nyheter*. 2 July, 6–7.

Hellström, B. 2003. *Noise Design: Architectural modelling and the aesthetics of urban acoustic space* Doctoral thesis, KTH, Stockholm: Bo Ejeby Förlag.

Hellström, B. 2010. Akustiska stadsplanerare efterlyses *Svenska Dagbladet* Under strecket, 9 Jan.

Hellström, M. and Gullbring, L. 2001. Vilka ideal helgar denna mässa? *Area* 2/01.

Hempel, C.G. 1942. The Function of General Laws in History *The Journal of Philosophy* 39 (2), 35–48.

Hempel, C.G. 1966. *Philosophy of Natural Science.* Englewood Cliffs NJ: Prentice Hall.

Hempel, C.G. and Oppenheim, P. 1948. Studies in the Logic of Explanation. *Philosophy of Science* 15 (2), 135–75.

Hermerén, G. and Lynöe, N. 2008. *Etik – en introduktion*, Upplaga 3, Etiska vägmärken 1, Statens medicinsk-etiska råd. Stockholm: Elanders.

Hermodsson, E. 1968. Vetenskapens frihet. In *Rit och revolution. Essäer och polemik* Stockholm: Verbum.

Heron, L. (ed.) 1993. *Streets of Desire: Women's Fiction in the Twentieth Century* London: Virago Press.

Hetherington, K. 1997. In Place of Geometry: The materiality of place. In *Ideas of Difference* edited by K. Hetherington and R. Munro. Oxford: Blackwell, 183–99.

Hillier, B. 1993. Specifically Architectural Knowledge. *Nordic Journal of Architectural Research* 2, 11–37.

Hillier, B. 1996. *Space is the Machine: A Configurational Theory of Architecture* Cambridge: Cambridge University Press.

Hillier, B. 2002. A Theory of The City as Object: Or, how spatial laws mediate the social construction of urban space. *Urban Design International* 7, 153–79.

Hillier, B. 2005. Between Social Physics and Phenomenology. Conference paper *Fifth Space Syntax Symposium*, 13–17 June 2005, Delft University.

Hillier, B. 2007. [1996] *Space is the Machine: A Configurational Theory of Architecture* Cambridge: Cambridge University Press, e-edition.

Hillier, B. 2008a. Space and Spatiality: What the built environment needs from social theory. *Building Research and Information*. 36 (3), 216–30.

Hillier, B. 2008b. The New Science of Space and the Art of Place. Toward a space-led paradigm for researching and designing the city. In *New Urbanism and Beyond – Designing Cities for the Future* edited by T. Haas. New York: Rizzoli.

Hillier, B. and Hanson, J. 1984. *The Social Logic of Space* Cambridge: Cambridge University Press.

Hillier, B. and Netto, V. 2002. Society Seen Through the Prism of Space. Outline of a theory of society and space. *Urban Design International* 7, (3/4), 181–20.

Hillier, B. and Penn, A. 2004. Rejoinder to Carlo Ratti. *Environment and Planning B: Planning and Design* 31, 501–11.

Hillier, B. and Sahbaz, O. 2008. An evidence based approach to crime and urban design. Or, can we have vitality, sustainability and security all at once?' http://www.spacesyntax.com/Files/MediaFiles/Hillier%20Sahbaz_An%20 evidence%20based%20approach_010408.pdf 2009-04-26.

Hillier, B., Musgrove, J. and O'Sullivan, P. 1972. Knowledge and Design. *EDRA* 3, 29/3/1-19/3/14.

Hillier, B., Leaman, A., Stansall, P. and Bedford, M. 1978a. Space syntax. In *Social Organisation and Settlement. Contributions from Anthropology, Archaeology and Geography. Part ii* edited by D. Green, C. Haselgrove and M. Spriggs. Great Britain: B.A.R. International Series (Supplementary) 47.

Hillier, B., Leaman, A., Stansall, P. and Bedford, M. 1978b. Reply to Professor Leach. In *Social Organisation and Settlement. Contributions from Anthropology, Archaeology and Geography. Part ii* edited by D. Green, C. Haselgrove and M. Spriggs. Great Britain: B.A.R. International Series (Supplementary) 47.

Hillier, B., Penn, A., Julienne, H., Tadeusz, G. and Jianming, X. 1993. Natural movement; or, configuration and attraction in urban pedestrian movement. *Environment and Planning B: Planning and Design* 20, 29–66.

Hollier, D. 1989. *Against Architecture. The Writings of George Bataille* Cambridge MA: MIT Press.

Hollingdale, R.J. 2007. Introduction. In *Dithyrambs of Dionysos* by F. Nietzsche. London: Anvil Press Poetry.

Holmqvist, B. 2009. *Till relativismens försvar: några kapitel ur relativismens historia: Boas, Becker, Mannheim och Fleck* Stockholm/Stehag: Symposium.

Holston, J. 1989. *The Modernist City: An Anthropological Critique of Brasilia* Chicago IL: The University of Chicago Press.

hooks, b. 1990. Homeplace: A site of resistance. In *Yearning: Race, Gender and Cultural Politics.* Cambridge, MA: South End Press, 41–50.

Howland, Mark (1985) 'On Becoming an Architect' *Perspectives* 5, Nr. 1, juni, 4–7.

Hughes, S. 1958. *Consciousness and Society. The Reorientation of European Social Thought 1890–1930* New York: Vintage Books.

Huizinga, J. 2003. [1949] *Homo Ludens: A Study of the Play-Element in [sic!] Culture* translated from Dutch by R.F.C. Hull. London: Routledge.

Hulme, M. 2013. Commentary 1: To know thy place. In the section 'Geography and the humanities'. *Progress in Human Geography* 37 (2), 306–9.

Hultin, O., Pontvik, A. and Söderlind, J. 1992. Staden, vattnet och planerarna. *Arkitektur* 1, 22–31.

Hultin, O. and Waern, R. 2002. Hammarby Sjöstad, Stockholm. *Arkitektur* 6, 34–9.

Huxley, A. 1963. *Literature and Science* London: Chatto and Windus.

Hylland Eriksen, T. 2004. *Rötter och fötter. Identitet i en föränderlig tid* translated from Norwegian by H. Dalén. Nora: Nya Doxa.

Hylland Eriksen, T. 2008. *Jakten på lycka i* överflödssamhället translated from Norwegian by J. Jakobsson. Nora: Nya Doxa.

Hyvönen, F. 2008. *Silence is Wild* Music album. Playground.

Imrie, R. 1996. Ableist Geographies, Disablist Spaces: Towards a Reconstruction of Golledge's 'Geography and the Disabled'. *Transactions of the Institute of British Geographers* 21, 397–403.

Imrie, R. 2003. Architects' Conceptions of the Human Body. *Environment and Planning D: Society and Space* 21, 47–65.

Imrie, R. and Street, E. 2008. The Autonomous Architect. Conference paper. *RGS-IBG Annual Conference*, London, 26–29 Aug. 2008.

Increased requirements for space in the urban environment [Ökade ytbehov i stadsbygden] 1965. International Federation for Housing and Planning. Stockholm: Kungliga Byggnadsstyrelsen.

Inghe-Hagström, J. 1987. Södra Station Stockholm. *Arkitektur* 7, 32–3.

Inghe-Hagström, J. 1997. Hammarby Sjöstad, Stockholm. *Arkitektur* 7, 32–4.

Isenberg, B. 2006. Sociologisk essäism – Essäistisk sociologi. Om en tankestils utveckling och aktualitet i en postdisciplinär tid. *Dansk Sociologi* 1/17, 87–110.

Israel, J. 1967. Sigmund Freud och psykoanalysen. In *Sociologiska teorier* edited by J. Asplund. Stockholm: Almqvist and Wiksell.

Israel, J. 1971. [1968] *Alienation. From Marx to Modern Sociology. A Macrosociological Analysis* translated from Swedish by the author, edited by A. Etzioni. Boston: Allyn and Bacon.

Israel, J. 1980. *Språkets dialektik och dialektikens språk* [*The Language of Dialectics and the Dialectics of Language*] Arlöv: Berlings.

Jacobs, J. 1958. Downtown is for People. *Fortune* 4, April.

Jacobs, J. 1992. [1961] *The Death and Life of Great American Cities* New York: Vintage Books.

Jacobs, J. 1993. Foreword to the Modern Library Edition. In *The Death and Life of Great American Cities*. New York: The Modern Library, xi–xviii.

Jansson, K. 2009. *Tillsammans. Bidrag till den etniska boendesegregationens geofilosofi* Doctoral thesis, Geografiska regionstudier 81, Uppsala University.

Jarry, A. 2005. [1897] *Dagarna och nätterna. En desertörs roman* [*Days and Nights: A Novel of a* Deserter] translated from French by I.I. Gadd and Y. Lindberg. Lund: Bakhåll.

Jay, M. 1994. *Downcast Eyes. The Denigration of Vision in Twentieth-Century French Thought* Berkeley and Los Angeles: University of California Press.

Johannisson, K. 1988. *Det mätbara samhället. Statistik och samhällsdröm i 1700-talets Europa* Stockholm: Norstedts.

Johannisson, K. 1997. *Kroppens tunna skal. Sex essäer om kropp, historia och kultur* Stockholm: Pan, Norstedts.

Johannisson, K. 2009. *Melankoliska rum. Om* ångest. *Leda och sårbarhet i förfluten tid och nutid* Stockholm: Bonnier.

Johansson, G. 1930. Storstadens problem. *Svenska Dagbladet* 12 April.

Johansson, J. 1989. Stad och stadsmässigt. *Arkitektur* 6.

Johansson, M. and Khakee, A. 2008. *Etik i stadsplanering* Lund: Studentlitteratur.

Johansson, P.M. 2003. Sweden and Psychoanalysis. *JEP European Journal of Psychoanalysis. Humanities, Philosophy, Psychotherapies.* No 17.

Johansson, P.M. 2011. Upplysningen i psykoanalysen. Sigmund Freuds sammansatta idéer om psykoanalysen som upplysningsprojekt. In *Sociologik: tio essäer om socialitet och tänkande* edited by C. Abrahamsson, F. Palm and S. Wide. Stockholm: Santérus.

Johansson, P.M. Forthcoming. Psykoanalys, konstnärskap och begreppet det reala. In *Psykoanalysen och humaniora.* Gothenburg: Daidalos.Johnston, R.J. 1989. Philosophy, Ideology and Geography. In *Horizons in Human Geography* edited by D. Gregory and R. Walford. London: Macmillan Education.

Johnston, R.J. 1997. W(h)ither Spatial Science and Spatial Analysis. *Futures* 29 (4/5), 323–36.

Jonas, H. 1954. The Nobility of Sight. A Study in the Phenomenology of Senses. *Philosophy and Phenomenological Research* 14 (4), 507–19.

Jonas, H. 1984. *The Imperative of Responsibility. In Search of an Ethics for the Technological Age* translated from German by H. Jonas and D. Herr. Chicago IL: University of Chicago Press.

Joyce, P. 2003. *The Rule of Freedom. Liberalism and the Modern City* New York: Verso.

Kalin, M.G. 1974. *The Utopian Flight from Unhappiness: Freud against Marx on Social Progress* Chicago IL: Nelson-Hall Company.

Kallstenius, P. (ed.) 1986. *Stockholm Bygger. Om 1980-talets byggande i Stockolm* Stockholm: Stockholmia.

Kallstenius, P. 1998. Utsikt från en bro. In *Stockholm blir stor stad. Tiden 1948–1998* edited by K-E Synnemar. Laholm: Byggförlaget.

Kallstenius, P. 2006. Ännu en årsring – Stockholms stadsutvecklingsområden. In *Stockholm Bygger 06* Stockholm: Stockholmia.

Kallstenius, P. and Pemer, M. 2005. Så läggs nu grunden till den framtida staden – ett credo för Stockholm. In *Stockholm, den växande staden* edited by U. Sörenson. Stockholm: S:t Erik.

Kant, I. 1992. [1798] Svar på frågan: Vad är upplysning? [An Answer to the Question: What is Enlightenment?] Translated from German by J. Retzlaff. In *Vad är upplysning?* edited by B. Östling. Stockholm/Stehag: Symposion, 25–36.

Kant, I. 2003. [1790] *Kritik av omdömeskraften* translated from German by S-O. Wallenstein. Stockholm: Thales.

Kant, I. 2005. [1790] *Critique of Judgement* translated from German by J.H. Berard. New York: Dover.

Karatani, K. 1995. [1983] *Architecture as Metaphor. Language, Number, Money* translated from Japanese by S. Kohso. Cambridge MA: MIT Press.

Kärrholm, M. 1999. Är rummet en maskin? Aspekter på Bill Hilliers konfigurationsteori. Degree project (edition without figures), Lund University.

Kärrholm, M. 2004. *Arkitekturens territorialitet. Till en diskussion om territoriell makt och gestaltning i stadens offentliga rum.* Doctoral thesis, Lund University.

Kärrholm, M. 2010. Space Syntax and Meta Theory. *The Journal of Space Syntax: Architecture, Urbanism, Society* 1 (1), 251–3.

Kärrholm, M. 2012. *Retailising Space. Architecture, Retail and the Territorialisation of Public Space* Farnham: Ashgate.

Katz, J. 1955. Ethics without Morality. *The Journal of Philosophy* 52 (11), 287–91.

Katz, P. (ed.) 1994. *The New Urbanism. Toward an Architecture of Community* New York: McGraw-Hill.

Kaufmann, W. 1974. *Nietzsche: Philosopher, Psychologist, Antichrist* 4th edn. Princeton NJ: Princeton University Press.

Kazmierska, N. 2010. Nu ska Stockholm bli Chicago. *Stockholm City* 28 Jan.

Kearnes, M.B. 2003. Geographies that Matter: The rhetorical deployment of physicality? *Social & Cultural Geography*, 4(2), 139–52.

Keller, A. 2006. Luma torg väntar på folk. *Dagens Nyheter* 11 July.

Kenny, A. 1963. *Action, Emotion and Will* London: Routledge and Kegan Paul.

Kern, S. 2004. *A Cultural History of Causality: Science, Murder Novels, and Systems of Thought.* Princeton NJ and Oxford: Princeton University Press.

Kierkegaard, S. 1987. [1843] *Either – Or. Part I* edited and translated from Danish by H.V. Hong and E.H. Hong. Princeton NJ: Princeton University Press.

Kim, Y.O. and Penn, A. 2004. Linking the spatial syntax of cognitive maps to the spatial syntax of the environment. *Environment and Behavior* 36(4), 483–504.

King, R.H. 1972. *The Party of Eros. Radical Social Thought and the Realm of Freedom* Chapel Hill: The University of North Carolina Press.

Kingsbury, P. 2004. Psycho-analytic Approaches. In *A Companion to Cultural Geography* edited by J.S. Duncan, N.C. Johnson and R.H. Schein. Maldon MA: Blackwell, 108–20.

Kjellén, A. 1985. *Flanören och hans storstadsvärld. Synpunkter på ett litterärt motiv* Stockholm: Acta Stockholm Studies in History of Literature.

Klarqvist, B. 1993. A Space Syntax Glossary. *Nordic Journal of Architectural Research* 2, 11–12.

Klarqvist, B. 1995. Att hela staden. Om urbana kvaliteter och planeringens imperativ. *Nordic Journal of Architectural Research* 8 (4), 153–9.

Klasander, A-J. 2004. *Suburban Navigation Structural Coherence and Visual Appearance in Urban Design.* Doctoral Thesis. Gothenburg: Chalmers.

Klosterman, R.E. 1985. Arguments For and Against Planning. *Town Planning Review* 56 (1), 5–20.

Knox, P. and Ozolins, P. (ed.) 2000. *Design Professionals and the Built Environment. An Introduction* Chichester: Wiley and Sons.

Koestler, A. 1967. *The Ghost in the Machine* London: Hutchinson and Co.

Koolhaas, R., Chung, C.J., Inaba, J. Leong, S.T. (eds) 2001. *Harvard Design School Guide to Shopping /Harvard Design School Project on the City 2.* Köln: Taschen.

Koskela, H. 1997. 'Bold Walk and Breakings': Women's spatial confidence versus fear of violence *Gender, Place and Culture* 4 (3), 301–19.

Krange, O. and Strandbu, Å. 1996. *Kjøpesenteret – handlemaskin og fornøyelsepark* Oslo: Pax Forlag.

Kremer-Marietti, A. 1999. Nietzsche's Critique of Modern Reason. In *Nietzsche, Theories of Knowledge and Critical Theory: Nietzsche and the Sciences I* edited by B.E. Babich. [Boston Studies in the Philosophy of Science 203] Dordrecht: Kluwer Academic Publishers.

Krogh, T. 1992. *Frankfurtskolan. En introduktion* translated from Norwegian by G. Sandin. Gothenburg: Daidalos.

Lacan, J. 2001. [1957] The Agency of the Letter in the Unconscious or Reason since Freud. Translated from French by A. Sheridan in Écrits: *a selection* [1966]. London: Routledge.

Laing, R.D. 1965. [1960] *The Divided Self. An Existential Study in Sanity and Madness* Harmondsworth: Pelican.

Laing, R.D. 1967. *The Politics of Experience and the Bird of Paradise* Harmondsworth: Penguin.

Larsson, Y. 2010. Stockholm saknar verktyg för byggboom. *Arkitekten* 4, p. 60.

Lawson, B. 1997. *How Designers Think: The Design Process Demystified* Oxford: Architectural Press.

Leach, E.R. 1978. Does Space Syntax really Constitute the Social? In *Social Organisation and Settlement. Contributions from Anthropology, Archaeology and Geography. Part ii* edited by D. Green, C. Haselgrove and M. Spriggs. Oxford: B.A.R. International Series (Supplementary) 47.

Lear, J. 2005. *Freud* Abingdon: Routledge.

Le Corbusier 1948. [1942] *The Home of Man* translated from French by C. Entwistle. In *The Home of Man* by Le Corbusier and F. de Pierrefeu. London: Architectural Press, 51–156.

Le Corbusier 1971. [1929] *The City of Tomorrow and its Planning* translated from French by F. Etchells. Cambridge MA: MIT Press.

Le Corbusier 1986. [1923] *Towards a New Architecture* translated from French by F. Etchells. New York: Dover.

Leder, D. 1990. *The Absent Body* Chicago IL: Chicago University Press.

Lefebvre, H. 1977. Reflections on the politics of space. Translated from French by M.J. Enders In *Radical Geography* edited by R. Peet. Chicago IL: Maaroufa Press.

Lefebvre, H. 1991. [1974] *The Production of Space* translated from French by D. Nicholson-Smith. Oxford: Blackwell.

Lefebvre, H. 1995. [1962] *Introduction to Modernity. Twelve Preludes September 1959 – May 1961* translated from French by J. Moore. London: Verso.

Lefebvre, H. 1996. *Writings on Cities* translated and edited by E. Kofman and E. Lebas. Cambridge: Blackwell.

Legeby, A. 2010. *Urban Segregation and Urban Form: From residential segregation to segregation in public space.* Licentiate thesis. Stockholm: KTH.

Legeby, A. 2013. *Patterns of co-presence: Spatial configuration and social segregation.* Doctoral thesis, KTH, Stockholm.

Lehrer, R. 1995. *Nietzsche's Presence in Freud's Life and Thought* Albany: State University of New York Press.

Levin, D.M. 1988. *The Opening of Vision: Nihilism and the Postmodern Situation* New York and London: Routledge.

Levin, D.M. (ed.) 1993. *Modernity and the Hegemony of Vision* Berkeley: University of California Press.

Ley, D. 1977. The Personality of a Geographical Fact. *The Professional Geographer* 29 (1), 8–13.

Ley, D. and Samuels, M.S. (eds) 1978. *Humanistic Geography. Prospects and Problems* London: Croom Helm.

Ley, D. 1981. Cultural/humanistic geography. *Progress in Human Geography* 5, 249–57.

Liebst, L.S. 2011. Useful(filling) Durkheim: Reconfiguring the Sociological Prospect of Space Syntax. Working paper.

Liedman, S-E. 2008. Skilda världar: Essä om Gottfried Wilhelm Leibniz och Martin Heidegger *Dagens Nyheter* 29 Sept.

Liliequist, B. 1997. Introduction to L. Fleck's *Uppkomsten och utvecklingen av ett vetenskapligt faktum.* Stockholm: Symposion.

Lilja, E. 2006. Förorten – den typiska Stockholmsstadsdelen. In *Stockholm Bygger 06* Stockholm: Stockholmia.

Lindblad, F. and Lindgren, C. 2009. *Välfärdslandets gåta. Varför mår barnen inte lika bra som de har det?* Stockholm: Carlsons Bokförlag.

Linn, B. 1998. *Arkitektur som kunskap* Stockholm: Byggforskningsrådet.

Linn, B. 1991. Arkitekturens referenser. En skiss av en grupp begrepp. *Nordic Journal of Architectural Research* 3, 41–56.

Listerborn, C. 2002. *Trygg stad. Diskurser om kvinnors rädsla i forskning, policyutveckling och lokal praktik.* Doctoral thesis. Gothenburg: Chalmers.

Livingstone, D. 1992. *The Geographical Tradition* Oxford: Blackwell.

Lofland, L.H. 1998. *The Public Realm – Exploring the City's Quintessential Social Territory* New York: Walter de Gruyter.

Löw, M. 2012. The intrinsic logic of cities: Towards a new theory on urbanism. *Urban Research and Practice*, 5 (3), 303–15.

Lowenthal, D. 1967. Introduction. In D. Lowenthal (ed.) *Environmental Perception and Behavior.* Research paper No. 109, Dept. of Geography. Chicago: Public Litho Service.

Lowenthal, D. 1975. Geography, Experience, and Imagination: Towards a Geographical Epistemology. In *Readings in Social Geography* edited by E. Jones. Oxford: Oxford University Press, 104–27.

Lukács, G. 1980 [1962] *The Destruction of Reason* translated from German by P. Palmer. London: Merlin.

Lundequist, J. 1989. Om det konstnärliga utvecklingsarbetet. *Tidskrift för arkitekturforskning* 2 (1–2).

Lundequist, J. 1991. Arkitekturforskning som kritik. *Tidskrift för arkitekturforskning* 4 (1).

Lyotard, J-F. 1984. [1979] *The Postmodern Condition. A Report on Knowledge* translated from French by G. Bennington and B. Massumi. Minneapolis: University of Minnesota Press.

McClintock, A. 1995. *Imperial Leather. Race, Gender and Sexuality in the Colonial Contest* New York, London: Routledge.

MacDonald, B.J. 1999. Marx and the Figure of Desire. *Rethinking Marxism* 11 (4), 21–37.

McDowell, L. 1995. Understanding Diversity: The problem of/for theory. In *Geographies of global change* edited by R.J. Johnston, P.J. Taylor and M.J. Watts. Oxford: Blackwell.

McDowell, L. 1999. *Gender, Identity and Place: Understanding Feminist Geographies* Minneapolis: University of Minnesota Press.

MacIntyre, A. 2007. [1981] *After Virtue. A Study in Moral Theory* London: Duckworth.

MacMurray, J. 1957. *The Self as Agent* London: Faber.

MacPherson, H. 2005. Landscape's Occular-centrism – and Beyond? In *From Landscape Research to Landscape Planning* edited by B. Tress, G. Fry and P. Opdam. Boston MA: Springer/Kluwer Academic.

Madanipour, A. 1996. Urban Design and Dilemmas of Space *Environment and Planning D: Society and Space* 14, 331–55.

Magnusson, L. (ed.) 2001. *Den delade staden* Umeå: Boréa.

Malcolm, J. 1981. *Psychoanalysis. The Impossible Profession* New York: Vintage Books.

Marcus, L. 1992. I stadens sken. *Magasin för modern arkitektur* 2.

Marcus, L. 1998. Stad – kärt namn med många barn. *Nordic Journal of Architectural Research* 11 (3).

Marcus, L. 2000a. Vad kan arkitekter? *Arkitekten* 6.

Marcus, L. 2000b. *Architectural Knowledge and Urban Form. The Functional Performance of Architectural Urbanity.* Doctoral thesis, KTH, Stockholm: Pointline.

Marcus, L. 2000c. The Need for Descriptive Methods in Architectural Research. *Nordic Journal of Architectural Research* 13 (1–2), 37–44.

Marcus, L. 2008. Spatial Capital and How to Measure it. An outline of an analytical theory of urban form. In *New Urbanism and Beyond – Designing Cities for the Future* edited by T. Haas. New York: Rizzoli.

Marcus, L. 2010a. Det nya Stockholm skapas i det tysta. *Svenska Dagbladet* 26 June.

Marcus, L. 2010b. Spatial Capital. A proposal for an extension of space syntax into a more general urban morphology. *The Journal of Space Syntax: Architecture, Urbanism, Society* 1 (1), 30–40.

Marcus, L. and Koch, D. 2005. Framtidens arkitektur ligger i det performativa. *Arkitektur* 4.

Marcus, L., Westin, S. and Liebst, L.S. 2013. Network buzz: conception and geometry of networks in geography, architecture and sociology. Paper for 9th *International Space Syntax Symposium* Seoul, South Korea, 31st Oct – 3rd Nov.Marcus, S. 1999. *Apartment Stories. City and Home in Nineteenth-century Paris and London* Berkeley: University of California Press.

Marcuse, H. 1955. *Eros and Civilization. A Philosophical Inquiry into Freud* New York: Random House.

Marcuse, H. 1964. *One-Dimensional Man. Studies in the Ideology of Advanced Industrial Society*. Marked up and corrected by A. Blunden. cartoon.iguw. tuwien.ac.at/christian/marcuse/odm.html.

Marcuse, H. 1968b. [1965] *Negations. Essays in Critical Theory* translated from German by J.J. Shapiro. Boston MA: Beacon Press.

Martin, J. 2002. *The Education of John Dewey. A Biography* New York: Columbia University Press.

Marx, K. 1977. [1859] *A Contribution to the Critique of Political Economy* translated from German by S.W. Ryazanskaya. Moscow: Progress Publishers.

Massey, D. 2005. *For Space* London: Sage.

Matless, D. 2003. Gestures around the Visual. *Antipode* 35 (2), 222–6.

Mattsson, H. and Wallenstein, S-O. 2009. *1930–1931: Den svenska modernismen vid vägskälet. Swedish modernism at the crossroads. Der schwedische Modernismus am Scheideweg* Stockholm: Axl Books.

Megill, A. 1985. *Prophets of Extremity. Nietzsche, Heidegger, Foucault, Derrida* Berkeley: University of California Press.

Merleau-Ponty, M. 1968. [1964] The Intertwining – the Chiasm. Translated from French by A. Lingis in *The Visible and the Invisible* Evanston IL: Northwestern University.

Merleau-Ponty, M. 2002. [1945] *Phenomenology of Perception* translated from French by Colin Smith Routledge Classics edn. London and New York: Routledge.

Merrifield, A. 1993. Place and Space: A Lefebvrian reconciliation. *Transactions of the Institute of British Geographers* 18 (4), 516–31.

Merrifield, A. 1995. Lefebvre, Anit-Logos and Nietzsche: An alternative reading of *The Production of Space. Antipode* 27 (3), 294–303.

Merrifield, A. 2004. The Sentimental City: The lost urbanism of Pierre Mac Orlan and Guy Debord. *International Journal of Urban and Regional Research* 28.4, 930–40.

Merrifield, A. 2006. *Henri Lefebvre. A Critical Introduction* New York and London: Routledge.

Merrifield, A. 2009. The Whole and the Rest: Remi Hess and *les lefebvriens français' Environment and Planning D: Society and Space* 27 (5), 936–49.

Merton, R.K. 1968. *Social Theory and Social Structure* New York: The Free Press.

Miller, E. 1930. The Analysis of Agora-Claustrophobia. *British Journal of Medical Psychology* 10, 253–67.

Miller Lane, B., Kåberg, H. and Creagh, L. (eds) 2008. *Modern Swedish Design. Three founding texts* New York: MoMA.

Molander, B. 1995. Mellan konst och vetande. Att ge verkligheten form och innehåll. In *Mellan konst och vetande.* edited by B. Molander. Gothenburg: Daidalos.

Molina, I. 1997. *Stadens rasifiering. Etnisk boendesegregation i folkhemmet.* Doctoral thesis, Geografiska regionstudier 32, Uppsala University.

Molina, I. 2007. Intersektionella rumsligheter. *Tidskrift för Genusvetenskap* 3.

Montello, D.R. 2007. The Contribution of Space Syntax to a Comprehensive Theory of Environmental Psychology. *Proceedings, 6th International Space Syntax Symposium,* Istanbul.

Moorcroft Wilson, J. 1987. *Virginia Woolf Life and London. A Biography of Place* New York: Norton.

Nasar, J. 1989. Perception, Cognition, and Evalutation of Urban Places. In *Public Places and Spaces* edited by I. Altman and E. Zube. New York: Plenum.

Nehring, C. 2009. *A Vindication of Love. Reclaiming Romance for the Twenty-First Century* New York: HarperCollins.

Niedomysl, T. 2006. Residential preferences for interregional migration in Sweden. In *Migration and Place Attractiveness* Doctoral thesis, Geografiska regionstudier 68, Uppsala University.

Nietzsche, F. 1968. [1901] *The Will to Power* translated from German by W. Kaufmann. New York: Vintage Books.

Nietzsche, F. 1982a. [1873] On Truth and Lie in an Extra-Moral Sense. In *The Portable Nietzsche* translated from German by W. Kaufmann. New York: Penguin.

Nietzsche, F. 1992. [1908] *Ecce Homo. How One Becomes What One Is* translated from German by R.J. Hollingdale. London: Penguin.

Nietzsche, F. 1997. [1886] *Beyond Good and Evil. Prelude to a Philosophy of the Future* translated from German by H. Zimmern. Mineola, New York: Dover.

Nietzsche, F. 1986a. [1878] *Human, All Too Human. Part One* translated from German by R.J. Hollingdale. Cambridge: Cambridge University Press.

Nietzsche, F. 1986b. [1878] *Human, All Too Human. Part Two* translated from German by R.J. Hollingdale. Cambridge: Cambridge University Press.

Nietzsche, F. 1999. [1872] *The Birth of Tragedy* translated from German by R. Speirs. Cambridge: Cambridge University Press.

Nietzsche, F. 2001. [1882] *The Gay Science* translated from German by J. Nauckhoff. Cambridge: Cambridge University Press.

Nietzsche, F. 2003. [1887] *The Genealogy of Morals* translated from German by H.B. Samuel. New York: Dover.

Nietzsche, F. 2007. [1891] *Dithyrambs of Dionysus* translated from German by R.J. Hollingdale. London: Anvil Press Poetry.

Nietzsche, F. 2010. [1986] *The Peacock and the Buffalo: The Poetry of Nietzsche* translated from German by J. Luchte and E. Leadon. London and New York: Continuum Books.

Norberg-Schulz, C. 1963. *Intentions in Architecture* Oslo/Bergen: Universitetsforlaget.

Nordström, S. 2008. *Illusionernas harmoni.* Doctoral thesis, Karlstad University Studies 55.

Nylund, K. 2001. Cultural Analysis in Urban Theory of the 1990s. *Acta Sociologia* 44, 219–30.

Nyman, K. 1989. *Husens språk.* Doctoral thesis, No. 9. Nordplan. Stockholm: Atlantis.

Nyström, L. 1999. Mot ett nytt stadsbyggnadsparadigm. In *Stadsarkitektur – form, kultur, liv* edited by L. Nyström. Karlskrona: Boverket, Stadsmiljörådet.

Ollén, G. 1949. *Strindbergs dramatik* Stockholm: Ronzo.

Ollman, B. 1969. Review of Henri Lefebvre's *The Sociology of Marx. The American Journal of Sociology* 74 (4), 435–6.

Ollman, B. 1976. *Alienation. Marx's Conception of Man in Capitalist Society* Cambridge: Cambridge University Press.

Ollman, B. 2003. *Dance of the Dialectic. Steps in Marx's Method* Chicago: University of Illinois Press.

Olsson, G. 1974. The Dialectics of Spatial Analysis. *Antipode* 6 (3), 50–62.

Olsson, G. 1977. Servitude and Inequality in Spatial Planning: Ideology and methodology in conflict. In *Radical Geography* edited by R. Peet. Chicago IL: Maaroufa Press.

Olsson, G. 1978. Of Ambiguity or Far Cries from a Memorializing Mamafesta. In *Humanistic Geography* edited by D. Ley and M.S. Samuels. London: Croom Helm.

Olsson, G. 1979. Social Science and Human Action or On Hitting Your Head against the Ceiling of Language. In *Philosophy in Geography* edited by S. Gale and G. Olsson. Dordrecht: D. Reidel.

Olsson, G. 1980a. *Birds in Egg: Eggs in Bird* London: Pion Limited.

Olsson, G. 1980b. Att tänka i säregna öglor. *Svenska Dagbladet* Under strecket, 23 Aug.

Olsson, G. 1980c. Om snedstreck och snedsprång. In *Maantiede, Eräitä perspektiivejä* No 26, edited by A. Paasi. University of Joensuu, Publications of Social and Regional Science, 9–22.

Olsson, G. 1984. Toward a Sermon of Modernity. In *Recollections of a Revolution* edited by M. Billinge, D. Gregory and R. Martin. New York: St Martin's Press, 73–85.

Olsson, G. 1985. Om Planeringens Paradoxer. *Nordic Journal of Human Geography*, 2.

Olsson, G. 1990. *Antipasti* Gothenburg: Korpen.

Olsson, G. 1991. *Lines of Power. Limits of Language* Minneapolis: University of Minnesota Press.

Olsson, G. 1993. Chiasm of Thought-and-Action. *Environment and Planning D: Society and Space* 11, 279–94.

Olsson, G. 2002. Glimpses. In *Geographical Voices* edited by P. Gould and F. Pitts. Syracuse: Syracuse University Press.

Olsson, G. 2007. *Abysmal. A Critique of Cartographic Reason* Chicago IL: Chicago University Press.

Olsson, G. 2008. Nordplan and Nordregio. *International Encyclopedia of Human Geography* Oxford: Elsevier.

Olsson, G. 2012. Review of *Reading Kant's Geography* edited by S. Elden and E. Mendieta in *Geografiska Annaler: Series B*, 94 (1), 83–87.

Olsson, S. 1989. Om gestaltningsprocessen. *Nordic Journal of Architectural Research* 2 (1–2), 95–99.

Online Etymology Dictionary www.etymonline.com

Osborne, T. and Rose, N. 2004. Spatial phenomenotechnics: Making space with Charles Booth and Patrick Geddes. *Environment and Planning D: Society and Space* 22, 209–228.

Östberg, G. 2005. Om att fatta det ogripbara. In *Risk och det levande mänskliga* edited by I. Brinck, S. Halldén, A-S. Maurin and J. Persson. Nora: Nya Doxa, 235–245.

Østerberg, D. 1966. *Forståelsesformer. Et filosofisk bidrag* Oslo: Pax Forlag.

Østerberg, D. 1990. Det sosio-materielle handlingsfelt. In *Kulturanalyse* edited by T. Deichman-Sørensen and I. Frønes. Oslo: Gyldendal Norsk Forlag A/S.

Østerberg, D. 2000. *Stadens illusioner* Gothenburg: Korpen.

Östnäs, A. and Werne, F. 1987. Arkitekterna och arkitekturforskningen. *Tidskrift för arkitekturforskning* 1 (1).

Ottomeyer, K. 1978. [1977] *Människan under kapitalismen* translated from German by K. Westerståhl and T. Lindén. Gothenburg: Röda Bokförlaget.

Page, M. and Mennel, T. (eds) 2011. *Reconsidering Jane Jacobs* Chicago IL: The American Planning Association.

Pahl, R.E. 1975. *Whose City?* Harmondsworth: Penguin Books.

Pain, R. and Smith, S.J. 2010. Introduction: Geographies of Wellbeing. In *The SAGE Handbook of Social Geographies* edited by S.J Smith et al. London: SAGE.

Pallasmaa, J. 2005. [1996] *The Eyes of the Skin. Architecture and the Senses* Chichester: Wiley and Sons.

Palmgren, Lisbet (1997) *Diktarnas, barnens och dårarnas språk* Stockholm: Natur och Kultur.

Parkhurst Ferguson, P. 1994. The *Flâneur* On and Off the Streets of Paris. In *The Flâneur* edited by K. Tester. London: Routledge.

Parsons, D.L. 2000. *Streetwalking the Metropolis. Women, the City, and Modernity* Oxford: Oxford University Press.

Philo, C. 2000. More Words, More Worlds: Reflection on the 'cultural turn' and human geography. In *Cultural turns, geographical turns: perspectives on cultural geography* edited by I. Cook, D. Crouch, N. Simon and J.R. Ryan. New York: Prentice Hall.

Pickles, J. 2004. *A History of Spaces: Cartographic Reason, Mapping and the Geocoded World* London: Routledge.

Pile, S. 1996. *The Body and the City. Psycho-analysis, Space and Subjectivity* London: Routledge.

Pile, S. 2010. Emotions and affect in recent human geography. *Transactions of the Institute of British Geographers* 35 (1), 5–20.

Pinder, D. 1996. Subverting Cartography: The situationists and maps of the city. *Environment and Planning A*, 28, 405–27.

Pinder, D. 2005. *Visions of the City* Edinburgh: Edinburgh University Press.

'Place Syntax Tool', Project presentation, NADA, KTH http://www.nada.kth.se/projects/prom03/pst/PST_Projektpresentation.htm 2006-07-06.

Plato 1991. [380 BC] *The Republic of Plato* 2nd edn translated from Greek by A. Bloom. New York: Basic Books.

Pløger, J. 1997. *Byliv og modernitet – mellom nærmiljø og urbanitet* Oslo: NIBRs Plus-serie, 1.

Prendergast, C. 1992. *Paris and the Nineteenth Century* Cambridge: Blackwell.

Projektbroschyr för Silverdals Torg http://www.nyahem.skanska.se/rdn_files/Projektbroshyr/PB%20SilverdalsTorg.pdf 2009-03-22.

Putnam, H. 1987. *The Many Faces of Realism. The Paul Carus Lectures* LaSalle: Open Court.

Rabe, A. 2004. Den felande länken. In *Sthlm at Large* edited by J. Åman. Stockholm: Färgfabriken.

Råberg, P.G. 1970. *Funktionalistiskt genombrott* Uppsala: Sveriges Arkitekturmuseum.

Rabinow, P. 1985 Discourse and Power: On the limits of ethnographic texts. *Dialectical Anthropology* 10, 1–13.

Rådberg, J. 1988. *Doktrin och täthet i svenskt stadsbyggande 1875–1975* Stockholm: Statens råd för byggnadsforskning.

Rådberg, J. 1991. Den moderna stadsplaneringens uppkomst – en fråga om historieperspektiv. *Tidskrift för Arkitekturforskning* 4 (4), 19–31.

Rådberg, J. 1997. *Drömmen om atlantångaren* Stockholm: Atlantis.

Ramirez, J.L. 1995. *Skapande mening. En begreppsgenealogisk undersökning om rationalitet, vetenskap och planering* Doctoral thesis, Nordplan 13:3.

Ramirez, J.L. 2003. Retorik som humanvetenskaplig kunskapsteori och metod i samhällsplanering – En idéöversikt. *Statsvetenskaplig Tidskrift* 2003/04, 106 (1), 55–74.

Rasmussen, E.S. 1964. *Experiencing Architecture* USA: MIT Press.

Ratti, C. 2004. Space Syntax: Some inconsistencies. *Environment and Planning B: Planning and Design* 31 (4), 487–99.

Read, S. 2004. Situated Livelihoods: The street in a social ecology. *Spacelab, Research laboratory for the contemporary city*, Delft University.

Reeder, J. 2010a. *Det tystade samtalet* Stockholm: Norstedts.

Reeder, J. 2010b. Psykoanalytisk psykoterapi och livsproblemen. Public lecture 28 April, ABF, Stockholm.

Renqvist, A-L. 2013. Review of F.W.J. Schelling *Inledning till filosofin. Tidskriften Respons* 2, 64–6.

Ricoeur, P. 1970. [1965] *Freud and Philosophy: An Essay on Interpretation* translated from French by D. Savage. New Haven and London: Yale University Press.

Rilke, R.M. 2009. [1910] *The Notebooks of Malte Laurids Brigge* translated from German by M. Hulse. London: Penguin.

Ritson, J. 1810. *Gammer Gurton's Garland or, the Nursery Parnassus* London: Hardin and Wright.

Roazen, P. 1979. [1975] *Freud and his Followers* Harmondsworth: Penguin.

Robbins, E. 1997. *Why Architects Draw* Cambridge MA: MIT Press.

Rockcastle, G. 2000. Ethics and the Built Environment. In *Design Professionals and the Built Environment* edited by P. Knox and P. Ozolins. Chichester: Wiley and Sons.

Røe, P.G. 2007. Urbanism in Suburbia – Suburban 'Minicities' as Fields for Cultural Change and Politics. Conference paper *Nordic Geographers Meeting*, Bergen, Norway 15–17 June.

Rogoff, I. 2000. *Terra Infirma – Geography's Visual Culture* London and New York: Routledge.

Rose, G. 2000. Geography and Psycho-analytic Theory. In *The Dictionary of Human Geography* 4th edn edited by R.J. Johnston, D. Gregory, G. Pratt and M. Watts. Oxford: Blackwell, 653–55.

Rose, G. 2003. Just How, Exactly, is Geography Visual? *Antipode*, 35 (2), 212–21.

Rose, N. 1999. *Powers of Freedom. Reframing Political Thought* Cambridge: Cambridge University Press.

Rosenberg, G. 2009. Vad kan bevisas? *Dagens Nyheter* 24 July.

Rose-Redwood, R.S. 2006. *Govermentality, the Grid, and the Beginnings of a Critical Spatial History of the Geo-Coded World.* Doctoral thesis, Pennsylvania State University.

Rudberg, E. 1992. *Folkhemmets byggande* Norrköping: Fäldts Bokbinderi.

Russell, B. 1946. *History of Western Philosophy* London: George Allen & Unwin Ltd.

Ryan, J.R. 2003. Who's Afraid of Visual Culture? *Antipode*, 35 (2), 232–7.

Sack, R.D. 1974. The Spatial Separatist Theme in Geography. *Economic Geography* 50 (1), 1–19.

Sandell, R. 1993. Vad är psykoanalys? Stockholm: *Svenska Psykoanalytiska Föreningen.*

Sandercock, L. and Forsyth, A. 1992. Gender. A new agenda for planning theory. *Journal of the American Planning Association* 58 (1), 49–60.

Sanders, J. (ed.) 1996. *Scenes from the City. Filmmaking in New York* New York: Rizzoli.

Sartre, J.P. 2004. [1960] *Critique of Dialectical Reason: Volume One* translated from French by A. Sheridan-Smith. London: Verso.

Sartre, J.P. 2006. [1985] *Critique of Dialectical Reason: Volume Two* translated from French by Q. Hoare. London: Verso.

Sawday, J. 1995. *The Body Emblazoned. Dissection and the Human Body in Renaissance Culture* London: Routledge.

Schafer, R.M. 1993. *The Soundscape: Our Sonic Environment and the Tuning of the World* Rochester: Destiny Books.

Schmid, C. 2005. *Stadt, Raum und Gesellschaft: Henri Lefebvre und die Theorie der Produktion des Raumes.* Stuttgart: Steiner.

Schorske, C.E. 1981. [1980] *Fin-De-Siècle Vienna. Politics and Culture* New York: Vintage Books.

Schroeders, H.W. 2008. The Felt Sense Of Natural Environments. *The Folio*, 21, 63–72.

Schumacher, J. 1993. *Falling Down* Film.

Seaford, R. 2006. *Dionysos* New York: Routledge.

Seamon, D. 1994. The Life of the Place. *Nordic Journal of Architectural Research* 7 (1), 35–48.

Seamon, D. 2004. Grasping the Dynamism of Urban Place: Contributions from the work of Christopher Alexander, Bill Hillier and Daniel Kemmis. In *Reanimating Places: A Geography of Rhythms* edited by T. Mels. Aldershot: Ashgate.

Seamon, D. 2007. A Lived Hermetic of People and Place: Phenomenology and space syntax. *Proceedings, 6th International Space Syntax Symposium*, Istanbul.

Seip, I. 1995. Vetenskapens estetiska dimension. In *Mellan konst och vetande* edited by B. Molander. Gothenburg: Daidalos.

Selboe, T. 2003. Litterære vaganter. Byens betydning hos seks kvinnelige forfattere. Oslo: Pax Forlag A/S.

Sennett, R. 1990. *The Conscience of the Eye. The Design and Social Life of Cities* New York: Norton.

Sennett, R. 1992. [1977] *The Fall of Public Man* New York: Norton.

Sennett, R. 1996. [1994] *Flesh and Stone. The Body and the City in Western Civilization* New York: Norton.

Sennett, R. 2008. [1970] *The Uses of Disorder. Personal Identity and City Life* Great Britain: Yale University Press.

Sennett, R. 2009. Sociology as Literature. Lecture, recorded. CRASSH Cambridge University, 2 April, http://www.youtube.com/watch?v=4ogeGVpBFZ0 2010-04-01.

Shapiro, G. 1993. In the Shadows of Philosophy. In *Modernity and the Hegemony of Vision* edited by D.M. Levin. Berkeley: University of California Press.

Sheiban, H. 2002. *Den ekonomiska staden: stadsplanering i Stockholm under senare hälften av 1800-talet.* Doctoral thesis, Lund: Arkiv Förlag.

Sheppard, E. 2008. Geographic Dialectics? *Environment and Planning A.* 40, 2603–12.

Shields, R. 1994. Fancy Footwork: Walter Benjamin's notes on *flânerie'.* In *The Flâneur* edited by K. Tester. London: Routledge.

Shields, R. 1999. *Lefebvre, Love and Struggle: Spatial Dialectics* London: Routledge.

Short, J.R. 1984. *An Introduction to Urban Geography* Great Britain: Routledge.

Sigurdsson, O. 2006. *Himmelska Kroppar. Inkarnation, blick, kroppslighet* Munkedal: Glänta produktion Logos Pathos No. 6.

Silverstone, R. 2007. *Media and Morality. On the Rise of the Mediapolis* UK, USA: Polity Press.

Simmel, G. 1995. Storstäderna och det andliga livet. In *Hur är samhället möjligt? Och andra essäer* Gothenburg: Korpen.

Simonsen, K. 1993. *Byteori og hverdagspraksis* Köpenhamn: Akademisk Forlag.

Simonsen, K. 2004. Networks, flows and fluids – reimagining spatial analysis? *Environment and Planning A.* 36, 1333–7.

Sitte, C. 2005. [1889] 'Author's Introduction', 'The Relationship Between Bulidings, Monuments, and Public Squares', and 'The Enclosed Character of the Public Square' from *The Art of Building Cities'* translated from German by C.T. Stewart in *The City Reader* edited by R.T. LeGates and F. Stout. USA and Canada: Routledge.

Sjögren, L. 2001. *Sigmund Freud. Mannen och verket* Stockholm: Natur och Kultur.

Sjögren, L. 2008. Inledning i *Samhälle och Religion. Samlade skrifter av Sigmund Freud. Band X* edited by C. Craaford, L. Sjögren and B. Warren. Stockholm: Natur and Kultur.

Skjervheim, H. 1996. *Selected Essays. In Honour of Hans Skjervheim's 70th Birthday* Bergen: The Department of Philosophy.

Skoglund, P. and Eklund, P. 1997. *Lugnet. Här går plåtvågor.* Stockholm: Byggförlaget.

Sleinis, E.E. 1999. Between Nietzsche and Leibniz: Perspectivism and irrationalism. In *Nietzsche, Theories of Knowledge, and Critical Theory: Nietzsche and the Sciences I* edited by B.E. Babich. [Boston Studies in the Philosophy of Science 203] Dordrecht: Kluwer Academic Publishing.

Smart, B. 1994. Digesting the Modern Diet: Gastro-porn, fast food and panic eating. In *The Flâneur* edited by K. Tester. London: Routledge.

Smith, D.M. 1997D. Geography and Ethics: A moral turn? *Progress in Human Geography* 21 (4), 583–90.

Smith, L.D. 1986. *Behaviorism and Logical Positivism: A Reassessment of the Alliance* Stanford CA: Stanford University Press.

Smith, M.P. 1980. Sigmund Freud and the Dialectics of Nature and Culture. In *The City and Social Theory* Oxford: Basil Blackwell.

Smith, N. 1979. Geography, Science and Post-positivist Modes of Explanation. *Progress in Human Geography* 3, 356–83

Smith, S.J. 1997S Beyond Geography's Visible Worlds: A cultural politics of music. *Progress in Human Geography* 21, 502–29.

Sobel, M.E. 1995. Causal Inference in the Social and Behavioral Sciences. In *Handbook of Statistical Modeling for The Social and Behavioral Sciences* edited by G. Arminger, C.C. Clogg and M.E. Sobel. New York: Plenum Press.

Sociotopkartan [*The Sociotope Map*] 2002. edited by M. Pemer, Stockholm's Office for City Planning.

Söderberg, H. 2002. [1905] *Doctor Glas* translated from Swedish by P.B. Austin. New York: Anchor Books.

Södergran, E. 1984. *Complete Poems* translated from Swedish by D. McDuff. Newcastle upon Tyne: Bloodaxe Books Ltd.

Söderlind, J. 1998. *Stadens renässans* Kristianstad: SNS Förlag.

Söderqvist, L. 2008. *Att gestalta välfärd: från idé till byggd miljö* Stockholm: Formas, Riksantikvarieämbetet.

Söderström, O. 1996. Paper Cities: Visual thinking in urban planning. *Ecumene/ Cultural Geographies* 3 (3), 249–81.

Södra Stationsområdet 1984. Programskrift för Södra Stationsområdet.

Soja, E.W. 1980. The Socio-Spatial Dialectic. *Annals of the Association of American Geographers* 70 (2), June, 207–225.

Soja, E.W. 2000. *Postmetropolis. Critical Studies of Cities and Regions* Oxford: Blackwell.

Soja, E.W. 2001. In Different Spaces: Interpreting the spatial organization of societies. *Proceedings, 3rd International Space Syntax Symposium*, Atlanta, A. Alfred Taubman College of Architecture and Urban Planning, Michigan, 1.1–1.7.

'Solna – the City of the Future' 2010. Ad from Solna Stad distributed by *Dagens Nyheter* 20 May.

Sörenson, U. (ed.) 2005. *Stockholm, den växande staden* Stockholm: St Erik.

Spacks, P.M. 1995. *Boredom: The Literary History of a State of Mind* Chicago IL: Chicago University Press.

Squier, S.M. 1985. *Virginia Woolf and London: the Sexual Politics of the City* Chapel Hill: University of North California Press.

Stanek, L. 2007. Space as Concrete Abstraction. Hegel, Marx and modern urbanism in Henri Lefebvre. In *Henri Lefebvre on Space. Architecture, Urban Research, and the Production of Theory* by L. Stanek. Minneapolis: University of Minnesota Press.

Steffner, L. 2009. *Värdering av stadsmiljöer. En metod att mäta upplevelse.* Doctoral thesis, Lund: LTH.

Sternudd, C. 2007. *Bilder av småstaden. Om estetisk värdering av en stadstyp* Doctoral thesis, Lund: LTH.

Stockholms översiktsplan *99.* 2000. Stockholm's Office for City Planning 2000:6.

Stonor, T. and Stutz, C. 2004. Towards evidence-based urban design http://66.102.1.104/scholar?hl=svandlr=andq=cache:7RjELT8vbcgJ:www. spacesyntax.com/downloads/SpaceSyntax_TowardsEvidenceBasedUrbanDesign. pdf 2007-08-11.

Strindberg, A. 1998. [1903] *Alone* translated from Swedish by E. Sprinchorn in *Ensam. Alone.* Norway: Geelmuyden.Kiese, 129–247.

Strindberg, A. 2000. [1901] *A Dream Play* in *August Strindberg Five Major Plays* translated by C.R. Mueller. Lyme: Smith and Kraus, 87–140.

Strindberg, A. 2008. [1894] *Deranged Sensations* translated from Swedish by M. Robinson. In *August Strindberg. Selected Essays* Cambridge: Cambridge University Press, 122–34.

Strömgren, A. 2007. *Samordning, hyfs och reda. Stabilitet och förändring i svensk planpolitik 1945–2005.* Doctoral thesis. Acta Universitatis Upsaliensis, Uppsala University.

Sundlöf, P. 2008. *Segregation och karriärposition: En studie av bostadsomgivningens betydelse för utbildning, sysselsättning och inkomst bland yngre i stockholmsregionen.* Doctoral thesis, Geografiska regionstudier 78, Uppsala University.

Svendsen, L.Fr.H. 1999. *Kjedsomhetens filosofi.* Oslo: Universitetsforlaget.

Svendsen, L.Fr.H. 2003. [1999] *Långtråkighetens filosofi* translated from Norwegian by U-S Rask. Stockholm: Natur och Kultur.

Svendsen, L.Fr.H. 2005. [1999] *A Philosophy of Boredom* translated from Norwegian by J. Irons. London: Reaktion Books.

Svensson, P. 2004 Tallbarstalibanism. In *Sthlm at Large. Handbok om framtidens Stockholm* edited by J. Åman. Stockholm: Färgfabriken.

Taleb, N.N. 2007. *The Black Swan. The Impact of the Highly Improbable* London: Penguin.

Taylor, C. 1985. *Human Agency and Language. Philosophical Papers 1* Cambridge: Cambridge University Press.

Taylor, C. 2003. Rorty and Philosophy. In *Richard Rorty* edited by C.B. Guignon and D.R. Hiley. Cambridge: Cambridge University Press.

Taylor, N. 2003. The Aesthetic Experience of Traffic in the Modern City. *Urban Studies* 40 (8), 1609–25.

Taylor, R.R. 1974. *The Word in Stone. The Role of Architecture in the National Socialist Ideology* Berkeley, Los Angeles and London: University of California Press.

Tester, K. 1994. Introduction. In *The Flâneur* edited by K. Tester. London: Routledge.

Thom, R. 1979a. At the Boundaries of Man's Power: Play. *Sub-Stance* 8, 4 (25), 11–19.

Thom, R. 1979b. Remarks for the Polylogue on Play. *Sub-Stance* 8, 4 (25), 36–8.

Thomas, J.M. 1996. Educating Planners: Unified Diversity for Social Action. In *Readings in Planning Theory* 2nd edn edited by S. Campbell and S.J. Fanstein. Oxford: Blackwell, 356–75.

Thrift, N. 2006. Space. *Theory, Culture and Society* 23(2–3), 139–55.

Thörn, C. Här utplånas mångfalden. *Arkitektur* (7), 68-77

Toffler, A. 1984. Preface to *Order out of Chaos. Man's New Dialogue with Nature* by I. Prigogine and I. Stengers. London: Heinemann.

Tonboe, J.C. 1985a. Fra byen till rummet. In *Farvel till byen? Danske bidrag till den byteoretiska udvikling* edited by J.C. Tonboe. Aalborg: Serie om offentlig planlægning 18, 5–29.

Tonboe, J.C. 1985b. Materialstrukturens dialektik. In *Farvel till byen? Danske bidrag till den byteoretiska udvikling* edited by J.C. Tonboe. Aalborg: Serie om offentlig planlægning 18, 49–78.

Tönnies, F. 1957. [1887] *Community and Civil Society* translated from German by M. Hollis. Cambridge: Cambridge University Press.

Torsson, B. 1995. Rummets språk och språkets rum. In *Mellan konst och vetande* edited by B. Molander. Gothenburg: Daidalos.

Toulmin, S. and Goodfield, J. 1963. [1962] *Universums byggnad. Den moderna världsbildens uppkomst* translated from English by L. Edberg. Stockholm: Natur och Kultur.

Trotter, D. 2004. The Invention of Agoraphobia. *Victorian Literature and Culture* 32 (2).

Tunström, M. 2009. *På spaning efter den goda staden. Om konstruktioner av ideal och problem i svensk stadsbyggnadsdiskussion.* Doctoral thesis. Örebro Studies in Human Geography 4, Örebro University.

Tunström, M. 2010. På spaning efter den goda staden. *PLAN* 1, 8–12.

Turkle, S. 1981. [1978] *Psychoanalytic Politics. Freud's French Revolution* Cambridge MA: MIT Press.

Ullstad, E. 2008. *Hållbar stadsutveckling. En politisk handbok från Sveriges Arkitekter* Stockholm: Intellecta.

Uppman, R. 2006. *I arkitektens öga. En yrkesmemoar* Stockholm: Carlssons Bokförlag.

Valentine, G. 1989. The Geography of Women's fear. *Area* 21 (4), 385–90.

van Zuylen, M. 2005. *Monomania. The Flight from Everyday Life in Literature and Art* Ithaca NY and London: Cornell University Press.

Vattimo, G. 1997. [1985] *Nietzsche. En introduktion* [*Nietzsche. An Introduction*] translated from Italian by W. Fovet. Gothenburg: Daidalos

Vaughan, L. 2007. The Spatial Syntax of Urban Segregation. *Progress in Planning* 67 (3), 205–94.

Vernant, J-P. and Vidal-Naquet, P. 1990. [1972] *Myth and Tragedy in Ancient Greece.* Translated from French by J. Lloyd. New York: Zone Books.

Vidler, A. 2000. Diagrams of Diagrams: Architectural abstraction and modern representation. *Representations* 72, 1–20.

Vidler, A. 2001. *Warped Space: Art, Architecture, and Anxiety in Modern Culture* Cambridge MA: MIT Press.

Walkowitz, J.R. 1992. *City of Dreadful Delight. Narratives of Sexual Danger in Late-Victorian London* Chicago IL: University of Chicago Press.

Wander, P. 2007. Introduction to the Transaction Edition. In Lefebvre, H. *Everyday Life in the Modern World* USA: Transaction Publishers.

Wästberg, P. (ed.) 1995. *Kärleksdikter. I urval av Per Wästberg* Stockholm: Bonnier.

Weber, M. 1994. *Political Writings* translated from German by R. Speirs. Cambridge: Cambridge University Press.

Westerståhl-Stenport, A. 2004. *Making Space: Stockholm, Paris, and the urban prose of Strindberg and his contemporaries*. Doctoral thesis, University of California, Berkeley.

Westin, B. 1999. Vandraren, drömmen och dikten: *Ensam*. In *Strindbergs förvandlingar* edited by E. Adolfsson. Stockholm/Stehag: Symposion.

Westin, S. 2004. Hammarby Sjöstad – en förlängning av Södermalm? Bachelor thesis, Gotland University.

Westin, S. 2005a. Att skapa stadsmässighet – en paradox? *PLAN* 5–6, 21–5.

Westin, S. 2005b. Stadsmässighetens paradox? En funktionalistisk diskurs i planläggandet av Södra Stationsområdet och Hammarby Sjöstad. Magister thesis, IBF and Dept. of Social and Economic Geography, Uppsala University.

Westin, S. 2010. Space Syntax and Geography. A Question of Logic and Dialectics. *The Journal of Space Syntax: Architecture, Urbanism, Society* 1 (1), 254–7.

Westin, S. 2011. The Life and Form of the City: An interview with Bill Hillier. *Space and Culture* 14(2), 227–37.

White, E.B. 1999. [1949] *Here is New York* New York: The Little Bookroom.

Whitehead, A.N. 2011. [1926] *Science and the Modern World* Cambridge: Cambridge University Press.

Whyte, W.H. 1990. [1988] *City – Rediscovering the Center* New York: Anchor Books.

Wide, S. 2005. *Människans mått. Om statistik, sociologi och världen som socialt vara* Stockholm/Stehag: Symposion.

Wigorts Yngvesson, S. 2009. Rädslan för passionen vår tids tragedi. *Svenska Dagbladet* Under strecket, 16 Dec.

William-Olsson, W. 1934. Stockholms inre differentiering. In *Stockholms inre differentiering* edited by H.W. Ahlmann, I. Eckstedt, G. Jonsson, and W. William-Olsson. Stadskollegiets utlåtanden och memorial No. 51.

Williams, B. 1972. *Morality: An Introduction to Ethics* New York: Harper Torchbooks.

Williams, B. 2002. *Truth and Truthfulness. An Essay in Genealogy* Princeton NJ and Oxford: Princeton University Press.

Wilson, E. 1977. *Women and the Welfare State* London: Tavistock.

Wilson, E. 1992a. *The Sphinx in the City – Urban Life and the Control of Disorder and Women* Berkeley: University of California Press.

Wilson, E. 1992b. The Invisible *Flâneur. New Left Review* 1/191 Jan-Feb, 90–110.

Winnicott, D.W. 1989. [1971] *Lek och verklighet [Playing and Reality]* translated from English by I. Löfgren. Stockholm: Natur och Kultur.

Winther Jørgensen, M. and Phillips, L. 2000. *Diskursanalys som teori och metod* Lund: Studentlitteratur.

Wirth, L. 1938. Urbanism as a Way of Life. *The American Journal of Sociology.* XLIV (1), 1–24.

Wolff, J. 1985. The Invisible Flaneuse: Women and the Literature of Modernity. *Theory Culture Society* 2 (37), 37–46.

Wolodarski, A. 1997. Sankt Eriksområdet, Stockholm. *Arkitektur* 7, 40–43.

Wolodarski, A. 2003. Med ordningens lekfullhet mot vattnet. In *Stockholms stränder* edited by E. Eriksson. Stockholm: Ordfront/S:t Erik.

von Wright, G.H. 1968. An essay in deontic logic and the general theory of action. *Acta philosophica Fennica*, Fasc. XXI. Amsterdam: North-Holland Publishing company.

von Wright, G.H. 1986. *Vetenskapen och förnuftet. Ett försök till orientering* Stockholm: Bonnier.

Wood, L.W. 2005. *Theology as History and Hermeneutics. A Post-Critical Conversation with Contemporary Theology* USA: Emeth Press.

Woolf, V. 1992. [1919] *Night and Day* London: Penguin.

Woolf, V. 1996. [1925] *Mrs Dalloway* London: Penguin.

Woolf, V. 2004. [1931] *The Waves* London: Vintage Books.

Woolf, V. 2005a. [1930] *Street Haunting: A London Adventure*. In *Street Haunting* London: Penguin, 1–15.

Woolf, V. 2005b. [1929] *A Room of One's Own*. In *Selected works of Virginia Woolf* Ware: Wordsworth Editions Ltd, 561–633.

Woolf, V. 2008. *Selected Diaries* edited by A.O. Bell. London: Vintage Books.

Yiftachel, O. 1998. Planning and Social Control: Exploring the Dark Side. *Journal of Planning Literature* 12 (4), 395–406.

Zumthor, P. 2005. *Thinking Architecture* 2nd edn Basel, Boston and Berlin: Birkhäuser.

Zupančič, A. 2012. Not-Mother: On Freud's Verneinung. *E-Flux* www.e-flux.com/journal/not-mother-on-freuds-verneinung/ 2013-04-17.

Index

www.ingramcontent.com/pod-product-compliance
Ingram Content Group UK Ltd.
Pitfield, Milton Keynes, MK11 3LW, UK
UKHW020359010325
455677UK00021B/533